THE YEAR 2000: *A Critical Biography*
of Edward Bellamy

the
year 2000

A CRITICAL BIOGRAPHY

OF

EDWARD BELLAMY

by SYLVIA E. BOWMAN

BOOKMAN ASSOCIATES
NEW YORK

To

My friends, relatives, and professors who, in the course of the years, have given me inspiration and encouragement

TABLE OF CONTENTS

LIST OF ILLUSTRATIONS

INTRODUCTION

The purpose of *The Year 2000: A Critical Biography of Edward Bellamy* is to trace the experiences and ideas of Edward Bellamy and his reactions to sundry problems of his epoch which culminated in the delineation of the Utopian society presented in *Looking Backward* (1888), America's most popular and influential Utopian novel, and its sequel *Equality* (1897). To achieve this objective, Bellamy's novels are viewed as the product of the social, economic, and political life of his era; of his immediate community; of his family environment; and of his experiences, interests, philosophy, and character. Bellamy's major publications—*Looking Backward* and *Equality*—are approached, therefore, from a psychological and sociological aspect; for Utopian novels can only be fully understood, appreciated, and evaluated when they have been fitted into the pattern of the author's life and thought and have been viewed in their relationship to the political, social, and economic conditions of their period.

The only dialectic consideration given to Bellamy's ideas is contained in the material about the ideas of reformers and reform movements with which Bellamy was acquainted. The reader interested in a more thorough dialectic study is referred to my thesis *Le Développement des Idées d'Edouard Bellamy* which I presented at the Sorbonne for a doctorate in 1952. In that work, a comparative study of Bellamy's ideas and those of the social and Utopian writers (prior to *Looking Backward*) of the United States, France, Germany, and England is presented. Copies or microfilms of this thesis are deposited in the libraries of the University of Paris, Harvard University, and Union College.

The Year 2000 contains—except for a brief section about the Bellamy movement—no study of the influence of Bellamy's ideas because the story of the international reaction to them could fill a sizeable volume. Such a volume—*Bellamy at Home and Abroad*—is now being prepared by me in collaboration with professors from many universities abroad.

The method of the presentation of the material which comprises *The Year 2000* is as follows: Part I, "The Educative Influences," presents the influences of the era and of the life of Bellamy which culminated in the writing of *Looking Backward;* the effect the publication of this book had upon Bellamy's life; and, in turn, the effect his experiences as a reformer had upon the writing of *Equality.* For the convenience of the reader, the material is chronologically organized; and the development of Bellamy's philosophy, his early literary works, his personal experiences, and his early interests in social and economic problems—as well as in socialist ideas—are presented in the era in which they were developed or in which their development was important in the life and writing of Bellamy. For the first time, an attempt has also been made to show the relationship of Bellamy's short stories and early novels to not only his philosophy of solidarity but his Utopian novels.

Part II, "The Ideal State: Origin and Development of Ideas for It," is devoted to an analysis of the ideas of *Looking Backward,* of the articles published by Bellamy, and of *Equality.* The study of these ideas is presented with the intention of demonstrating the following: (1) Bellamy's plan for the society of the year 2000; (2) the reflection of the social, economic, political, religious, and intellectual life of the period in Bellamy's ideas for the ideal state; (3) the contribution the life and character of Bellamy made to the acceptance or rejection of certain ideas; and (4) the development of Bellamy's social thinking in the interim between the publication of *Looking Backward* and *Equality.* To avoid repetition of ideas, only those presented as arguments for, explanations of, or substitutes for those of *Looking Backward* are noted. Frequent references are made—directly and indirectly—to the material in Part I, which, since it contains the life and the philosophy of Bellamy, may be considered as the foundation for Part II.

The content of *The Year 2000* is based almost entirely upon the published articles, novels, and short stories of Bellamy and upon his unpublished manuscripts and journals which were deposited, with the sanction of the Bellamy family, in the Houghton Library of Harvard University by Arthur E. Morgan, Bellamy's first biographer. Many extracts from the unpublished material were printed in

Morgan's *Edward Bellamy* and in his *Philosophy of Edward Bellamy;*
and many of the almost unreadable manuscripts which were "translated" and typed by Mr. Morgan's assistants are also deposited at
Harvard University. *The Year 2000* is based upon the original
manuscripts, however, and all of the material quoted is from them
since some errors were found in the Morgan typescripts when they
were compared with the original papers. Since all of the manuscripts and journals (which the Bellamy family discovered in a
forgotten trunk when Bellamy Earnshaw, a grandson of Edward,
was searching for stamps on old letters for his brother David) were
not read by Mr. Morgan, this is the first work which is the result
of a consideration of all of these papers.

Other material deposited at Houghton Library which was used
included the letters of Edward Bellamy to William Dean Howells
and to Thomas Wentworth Higginson, the unpublished biography
of Bellamy by Mason Green, and the unpublished autobiography of
Cyrus Willard. The Green biography (which was purchased from
the author by Paul Bellamy, Edward's son) contains some material
not otherwise available, for it was gleaned from the early journals
and letters of Bellamy which were consumed by the fire which
destroyed Green's residence in Rutland, Vermont, while he was
writing the biography.

Other material in *The Year 2000* is based upon data gathered
from letters, telegrams, and a journal which are still in the possession of Mrs. Marion Earnshaw (Bellamy's daughter) and from interviews with members of the family. During the course of a two-
months' stay in Springfield, Massachusetts, I had the privilege of
having almost daily conversations with the late Mrs. Edward
Bellamy and with Mrs. Earnshaw whose willingness to discuss their
husband and father, respectively, aided me in securing numerous
enlightening facts and anecdotes which are included in *The Year
2000.* Mrs. Earnshaw also conducted me on a tour of Chicopee and
of Chicopee Falls; showed me the old Bellamy home, the mills, and
the residences of the mill workers; and described the town as it had
appeared in her early childhood.

Interviews were also had with the late Paul Bellamy, editor of
the Cleveland *Plain-Dealer* until his retirement; with Charles Bellamy,

Edward's nephew; and with members of the Chicopee Falls, Boston, and Springfield communities who, it was hoped, would remember Edward Bellamy. The last-mentioned interviews were of no avail except that they showed that Edward Bellamy had become a legend in the communities in which he had lived.

Much of the material in *The Year 2000* which shows Bellamy's reactions to his times or his early ideas about sundry problems was gathered from the *Springfield Union,* the *Penny News,* and the *Daily News.* The editorials written by Bellamy from 1872 to 1878 were painstakingly identified; and they and his book reviews were then studied for a knowledge of his reading, his literary criticism, and his ideas about the social, political, and economic scene. These newspaper files were also perused for data about the life of Bellamy and for a view of the period in which he lived. Of all of these newspapers, the *Union* was the most valuable source of information, for the *Daily News* contained, during the period Bellamy wrote for it, very few editorials and no book reviews.

A painstaking study was also made of the complete files of *The Nationalist* and of *The New Nation* for data regarding Bellamy's activities and the development of his ideas after the publication of *Looking Backward.* The articles written by Bellamy for *The New Nation* were identified; and all other articles of his—as well as articles and books written by others about him, his ideas, and his era—were also inspected, as were several unpublished theses.

For the sections of *The Year 2000* about Bellamy's early novels and short stories, a thorough study was made of his unpublished manuscripts and journals, of the collection of his short stories, *The Blindman's World,* and of the early novels: *The Duke of Stockbridge, Six to One, Dr. Heidenhoff's Process,* and *Miss Ludington's Sister.* A search through magazines and journals (popular during the period but whose contents are not listed in various indices) resulted in the unearthing of several of Bellamy's hitherto unlisted short stories and early articles. Many periodicals published in and around New York and Boston during the early period of Bellamy's career were not, however, accessible; and it is possible that some of these may contain other works by Bellamy.

Although no letter, manuscript fragment, or journal that could be read was left unread in amassing the data for *The Year 2000,* this material could not have been available had it not been for the helpfulness of the Bellamy family and for the work done by Mr. Morgan whose books about Bellamy are important pioneer studies and whose collection of correspondence and notebooks—also deposited in Houghton Library—contained some interesting material. The unorganized Bellamy manuscripts deposited at Houghton Library could not have been used, however, had it not been for the cooperation of Miss Carolyn Jakeman and the staff of Houghton Library who prepared the material so I could read it.

I am also grateful for the usage of material contained in the following libraries and for the courteous helpfulness of the staff members: Bibliotheque Nationale, Bibliotheque de la Sorbonne, the Boston Public Library, the Athenaeum Library, the Massachusetts Historical Association Library, the Springfield Public Library, the Connecticut Valley Historical Association Library, the Chicopee Public Library, the New York Public Library, the Antioch College Library, the John Crerar Library, the Julia Newberry Library, the Milwaukee Public Library, the St. Paul Public Library, the Fort Wayne Public Library, and the Lane Public Library of Hamilton, Ohio. I wish also to express my thanks for the aid given by Mr. Frank Kelly, managing editor of the Springfield *Daily News,* who made it possible for me to use the files of the *Penny News* and of the *Daily News.*

My appreciation for the reading and criticizing of the manuscript of *The Year 2000* must also be expressed. Among those friends, colleagues, and former professors whom I wish to thank are: Professor Maurice le Breton, director of the Institute of English and American Studies, the University of Paris; Mr. Herman O. Makey, retired instructor of English; Mr. Robert Wise, Purdue University; Dr. Richard Neil Kramer, Tri-State College; Mr. Philip Headings; Miss Jean Warfield; Mr. B. Tone; Miss Katherine Yaple; Miss Helen Kellogg; and Miss Helen Griesmer.

Sylvia E. Bowman
Fort Wayne, Indiana

CHAPTER I

THE YOUNG PHILOSOPHER (1850-1873)

In the middle of a winter night of the year 1886, Edward Bellamy, a slightly built young man of thirty-six, entered the lamp-lighted sitting room of his home in Chicopee Falls, Massachusetts; and he walked with wiry, self-contained, graceful movements toward the sloping top of his battered, old-fashioned desk. In his hands he carried a cup of steaming black coffee and a small glass of whisky—for these were the stimulants which were to enable him to force his frail, tubercular, dyspeptic body to work through the night. Sitting down at his desk and alternately sipping the coffee and the whisky, he glanced over the page of copy which lay before him—a page which was to be one of many which, after having been painstakingly revised, were to comprise *Looking Backward*, the most widely read and the most influential Utopian novel ever to be written by an American. With a gesture of impatience, Bellamy tossed the rejected page to the already cluttered floor; then, picking up his pen, he began to write so rapidly that his script appeared to be a type of personal shorthand.

As he paused to think, the swarthy face which he lifted toward the lamp showed lineaments which bespoke kindliness, thoughtfulness, and geniality. As he pondered over the next sentence, he ran his hand through his dark brown wavy hair which was sprinkled with strands of silver or he brushed back with sensitive finger tips a wing of his carelessly trimmed mustache. When the words or the ideas for which he searched came to him, his frank yet introspective grey eyes kindled with satisfaction and interest—and once again he picked up his pen to write hastily the words which not only were to make him famous but were also to change the tenor of his life.

If, in one of those moments when he had paused to reflect, Bellamy had asked himself why he was drafting a plan for an ideal society and if, as he searched for the answer, he had been able to review objectively the effects of his early environment, his youthful aspirations, and the experiences he had had in the world of men, he would doubtless have concluded that they had all contributed toward preparing him for the moment when he would feel compelled to begin the book which was to present an ideal world which would enable men to be and to achieve what he had himself aspired to be and had dreamed of achieving.

1. The Boy of Chicopee Falls

When Edward Bellamy was born on March 26, 1850, in the two-story brick residence of his father, the Reverend Rufus King Bellamy, Chicopee Falls was already an industrial town. The majestic river—dotted with islands and lined with trees and called Chicopee, "river of elms," by the Indians—had played an important role in the industrial development of the town; for, shortly after the first settlements had been made, the settlers had harnessed the river power to work the grist and saw mills they had erected. By 1810, the first cotton mill was in operation; and, by 1836, the first labor strike had occurred. By the late 1880's, Chicopee Falls was famous for its cotton factories and its manufacturing plants which produced armaments, bicycles, knitting machines, and agricultural implements.

Shortly after Edward's birth, the Bellamy family moved to the large white frame house shaded by maple trees and surrounded by a large yard where Bellamy was to live the remainder of his life. This dwelling was but a short distance from the beautiful river, the drab brick cotton mills, and the row upon row of stark, yardless, treeless, dreary brick tenement houses where the factory workers lived. Adjacent to the Bellamy dwelling were also the spacious homes of the factory owners and agents whose power a young Bellamy was to describe as being feudal—for these men moulded the destiny of the people, hired and fired the ministers, and eventually determined the nature of every social and public enterprise. As he watched the bedraggled, stunted, poorly paid children whom he saw coming and going to their work in the factories, Bellamy denounced a civilization which so sacrificed human rights and well-being—and it seemed to him that the industrialists and their representatives who so victimized the youth of the nation were worse than the Napoleons of the world.

The environment of the home of a Baptist clergyman and the characters of his parents had prepared Bellamy for this compassionate and indignant reaction to the exploitation of humanity. His father, a witty, intelligent, robust, and rather liberal-thinking minister for his time, was "honored all over Western Massachusetts and especially loved for his quiet and modest ways of 'going about doing good' among the people of his charge." His mother, Maria Putnam Bellamy, though less popular because she was more austere and reserved than her jolly, effervescent husband, was no less kind to her fellowmen.

In the character of Mrs. Bellamy, one discerns the stiff unbending qualities associated with the Puritans as well as their sense of duty. To her, the two most important things in the finite existence of man were revealed religion and a high aim in life. She frowned upon self-indulgence, for "the main purpose in life" was "to be discipline of the heart, soul, and mind"—and a life barren of gratification of the senses was to be deemed not a misfortune but a benefit. To this austere woman, shams and affectations were despicable; conversations lacking substance were contemptible; and courage was a duty.

Edward's life was influenced not only by his mother's attitude toward a high purpose in life and by her piety but by her favoritism which had previously rested upon his brother Packer, who had died in Europe in April, 1868. Edward was thenceforth to be in more ways than one his mother's boy—for, like her, he was reserved and reticent. Despite his reticence, he was to be more in rapport with his mother than with anyone else, and all of his life he was to spend hours conversing with her about books and ideas—and this, perhaps, was as it should have been, for she had helped to form his interests.

Mrs. Bellamy was an exceedingly well-educated woman for her time, and this had been due in part to the decided ideas relative to the necessity of educating women which her father, the Reverend Benjamin Putnam, a Baptist minister of Springfield, Massachusetts, had entertained. Mrs. Bellamy had, therefore, been sent to a female academy where she had read Latin and Greek. Her letters to Mrs.

E. H. Gorham, written long after her formal education had terminated, show her continued delight in study and in teaching. This interest in reading and studying and her serious attitude toward living were reflected in her guidance of her children; for, when one of them had an idle moment, she commanded him to get a book—and she meant an informative book of history, for she regarded novels and newspapers as a mere waste of time.

As a result of her intellectual guidance, the boys Frederick (born April 14, 1847), Charles (born May 7, 1852), and Edward were a source of wonder to their cousins because of their earnest, lengthy discussions of vital problems and ideas. As the Bellamy family sat around the table at meal time, the lads would frequently become so ardently argumentative that the Reverend Bellamy would summarily end their discussion by banging the table with the handles of his knife and fork and by shouting above the din: "Sing Old Hundred! 'Praise God from Whom all blessings flow. . . .' "

Although Edward attended the local educational institutions during his boyhood, the most important aspect of his education was his voluntary reading which his mother so greatly encouraged. From the day that he learned his letters, the quiet, earnest boy was an insatiable reader of the biographies of great men and of tales of adventure. As a result of his literary fare, he lived in a dream world in which he aped the actions of his heroes. From the books he read, he formed also his ideas of "life and action" which led him to regard "with serene contempt or rather a total indifference" the "men and women whom he saw in the world about him"; for, "from his intercourse with heroes and kings, he had gained a royal air in regarding the common hero." The end result of this effect of his reading was that "when he came to go out in the world, it was with profound surprise and bewilderment that he found these common people quite capable of obstructing his course." Because of having lived with his head in the clouds, he was—Bellamy wrote in his unfinished autobiography—"as utterly out of joint with the world as Don Quixote in his library."

Because of his reading, he had also dreamed of the role that he would himself play in the world, and of these ideals and plans he wrote—with great indefiniteness—that they were as "definite

as they were prodigious." He had not failed to perceive, however,
"the necessary and utter pettiness of all achievement undertaken in
the selfish spirit as contrasted with the infinite scope of unselfish
aims." Introvert that he was, he was "therefore greatly troubled
in his mind" because he feared that his "lofty aspirations might
spring from a selfish love of fame, of personal credit. This point
he never fairly got over. At times he felt that the service of humanity was chief motive, and at other times he explained his ambitions,
if not on an unselfish yet on a neutral basis, by ascribing them to
the natural passion of the human nature to fully expand, exert, and
express itself in activities. In this desire to escape self, he became
greatly captivated by the idea of service. He would, in fine, shuffle
off the responsibility of being selfish upon somebody else, either
God or humanity, by devoting himself to them."

For a time, Bellamy the boy thought of serving mankind by
being a soldier; his environment, that of the Civil War, and his
reading of the lives of Napoleon, Nelson, and Mohammed, probably
influenced him. At the age of ten, he recorded in his journal the
list of characteristics which he thought a good soldier should possess
and which he deemed it necessary to acquire because of his forth-
coming military career. This list is of interest not only because
of the qualities listed—self-control, obedience, ambition, quickness
of decision, determination, bravery, and love of his profession—but
because of the reasons given for developing them which indicate
the youth's precocity and his logical thinking.

Bellamy's initial compositions display his early interest not only
in militarism but in social and historical questions. At the age of
ten in a childish essay entitled "A Law for the Republic of San
Domingo," he proposed that the lazy natives be reformed by being
given farm land and by being forced by law to till it. The government was to buy the surplus produce and each year it was to give
more land to the people. Wrote the youthful Utopian: "The
people Must and Cannot help in a short time being interested in it."
At the age of thirteen, in "Does Time Establish a Usurpation," he
maintained that "time cannot change evil to good nor make a rightful inheritance out of a usurpation."

One of the most interesting of these youthful literary exercises is the composition "Considerations upon Divorce" which, despite the prejudice against divorce of this era, logically shows the benefits and wisdom of divorce between incompatible persons if children are not involved. Other compositions—"Treason" (November 30, 1861), "Ensigns" (January 16, 1862), "Islamism" (February 26, 1862), "Physical Decadence of the Race," "Philip and Alexander" (October 17, 1863), "The Marshalls of Napoleon," and "Notes on Military Tactics"—indicate his interest in military heroes, history, and religion.

Several of the essays written in the 1860's and the early 1870's indicate Bellamy's participation in the social clubs and lyceums of Chicopee Falls. "The Force of Flattery" (July, 1863) was read to the Ignota Club; and at least two other talks were given on social questions by Bellamy to the village lyceum group. That Bellamy profited by these discussions may be deduced from the fact that years later in his editorials in the *Springfield Union* he frequently suggested that his readers seek self-improvement by joining such groups as well as by reading widely. His experiences also contributed to a description of the social club of C - - - - in his short story "The Old Folks' Party."

When Bellamy's dream of a military career was shattered in 1867 by his inability to pass the physical examination for entrance to West Point, his mother pondered over the advisability of not sending him to college and of keeping him at home because of his frail health and his youthfulness. She felt that he had already received an education in Latin, Greek, algebra, and geometry comparable to that given by the best preparatory schools, and she did not doubt that, if he remained at home, he would find ways of spending his time profitably.

2. Union College, Then Germany

Bellamy did not, however, remain in Chicopee Falls, for he entered Union College of Schenectady, New York, in 1867. His education there, however, was again to be gained in the library and through discussions; for Bellamy was again to show that—as his brother Frederick observed—his education from the beginning had been that of a recluse, "chosen by a recluse . . . who began to think for himself in very early life." A reader devoted to the college library and not a student tied to textbooks, Bellamy took, therefore, no regular courses but prevailed upon one of the professors to give him a special course in literature. His program of reading was probably based upon the aims set forth in his "Necessary Self Education" which is dated October, 1867. This outline is of particular interest because it reveals Bellamy's interest in political economy and also his concern with his own mental and moral development so as to prepare himself to follow his high—but unspecified—purpose in life.

In the first three sections of this outline, Bellamy stated his aim of becoming thoroughly acquainted with the ancient and modern social and political history of the world; with physical and political geography; and with political science. In the other seven remaining sections, he declared his intention of studying thoroughly Spanish, French, military science, mental science, and logical demonstration. He intended to practice public speaking and writing as much as possible and to study human nature as he saw it displayed by others and as he watched it develop in himself. All of these preparations were necessary, he wrote, for "the accomplishment of those purposes in life to which I have appointed myself."

Bellamy also intended to prepare himself morally and physically for the role he was to play, for he noted that his "moral education" was to have the purpose of preventing his "yielding or departing from . . . [his] high purpose through any temptation of personal reputation or indolent repose, or any other influence whatever." His "physical system" was to have "such care and strengthening and discipline as shall prepare it to be the effective instrument of . . . [his] mind through life."

While attending Union College, Bellamy belonged to the Alpha Kappa Epsilon fraternity, and, if one is to judge by his description of the conversations of the college boys in "Pott's Painless Cure" (1879), he enjoyed the opportunity which the fraternity and college life afforded for the discussion of ideas. Ten years after he had spent his year at Union College, Bellamy assessed college life in a book review of *Student Life at Harvard* in terms which must have been influenced by his own memories; he wrote: "It is at this epoch that the mind first arouses, that ambitions first stir, that the most permanent expressions of life are received. It is a time of storms and convulsions, when the great passions of love, art, and ambition, clothed in a majesty they lose in after days, first accost the mind. The earth and its kingdoms are spread out before the dreamy youth in all the gilding of sunrise. It is a *coup d'oeil* never but once beheld. College life, to be adequately treated, needs the heart of a poet and the head of a philosopher."

Though Bellamy was to describe Union College in "A Positive Romance" as a "little one-horse institution, . . . blue as a whetstone in its orthodoxy," it is probable that some of the ideas that first accosted his mind while he was there were those of Auguste Comte and of the socialists. That he must have discussed socialism in some form or another during his college days is indicated by a letter written to him after the publication of *Looking Backward* by a former fellow student who assured Bellamy that the book was just like the "Ed of Old Union." Further evidence to support this supposition is to be found in a statement made by Frederick Bellamy to the effect that Edward had read and talked about socialism before he went to Germany.

Bellamy had reluctantly gone to Europe in 1868 to join his cousin William Packer who had been with Packer Bellamy when the latter had died while touring the Continent for his health. Edward's reluctance to make the trip had been due to his dislike of accepting financial aid from his mother's wealthy sister Mrs. Harriet Packer—or, for that matter, as he was to show later, from even his own father or mother. Bellamy's mother had insisted, however, that, in the case of the proposed trip to Europe, her son had to "make the sacrifice" and forget his "selfish pride."

When Edward had acceded to her demands and had joined his cousin William, the two young men were installed by Mrs. Packer in a German home in Dresden where they spent the winter of 1868-1869 learning to write and read German and attending lectures. Though his story "Lost" and some unfinished stories are based upon this European sojourn, very little was actually recorded by Bellamy or others about this period of his life. His brother Frederick wrote that Edward's letters to him from Europe were full of German socialism which "he had read and studied much at home." After the writing of *Looking Backward,* Bellamy stated in an article that the sight of the poverty and slums of Europe had first awakened him to the inhumanity of man to man and that he and his cousin had had long discussions as "to the possibility of finding some great remedy for poverty." When a newspaper reporter asked him if he had imbibed his socialistic ideas in Germany, Bellamy replied with a twinkle, " 'Sir, the only thing I learned to imbibe in Germany was beer.' "

Whatever the effects of this sojourn may have been upon his humanitarian or socialistic ideas, Bellamy's articles—published several years later in the *Springfield Union*—show that he did learn to appreciate the tenor of German life. To Bellamy, Americans had much to learn from the Germans who enjoyed nature, had outdoor summer houses and beer gardens, and, from all of these, had found a placid contentment which contrasted to the hustle and bustle of American life. Furthermore, Bellamy believed that a real appreciation of and a cordial sympathy with German life could give a "lifelong educational benefit and mental broadening."

Leaving Chicopee Falls to go first to Union College and then to Europe must have been a profound experience for Bellamy who hated change and who was greatly attached not only to his mother but to his home. In "Hooking Watermelons," he portrayed the joy of coming home and surprising his mother and of talking with her. Elsewhere he wrote that the ties and associations of home flourished perennially in the heart upon which they were so deeply engraved that they seemed like "innate principles"; and he described love of home as "one of the strongest, the purest, the most unselfish passions that human nature knows. . . ." Throughout his life, his journals were to record his discomfort when he was forced to leave familiar surroundings, and his desire, when it was necessary to do so, to find some means of postponing his journey.

Despite his deepseated love of home and family, there was, however, rebellion in Bellamy's heart against family ties and the bondage of all love. The cause of this revolt seems to have been his sensitive reactions to the sufferings of at least his mother because of his unorthodox religious beliefs, for in 1872 he recorded in his journal: "Then also if one has a religion he is in misery till at least the closer circle of friends are in the particular ark with himself. This alone in religious communities is a great drawback on the pleasures of loving and being loved. I doubt not that often times in New England where people take their religion so earnestly parents of strong dogmatic convictions have suffered more from the irreligious dispositions of children than any satisfactions of parentage have compensated."

3. Religious Experiences

Religious observance was a dominating factor in the routine life of the Bellamy family, for family prayers were held at least twice every day and each child had his own prayers to be said in private. When Edward had reached the age of discretion, the subject of many of the prayers said by the family was that he would be visited with the light. That these prayers were answered is testified to by the fact that on April 13, 1864, Edward was baptized in the Baptist Church of Chicopee Falls.

"The emotional experience" of this "religious conversion" was recorded by Bellamy in his unfinished autobiography. Because of it, "he came to feel a sense of intimacy and to enjoy an indescribably close and tender communion with what seemed to him a very real and sublime being. The mental and moral revolutions of later years never blotted from his mind the strange and touching experiences of this epoch." Prayer became to him "a deep and awful pleasure," for "it was to him a sensation at once of almost sensuous happiness as of ineffable sublimity when at such times his heart seemed to throb with that of deity and his soul seemed fused and melted in perfect unison with the divine." It seemed to him that he was bound "to the infinite" with "a love more tender and passionate than any with which human charms ever moved him." During this period of intense reaction, he hastened home from school to pray, for he wanted "only to be with God." "In after years he used to preserve an old chair which had been his oratory and no memento did he so cherish as that, for it recalled the most ecstatic hours of his life."

As a result of this profound experience, Bellamy "saw the world with new eyes" and felt that there was "no other business in it save God's service" and "no other reward save communion with Him." As a result, he "ceased to feel any interest in any reading which did not relate to this subject," and, though he did not renounce his "earlier ambitions," "they were in suspense." As he pondered and read, he concluded "that the only bond of brotherhood between men must be their brotherhood in Christ."

Because of its very intensity, Bellamy's religious fervor could not last, but it was to have four important consequences. Firstly, Bellamy read so widely in the field of religious literature and became so well-versed in the *Bible* that he out-quoted even the missionaries who traveled with him on the ship on which he sailed to the Sandwich Islands. In his editorials written for the *Springfield Union,* he showed interest in the religious movements and literature of his day; and he frequently quoted Biblical passages or made allusions to Biblical stories. His famous parable about the water tank in *Equality* was also written in Biblical style.

Secondly, the Christian ethics of the brotherhood of man and of the Golden Rule remained the bases of Bellamy's guiding philosophy; and he sought, in the fashion of the social gospelers, to make them the foundation of economic and political life. Thirdly, his eventual rejection of orthodox religion stimulated his thinking and caused him to speculate further about the ideas of God, man's relationship to the finite and the infinite, and the effects of sin. He became in himself a continuation of the Reformation and eventually formulated his own religion of solidarity, which he put in concrete form about 1873. This philosophy substantiates and ties in with the Christian teaching of the brotherhood of man and with the tenet that man finds his life only by losing it. Fourthly, his profound and ecstatic religious experiences were later paralleled by Wordsworthian and Whitmanesque reactions to nature.

The story of Bellamy's loss of religious convictions and the reasons for it is not related in his autobiography. However, in the autobiographical story of Eliot Carson—which Bellamy was evidently writing in the later 1870's while on his trip to the Sandwich Islands— he recounted the religious turmoil of the character Edna, who converses with Eliot. Both characters seem to represent Bellamy, for when Edna tells of her emotional disturbance due to her lack of faith, Eliot tells her of the new religion that will be evolved. From this journal and from scattered jottings in others, it is therefore possible to piece together the story of the cause of Bellamy's loss of faith, his flounderings in the sea of despondency after it, and his search for a substitute for the rejected religion of his parents.

Generally, contributing factors to his intellectual renunciation of the articles of religious faith of his parents are to be found in the conflict of religion and science, which made Bellamy's era one of religious discussion, and in the conflicting dogmas of the churches. Bellamy, who frequently discussed the intellectual chaos of his age in his journals, editorials, and book reviews, noted, in his journal of July or August of 1871, that nothing in religion or politics was "considered any more to be axiomatic" and that the "world intellectually speaking seems to be living in a sort of hand-to-mouth style." To him, his epoch was one which was trying to prove all things and was able to hold on to nothing. He attributed this tendency not only to the intellectuality of the period but also to the stupidity of most of the hitherto accepted truths. Though he did not doubt the existence of abstract truths, he did feel that better ones than those to which the world had clung could be discovered.

Scepticism, wrote Bellamy, was the disease of his time—and the only definite things in "modern scepticism are scientific theories which would take volumes to refute or even to state, philosophical theories very complex." Of these theories, he classified Darwinism "as the most original and noteworthy philosophic idea of the nineteenth century" and as the one that had "made more talk in the world than any scientific theory, ancient or modern."

Specifically, the religious tenet which proved so disturbing to Bellamy himself was the Calvinistic doctrine which maintained that the majority of souls born go to hell. Bellamy rebelled at this acceptance of a God Who demanded that man be willing to be damned for His sake—and, like Herman Melville and Samuel Clemens, he was also unable to reconcile the idea of a benevolent deity with the widespread deviltry and misery which he saw in the world. Because of the "hideous atrocity of life," Bellamy could not consider

God as responsible for the creation of the world nor Christ as a god; he could, however, love Christ—he wrote—if he considered Him as a man who had sought to succor those in need. Bellamy concluded, therefore, that a God permitting such suffering in the world was "fatal to the conception of an omnipotent deity with sympathies and affections like those of a good father" and that those who maintained that He was the fatherly overseer had to account for the misery of the world.

The theories advanced to explain the presence of human suffering—such as that of compensation and that stating that suffering was necessary for the development of virtue—were rejected by Bellamy. The theory of compensation was not only an "impotent device of mortals for making good the blunders" but was also an impossibility since earthly joys could be enjoyed only on earth; the missed joys of childhood, for example, could only be made up to a person if he could again be a child.

In discussing the idea of the development of virtue through suffering, Bellamy pointed out that virtues were but the remedies of the world's ills; and if the world were healthy, he argued, self-control, continence, and temperance would be vain, useless, and obsolete. Furthermore, if one fully accepted this idea of the benefit of suffering, charity would have to be regarded as opposed to God's will. To Bellamy, it seemed that most men had developed a more loving and compassionate disposition and a greater hatred of suffering than the exponents of this idea, than nature, or than God. God was, wrote Bellamy in his journals of 1870-1875, comparable to the man who idly destroyed ants with his cane while he was talking and was indifferent to the afflictions he bestowed upon them.

The effect of Bellamy's loss of religious faith as a result of these considerations was that he realized the significance of religion to man and that he, like his character Edna, felt like a lonely outcast. He missed the inspiration that came from divine communion, and he desired to attain once again the blissful sense of security of one who had faith. He longed to worship and to believe, not only because of these lacks but because of his need to have something to love, and this necessity he described as being akin to that of a child who, longing to express affection, feigned life in a doll. Man, decided

Bellamy, needed to worship; for it, like love of a woman, was beneficial in that it carried man out of himself—and self-forgetfulness was the means of his entering his godhead.

Bellamy's desire to have something to worship and his despair led not only to a vacillating search for something to which he could pin his belief and his loyalty but also to Werterean moods of bitterness and a "profound life weariness." For a time the Nirvana of the Buddhists seemed the ideal state, but his "faith never did stay where it was pinned." As an antidote to his wearying search and his grief, he wished to lose himself in physical love of a woman, but he feared this to be impossible since he was "too thoroughly self-conscious," "too well acquainted with the mechanism of" his emotions to be able to do so more than temporarily—and then it would have been with a full knowledge of what he was doing!

By October, 1872, Bellamy, because of the "jarring multiplicity of creeds and philosophies and sentimentalities," concluded that the one thing that might be right would be to "act out himself" and to be "thoroughly and fully a man." He reasoned that since God had given man his instincts, he could perhaps best please Him by "conscientiously fulfilling his instincts one and all"; in this way, he might also find his place in the universe. "This rudimentary religion," or this credo for living, would not be a "repetition of the meaningless jingle of words about doing right whatever befalls" nor would the pattern of conduct it would entail be based upon the rules of the "morality mongers and religionists"; instead, it would permit him to be a "law unto himself." It would, however, inculcate a hearty dislike of sham, conventionalities, and self-misrepresentation. The experiences which doubtless resulted from the adoption of this substitute for religion which would permit full play of his instincts probably contributed to Bellamy's attitudes toward Nemesis, toward the many stages of a man's development, and toward sin as he expressed them in *Dr. Heidenhoff's Process* and in *Miss Ludington's Sister.*

4. The Religion of Solidarity

The final result of Bellamy's search was to be, however, something far less elemental than his being a law unto himself, for he was to write in 1873 his "Religion of Solidarity," an exceedingly redundant essay in which he gave his philosophical explanation of "his relations to the infinite around him," for this seemed to him one of the purposes of all religion. The personal significance of this achievement may be deduced in part from this declaration which Bellamy wrote in one of his journals: "This life is a mystery, men say, and . . . go about their business. This life is a mystery I say and do no other thing till I solve it in some measure at least. That mystery includes all things, and therefore until I know what I am doing I will do nothing. I will not live at random as men do. It is not that I necessarily expect to solve it. Not at all. It is merely that in the presence of that mystery none of the affairs in which men interest themselves seems to have any importance or attraction whatsoever."

That Bellamy was at least partially satisfied with his solution of the question of man's relationship to God, to man, and to the universe was proved not only in 1887 when he re-read the essay and re-affirmed its contents as being his "ripe judgment of life" but in the years in which he published his Utopian novels. The ideas contained in this philosophy appeared also, however, in his other novels, his short stories, in the unpublished Eliot Carson story, and in his journals.

In the "Religion of Solidarity," God was no longer an idol set above man, the inferior being, who was to worship Him blindly on faith. He became the "All-soul"—or the "not-self," the "universal," the "centripetal force," the "infinite." A portion of this universal spirit—or God—existed in all men, and its presence was evidenced by man's instinct to merge himself in others, to get out of himself. Man was, therefore, a manifestation—or the fragment but not the microcosm—of the All-soul, and was, therefore, testimony of the actual existence of God, Who was impersonal in that He "interpenetrated all forms of being." This divine essence— which Bellamy also called the "inner ego," the "noumenal self," and the "real self"—dwelt in all men; and, though it might be more developed in some than in others, it made all men half-gods or potential Christs. Because all men contained a spark of the divine, they were brothers.

Juxtaposed to this universal spirit in man, which made him a part of God and the brother of all men, was the individuality which Bellamy defined as man's personality, his selfish appetites, or the qualities which made him a mortal and at the same time separated him from other men. Individuality could, however, be submerged by actual experiences and by conscious cultivation which would permit man to achieve an objective view of all individuality and to see its infinitesimality. The methods of developing the impersonal—or of entering into the godhead—were meditation, introspection, generous and self-sacrificing actions, and appreciation of the beauties of nature.

To Bellamy, nature was an "auxiliary to man," and the reactions of the sensitive person to it were better proof to him of the "underlying unity and common origin of life" than Darwin's theory. In recounting his own emotional reactions to a beautiful landscape, Bellamy described his urge to enter into and possess the beauty before him as a "passionate desire, I had almost called it lust" which amounted to "a veritable orgasm" which left him weak and listless. He also, however, delineated these reactions and their multiple sources thusly: "The psychical phenomena to which I have referred are those sentiments of intense and mysterious sympathy excited by sublimity and beauty in nature or in men and in art, whether in repose or in action: the emotions of transport, ecstasy, and trance under the influence of music, of majestic imaginations, of enthusiasms of every class."

Though Bellamy had described his physical reactions to the beauty of nature in terms of physiological reactions, he also described them as "mental experiences . . . distinguished from all others by a certain unearthliness; there is no blood in them; they are marked by what may be called a vague intensity. They are independent of the intellect and unconscious of the being. They belong to another world than the intellect, than the body. They seem to rise to a higher vault . . . over . . . the animal and mental life. They are, in short, spiritual—different not in degree but in kind from the phenomena of the mind and the body to which no analysis can reduce or assimilate them."

Whether his reactions were physical, mental, or spiritual, Bellamy was intrigued by them, for to him "this side of human nature, opening on infinity, these unexplored countries of the soul, these mysterious emotions that seem to have no speech nor language" might contain a "clue to the enigma of human life, beyond seeking which I know nothing worth while in this existence."

Bellamy, like the romantic described by Kingsley as a man whose moods were determined by the thermometer, felt "most intimately, tenderly" the presence of the universal spirit in all things in the spring, and he rejoiced to "claim the trees and flowers as brothers and sisters in God's great family." Winter, however, had the effect of "shutting up the universal side of his soul and [of] concentrating his sensations to the individual side." Winter or summer, a slight illness which left him languid "brought the soul wonderfully into the impersonal mood" and made "it long for absorption into the grand omnipotency of the universe by death, as it does not in times of vigor."

Bellamy did not, however, reserve his descriptions of the effects of communion with the universal for notations in his journals; for he portrayed its effects in his first, anonymous novel, *Six to One* (1878), in which the character Addie Follet has a mystical passion for the sea. Because of her devotion, she has so cultivated the impersonal side of herself that it seems to her that no "human being could call forth the exalted and intense emotions which the sea elicited and satisfied." Another character, Edgerton, who is ill, is used to show the curative effects of "resting on the heaving bosom of infinity," the sea; from this experience, he receives a "sense of moral, mental, and physical health and balance."

In his short stories, Bellamy also depicted the arousal of the impersonal in man as the result of varied stimuli. In "An Echo of Antietam" (1886), it resulted from mass feeling, martial music, patriotism, and the desire for self-sacrifice. In "The Cold Snap" (1875), an emergency promoted a feeling of solidarity which was the result of the impersonal in man; and, in "Deserted" (1878), the longing to attain perfect insight and sympathy by one who appreciated nature was portrayed. At election time, wrote Bellamy in the manuscript entitled "Joseph Claibourne," each American felt the "vast pulse of the national heart, and for a little time the meanest soul" had "an inkling of the life universal of which the life of the individual" was "so small a function."

As Bellamy indicated in this last quotation, the universal or centripetal force which bound people and things together was the all-important aspect of man. The individuality was to be regarded as narrow and petty—as the force causing division and preventing fusion. It was the universal or impersonal in man which made him sympathetic with all things; which enabled him to recognize the pettiness of the subjective reactions which resulted from his narrow self-concern, or individuality; and which made him capable of being more than a mere animal. Bellamy defined the impersonal as the source of all that men "call greatest, noblest, broadest, most inspired and most enthusiastic, most self-devoting and devotedly self-asserting, the most perfect enjoyment of beauty, the purest and most intense of our psychical faculties." It was the source, in short, of "all our emotions and our moods . . . by which we are greater than our individualities." This "unconsciousness of personality" did not, however, "imply unconsciousness of being . . . but rather a deeper, stronger pulse of being than is consistent with a vigorous assertion of the individuality."

Vigorous assertion of individuality without development of the impersonal resulted, wrote Bellamy, in "human oxen" and in the feeling that the individual was the center of the universe. When this happened, the individuality became the "dungeon of the soul." People were often, however, incapable of "soul culture," and these were they who did the work and business of the world—and Bellamy admitted that if this group did not exist, "we might otherwise have to make slaves of some to get the business done at all." Those incapable of such spiritual culture were most unfortunate because their lack of unselfishness and impersonality deprived them of an intellectual and spiritual refuge which would not only give them peace in time of trouble but save them the ennui that resulted from living only in the individuality. To Bellamy, there was no way of mitigating the sorrows of life comparable to that of retreating to the serene plane of the impersonal.

Bellamy recognized, however, that individuality was not to be wholly condemned, for it made possible not only the expression of the universal but the joys that came from individual life. Bellamy also realized that the individuality, or centrifugal force, preserved "that variety in unity which seems the destined condition of being." Each force played, therefore, its necessary role in life—but Bellamy thought that as man progressed the impersonal would play a greater and greater part.

It was, said Bellamy, the universal force in man that created attraction between different individualities, and it was, therefore, the heart of all love. Since the individuality of man prevented his being absorbed by, or his absorption of, the loved one—which complete soul-fusion he desired—this universal longing was also responsible for much of the pathos and disappointment of life and love. The love man bore for woman, for his fellows, for his nation, and for ideas—which resulted from his forgetting himself and from his developing sympathies—was a development of the impersonal, for it alone produced the unselfishness which was the "root and flower of all true religion." This love and this unselfishness were also the basis of the brotherhood of man, or of solidarity.

Though Bellamy stated that the impersonal prompted men to acts of self-sacrifice and unselfish service, he admitted that he had difficulty in showing its specific operation. In his plot for a short story about a man who was capable of generous deeds only when drunk, Bellamy compared doing good to a form of intoxication. On the other hand, he stressed that man was as obliged to obey the generous impulses of the impersonal as he was to answer the needs of his physical being; if both were not considered, a penalty would have to be paid. Since expression of the impersonal was essential to the life of the "not-self," a moral code prompting man to live a more impersonal life was not just a doctrine but a basic recognition of the fact that unselfishness was a natural appetite which had to be satisfied. No man, wrote Bellamy, no matter what he desired, could be completely self-centered; though he might try to be, the impersonal would break through in even the most unlikely persons and result in deeds of heroism and self-sacrifice.

The reward of developing the impersonal was a soul that had "exchanged its infinite want for an infinite fullness" and felt no more "lonely and isolated in creation but rather a sense of intimate sodality." Through unselfish acts, man became enfranchised of self and hence truly virtuous. To Bellamy, self-sacrifice and generosity were the greatest virtues; and, because they had their own bases in the absolute or in the All-soul, they were the natural virtues. By way of distinction, chastity, for example, was classified by him as an artificial virtue because it stemmed from social conventionality rather than from the absolute.

Bellamy anticipated two stages in the development of this impersonal force in man; one was to be that of enthusiasm for humanity, upon which he based the achievement of the Utopian society depicted in *Looking Backward* and in *Equality*; the other was to be that which would evolve a new race of men able to communicate their ideas without speech, and upon this he based "To Whom This May Come" (1889). During the first stage of development, men would realize that "life is hid in our brethren, in the race" and not in the petty self; as a result, they would cease mangling their own bodies by oppressing their fellows. Selfishness would be recognized, therefore, as suicide, and the "warm glow of sympathy and fellowship between men" at Christmas would suffuse society. This enthusiasm for humanity, which was also the heart of Christianity, would show men "the essential unity of the individual with the immortal race of man, and . . . [their] obvious duty to forget self in its service." The symbol of this centripetal force which would bring man, the individualist, back to bind him to humanity—his greater self—would be woman.

The second stage of development would lead to further growth of this "impersonal side of . . . [men's] natures" in which was "found the apotheosis of humanity, which has been its aspiration ever since Adam and Eve ate the apple in the hope of being as gods." The susceptibility of the soul to nature, as had been seen in the Wordsworthian school, was the result, thought Bellamy, of man's beginning to reach after the infinite. He reasoned that if culture could add such a province to human nature within a century, it surely was not too visionary to count upon a still more complete development of the "subtle psychical faculties."

Bellamy reasoned that if these more sensitive people whose psychical faculties and impersonalities were highly developed were encouraged to mate, a type of people might in time be produced such as that which inhabited the island of the mind readers in "To Whom This May Come" or that which, in "The Blindman's World," respected the solidarity of the race and the inner ego of man. In this stage of development, the life of the soul would have achieved its proper significance—and what Bellamy meant by this may be deduced from the following statement: "The truth is . . . that the life of the soul is accepted by us as a point of faith rather than realized as a fact. It is present to our intellects rather than to our consciousness. That is wrong, all wrong. The life of the soul should be with us a life as real, as substantial, as positive as that of the body. This I believe to be the next development of human nature, and a development it will be which will realize the potential divinity of man. We should not regard the soul as something super-added to the body, but the body to the soul."

Bellamy also expressed in his "Religion of Solidarity" his ideas relative to the fate of the soul after the death of the body. As a part of the All-soul, the soul of man was infinite, inexhaustible, and a constant quality. It belonged to the eternal state, and the body was merely its temporary hotel. During life on earth, the soul existed quite separately from the brain; and when the brain died, the soul lived on, though it ceased to have any further experience of thought. At the moment of death, it returned to the "ocean of circumambient life whence it came and must return," and there it dwelt in a state of "impersonal, unindividual, diffused consciousness" which Eliot Carson described thusly: "I find rest . . . a sense of lofty calm in imagining my future life as being so far impersonal and even unconscious as may be implied in an entire lack of individualities. I love to dream of my spirit as something interfused in the light of setting suns, broad oceans, and the winds. If you say that such impersonality means a merely unconscious existence, I will not quarrel with you. I am quite content that it should be so. But is it necessarily so? Are sense of personal limitations and the consciousness of existence necessarily inseparable? May we not dream of a mode of existence at once conscious and yet unindividual?"

Bellamy's conception of death robbed it of its sting, for he believed that just as man looked upon the death of a flower as a part of the frame of nature, so should he regard his own demise. Fear of death existed, he thought, because men did not actually believe in the soul or because the soul was merely a point of view and not a "fact of consciousness" to them. If man developed his spiritual side, death would become nothing more than "a slight and obvious step in natural evolution." That Bellamy had developed his spiritual side and that he had found solace in his philosophy were proved when he faced death in September, 1874, with equanimity and when he died in 1898 with the words, "I am but stepping into another room."

Bellamy's philosophy of solidarity not only permitted him to face death without fear but gave him at one time a feeling of superiority. It is probable that he was being autobiographical when, in "A Positive Romance," he described a young man, who after an unorthodox religious experience, regarded the rest of the world as "still groping in the mists of childish superstition." His new religion permitted him to show in "A Tale of the South Pacific" how people—because of ignorance and superstition—could worship a god who did not exist. His philosophy was also doubtless responsible for his withdrawing his membership from the Baptist Church in June, 1882, the year his father retired from the ministry.

In summary, Bellamy's religion of solidarity was not only the result of his spiritual and intellectual search to discover the mystery of man's relationship to the finite and the infinite but the result of the Christian ethics which had been an integral part of his early environment and of his mother's ideas of unselfishness, self-sacrifice, and the importance of the spiritual life of man. His religion was also in keeping with his spiritual mysticism, his emotional longings and sensitivities, his introspection, and his independence. He wrote: "What I want to know is why in the name of creation should I bow down to anything. I am. I know not that anything else is. If there be anything else, I deduce its existence from myself who am major premise in all metaphysics. To bow down then to aught I deduce from myself is flat idolatry, and catch me at it! I am; others may be; and shall the real worship the imaginary, the actual the possible? Good Lord deliver us from such folly." In all fairness, however, it must be added that Bellamy realized that there might be some personal-impersonal force which it was beyond the mind of man— in its present state of development—to perceive, and that there might be a "hierarchy of beings above ourselves just as there are grades below."

Aside from these personal influences, Bellamy's religion of solidarity was undoubtedly the result also of his wide reading and of the intellectual atmosphere of his era. In his religion there are reflections of the enthusiasm for humanity of the "noble and fascinating theories" of Auguste Comte; of the ideas of the *me* and the *not me* of Emerson, the Swedenborgians, and the Brahmins; and of the conception of absorption into the divine essence as set forth by Plotinus. The essay contains also the romantic's ecstatic, mystical conception of the relationship of man to nature such as is found in the poetry of Walt Whitman, as well as the idea of the submergence of the individual for the common good found in the philosophies of Epictetus, Marcus Antonius, Fénelon, Christ, and countless others.

Bellamy's religion of solidarity is not important, therefore, because of its originality of thought; it is important because of the role it played in the formation of the ideological basis of Bellamy's fiction. As will be seen in Chapter II, Bellamy was concerned in his minor fiction with the problems of the impersonal and the individuality; and in his Utopian novels—his major fiction—he tried to create a world which would further the growth of the impersonal. In Bellamy's Utopian novels, the principles of the religion of solidarity not only determined the type of church and the religion of the ideal state but affected it politically, economically, and socially.

CHAPTER II

LAWYER AND WRITER

1. The Lawyer

When Edward Bellamy returned to the United States in 1869 from his year of travel and study in Europe, he began the study of law in the office of Leonard and Wells in Springfield, Massachusetts. His reasons for preparing for the legal profession are to be found not only in the interest he had evinced for law and government in his already-mentioned outline for his self-education but also in his notation in the Eliot Carson journal. In this autobiographical story, Bellamy stated "he had had in his mind's eye when taking to the law . . . the arguing of great constitutional questions, the chivalrous defense of the widow and the orphan against their oppressors, and the vindication of accused and sorely beset innocence."

After having studied for two years in the office of the Springfield law firm, Bellamy passed his bar examinations in 1871 with such brilliance that he was immediately offered a partnership by Mr. M. B. Whitney, a well-known Westfield lawyer. Bellamy refused this offer, however, and opened his own practice in Chicopee Falls. The youth who had dreamed of protecting widows and orphans had as his first case the eviction of a widow for non-payment of rent. His reaction to this experience was so profound that he became disgusted with being a "public blood hound" and forthwith took down his shingle.

As a result of his experience as a lawyer, Bellamy criticized the profession in his novels and editorials as being the upholder of the plutocracy. He benefited, however, from his study of law, for it not only had trained him to think logically but had given him the knowledge of law and government that a would-be social reformer should have. Bellamy himself recognized that this training had been an asset when, years later, he wrote "that unless a man knows something about law . . . as to how the world has been and is governed, he's unlikely to be a sound adviser as to how the present methods can be improved on. The man who undertakes to mend a machine must understand it as it was made."

2. Journalist

After his disillusioning but intellectually profitable essay in the legal profession, Bellamy began another phase of his life which also contributed to his education as a reformer; he began to write for the newspapers. As a writer of editorials, he sharpened his mind and his pen on the affairs of the nation; as a literary editor, he developed his critical faculties, discussed the techniques of fiction, and kept in touch with the ideas current in the books and magazines of the era. During this period he also began his own literary career as a successful writer of short stories and novels.

While Bellamy was still residing in Chicopee Falls, his first known published article, "Woman Suffrage," appeared in the March, 1871, issue of Theodore Tilton's radical weekly, *The Golden Age*. In September, his cousin William Packer wrote Bellamy that he had interviewed Mr. Carleton L. Lewis, the managing editor of the *New York Evening Post* and a neighbor of the Packer family, and had applied for a "literary situation" for Edward on this newspaper. William reported that he had also referred Lewis to Bellamy's article in *The Golden Age* and that he had suggested that he seek information about Edward from Colonel T. W. Higginson. William had also told Lewis that Edward's studies in political science and law, as well as his propensity to think out his own political creed, would make him a person well qualified to write about home politics and current questions of the day. As a result of William's recommendation, Lewis requested that Edward send him a sample editorial.

Bellamy evidently not only submitted the sample editorial but received encouragement from Lewis, for in November he went to New York City to live. Instead of accepting the hospitality offered him by his wealthy relatives, the Packers, the proud young Bellamy asserted his spirit of independence and secured a room for himself in Stuyvesant Square. Though the days that followed were filled with the struggle to remain economically solvent, Bellamy adamantly refused to accept the money which even his mother and father sent him.

During this period in New York, Bellamy contributed articles whenever he could to the *Post,* which was engaged at this time in a reform movement relative to tenement evils, sanitary regulations, and corrupt politics as exemplified by Boss Tweed and his gang. Bellamy wrote two other articles—"Railroad Disasters" and "National Education"—which were published in *The Golden Age.* He also spent some time helping his brother Frederick, who was a partner of the Rowe Company which was seeking to publish a book by including advertisements in it. It is also probable that, following Frederick's advice, he was writing articles for the *Boston Daily Globe,* which had just begun publication.

According to the statements made by Frederick, he introduced Edward at this time to Albert Brisbane, "whose theories interested" his brother deeply. Edward, however, made no mention of this meeting in his journal of this period—nor did he make any other comments about his stay in New York except that he had "met with good success" and that he had experienced there some of the profound hours of his life. He did, however, write in his journal on June 4, 1872, a sentimental farewell to his room. Years later when Bellamy made some notes for a sequel to *Looking Backward,* he was doubtless thinking of this period of his life when he wrote that a young cousin was to go to the city, find it "hard to live," see a lot of suffering, and become a Nationalist.

Edward's leaving New York to return to Chicopee Falls seemingly was the result of his father's advice. In May, 1872, the Rev. Bellamy had written Edward that part of the staff of the *Springfield Republican* had purchased the *Springfield Union* with the intention of publishing it as a pro-administration paper. After apprising Edward of these facts, the Rev. Bellamy advised him to apply for a job and then added: "I don't know as it would suit your ideas, or your *politics,* if you have any just at this time. But as the two papers take opposite sides you might pay your money and take your choice."

Bellamy's choice was evidently the *Union,* for by the late summer of 1872 editorials and book reviews in his style of writing and thinking began to appear in its columns. From 1872 until December, 1877, Bellamy was to hold the position of editorial writer and literary editor on the staff of the *Union*. As one reads the numerous editorials and weekly one-to-three column book and magazine reviews that he wrote, one marvels at his indefatigable industry.

The editorials are of interest because of their wide range of subject matter and because of their revelation of Bellamy's clear thinking and logic and of his sense of style and form. The subject matter ranges from women's fashions and the weather to the suffrage movement, the Grangers, local and national politics, and co-operative movements. Frequently the idea discussed in an editorial is one that was suggested by a book or a magazine article which Bellamy had reviewed.

Bellamy's method of presenting his material was to begin his editorial with a succinct presentation of the theme and then to devote the central section to the exposition of it. In the last section, he rounded off the discussion with either a summarizing or a penetrating and striking observation. At this period of his writing, Bellamy quoted generously from the *Bible* and from the classics of all ages—and sometimes the reader surmises that he made liberal usage of Bartlett's book of quotations. Bellamy's sentence pattern is also distinctively his: no other writers on the staff compare with him in the use of compound and complex sentences—nor in the employ of telling illustrative analogies from nature and everyday life.

The books which Bellamy reviewed related to religion, science, history, and other subjects, but those that predominate are novels and biographies. His reviews of magazine articles are of particular interest because they reveal his interest in subjects such as psychology, sanitation, housing, and political science. Because Bellamy infused his book reviews with his personal ideas about life and the ideologies he was discussing, they are particularly valuable indications of his reactions, interests, and thinking during this formative period of his life about which little else is known. Because of his criticisms of the style and the technical methods of the novels he reviewed, Bellamy developed also, without doubt, his own ideas of effective methods of presentation of material.

Bellamy reviewed many French, German, and English novels; and his opinions show him to have been particularly fond of the works of George Eliot, George Sand, Hardy, Thackeray, Dickens, Charles Kingsley, Bulwer-Lytton, Howells, Hugo, Clemens, and Turgenieff. His comments show that he had little good to say about Bret Harte; was in doubt as to the merits of Walt Whitman; and thought Henry James, Jr., to be the most promising writer of his day.

In comparison to the book reviews written by Bellamy, those written before and after he was literary editor of the *Union* are flat, inept so far as critical acumen is concerned, and uninteresting because of the impersonality of the perfunctory reviewers. Many of the comments Bellamy made about the novels he reviewed are often as pithy as those of Edgar A. Poe, who never spared the author's feelings. Of M. T. R. Hamilton's *Cachet,* Bellamy wrote, for example, that "the literary style is beneath criticism." Of Joaquin Miller, he said: "Joaquin Miller's work, nominally upon the Modocs, whom he admires, but really and chiefly upon himself whom he admires more, and his wife, whom he admires less, will soon be out."

His career with the *Union* terminated late in December, 1877, when Bellamy, who had been suffering from fainting attacks and generally poor health, journeyed with his ailing brother Frederick to the Sandwich Islands. Arriving in San Francisco on January 11, 1878, they sailed for the Islands, which they reached on the last of February or the first of March. In a letter to Charles, Edward stated that he and Frederick were having an "infernally good time" and that they were not sick enough to have their health interfere "with recreation, however it may be with work." Returning to San Francisco, the brothers left for home on April 9, although Edward wrote his parents that he would have left a week sooner "if I had only to consult my own tastes, but Fred is not such a home body as I am and wants to see the last dog hung."

Although Bellamy kept a journal, the "Hawaiian Notebook," during this trip, it contains very little information about the scenes visited or the experiences enjoyed by himself. Two of his short stories, however, show the influence of this trip: "Deserted" (1879), which contains an excellent description of the Nevada desert and an amusing episode about two people's attempt to make the Indians think they are phantoms; and "A Tale of the South Pacific" (1880), which relates the experiences of travelers and missionaries from the good ship "Moonbeam," who, when they go to see the volcano Kilauea, hear a native tell a story about a white man who became a selfish god to the credulous and ignorant natives. In the last-mentioned story Bellamy wrote that the narrator had been drawn to these regions by a desire "dating from the perusal of *Robinson Crusoe* to behold a genuine Polynesian Island, ere yet its primitive people should have succumbed in the effort to grapple with the philosophy of clothes and all that it implies."

The most important—or at least the most revealing—work that Bellamy was mulling over and writing during this trip was, however, the Eliot Carson story which, although it was never to be completed, was to occupy him intermittently for almost twenty years. In this story, which had first been conceived in order to propose the starting of a modern hermitage dedicated to the study of ideas and the perpetuation of religion, Bellamy wrote of Eliot's withdrawal from business affairs in order to devote himself to the development of his mind and his soul through reading and meditation. Eliot, who—like Bellamy at the moment—was nearing the age of thirty, was discontented with the life he had been living; for, as he surveyed the past ten years, he realized that he had had little time for the development of his soul and had added little to his knowledge of the marvel of his own life.

Like the Eliot Carson of the "Hawaiian Notebook," Bellamy retired from the world of business after his return to Chicopee Falls. He devoted himself to a literary career, and published from 1878 to 1880—the year he again devoted himself to journalism—three novels and seven short stories. Bellamy's retirement from the *Union* was the result not only of his poor health and his attitude toward the basic purpose of life but of the encouragement to pursue a literary career which the publication of his novels and short stories—while he was still a member of the *Union* staff—had given him.

3. Bellamy's Minor Fiction

From 1875 to 1889, Bellamy published twenty-three known short stories in some of the best magazines of his day—*Scribner's, Atlantic Monthly, Harper's Monthly, Appleton's Journal, Lippincott's, The Century, Good Company,* and *Sunday Afternoon.* Although his name is associated today with the internationally famous Utopian novel *Looking Backward* and with its successful sequel *Equality* (1897), Bellamy was recognized by the readers and by the editors of his own epoch as the writer of highly imaginative, psychological, and speculative short stories and novels.

During the period from 1878 to 1884, Bellamy wrote four novels which were also not ignored by either the reading public or the critics: *Six to One* (1878); *Dr. Heidenhoff's Process* (1878-9; 1880); *The Duke of Stockbridge* (1879; 1900); and *Miss Ludington's Sister* (1884). Of *Six to One,* Clark W. Bryan, editor of *Good Housekeeping,* wrote in 1889 that it had "made something of a hit" and that it—though an anonymous publication—had brought Bellamy's name as a novelist into "quite as great prominence with the public as it has had at any time since until the publication" of *Looking Backward.*

When *Dr. Heidenhoff's Process* was published, one of its most enthusiastic reviewers was William Dean Howells who predicted that Bellamy was to be the literary successor of Hawthorne. Eighteen years later when Howells wrote the preface to the posthumous collection of Bellamy's short stories, *The Blindman's World* (1898), he stated that this novel—the first of Bellamy's novels that he had read—had impressed him as being "one of the finest feats in the region of romance which . . . [he] had known" because of the author's ability to "make the airy stuff of dreams one in quality with veritable experience."

Howells' interest in *Dr. Heidenhoff's Process* resulted in his writing to Bellamy personally, in his recommending the novel to its British publisher, and in his offering to read any of Bellamy's future manuscripts with a view to their publication. Because of this generous offer, Bellamy sent Howells the manuscript of *Miss Ludington's Sister;* Howells criticized the work and, after Bellamy had revised it, not only introduced it to its publisher but reviewed it more than favorably in the *Century*.

By 1886, Bellamy was such a well-recognized writer of short stories that George Parsons Lathrop, the son-in-law of Nathaniel Hawthorne, recommended him to editors of publications; and after *Looking Backward* had become nationally famous, Bellamy could have reaped a financial harvest had he not refused the proffers of editors like Horace Scudder of the *Atlantic Monthly* who were eager to publish his fiction.

Bellamy had decided, however, that he would cease to write short stories—and for cogent reasons. In his letter of 1890 to Horace Scudder, he presented the following explanation of his decision: "It would indeed be a delight to me to revert to those psychologic studies and speculations which were the themes of my earlier writings. But since my eyes have been opened to the evils and faults of our social state and I have begun to cherish a clear hope of better things, I simply 'can't get my consent' to write or think of anything else. As a literary man I fear I am 'a goner,' and past praying for. There is a sense in which I am very sorry for this, for I had much work laid out to do, and should have greatly enjoyed doing it. There is one life I would like to lead and another I must lead. If I had only been twins!"

Bellamy seemed, however, to have another, deeper reason for not consenting to write short stories. This reason is implied in a letter written to him in 1889 by Sylvester Baxter who obviously was replying to ideas that had been expressed by Bellamy: "Your views are level headed. It is of course best not to entangle our movement [the Bellamy or Nationalist] by making people regard us as flighty, yet I hope some time to see that article published, and if publication is delayed too long, to have the pleasure of reading it. As to your stories, there is no danger from that source. Those who understand them will understand you; those who do not will enjoy them as 'brilliantly imaginative,' and not be disposed to impeach your common sense."

Bellamy must have thought, therefore, that the publication of more short stories would increase his reputation as a writer of imaginative, out-of-this-world fiction and that such repute would hinder serious consideration by the public of his ideal society. He also quite obviously feared that, unlike Baxter, the average reader would not see the underlying significance of his stories. And that Baxter did understand their thematic relationship to *Looking Backward* is evidenced in his article published in 1889 in the *New England Magazine* in which he hinted that a study of Bellamy's early fiction might show such a connection—a suggestion that was repeated in articles by Katherine Woods in 1898 in *The Bookman* and by Robert L. Shurter in 1933 in *American Literature.*

Despite the comparative indifference of recent writers about Bellamy—such as Arthur Morgan and Joseph Schiffman—to the suggestion of Baxter, a study of Bellamy's early or minor fiction does show his preoccupation with ideas which were to be developed in one way or another in his famous Utopian novels or which were to be important in the formation of the objectives which his ideal society was to attain. Furthermore, an analysis of these early novels and short stories shows the relationship of the themes of both his minor and major fiction with the ideas Bellamy expressed in his "Religion of Solidarity" which he completed about 1873—but which, as has already been noted, he re-read and re-accepted as "his ripe judgment of life" as late as 1887, the year before the publication of *Looking Backward.* The ideas Bellamy expressed in his "Religion of Solidarity" about the presence of the universal spirit in man, the methods for and the possibility of developing the impersonal in man, the result of the development of the impersonal in creating social solidarity, and the criticism of a society which did not encourage such development all found expression in the basic themes of his minor fiction.

4. Themes: The Impersonal, the Individuality

Bellamy's first novel, *Six to One,* which has hitherto been considered "a light summer novel," is a fictional exposition of Bellamy's philosophy of man's relationship to the universal spirit in nature which, in this case, is represented by the sea which Bellamy considered to be more appealing to youth than the mountains. Addie Follet, the heroine, epitomizes the mystical rapport with nature which develops the impersonal in man; and Kate Mayhew (one of the six girls who pursue Edgerton, the convalescent newspaper editor) represents the person imprisoned in the individuality. Edgerton, who might well have been Bellamy himself, goes to the sea to have his health restored and finds in its impersonality—and in the development of the impersonal in himself—renewed vigor. Although Edgerton finds both Kate and Addie attractive, he loves Addie who finally resolves the conflict between her love of the sea and of Edgerton by surrendering to and accepting his love. The surrender comes, however, after she is almost literally drowned by the sea—and has, of course, been rescued by Edgerton. Her surrender to Edgerton's love does not mean, however, that she has denied the impersonal, for Bellamy believed that love of human beings also developed it.

In describing the effect of Addie's mystical communion with the sea, Bellamy employed terms quite similar to those he had used to describe his own reactions. Addie's experience was intensely emotional—one which made her, like her creator, wonder if "a human being could call forth the exalted and intense emotions which the sea elicited and satisfied." Through her "mystical passion," Addie found release from self and personal thoughts and was refreshed because she had been elevated out of the personal sphere—and the same was true of Edgerton. Edgerton, in one of the many conversations in the novel about the personal and the impersonal, also made the following significant remark: ". . . by the cultivation of the impersonal side of our natures is to be found the apotheosis of humanity, which has been its aspiration ever since Adam and Eve ate the apple in the hope of being as gods."

The final result of the development of the impersonal in man is shown by Bellamy in his short story "To Whom This May Come" (1889). In this short story, Bellamy depicted the influence of the development of the impersonal upon love and understanding of others; upon the mental and physical health of the individual; and upon the social order. The narrator of the story is a shipwreck victim—an individual who can never attain enfranchisement "from the false ego of the apparent self"—who is washed by the sea to an island in the Pacific inhabited by the mind-readers—people who no longer rely upon oral communication of their ideas.

The results of their having perfected their ability to read the minds of others are: complete justice, for everything can be seen against its background, and misjudgments of characters and incidents are, therefore, rendered impossible; satisfying friendships, for they are marked by complete understanding and sympathy; satisfactory communication of ideas, for thoughts are totally disclosed as they cannot be in oral communication; rapturous love, for mental sympathy and understanding are added to physical passion; generosity of judgment, for all recognize their own and others' frailties; and complete self-knowledge, for each sees himself as others see him. Because these people are capable of putting themselves in others' places and are, therefore, sympathetic and understanding, they have no hatred, no envy, no uncharitableness.

The mind-readers are also objective toward their own individualities, and this attitude is due to their impersonality which is engendered by their seeing their mental and moral selves reflected in others' minds. To them, the inner self of the "Religion of Solidarity" is the "essential identity and being," and their minds and their bodies are but its garments of a single day. The effect of this "instinctive consciousness" is a "sense of wonderful superiority to the vicissitudes of this earthly state and a singular serenity" in the midst of all the misfortunes which befall the individuality. Enfranchised "from the false ego of the apparent self," these people are truly the lords of themselves. The mind-readers, because of their mental development, as well as their development of the impersonal, have become a race of perfected people.

Bellamy portrayed in "The Cold Snap" (1875), "Jane Hicks" (1879), and "An Echo of Antietam" (1889) the way the impersonal could be developed. In "A Positive Romance" (1889) he not only considered the way the impersonal could be developed but showed how it acted as a centripetal force and how it resulted in the enthusiasm for humanity which became the basis of social solidarity. In "A Mid-Night Drama" (1877), "Extra-Hazardous" (1877), "Hooking Watermelons" (1877), "That Letter" (1880), and "Two Days' Solitary Imprisonment" (1878), Bellamy demonstrated the way qualities of the individuality such as jealousy, vanity, pride, and suspicion could affect human relationships.

The impersonal and social solidarity are developed in the characters and in the community of "The Cold Snap" by an onslaught of zero weather which caused "the general exaltation of spirit and suspension of the conventionalities" which resulted in "an increase of mutual respect" and "that sense of fellowship which springs up between those associated in an emergency."

Another emergency—war—is responsible for the development of the impersonal in "An Echo of Antietam." A simply narrated but often moving tale of a young woman and her lover who are separated first by war and then by death, the story contains very little action; for Bellamy was primarily concerned with depicting the horrors of war, the sacrifices demanded of women and men, and "the mystic gain" of self-sacrifice. One of the most important and best descriptions in the story is that of the engendering of the spirit of self-sacrifice and of unity in the masses by the roll of the drum, the flag, and the marching men.

The joy of giving—of doing generous deeds—is shown in "Jane Hicks," a story based upon a conflict between Jane, a poor factory girl, and the rich mill owner's wife over the latter's desire to reward Jane financially for saving her little son's life. Jane, who had always wanted to do "fine things" for people, feels that the reward for doing them is the feeling the action engenders in the doer; she refuses, therefore, the material reward which she says would spoil her feeling.

One of the most important of Bellamy's short stories is "A Positive Romance" (1889)—a bizarre story, based upon the ideas of Auguste Comte, about a young man who had been introduced to Positive worship of women while in college and who narrates his experiences to his friend after the two have attended an opera and have begun a discussion about the reasons for man's adoration of women and for woman's role as the inspiration of art and literature. They conclude that woman is worshipped not because of her beauty but because of "the mystical suggestiveness of it." Woman represents the race—or humanity; and it is through her that man, the individualist, is brought back to the race and fused with humanity. The story emphasizes that enthusiasm for humanity demands self-sacrifice and declares that "the supreme object of the individual love and devotion should be humanity"—an idea which is also "the heart of the old religion," as well as of Bellamy's "Religion of Solidarity" since such a devotion to woman and to humanity developed the impersonal or the universal spirit.

As has already been indicated, Bellamy was also interested in showing in many of his psychological stories the divisive qualities of the individuality. In "Pott's Painless Cure"—one of his cleverest and most entertaining stories—and in "A Mid-Night Drama," he exposed the deceits practiced in courtship. Because of vanity, pride, the desire for approbation, or self-interest, the individual sacrificed his character. Bellamy had touched upon this theme in *Six to One*; and in his Utopian novels and in "A Love Story Reversed" (1888) he so changed the practices of courtship that women could declare their love, that hypocritical attitudes were frowned upon, and that love and understanding were the bases of marriage.

In two of his short stories—"Two Days' Solitary Imprisonment" and "That Letter"—Bellamy portrayed the divisive effects of doubt, suspicion, and jealousy upon human relationships. In "Hooking Watermelons" and in "Extra-Hazardous" he touched upon the themes of the divisive influence of social classes—of pride in class. In these two short stories, Bellamy also introduced the moral question of ownership of property. In "Extra-Hazardous" his hero says: "I am sick at heart of this lying sham of mine and thine. I know not, no man can know for certain, in this war of equities, what or how much is rightly his and rightly another's. I leave such controversies to others. I am tired of this grab etiquette at the table of life. I do not ask for a great portion, but what I do have I want to be able to eat with a good conscience, with assurance that it is mine. To that end I would gladly concede that everything of right belongs to others, so that my claim to at least what they freely give me ought to be clear."

Bellamy's most trenchant early criticism of the divisions of society wrought by poverty and riches and by illiteracy and literacy—as well as by the selfish greed of men—was presented in *The Duke of Stockbridge* (1900) which was first published in serial form in 1879 in the *Berkshire Courier* of Great Barrington, Massachusetts—a newspaper owned and published by Clark W. Bryan who had, as part owner of the *Union,* been Bellamy's employer for five years. In this historical novel, Bellamy, as has been pointed out by Arthur Morgan and Alice Stone Blackwell, presented the first accurate picture of the causes of the Shays' Rebellion.

Bellamy presented the story of the Shays' Rebellion in a fashion which arouses sympathy for the debt-ridden, cheated farmers who are at the mercy of the banker, the storekeeper, and the rich who control the lawyers and the legislature. Many of the dispossessed had fought in the Revolution only to languish afterwards in debtors' prisons—and to wonder if they had not exchanged the rule of the king for that of the plutocracy.

Though the setting of the novel is 1786 and though the crisis pictured is that of the first post-Revolutionary War revolt against the unjust use of property and power by the plutocracy, the situation depicted is one which Bellamy saw as existing in the 1880's and one which he criticized in the same fashion in his Utopian novels. In this early novel the tyranny of wealth is also shown to have set aside democratic institutions: the common people have no social or cultural equality; they have no freedom from bondage to the rich; and they have no economic or legal equality. The people are discontented; reforms are broached; but the attitude of the ruling class, as it is expressed in the following quotation, is similar to that of the Gilded Age toward the strikers when the militias were summoned to quell them: " 'I much err,' said Squire Woodbridge, 'if the stocks and the whippingpost be not the remedy their discontent calls for. . . . These numbskulls must be taught their place, or 'twill shortly be no country for gentlemen to live in.' "

5. Themes: Sin, Man's Development

In his other short stories concerned with the qualities of the individuality of man, Bellamy was greatly preoccupied not only with the sins to which they contributed but also with the effect guilt had upon the sinner's inability to develop the impersonal, to forget his past. Bellamy's concern with the problem of guilt and sin was not, however, unique, for many authors of the nineteenth century were preoccupied with it. Hawthorne in *The Scarlet Letter* and in *The Marble Faun* had shown that sin did not always become the spiritual

gangrene of the moralists. Dostoevsky saw that sin could be a corrupting or a blessed influence—or that it could mean nothing. Hardy
portrayed the conflict between man's instincts and social mores. During the nineteenth century there was, therefore, not only much
consideration of the problem of evil in literature but also a changing
attitude toward man's responsibility for his sins and his virtues.
Man was being considered more and more as a product of the social
order, and criminals were beginning to be regarded as pathological
cases.

In Bellamy's reviews of the 1870's of such books as Wilkie
Collins' *The New Magdalen,* Thomas Hardy's *A Pair of Blue Eyes,*
and Alice Cochran's *Bessie Lang,* Bellamy voiced his approval when
the author treated the case of the erring woman with commiseration
and understanding. In his reviews of Berthold Auerbach's *The
Convicts,* he commented that the story was of interest because it
showed the attempts of criminals to live down their pasts; and he
stated that suggestions from any source about the means of restoring
self-respect for such people would be welcome. When he reviewed
the anonymous novel *Betty's Strange Experience,* he wrote: "Like
[the same author's] *Mercy Philbrick's Choice,* this story is wholly
devoted to tracing the morbid working of a woman's mind under
the joint influence of love and a perverted and sick conscientiousness.
Betty's own history illustrates the fact that too much conscience is
as injurious to the happiness of one's self and others as a certain
amount of actual depravity."

These comments of Bellamy about the considerations of others
of the problem of sin are of importance, for Bellamy had expressed
in the "Religion of Solidarity"—as well as in his journals and other
manuscripts—ideas about the genesis of morality and the dangers
of a too-active conscience which contrasted with Calvin's idea of
innate sin and with the morbid, Puritanical concern with repentance, atonement, and punishment. Bellamy's own stories and the
novels which are devoted to the problem of sin and the stages
of man's development of the individuality—*Dr. Heidenhoff's
Process, Miss Ludington's Sister,* "Lost" (1877), "An Old Folks'
Party" (1876), "A Summer Evening's Dream" (1877), and "The
Blindman's World" (1886)—are closely associated not only with

the ideas he included in the "Religion of Solidarity" but with those of other authors of the epoch.

The introspective, philosophical Bellamy was fascinated by the mental and moral disintegration of man; and, because of his sensitivity and his imagination, he found that "the smallest sin, if tasted fully and with a refined and philosophic palate" was enough to "satisfy the devil himself." Though enthralled by the frailties of the individuality, Bellamy deemed them of slight importance in comparison to that of the universal self. Like slight deformities they "should be regarded in the same spirit by the possessor as incidental to a merely temporary and insignificant phase of the eternal and universal life of the soul, like a pebble in the shoe on a day's march, . . . unpleasant enough certainly but not to be made ado over except by very womanish folk. No, no . . . there is in no wise the slightest difference in kind between physical and mental or moral deficiencies or desires as regards the greater or less degree of identification which our real being has with them. To our real being, such things do not stick. As well think to paint the wind as to affect the soul with any phase of this transient and trifling experience as human beings."

Bellamy realized, however, that a sense of guilt could so often distort the "very womanish folk"—the very religious persons—that they would be so plagued by their consciences that they could live only in their individuality, in their past. And this condition was dangerous for it halted the development of the impersonal which would enable them to expand and grow, to forget selfish concerns, and to live a full life with and for their fellow men. Furthermore, reasoned Bellamy, the man who castigated himself as a sinner might, if he were living in another era, deem himself virtuous—for "the sins of one age" were "the virtues of another."

As Bellamy reasoned about sin, he concluded that it was not a "positive thing" or "anything objective" but a "state of mind and not a course of conduct." Sin was a state of mind because the mental attitude which caused a man to regard his action as sinful was created by principles or mores instilled in youth, and over these man's will or intellect had no control. To Bellamy, man "in his relations to the prodigious and incomprehensible jumble of attributes, prejudices, powers, habits, etc., which make his nature" was as a "stumbling and fumbling child being carried about by an elephant" which he fancied he was driving. Bellamy concluded, therefore, that the "mental phenomena called moral instincts" were "reducible to acquired experiences or mere prejudices."

The prejudices and the principles which formed the habits of the mental and moral system had an importance, however, which could not be exaggerated; for they were the source of reactions which could be devastating in their effect—though it was doubtful, asserted Bellamy, that they were very effective as the motivators of moral action! Bellamy questioned the share such moral principles had in human conduct, for he reasoned that man's most important relations with his fellows depended upon his "natural instincts of affection," sympathy, and habit, and that his relationship with the world about him was ruled by his self-interest which might, however, be glossed over with a moral motive—or be so channeled that it could be made to serve society.

Bellamy also concluded that the contrast between the actions of men and their principles seemed to be the result of man's having invented "virtues and refinements . . . beyond or at variance with the morals of the Creator and the severe tenor of the universe." The result was "a house divided"—and this house was doomed to fall because of the mental discomfort created by the disturbance of the conscience which was formed by the moral principles man had been taught.

Bellamy was principally concerned, therefore, with the reactions suffered by a person who had a strong sense of right and wrong because of his religious principles or prejudices. Such a person, thinking his action to be evil, would suffer from remorse and guilt and from a loss of self-respect. On the other hand, a person lacking moral sensibilities or principles might be a sinner but remain uninjured so far as his integrity was concerned; for there would be no conflict between his conscience and his actions. Bellamy wrote that "a tender conscience has ruined far more men and women than it has ever saved. When one has fairly taken to a course opposed to current opinions, the less conscience he has, the more hope for him. More men might be saved by persuading them that their crimes were justifiable, than by persuading them that they are censurable."

As a result of his cogitations about the effects of guilt and remorse, Bellamy evolved a theory about the stages of the development of the individuality which would permit men to take a healthier attitude toward their sins—and this idea was related to his philosophy of solidarity. Bellamy wrote: "The being of today has no identity with the being of yesterday (except that of the soul solidarity through which he is one with past, future, and all things) but only a connection of memory differing only from his memory of other things in being an inside view. Time daily recreates our individuality. As regards that part of our being we are that we are, and that only, not that we were, or that we shall be. It is the soul of solidarity alone that is the same yesterday, today, and forever to which time is irrelevant having power over the individual only."

In his theory about the stages of man's development, Bellamy sought to portray the way time and experience recreated man's individuality. The evil actions of a person—if they were regretted and repented of—were done by a person who no longer existed; and he was, therefore, no longer capable of the deed and he was also no longer culpable. The "tender conscience" would no longer ruin the life, therefore, of the man who, like Bellamy himself, accepted the idea that "each epoch of life is its own." Bellamy first exploited the ideas about the changing individuality of man in "The Old Folks' Party" (1876) in which the young people of a village social club decide to masquerade as the ghosts of their future selves—as they will be fifty years later. Henry Long, the spokesman for the author, offers his theories about the different stages in a man's development and suggests that people should speak of their past selves in the third person. To Henry, mortality is seen in the change from one personality to another—a change which may be so great that little persistent identity may remain. As a result of listening to Henry's ideas, the group at the party realizes the fragility of personal identity; and the party, in reaction to the depression created by this realization, ends in mild abandonment.

In "Lost" (1877) Bellamy related the story of Charles Randall who returns to Germany to marry Ida Werner, the girl who had loved him when he was a student there and whom—after his return to the United States—he had cruelly neglected while sowing his wild oats and furthering his career. When, after a frantic search, Charles finds Ida, she is a matronly woman with children; and his romantic memory of her, based upon her past self, is shattered. Charles then realizes that the past Ida is no more—she is dead. He reasons also that he can never make amends with the suffering girl he had deserted, for she had continued to exist only in his memory. The girl of the past has not even a soul that he could love, for only death could secure the soul. To Charles, therefore, immortality becomes a mockery unless it has manifold phases which provide for the multiple souls of men. As a result of all his cogitations, Charles also realizes that he too has changed; for, had he not, he would never have considered making amends to Ida.

The theme of the stages of man's development received a more whimsical treatment in "A Summer Evening's Dream" (1877), a love story about a middle-aged couple, Lawyer Morgan and Miss Rood. Lawyer Morgan, who lives in the past and who is in love with the Miss Rood of the past, believes that, if one but wishes it fervently enough, former identities may be brought to life. One autumnal evening, he takes Miss Rood for a walk; and, in the dim light, he thinks he sees the materialized spirit of the youthful Miss Rood. His hallucination is furthered by the young girl Mabel whom he mistakes for his love, for she knows his story. As Mabel walks with him, she pretends to be the Miss Rood of his memory; and she suggests that he propose to her because she has dreamed that when they are old they will still be unwed. Morgan promises that the dream will not come true; and, when he returns to Miss Rood, he proposes because he recognizes her identity with her past self.

The danger of a memory of the past is also the problem of *Dr. Heidenhoff's Process*; but in this novel two sorely beset, sensitive creatures—Henry Bayley and Madeline Brand—live shadowed, ruined, unhappy lives because of their sense of guilt until they commit suicide. They represent, therefore, the "tender conscience" which may destroy people; and the problem, since they can find no comfort in religion, is to discover a method which will salvage such doomed souls—souls actually doomed to live in the dungeon of their past individualities. The solution found by Dr. Heidenhoff is one which—like a lobotomy operation or shock treatments—blacks out the memories of such people and permits them, therefore, to face life anew, to continue to grow and expand.

Dr. Heidenhoff explains the principle upon which the treatment is based thusly: "Acts merely express the character, and give it a tendency in a particular direction. And that is why I say, if memory were abolished, constitutionally bad people would remain at their original and normal degree of badness, instead of going from bad to worse, as they always have done hitherto in the history of mankind. Memory is the principle of moral degeneracy. Remembered sin is the most utterly diabolical influence in the universe. It invariably either debauches or martyrizes men and women, accordingly as it renders them desperate and hardened, or makes them a prey to undying grief and self-contempt. When I consider that more sin is the only anodyne of sin, and that the only way to cure the ache of conscience is to harden it, I marvel that even so many as do, essay the bitter and hopeless way of repentance and reform. In the main, the pangs of conscience, so much vaunted by some, do most certainly drive ten deeper into sin where they bring one back to virtue."

Though the sinner might suffer enough remorse and repentance to balance the moral account, he could not make atonement for his sin because of the various stages in the development of man—a theme Bellamy also fully developed in *Miss Ludington's Sister* (1884). Miss Ida Ludington is an aged spinster who has separated herself from the present and the future in order to live with her memories of the past. She had been a beautiful girl until her beauty had been destroyed by an illness; and, after she had recovered physically, Miss Ludington had considered herself dead and had mourned her own demise by hanging crape around her portrait. And, indeed, the beautiful, the youthful Miss Ludington was really dead—for no Messiah had ever promised her any resurrection from the death of change.

With Miss Ludington lived her nephew Paul who fell in love with the Miss Ida of the portrait and who came to believe that she was "neither lost nor dead, but a living and immortal spirit." To Paul, the word "man" was a collective noun which stood "for a number of distinct persons . . . having certain features of resemblance." These distinct persons were related only by succession, for they could be very unlike one another mentally, morally, and physically. One might, for example, be vicious and depraved, and the other be upright, virtuous, and a hater of iniquity. In some instances, however, harmony and likeness might be found, for the ideals and habits of youth might also be those of adulthood.

Since man had manifold stages in his life and since the soul, like the body, changed during the career of life, Paul reasoned that each of man's many souls should have its distinctive immortality. If the soul were regarded as unchanging, as the same for the fiery youth as for the dotard, then it was—as Bellamy believed it to be— "nothing more than a colorless abstraction, without destructive qualities of any kind." If there were to be any intelligible or satisfying conception of immortality, it had to allow for these multiple souls.

When Paul expounded his philosophy to Miss Ida Ludington, her retrospection became anticipation; for she saw the futility of treasuring her past self since she now believed that God would restore it to her in His "eternal present." As a result of Paul's philosophy which is described as a "modification of the curious East Indian dream of metempsychosis, according to which every soul is supposed to inhabit in turn innumerable bodies," Paul and Miss Ludington became the victims of a plot. When Mrs. Slater, a life-long friend of Miss Ludington, heard their ideas, she persuaded them that the soul of the young Ida might be materialized by a spiritualist medium.

When Paul and Miss Ludington attended a séance, the spirit of the young Miss Ida was materialized, and she was taken to live with Paul and her spiritual sister, Miss Ludington. When the materialized spirit—who is really Ida Slater, the daughter of Miss Ludington's old friend—fell in love with Paul, she was filled with remorse and guilt. As a result of this reaction, she ran away from the Ludington home, but she left a note exposing the duplicity practiced by herself, her parents, and the medium. Paul and Miss Ludington forgave her, however, for her repentance had offset her offense; "in their eyes the past was good or bad for itself, and the present good or bad for itself, and an evil past could no more shadow a virtuous present than a virtuous present could retroact to brighten or redeem an ugly past. It is the soul that repents which is ennobled by repentance. The soul that did the deed repented of is past forgiving." When Paul and Miss Ludington found Ida and explained their attitudes, she saw that she had "no responsibility for her past self" and was freed of her sense of guilt.

In "The Blindman's World" (1886) Bellamy presented, in the form of a manuscript, the story of the Martians who have been freed from the curse of memory, who have developed the spiritual aspects of themselves, and who have learned to recognize the essential unity of all things. Unlike the people of the earth, the Martians live only in the present and the future. They know their futures just as men on earth know only their pasts, and to them it seems "equally rational that the mental vision should range forward, as it does with us, illuminating the path one is to take, rather than backward, as with you, revealing only the course you have already trodden, and therefore have no more concern with."

Since the Martians are able to foresee their futures and since they also recognize that each life is a part of the whole, they do not wish their lots to be different: "No person could ever thoughtfully wish anything different, for so closely are all things, the small with the great woven together by God that to draw out the smallest thread would unravel creation through all eternity." Since they know all that is to happen to them, they have the pleasure of anticipation; knowing when they will die, they are relieved of uncertainty and are ready for death when it comes because they have lost their interest in life. As a result the Martians have separated love from sorrow and suffering; and they have no fear of death, no fear of others, no hatred, no jealousy, and no desire to compete with others. They too have been freed of the burden of the individuality—memory of the past—and they are capable, therefore, of perfecting themselves.

Bellamy's concern with the problem of guilt—as well as with its cure—which is reflected in these short stories and novels was the result not only of the interest of his era in sin but of his own experiences. When searching for his religious credo, Bellamy had decided to "act out himself" and to forget the rules of the "morality mongers." As has already been noted in Chapter I, this period was followed by one of self-contempt and depression, for fearful had been "the nemesis of defied prejudices." Bellamy, who also believed that each epoch of life was its own, had doubtless found surcease from guilt and mental equilibrium by applying his belief to his own case.

6. The Importance of the Minor Fiction

Bellamy's minor fiction is important to the student of his life and ideas because it was the result of a highly personal ambition. This aspiration caused his fiction (1) to contain autobiographical material, (2) to reveal his ideas and interests, and (3) to pave the way technically and ideologically for his major works, *Looking Backward* and *Equality*.

Bellamy not only considered himself the "major premise in all metaphysics" but sought to know himself through his fiction. As he wrote in his journal of the 1870's, his motive for writing was "chiefly to see . . . [himself] reflected from the page." By studying himself and then by creating a reflection of himself in material things, Bellamy felt that he might come to know himself. To him —as to the mind-readers—self-knowledge was achieved "only at second hand, through something else." The exhilaration and the self-knowledge which came from this process—as well as the method itself—were described by Bellamy in "Two Days' Solitary Imprisonment": "Timidity is generally associated with imagination, if not its result, and Joseph, although he concealed the fact pretty well under the mask of reticence, was constitutionally very timid. He had an unprofitable habit of taking every incident of possible embarrassment or danger that occurred to his mind as the suggestion for imaginary situations of inconvenience or peril, which he would then work out, fancying how he would feel and what he would do, with the utmost elaboration, and often with really more nervous excitement than he would be likely to experience if the events supposed should really occur."

This "deepest reason" which impelled Bellamy to write accounts not only for the type of fiction he wrote but for the ideas embodied in it. Bellamy himself described his fiction as the "attempt to trace the logical consequences of certain assumed conditions." As a result, his novels and his short stories were primarily concerned with the working out of a situation, a problem, or an idea; and the characters were flat, the action was limited to the motivation of the exposition of the ideas, and the dialogue was concerned with them. The importance of this type of fiction and of these techniques lies in the fact that Bellamy was preparing for the writing of *Looking Backward*. In this novel, Bellamy took, however, the troubled conditions of his time and the ideas that had been broached as their solution; and he traced them to their logical conclusion: the ideal state. He presented his picture of his society and its principles through the dialogue of flat characters.

As might be expected because of Bellamy's avowed aim in writing fiction, many of his minor short stories and novels contain autobiographical material. In "Pott's Painless Cure" (1879) there is, for example, an excellent description of a bull session such as Bellamy might have attended when he was a student at Union College. In "Taking a Mean Advantage" (1879), Bellamy presented a psychologically accurate picture of a drunkard who tries at a party to convince others that he is not inebriated—and Bellamy himself often drank excessively. The hero of "That Letter" (1880) thinks of the advantages of marrying a woman ten years his junior; and this is exactly what Bellamy did in 1882. In "A Superfluity of Naughtiness" (1877), the young man elopes with the adopted daughter of the household; and Bellamy married his father's ward.

Scenes familiar to Bellamy are also delineated in his fiction. The opening chapter of *Dr. Heidenhoff's Process* contained such an excellent picture of one of the Reverend Bellamy's prayer meetings that mere mention of the novel always irritated him. "Deserted" and "A Tale of the South Pacific" contain scenes which Bellamy saw on his trip to the West and the Sandwich Islands. Descriptions of his own home and of Chicopee Falls are to be found in "Hooking Watermelons," "Jane Hicks," "Taking a Mean Advantage," and "A Providence."

Bellamy's minor fiction reflected not only his interest in Transcendentalism, Positivism, and the ideas contained in the "Religion of Solidarity," but also his fascination with the psychic experiments of his era in mesmerism, spiritualism, clairvoyance, and dreams. The newspapers of the period were filled with accounts of miracles performed by mesmerists and spiritualists and of the stupendous feats of mind-reading performed by Albert Brown and Katie King. One of the most sensational of these stories related how a spirit had been materialized into the form of a pretty girl during a Philadelphia séance—a phenomenon busily investigated by reputable scientists. Although Bellamy declared that spiritualism had no hold upon him, he used this story as a basic part of the plot of *Miss Ludington's Sister* and of "A Summer Evening's Dream." He was perhaps encouraged to make this usage because he had reviewed two novels which discussed such materializations: Florence Marryat's *Open Sesame* and Theophile Gautier's *Spirite*.

Mesmerism was referred to in the "Mid-Night Drama" and played an important role in the plot development of "The Blindman's World" and of *Looking Backward*. One of Bellamy's cleverest but apparently unused plots was for a story which would demonstrate how hypnotism could be used to erase the dull moments of life and to permit men to experience only the important events. They could then, as Bellamy expressed it, enjoy the raisins without so much dough.

Bellamy himself began his own investigation of one realm of psychic phenomena—dreams. In the 1880's he started a notebook in which he intended to record without "alteration or embellishment" his dreams. As he wrote in 1886 to T. W. Higginson—whose *Monarch of Dreams* he had just finished reading—Bellamy believed that dreams had a logic of their own. Although he recorded one dream which, if he could have read a Freudian interpretation of its logic, would have embarrassed him mightily, his experiment is important because it exemplified his desire to acquire and investigate all knowledge.

Bellamy was intrigued by these psychic interests of his age because of his omnipresent desire to solve the mystery of the finite and the infinite. He hoped that the scientific investigations of such scientists as Agassiz, Alfred Wallace, and Professor Crooks of the manifestations of psychic phenomena would lead to the discovery of some new laws of human nature. "Men," wrote Bellamy, "have been dimly conscious of the unexplored region within them" but "they have been terrified when but heeding its borders." The pushing back of these borders might, hoped Bellamy, result in new worlds "for the mind to live in" and in the development of "those majestic intuitions which put us in sympathy with infinite things."

The culmination of Bellamy's preoccupation in his minor fiction with the themes of the "Religion of Solidarity" and of his interest in finding new worlds for the mind to live in which would aid men in developing the impersonal was the creation of his Utopian world which he so successfully delineated in *Looking Backward* and in *Equality*. His objective was to create a moral society which would make it possible for the ideal man of the "Religion of Solidarity" to exist—and which would not permit the divisive characteristics of the individuality to exert themselves in any way not beneficial to the society. The emotional and the religious basis—as well as the motivator—of the organization of this society was enthusiasm for humanity which promoted solidarity, the development of the impersonal, and the acceptance of Christ's behest that man should love his neighbor as himself.

Bellamy's minor fiction must, therefore, be considered as important in his development of ideas which were to be—as will be seen in Part II—basic principles of the ideal society which had as its major objective Bellamy's own purpose in life: the spiritual and intellectual development of man. Once again, therefore, Bellamy was to project his own personality, character, ideas, and interests; and once again he was to "attempt to trace the logical consequence of certain assumed conditions" and tendencies in order to create fiction in which—like the characters of "The Blindman's World"—he would permit his "mental vision" to "range forward . . . illuminating the path one is to take."

8. The Publisher (1880-1884)

Before Bellamy wrote *Looking Backward,* he had—as he wrote Howells in 1881—forsaken "literature . . . and been wholly absorbed in money-getting as proprietor of a new daily newspaper here in Springfield, 'The News'. Thanks to the good luck which has attended the enterprise, I foresee already and ere long a time of leisure and serenity when I shall be free for fresh essays in romance. Then you may hear from me. . . ."

The newspaper venture referred to in this letter had been started by Edward and his brother Charles in February, 1880, when they had founded a tri-weekly called the *Springfield Penny News*. Though Charles was nominally the publisher and Edward the editor, both did any work necessary for the success of the paper. That their efforts were successful was proved by the fact that by May the paper was being published as a daily, *The Daily News*. By September, the circulation had reached 4,400; and, by October, the success of the paper warranted the establishment of larger offices at 38 Taylor Street and the purchase of a double cylinder press. On December 9, 1880, *The Daily News* rooms were gutted by fire. Despite this catastrophe, the paper did not cease publication, for other printing companies set the type and printed the paper for the Bellamy brothers. Since the press and the stock had been fully insured, no great loss was sustained.

The aim of the *Penny News* had been to interest the reader but not to do so "by spicing . . . [its] columns with questionable personalities." The aim of *The Daily News* was, however, more explicitly and fully stated in January, 1881, when the paper carried the publishers' announcement of policy. According to this manifesto, the publishers did not aspire to make the paper the exponent of art and literature, to ride any hobby, nor to appeal to its readers by publishing "scandalous items" or "tales of shame and dishonor." Though the "events of the day, foreign and domestic" were to be reported, there were to be no "tedious and long drawn out accounts of family reunions and centennials." Furthermore, the news reported was to be presented in a graphic, accurate style which would save the readers from "reading through a column of words for what might be condensed in one sentence." "Determined not to inflict the first weariness on its readers," *The Daily News* wanted "no dull paragraphs." If it were "thrown aside with a yawn," that would be, wrote the publishers, "a more terrible blow to the proprietors than the fire which had invaded their printing office, or the dullest season when advertisers" could not "afford the price of type and white paper."

The publishers also declared the independence of their newspaper, for it had "no favorite railroad corporations which it" was
"bound to support and screen at all times." It had also "no per-
emptory stock holders to whose whims and small ambitions the
paper" had to bend and "thereby insult the public sense." To
Bellamy and his brother, this declaration was a criticism of the
newspapers of the era and of the powers behind the editors who
controlled their ideas and policies and thereby destroyed the freedom
of the press. Because of their recognition of this situation, they
wished to publish "the people's newspaper." The extent to which
the brothers went in serving the people may be seen in the paper's
news, its editorials, and, during a period of depression, in its offer
to print gratis "advertisements for persons desiring situations, or
wanting help."

When the paper published news about strikes, it sought to
present an accurate picture of the underlying causes. The same
objective and truthful attitude toward the formation of public
opinion was to be seen when, during an election campaign, both
parties were represented with supporting editorials, for each brother
had evidently assigned himself to one of the parties. Editorials,
however, were rarely published except in times of crisis or of political campaigns.

One of the most interesting of the feature articles was a column
published intermittently which contained conversations with a character called Isaac. In these conversations which discussed such things
as communal kitchens, one may see not only the germs of the ideas
to be discussed a few years later in *Looking Backward* but also the
dialogue technique which Bellamy had already developed in *Dr.
Heidenhoff's Process* and in *Miss Ludington's Sister* and which he
was to employ with such skill in his Utopian novels and in his
"Talks on Nationalism" which he published in *The New Nation,*
his own reform publication.

In 1884, the future of *The Daily News* seemed questionable.
The circulation had fallen during a period of depression, and a
competitor—*The Daily Democrat*—had cut so deeply in the field
of the *News* that its publishers considered selling the paper to its
rival. Edward tried to persuade Charles to cease publication, but

Charles preferred to continue the fight alone and, therefore, agreed to assume all financial indebtedness so as to prevent any loss to Edward. So, while Charles struggled to make the newspaper the success it eventually became, Edward retired once more from the world of business to devote himself to his literary career—to the writing of such short stories as "An Echo of Antietam" and "The Blindman's World" and such novels as *Miss Ludington's Sister* and *Looking Backward.*

CHAPTER III

WHY A FATHER WROTE A UTOPIAN NOVEL

1. Marriage and Fatherhood

In his stories picturing family life, Bellamy often described a young girl who is a sister: in "The Cold Snap," she is Ella, who plays the melodeon; in "Hooking Watermelons," she is Amy, to whom the brother Arthur, although he is ten years her senior, enjoys talking because she is so refreshingly natural; and in "Providence," she is Kate. In the novel *Dr. Heidenhoff's Process,* Madeline Brand at the prayer meeting is the same child grown to maturity; and in "That Letter," she is the Grace Harrison whom Farrell Bainbridge intends to marry. To Farrell, marriage to Grace, who is ten years his junior, seems a means of achieving what he wants in a marital relationship. He had observed that his friends who had married women younger than they had obtained a deference which wives more nearly their own ages would not have given them, and Farrell had "always had a notion that he would like to be the head of his household."

The child and the woman who was the model of these portraits and the probable cause of these speculations about marriage was Emma A. Sanderson, who, having become the ward of the Rev. Rufus King Bellamy in 1874, had come to live in his home. Emma's parents had been divorced in 1872; and her mother, because of her health and her financial condition, found it wise to send her daughter to live with the minister, who had promised to educate and support her. Though both Charles and Edward witnessed the papers of guardianship, the child Emma, then thirteen, first saw her new brother Edward when he came in a buggy to take her to Chicopee Falls. Her first impression of him was that he was a very serious and pimply-faced young man.

Edward was extremely kind to the ward of the family. Shortly after her arrival, he took her chestnut-hunting. When they arrived in the woods, Emma found quantities of chestnuts which she happily gathered—and it was not until many years later that she discovered that Edward, not wanting her to be disappointed by a futile search, had purchased the nuts, spread them on the ground, and then guided her to the appropriate spot. It was also Edward who not only gave her her first jewelry—a gold necklace—but who, more important, conversed with her, helped her with her Latin (which she said he read as fluently as English), and enjoyed hearing her play the melodeon and sing.

Edward's friendliness for the girl whom he called "Tugs" is displayed in the letter he wrote to her in 1881 when she was away on a visit: "Your letter came only to hand. I am sorry your eyes are troubling you and should advise not singing or playing from notes in the evening. It is good to know that otherwise you are having a first rate time and bursting the buttons off your dress. Go on and do so some more. You say nothing about coming home and no doubt that is far from your thoughts as yet. That's right. Go in and have a good time and stay as long as they will keep you, for though we should be happy at any time to see you, we could scarcely offer you so much fun as you are having now. Father is going to stay in Brooklyn over another Sunday, that is next Sunday, and as yet we hear no talk of mother's return and hope not to for some time yet. We are doing very well at home in spite of the smallness of the family, and sounds of merriment are heard from the pastor's residence to a late hour every night. You can write to mother at No. 2 Grace Court as usual. Yrs. in a highly friendly spirit, Ed."

The beautiful young Emma who was nearing her twenties at this time was possessed, however, of more than a "highly friendly" feeling for Edward. Whatever Bellamy's unrevealed emotional reaction to her may have been, he told her not long after this letter was written that he had no intention of ever marrying and that, if she wished to have the normal life of a woman, she should attach her affections to someone else.

Though Bellamy's journals show that he had succumbed to the charms of women, had suffered the ecstasies of love, and had probably been an experienced lover, they also—as do his short stories—reveal his resolution not to marry. In May, 1873, he wrote that it was spring and that he was having "little touches of the tender passion," but nine months later, on January 1, 1874, he amusingly appended the following statement to this entry: "Is it my mood now? No. The ground is covered with snow and I am as dull as the earth. Who could love in Winter? Certainly not I. Once a year I love, in the Springtime and in the Summer, but not in Autumn much less Winter. I can not compass it. On these cold nights I can indeed take a certain gross warmingpan view of that suffusion of the vision, that fusing and melting of all the hard sense of self in a languor of passion that is only possible in the Springtime when the nuptial of earth and sky are consummating the epithalamium of the returning birds. Then indeed the earth is one bridal bower and the conscious air is laden with solicitations to love. He who would not love then is worse than a clod; he who talks of love at any other season is no better."

Bellamy was again in love later in 1874, and, like all lovers, he marvelled that his "sweet mistress" found him so lovable; that her love charmed away his blemishes and weaknesses; and that she, who was so much "purer, finer, better than" himself, so unselfishly became interested in all of his selfish interests. Love of God, he wrote, did not compare for richness and variety of emotions to love of a woman, which inspired reverence, protectiveness, idolatry, and self-forgetfulness in a man. God's love contained no surprises and caprices, but, wrote Bellamy, "the fact that God had it in Him to make a woman shows that He must be a good deal more interesting a personage than the theologians make Him out."

The persons to whom Bellamy was so fleetingly devoted during his springtimes of love are unknown, but he was reputedly deeply in love with his first cousin Julia Putnam Cross, whom he could not marry because the families objected to a marriage between cousins. However shallow or however deep his love may have been, Bellamy was coldly objective in his attitude toward marriage—and whether this attitude developed before or after his love for Julia it is impossible to ascertain.

In the 1870's Bellamy displayed his objective attitude toward marriage when he wrote in his journal that love came to "all men in their turn" and that he wondered if "this absurd passion" would outflank his rational attitude toward matrimony. In October, 1872, he recorded his qualms about the benefits of all kinds of love, for, though one might find "manifold pleasure in love and warm sympathies," love was also tyrannous and hampering.

Bellamy recorded in his journals and in his short stories the hampering effect of matrimony. In one journal entry, he wrote that marriage forced a man to give "god, nature, and the books the go-by," for a husband had to devote himself to earning a living. In *Six to One* (1878) he wrote that "matrimony begins with kisses, but it ends with bread and butter; the mouth is the alpha and omega of the tender passion. It begins by making idealists of us but ends in making us materialists." For this reason, marriage, he wrote elsewhere, was a chain that not only riveted a man but killed his generosity, for the dependence of others upon him made him grasping and unscrupulous. Furthermore, any man wishing to experience sorrow had only to court love and end by getting himself a wife and children.

Marriage was particularly hampering for the philosopher or for the artist whose two foes were laziness and marriage; of the latter Bellamy wrote in "Pott's Painless Cure": "Hitch Pegasus to a family cart and he can't go off the thoroughfare." In order to study and develop himself, Eliot Carson denied himself matrimonial bliss and retreated to a hermitage. To Bellamy, "the rivals of women are three—the love of combat, of study, of wine. It is strange how in the morning, when love of action and the desire of strife is strong in a man, the charms of a woman, which last night filled him and seemed the only worthy things in life, have paled and taken on a forced artificial effervescence." As a result of this observation, he concluded that one should "never propose to a woman in the evening but in the morning. If you feel like it then, you may be tolerably sure that your passion is real and not the mere evening hectic. We are all hectic in the evening, all passion is created."

After Edward had bluntly told Emma Sanderson of the attitude he had adopted toward marriage, the beautiful young girl began to associate with the youths of the village; and, before too many months had passed, she came home one day to announce her engagement. Edward accepted the news in silence—but from that day on he was so coldly polite and so morose that Mrs. Bellamy eventually suggested that Emma go to Springfield to live with her mother. Since Emma was giving music lessons to some village children and was also singing in the Baptist Church choir, Mrs. Bellamy advised her that she could return during the weekends to fulfill these obligations. When she returned to Chicopee Falls each weekend, Emma found a moody, sombre Edward who had little to say to her.

One Sunday evening her fiancé arrived to escort her to the evening church service. When he whistled for her—for she did not dare have him enter the house because of Edward's dour demeanor—she went to attire herself for the street. While she was putting on her hat, Edward came into the room, took her in his arms, and said: "You can't go. You're my little girl and I can't let anyone else have you." Thus did Bellamy's emotions outflank his prejudices against matrimony—and cause him to propose early in the evening!

Edward married Emma on May 30, 1882. This is one of the most important dates in the life of Bellamy, for his marriage and his subsequent fatherhood were to complete his education and to provide the emotional impetus which would eventually make of the would-be hermit a reformer.

Emma Bellamy, described by a contemporary as "very much in love with Ed tho [sic] not an intellectual type," was the wife Bellamy had surmised a younger wife would be in "That Letter." Edward was the head of the household, and he asserted his prerogatives by holding the purse strings, by giving his wife minute but thoughtful advice as to what trains to take where and when, and by taking vacations at the seashore alone when he felt the need, while she stayed home to care for the children, Paul (born December 26, 1884) and Marion (born March 4, 1886).

That Edward was, however, a thoughtful, appreciative, and loving husband is proved by his letters and his actions. Though he was opposed to the wearing of jewelry, he purchased a diamond and emerald ring for his wife while on a trip to New York City and informed her of it in a letter saying: "I've got it . . . but it's dead against my principles." In a letter written to her on their second anniversary, he wrote that he had married her because he could not get along without her and that he had never found a time when he could do so. In March, 1884, he wrote: "I have felt since you have been gone what it is to be a bachelor once more, and perceive plainly that I did a very sensible thing when I got married. It is not good for a man to be alone." In May, 1887, Edward sent the following note to his wife by a special messenger, Mrs. Charles Bellamy: "Dear Emma—it occurs to me that you forgot to kiss me when I came away. I'll excuse you this time but don't let it happen again."

Though Mrs. Bellamy was not the wife who could be Edward's intellectual companion and though she did not appreciate his literary endeavors until long after his death, there can be no doubt as to the depth of Bellamy's love for her—or of hers for him. He disliked being away from her and from his home. When he was, his letters constantly expressed his desire to be reunited with her and he kept her posted about his plans by telegram. When Mrs. Bellamy herself was so preoccupied with the activities of the Hampden County Music Association that she was gone for a day at a time, Bellamy remarked to his children: "We'll have to have a painting of Mrs. Bellamy so we can remember what she looks like."

When the children were born, Bellamy was a kind and loving father, and he sought—albeit in a somewhat absent-minded fashion—to help his wife rear their children. When they were preparing to move into an apartment (which they occupied only a few months, for when Bellamy's father died in 1886 they returned to live with Mrs. Bellamy), Emma wrote a friend that she had been able to do little about preparing their new home because of her pregnancy but that "poor Ed is worn out doing and 'forgetting' errands of various kinds."

Edward was, however, more efficient in walking the floor with the babies when they cried with colic and in entertaining them. When they grew older, he took them for long walks; taught them to garden; and often enthralled them and their friends with his stories while they sat in the sun in the enclosed space, formerly a chicken yard, which Edward called their hen-parlor. He guided their reading, introduced them to the library, and taught them the "Lord's Prayer." He never, however, permitted them to repeat the submissive passages of the prayer, for he said that God did not want submission from any man.

Edward's disciplining of his children was frequently done by remote control, for, if they were fighting or being rowdy, he would look up from his book to say: "Emma, do you see what *those* children are doing?" He himself rebuked them sternly, however, if he found them lying, being intolerant, or being inconsiderate. After having flayed the culprit with his tongue, he would gather the by-then-crying child in his arms and say: "There, there, there! Papa's little lamb! Papa loves you!" He wished always to assure his children that he loved them but disliked their faults.

He sought also to inculcate in his son and daughter unselfishness and respect for the rights of others. One evening when the Bellamy family was eating its Sunday supper, Paul, without asking whether anyone else wished the last piece of creamed toast, took it. His father, indignant because of his son's lack of consideration of others, ended the tirade he delivered to him with these words: "No son of mine will grow up to be a hog!"

Several mornings later when Mrs. Bellamy was serving the small boy his breakfast, she said: "Paul, you'll soon be eight years old."

Paul glumly answered: "Yes, eight years old—and a hog!"

After his father's death, Paul showed, however, that his father's training had not been wasted. Desiring to go on a camping trip and having to earn the money for it, Paul, a slightly built lad of fifteen, obtained a job in a nearby factory in the shipping room where he worked from six-thirty in the morning until six in the evening. When he came home at noon for lunch, he was so exhausted that he would lie on the floor of the living room, and it was there that his sister served him his meal. When he quit the job to go on his vacation, he gave his mother money for a vacation for his sister.

Marion too had her lessons in self-sacrifice. Because she was susceptible to respiratory infections, her father bribed her to follow a regime of physical exercises to develop her chest and lungs. The child hoarded her money to buy a walking doll which she had seen in a store, and when she announced just before Christmas that she was spending her $4.07 for the doll, her father chided her for the selfishness which prompted her to spend all of her money on herself, and he frequently referred to the subject. When her mother finally took her to the store, Marion stood before the show case, gazed at the coveted doll, cried—and bought another for $1.98. Though she never forgot the doll she denied herself, her father was jubilant because she had conquered her selfishness.

Bellamy's pride in and his love for his children were reflected in his actions and his letters. In 1886, he wrote to his wife from the Packer farm that "Mr. Bob [Paul] seems to me more than ever a paragon of babies, a marvel of affectionateness and hard common sense, a boy of a thousand, and the little girl's pretty face is constantly before my mind." If one of the children were ill when he was away from home, he expected Mrs. Bellamy to send him a daily telegram about the child's progress. When Marion was seriously ill with dysentery after the publication of *Looking Backward,* Bellamy canceled a series of lectures in order to stay home to nurse the child day and night for four weeks.

What his wife and his children meant to his development and to the writing of his first Utopian novel was recorded by Bellamy in the Eliot Carson journal. He wrote that, in the book which was to be entitled *Man, Woman and Child,* he should "make it clear that in seeking to wed Edna, Carson was not moved by the ideal view of Woman which he afterwards developed but by the pure natural passion of sex. Let his development in this come after marriage."

What this development and experience had actually been, Bellamy also recorded in his notebook in regard to the reasons Eliot Carson became a reformer: "[Eliot] falls in love, constrained by nature back to the world, again with his kind. Then his child came, not anticipated with much pleasure. Submitted to. With it comes a revelation of his oneness with posterity. Next he has a girl. With this his oneness with mankind. He cannot thenceforward bear the thought of leaving his children, anyman's, anybody's children to struggle in such a horrid world as this. Cured once for all of Hermitism and self-absorption, he plunges with enthusiasm, with tremendous earnestness into the study of social conditions and develops nationalism."

The sensitive, emotional, reticent, shy Edward Bellamy had coined his philosophy of solidarity out of his heart, his rebellion

against religion, his love of nature, and his frustrations; and he
had sought to study himself and to develop himself in his library.
He had entered the world of law and of journalism only to retreat
from its disillusionments and its unsatisfactory life of the mind and
the soul. To the lonely, proud, introspective Bellamy who wished
to be a self-sacrificing servant of humanity, a retreat to a hermitage
had seemed the only answer for one who wished to grow spiritually
and mentally.

It was, however, through the ties of matrimony and family—
"through woman and child"—which he had rebelled against as
curtailing the artist's progress, that he was finally to find his identification with the race and to learn that "selfishness is suicide." Because woman, the centripetal force, had brought him back to humanity and to his greater self and because his children would have no
security in the world of his day, Bellamy ceased to be a sentimentalist
in his study and became a practical reformer who sought to outline
and then to establish an ideal world.

Bellamy's ideal world was, however, based upon the world he
knew and his reactions to it. When *Looking Backward* was published, his contemporaries regarded it as a "looking glass well
polished and backed" of their world; and Bellamy himself admitted
in a public address that it contained nothing which could be "said
to be greatly in advance of public opinion." A general glance at
the political, social, reform, and literary conditions of the times in
which the mature Bellamy lived and a cursory glance at his reactions
to them are, therefore, enlightening.

2. Economic Revolution

At the end of the Civil War, President Lincoln had expressed,
in a personal letter addressed to the Honorable W. R. Ellis, his fear
of what might happen in the post-war era: "I see in the near future
a crisis arising that unnerves me and causes me to tremble for the
safety of my country. By a result of the war, corporations have been
enthroned, and an era of corruption in high places will follow and
the money power of the country will endeavor to prolong its reign
by working upon the prejudices of the people until all wealth is
aggregated in a few hands and the Republic is destroyed. I feel,

at this point, more anxiety for the safety of my country than ever before, even in the midst of war." Many years after this letter was written, Bellamy confirmed the fulfillment of Lincoln's fears when he stated that the conditions in industry, society, and politics indicated that portentous times had befallen the great American experiment in democracy on which the last hopes of humanity had been pinned.

Lincoln had doubtless realized that the unity of the nation which the Civil War had been fought to preserve was likely to be destroyed by the rapacious greed of the money kings who, because of their wealth, could corrupt the agents of the people and thereby make the government their tool. The factors which had created this centralization of wealth were the need of supplies for the army, the rapid expansion of the railroads, the employment of steam power, and the invention of machinery which required greater investments of capital but made mass production possible.

During the period from 1860 to 1874, the United States had risen from fourth to first place in the world for its volume and value of manufactured products. Before 1860 less than 36,000 patents had been issued, but between 1860 and 1900 over 640,000 were registered. Railroad construction had been doubled in 1870 and by 1880 it had been trebled. In 1876 Bellamy commented that mechanical progress was a characteristic of the period and that all other progress largely depended upon it.

This rapid expansion of transit and communication facilities, of the utilization of machinery, and of the development of large industries had enriched many men, and the number of millionaires had grown from three in 1860 to thirty-eight in 1890. Among these empire builders were such men as John D. Rockefeller, founder of the Standard Oil Company; Andrew Carnegie and Henry C. Frick, consolidators of the iron and steel industry; and Jay Gould and Jim Fisk, whose chicaneries, developments, and speculations were manifold and notorious.

Though these shrewd financiers developed the manufacturing and the communication facilities of the nation in a remarkably short time, they not only brought in their wake political corruption, speculative frenzy, and panics but they destroyed free competition—except

in the labor market. Their era was infamous as the "Nadir of
National Disgrace" because of its political scandals such as the
Credit Mobilier and the Whiskey Ring. In New York, the reign
of Boss Tweed and Tammany Hall increased in two and a half
years the city debt by seventy million dollars and left the city an
unfinished courthouse which had already cost eleven million dollars—according to the bookkeeper's record, one plasterer had earned
$138,187 in two days!

In 1873 a Congressional investigating committee reported that
"the country is fast becoming filled with gigantic corporations, wield-
ing and controlling immense aggregations of money and thereby
commanding great influence and power. It is notorious in many
state legislatures that these influences are often controlling so that
in effect they become the ruling power of the state." Bellamy himself noted in a *Union* editorial that the New York *Nation* had
charged the Senate with becoming a "capitalist's chamber" and that
Theodore D. Woolsey, ex-president of Yale, had wondered in 1876
if there were such a " 'poison in the political system that there was
no cure for it' " and if the republic would " 'run into a degenerate
form of polity within the next hundred years.' "

In an editorial relative to a poem which the Rev. Dr. J. G. Holland had read in 1874 at a reunion of Civil War veterans, Bellamy
wrote that the poem was the product of the times, for it voiced "the
anguish which every patriot felt in these latter years at the corruption
in our public affairs, the dry rot in our social and business morality,
and the degeneration of public opinion, an anguish that has led
many once earnest and hopeful patriots to a temper of bitter cynicism,
while over-whelming nobler souls with a weight of unmixed sorrow. . . . Was it worth while to save the nation from slavery and
secession merely to fall a victim to social and political corruption?"

In another *Union* editorial Bellamy quoted at length from
Montesquieu in order to show that a popular government could not
exist without virtue and that, when avarice entered the hearts of
men, they rebelled at all restraint and at all laws. The inevitable
result was that the public treasury became the patrimony of a few
private individuals who became the only power of the commonwealth. To Bellamy this minority of the wealthy made "the weight-

iest trusts and dearest interests of the republic" its "trading capital" in its game "of personal ambition."

Mercantilism, the principle of private business so dreaded by Thomas Jefferson, and the millionaire, the American ideal and hero, had conquered the republic. Not only the politicians were corrupted by special interests such as the railroads, which wanted enormous government loans and huge grants of land to finance and to make exorbitantly profitable their ventures, but every phase of national life was affected by the successful industrial consolidations and by the financial machinations of the business tycoons. It seemed to Bellamy that a revolution had occurred which made the Declaration of Independence mere verbiage, for the government which had been established for the protection of the life and liberty of all individuals had become a plutocratic oligarchy which insured and secured blessings only for the few.

Bellamy expressed this same attitude in an editorial of 1877 in which he wrote: "There is no probability that we shall ever give up the name and title of a republic. The name is safe enough: but how about the reality? The old states of Greece were republics; so were the medieval states of Europe; and they also were not. They were republican in that they allowed no king or emperor; but as to popular liberty and security they were as imperial as if they had never broken with the Caesars. They were oligarchies, with a dozen or a hundred kings instead of one. That is our drift." He also warned the laborers, who hoped that legislation would restore their prosperity, that the government could do nothing; for it was "but a cockle shell, rising and falling on the waves of the vast ocean of trade and industry, and can no more control its motion than the boat can change the movement of the tides which bear it."

In the year following this editorial, Bellamy had one of his wealthy characters of *The Duke of Stockbridge* remark that to have ridded themselves "of a king only to fall into the hands of a democracy" would be a bad exchange for the rich. The poor characters of this same novel remarked that they had merely exchanged the rule of the king for the rule of the plutocrats. The end result of such conflicting attitudes was delineated by Bellamy in a magazine review in which he called attention to an article by Professor Goldwin

Smith predicting the termination of popular government and then remarked that W. R. Greg had predicted in *Rocks Ahead* that either property would wrest the voting power from the working classes or the latter would wrest property from the former in order to restrain its accumulation and to direct its division. Though Bellamy as early as 1872 had stated that the rich were not to blame for the unequal distribution of wealth since they were but products of the system, he foresaw that the discontentment of the masses would force the capitalists to seek a "stronger form of government" which would put the already perishing republic completely out of existence.

In his portrayals of the results of a competitive system which permitted the rise of monopolies and plutocrats to a position of control in the country, Bellamy showed also his concern about the social, economic, and ethical effect of this condition. He feared that, as the strongest, or the most ruthless, continued to amass wealth, a social order based upon caste would develop in which the middle class and the proletariat would be reduced to the position of lackeys and eventually of serfs. Since education and business opportunities depended upon the possession of money, the door to life and opportunity would be shut for these classes; and the inevitable result would be the end of the American dream of social equality, of equality of opportunity, of liberty and independence for all, and of the right to the pursuit of happiness.

The social order resulting from this highly competitive form of society was, said Bellamy, no better than a state of barbarism, since an internecine strife which made men beasts of prey existed. Men, instead of working together in fraternal co-operation and unselfishness, were pitted against each other in a brutal, selfish struggle for the very sustenance of life. This predatory state was demoralizing, for it developed in men their selfish or individual instincts and not their generous or universal ones. To be moral or to carry the idealistic dreams of youth into this economic battle for life which recognized no ethical code was impossible, for men, if they were to survive, had to conform to the methods used in the fray. This conformity to the morals of the market place Bellamy sardonically pictured, in "Extra-Hazardous" (1877), as being ample excuse for becoming a tramp: the life of a tramp permitted a clear conscience, but that of the man who earned his bread was such that he felt himself to be a cheat—and his bread was correspondingly sour.

The need and the desire for wealth, the belief in individualism, and the moral laxity of the times which permitted the extenuation of the rascalities and dishonesties of the plutocrat resulted in a society comparable to that of the Gypsy because of its "proverbial dishonesty" and "thievish cunning." Though this society might be called Christian, it not only embodied an anti-Christian spirit but it prevented the following of the Christian concept of the Golden Rule. Though the Romans had regarded the qualities of the huckster with disdain, these same qualities of greed and self-seeking were considered by Americans to be the foundation and the cohesive force of society. Since these characteristics were actually anti-social, they were detrimental to the achievement of brotherhood and a recognition of the common good. Because men believed in individualism and because they suffered or witnessed the social abuses that were its result, they were pessimistic and melancholy; they felt man to be depraved; they disliked themselves and despised their Creator; and they were, as a result of all of these reactions, irreligious.

The general economic results which Bellamy portrayed as the effect of the competitive system were closely allied with its political, moral, and social results; for they were a loss of personal liberty and independence, of social equality, and of equal opportunity. The consolidation of industries to avoid the wastes of competition and the prohibitive cost of the machinery which made mass production possible resulted in the disappearance of the small producer and of the craftsman and, therefore, in the destruction of individual initiative, equality of opportunity, free competition, and independence of the laborer. The ever-increasing army of the proletariat which resulted forced men to bargain for work and to compete against one another; and, said Bellamy in *The Duke of Stockbridge,* the necessity of living made enemies of those who had the same social status, the same needs, and the same difficulties to surmount.

Though the laborers had attempted in self-defense to ape the methods of the monopolists and had combined to form unions, which brought about strikes, bloodshed, and lack of production, the benefits derived were only temporary. This was true because, as Bellamy pointed out in an early *Union* editorial, "the command of great pecuniary means, in any department of business," gave a "command of other men's muscles and brains—their labor. The very rich can make their own terms with the agents of their work, and they do it, as a rule, so as to realize excessive profits." Under such a situation, as Bellamy observed in a later article, the employers could and did resort to going on strike themselves by shutting down their plants or mines until the starving workers were forced to accede to the terms offered them. When the laborers were so at the mercy of their employers because they were dependent upon them for their livelihood, they were little better than slaves.

The end result of such a system and such profits was the growth of the number of millionaires, whose existence, "especially in a democratic country," seemed to Bellamy to indicate "a deep disease in our civilization" which contributed to another symptom of its illness—"the miserable poverty everywhere elbowing this wealth and luxury." America, "instead of being as once the country where the greatest equality of wealth prevailed," had become, wrote Bellamy in another editorial, "the country where the inequalities of wealth are most excessive."

Specifically, Bellamy condemned the monopolistic-capitalistic order because of its injurious effect upon the production of wealth by portraying its tendency to restrict production by raising prices. When an increase in price occurred without a corresponding raise in wages, the result was to diminish the purchasing and consuming power of the public and, subsequently, to decrease production, the sole basis of wealth. As will be seen in later chapters, Bellamy also condemned the industrial order because of its economic wastes, its influence in halting progress in the development of inventions and philosophical ideas, its prevention of the cultivation of the best leadership and minds of the nation, and its depriving the individual of leisure which might be used for self-cultivation.

Bellamy also saw, however, that the industrial system he so caustically criticized had contributed to the progress of the country and had played a necessary role in the evolution of the race. For the sake of the nation, this evolution had to be continued so that something better could be achieved. The alternative he pictured thusly: "Such . . . is the condition of political corruption, of social rottenness, of moral degeneracy, of industrial oppression, confusion and impending ruin which has resulted from the overthrow of our republican equality by the money power. If you would learn how republics perish, shut up your musty histories of Greece and Rome and look about you."

The actual conditions which Bellamy saw when he looked about were responsible not only for this pessimistic view of the future of the United States but for his creation of a Utopia which was to incorporate many of the ideas and reforms which had been formulated by others as a means of ameliorating these same conditions. To understand not only why Bellamy wrote his Utopia but to comprehend his criticism of his world and his picture of the ideal world, one must see some of the facts which confronted him.

3. The Laborer

Although free competition was decreasing in the industrial world because monopolies like the Standard Oil Company could combine with the railroads, freeze the shipments of competitors, and force them to sell or go bankrupt, freedom of competition was not an idle theory but a principle of trade in the labor market. And yet though adults and children competed with one another for jobs, the total income of the working family was barely sufficient to keep body and soul together. According to the Rev. C. A. Cressy, the total average annual living expenses of a Boston workingman's family in 1883 was $754.42—but the head of the family could earn only $558.68. The deficit that existed forced the wife and children to help maintain the family.

It is not surprising, therefore, that the Illinois commissioners of labor statistics reported that " 'one half of the intelligent workingmen are not even able to earn enough for support without depending on the labors of wives and children' " or that in 1883 in the state of Massachusetts alone 28,714 children under sixteen were employed in industrial establishments. In 1880 a total of 1,118,356 children under sixteen were employed in various industries throughout the nation; and in June, 1884, an article published in the *North Ameri-*

can Review stated that in Pennsylvania "herds of children of all ages, from six years upward, work in the coal breakers, toiling in dirt and air thick with carbon dust, from dawn to dark of every day in the week except Sunday." Because children of ten and twelve years of age were also working a ten-hour day in factories, it seemed to Bellamy "that modern industrial development" had become "the most formidable rival of the school-house" and that the nation needed to organize clubs for the prevention of cruelty to children.

Though it was necessary for the whole family to work, employment was not easily found because of the large body of unemployed that had been created by the industrial revolution; by the movement from the farm to the city; and by the influx of immigrants due, in many instances, to the posters and pamphlets presenting a glowing picture of the promised land which had been distributed by companies desiring cheap labor. Since the recently arrived Germans, Irish, French, Italians, or Chinese could underbid the American worker because of their lower standards of living, they were disliked; and racial prejudices and battles were rife. Bellamy wrote in the *Union* that this "influx of foreign cheap labor" created a hardship for the laborer; for it operated "to depreciate his currency, labor," which was "worse for him than a depreciation in common currency which would affect all classes alike, for this affects him alone while other classes get him at their mercy. . . ."

Bellamy observed that many of these foreign laborers lived in boxes, and Collins G. Burnham stated in an article about the city of Chicopee that many families were living in holes dug in the river bank. The living conditions of the native laborers were not, however, much better, for, wrote Dr. Frank Draper, their homes were so crowded and so unsanitary that the inhabitants suffered physical and moral vitiation. While charitable organizations were reporting that the laborers in New York were "living on the verge of starvation" and while the Bostonians were denying that the city contained any destitution although 3,300 people had gone to the poor house in one year and 12,583 families had been fed by public charity in sixty-nine days, the "American Medici" were building their palaces and filling them with treasures. The Vanderbilts, for example,

erected their cottage "The Breakers" at Newport and their house in
Asheville at a total cost of six million dollars.

Despite such evidences of the wealth of the nation, the laborer
seemed inextricably caught in a mesh of circumstances which he could
not control. Once upon a time, he could have moved westward and
have established himself as an independent farmer; but, by the
1890's, the frontiers were closing and the farmer had little more
security than the laborers. Indeed, the industrial slums were matched
in every state by the rural slums inhabited by the roving farm hands
who worked seasonally, the dispossessed farmers, and the farmers
who wrested a meager living from exhausted, exploited soil. The
days foreseen by Carlyle and DeTocqueville seemed to have arrived
—and the pictures of destitution of the period parallel those presented decades later by John Steinbeck in *The Grapes of Wrath.*

The farmer, always at the mercy of draughts and grasshoppers,
was also caught in the clutches of the capitalists. The speculators
and the middlemen played with his produce for their own profits,
and the railroads levied fares at their own discretion upon his produce. The large bonanza farms, owned by the bankers and the railroads and often consisting of as much as 75,000 acres, were also
a threat to the small farmer. Tilled only for profit by seasonal
industrial armies supplied with the latest farm equipment, these
farms not only created a surplus of produce but, because of discriminatory arrangements with the railroads, shipped it more cheaply.
In *Land and Labor,* William Godwin Moody stated that this non-
resident ownership of the bonanza farms resulted in the skinning of
the finest land, in the amassing of great fortunes, in the impoverish-
ment of the people, in the growth of a large group of transient
workers, and in the prevention of the settlement of certain large
areas.

The financiers had obtained control of these large tracts by
devious means and by mortgages. One large bonanza farm in
Dakota was controlled by a group of Eastern capitalists who had
"exchanged some almost worthless Northern Pacific bonds for the
company's government granted lands." Western farm lands were
heavily mortgaged, and the rates of interest were so high that payment of the principal sum was impossible and that of the interest

alone a hardship. A table of the profits on different types of investments showed that profit on farm lands was 2 percent but that profit on farm mortgages was 7 percent. To those concerned about the fate of the farmer, it seemed that he was, in view of these facts, doomed to become like his European cousin—a tenant. To men like Bellamy, this seemed only another instance of the sudden duplication of the oppressive conditions of Europe.

Factory laborers, artisans, farmers, and even the financiers themselves found no security in this age of economic anarchy which Gronlund, Bulwer-Lytton, and Bellamy compared to the days of the decline of the Roman Empire because of its mad chase for wealth and its paucity of ideals. In *The Gilded Age,* Mark Twain and Charles D. Warner depicted the speculative fever of the age which seemed to increase each year as the American public became more gullible or more infected with the desire to gain money without working for it.

In September, 1873, the mad, feverish chase ended with the most severe panic then known in the history of the country; the Jay Cooke Company had failed and the Northern Pacific Railroad had collapsed. During the next three years, twenty thousand businesses failed and suicide was rife. During the following six years, almost three million of the forty million Americans were unemployed, and those who were employed had sustained enormous wage cuts.

In 1884 another depression occurred which was to last until 1886. This and other long-lasting periods of crisis were to be severe enough to serve a profound purpose. As a result of the rapid growth of monopolies, of the unlicensed speculation, and of the exploitation of the worker and the investor, the pattern of American life was to be changed, for the people and their leaders were to seek to discipline industry. Even conservative Thurlow Weed was to prescribe radical treatment for the speculators who caused panics and for the usurers who loaned them money at one percent a day, for he advised that they be hanged by the neck in the streets which they had desecrated. Others were, however, to seek more lasting and permanent corrections, for, discounting the theory of Professor Stanley Stevons that the great periods of financial distress were caused by sun spots, they were to lead the people in a counter-revolution.

4. Reform Movements

In the early 1870's Bellamy described the reform spirit of his chaotic, iconoclastic age in these words: "No ancient institution, whose deep roots rise from the first strata of human experience, remains unmolested by its searching criticism, its unsurpassing dissection. No principle of morals, to which the adherence of an undoubting past has been recorded, commands for a moment its reverence. All religions, all moralities, all social conditions, and relations and institutions of law and government are cited in turn before the tribunal of the popular judgment, there to render good and sufficient reason for their existence and claims or cease them forever."

Bellamy attributed this spirit and the "political and social delusions" which were springing up like weeds to "the hard times and general discontent," for, he wrote in a *Union* editorial, "when men are so ready to lend their ears to all who will promise 'new things,' professional reformers are naturally a numerous class." The word "reform," he wrote in 1876, had been so overused that the public was prone to react to it with a cynical grin because it had been appropriated too frequently by knaves or had been used to cover political spite and demagoguery.

During this period "social idealism, once the struggle of individuals, was organized and put on a business basis" and became as good entertainment as the theater. Among the different reform movements which appeared were those—to mention only a few—which sought to improve prison conditions; to liberalize religion; to prevent cruelty to children; to halt the consumption of tea, coffee, and spiritous beverages; to revolutionize the wearing apparel of women; to obtain the vote for women; to improve conditions in insane asylums; and to reform the educational system.

Aside from these specific but often sporadic reform movements, there were also the social revolts of the farmers and the laborers who, patterning after the monopolists, had forsworn their individualistic tendencies and had turned to collective agencies as a means of obtaining legislation which might remedy their situations. As Frederick Jackson Turner has indicated, the western settler "began to lose his primitive attitude of individualism, government began to look less like a necessary evil and more like an instrument for the perpetuation of his democratic ideas. In brief, the defenses of the pioneer democrat began to shift from free land to legislation, from the ideal of individualism to the ideal of social control through legislation by law."

Although the American farmer had revolted in Bacon's Rebellion before and in the Shays' Rebellion after the Revolution, these revolts were short-lived in comparison to the nation-wide, organized protests that the usually phlegmatic sons of the soil were to make in Bellamy's period against the monetary system, the railroads, the growth of trusts, the middlemen, and the corruption in officialdom. The three major organizations of protest of the middle class—for the small business man joined the agrarians—were Greenbackism, Grangerism, and Populism.

Greenbackism, popular in the 1870's, was akin to the individualistic radicalism of the 1840's and 1850's as expressed in George Evans' freelandism, Horace Greeley's Homesteadism, Edward Kellogg's currency reformism, and Josiah Warren's early philosophic anarchism. The Greenbacks, who stood for private ownership and individual control, denounced the middleman, the broker, the railroads, and monopolistic control.

The National Grange of the Patrons of Husbandry, or the Grangers, was organized in 1866, and its membership consisted of independent farmers, but it had an influence upon the labor movement also, for it had formed by the 1880's connections in many states with the Knights of Labor. The objectives of this organization, as cited by Grand Master Adams at the St. Louis convention and recapitulated by Bellamy in a *Union* editorial, were to dispense with the middlemen, to establish co-operative buying and selling, to sell produce directly to the consumer, and to achieve government regulation of the rates of transportation.

The Grangers became a political power in the West, for by 1873, as Bellamy noted in an editorial, thirty-two states, two territories, and Canada contained 12,000 Granges. By the middle 1870's, the total membership was 2,500,000. In 1873, Ignatius Donnelly, who was later to help write the People's Party platform, was chosen chief lecturer of the Grange, and in one of his speeches he proclaimed: " 'Wherever amid the fullness of the earth a human stomach goes empty, or a human brain remains darkened in ignorance . . . there is wrong and crime and fraud. . . .' "

The story of the Populists, or the People's Party, which was a motley assortment of farmers, merchants, laborers, professional people, prohibitionists, suffragettes, Bellamyites, and socialists will be related in Chapter IV because of its relationship to the life of Bellamy as a reformer and its influence upon the development of his ideas.

The agitation of the farmers was, however, a very quiet affair in comparison to the great upheavals, riots, and strikes which were caused in the 1870's and the 1880's by the labor unions which had begun to organize in the decade that the Civil War ended. The labor union movement was in part a result of the abolition movement, of expanded communication facilities, of the change from prosperity to adversity, of the immorality of the business practices of the day which resulted in fortunes for the few and poverty for the many, of the concentration of labor in large factories, and of the importation of foreign labor which created antagonism between employers and employees. To these factors might be added the lack of personal contacts between employee and employer when the latter was replaced by an invisible, impersonal board of directors which determined the policies of the great corporations.

In the 1860's the locomotive engineers, the cigar makers, and the bricklayers founded their unions, and the National Labor Union, the Labor Knights of St. Crispin, and the Knights of Labor were organized. By 1870 there were thirty-two national trade unions in the country, and each large city had its labor paper and its workingman's library. The panic of 1873 and the consequent widespread industrial difficulties and unemployment brought death to the unions, and, by the end of the decade, only about eighteen percent were surviving. The difficulties caused by the labor groups in the 1870's and the 1880's struck fear, however, into the hearts of the conservatives and began in the West, after the Haymarket Riot of 1886, a reign of terror which eventually caused a change of tactics on the part of the labor unions.

Of these early organizations, the Knights of St. Crispin and the Knights of Labor were the most influential. The Knights of St.

Crispin was established on an international basis by 1869 and numbered at one time nearly a hundred thousand members. This organization, which was quite influential in Massachusetts, sponsored a program that went beyond that of most unions, for its declared, ultimate purpose was the establishment of co-operative production and trade. The Knights of Labor also sponsored a co-operative industrial system and advocated that the government control all transportation and communication facilities.

Bellamy, who noted the effort to establish co-operatives in the United States and elsewhere, thought that co-operation seemed to be the tendency of the time. Professor R. Ely wrote in *The Labor Movement in America* (1886) that success had attended this movement and that it had never been "so truly a live vigorous force, full of promise as it is today." The forms of co-operative production included profit-sharing or industrial partnership, the association of laborers who conducted production on their own account, and the unions of producers who were not in the employer class.

The first large co-operative industry—except for the cod and mackerel fisheries which had been organized on that basis in the 1730's—was that of the workers in iron which was organized by William S. Sylvis, founder of the Iron Moulders International Union. By 1870 fourteen co-operative foundries had been established in New York, Ohio, Massachusetts, and elsewhere. *The Iron Moulder's International Journal* stated that co-operation should command the attention of all workers, for it was the only true remedy for "low wages, strikes, lockouts, and a thousand other annoyances to which workingmen are subjected."

The Knights of Labor, which hoped to introduce co-operative production as a means of ultimately destroying the industrial competitive system, owned one hundred co-operatives by 1886. Other co-operative producers were the Co-operative Coopers of Minneapolis, Minnesota, which, started in 1874, had a million-dollar-a-year business by 1886; the Carpenter Co-operative of Decatur, Illinois; and the Co-operative Manufacturing of Easton, Pennsylvania, which produced shoes and boots.

Distributive co-operatives flourished because they were more easily organized than the producer ones. They ranged in form of

organization from those organized to buy in lots (such as the Roch-
dale Co-operative Society of Washington, D. C., which consisted
mostly of government employees) to co-operative stores (such as
the highly successful Philadelphia Co-operative Society). Wherever
these co-operatives made progress, they were invariably associated
with some labor or union organization; and the motive behind their
organization was the eventual replacement of the competitive order
with one based upon combination, unity, and partnership. Besides
the already-mentioned Knights of Labor and the Knights of St.
Crispin, the more important organizations which sponsored such
co-operatives were the New England Protective Union, the Patrons
of Husbandry, and the Sovereigns of Industry.

Many of these distributive co-operatives were highly successful,
and, in the case of the Granger organization, they saved the members as much as twelve million dollars a year. In 1876, the Grangers
owned five steamboat or packet lines, thirty-two grain elevators, and
twenty-two warehouses for storing goods. The largest store operated
by the Sovereigns of Industry was located in Springfield, Massachusetts, and it was so successful that it was able to build in 1875
the "Sovereign's Block" at a cost of $35,000. In 1878 President
William E. Earle said that the store's sales had amounted to $119,000
during the preceding year. Professor Ely noted that in the 1880's
the establishment of such co-operative institutions had reached a
new high, and he estimated that in 1886 they had done over twenty
million dollars worth of business.

Though the co-operative movement sponsored by the labor
groups may not be well known, the average citizen is well aware
of the turmoil of the 1870's and the 1880's caused by the terrorism
of the Molly Maguires, the demonstrations of the anarchists and
socialists in Chicago and New York, and the use of the state and
federal militias to quell the strikers. Though the year 1877 was
called "the bloodiest year in American Labor," it was followed by
the Gould Strikes of 1884, the Haymarket Riot of 1886, and the
Pullman Strikes of 1894. Between 1881 and 1906, over 36,000
strikes and 15,000 lockouts occurred which involved from six to
nine million laborers.

As a result of this conflict, the capitalists and the citizenry were alarmed. Newspapers warned the people that "the money interest of every citizen in crushing a mob on the instant it raises its hydra-head, is as great as in putting out a fire that has caught in his woodshed." The capitalists of the nation became vitally interested in the new armories appearing all over the country, in the re-organization of the state militias, in manuals on riot duty which became prescribed reading, and in the establishment of private armies. For a time, the chief function of the militia, wrote Bellamy, seemed to be to "overawe strikers and suppress disturbances of discontented workingmen." In 1894 he wrote: "We are being taught by object lessons of startling frequency that our industrial system, like the political systems of Europe, rests in the end, upon the bayonet."

5. Socialism

The attitude taken toward the cause of the strikes and the conflict between capital and labor was not, for the most part, that expressed by James F. Hudson in 1887 in an article published in the *North American Review*. Hudson asserted that the extortionate cost of monopolies, pools, and trusts had to be reckoned not only in the terms of the hatred and contempt for the law which they bred but in terms of the socialist agitation which had been their result. Such anarchist outbreaks and such socialist agitation could be prevented, he wrote, only "by abolishing the power of corporations to control the necessaries of life, and by enforcing the laws against conspiracies of wealth, as well as against conspiracies of poverty."

In the newspapers of the 1880's the strikers were denounced as socialists and anarchists and their principles and actions were declared to be the result of foreign influences—of the immigrants who helped form the laboring population. It was true that the Grangers, the Sovereigns of Industry, the Knights of Labor, and other labor and reform groups advocated socialist principles; and it was also true that the influx of Germans (following 1848 after the "Exceptional Law" was passed by the German Parliament against socialists) and the French (in 1871 after the suppression of the Commune) had stimulated the spread of socialist doctrine. It was not true, however, that socialism was wholly of foreign importation or caused by the foreign element. The growth of socialism in the United States in the 1870's and the 1880's was an indigenous product of the social and economic conditions of the country. It was but an illustration of Hegel's theory: the capitalistic system of acquisition was calling into being a force which challenged its authority— and its challengers were native as well as foreign-born Americans who saw the beginning of the end of the American dream of plenty, liberty, and equality of opportunity for all.

Americans since the day of Thomas Jefferson had been involved in a discussion as to the sphere of the state: was it to be increased or diminished? The problem of whether the government was to be "of the people, by the people, and for the people" or for the powerful few was also not only an old one but one recognized by Lincoln in 1861 in an address to Congress when he said: " 'There is one point to which I ask your brief attention. It is the effort to place *capital* on an equal footing with, if not above *labor,* in the structure of this our government. Let them, the people, beware of surrendering a political power which they already have, and which, if surrendered, will surely be used to close the door of advancement against such as they, and to fix new disabilities and burdens upon them, till all liberty shall be lost.' " The Civil War established the supremacy of the federal government over the states, but, in the post-Civil War period, the question, said Colonel T. W. Higginson, seemed to be whether the citizens of the United States would choose organized capitalism or organized government!

The discussion of socialist tenets was also not new; for the United States had, even before the Civil War, a body of socialist literature and a history of socialist agitation. During this period of Owenite and Fourieristic agitation and of socialistic and co-operative settlements, state socialist Thomas Skidmore had presented in *The Right of Man to Property* (1829) socialist ideas in almost Marxian terms and had started a short-lived socialist movement. In *Sources and Effects of Unequal Wealth* (1826), L. Byllesby had given an excellent analysis of economic exploitation; and in the *Essay on the Distribution of Wealth* (1824) William Thompson had portrayed the social evils resulting from unequal distribution of property and had advocated that mutual co-operation replace the capitalist system. In 1840, Albert Brisbane had published his *Social Destiny of Man;* and in 1854, Adin Ballou had advanced in *Practical Christian Socialism* the theories of Christian socialism which had been the basis of his colony at Hopedale, Massachusetts. During this period George Henry Evans waged war against all forms of property accumulation through land, usury, or speculation; and he maintained, as had Jefferson, that man held land in usufruct only and that the right to live entailed the right to land.

Aside from the New York German Communist Club (1857), the first large, organized society to propagate the idea of socialism was the German Gymnastic Union, or Turnverein, which by 1850 was organized on a national basis. The platform adopted in Philadelphia in 1850 "proclaimed the promotion of socialism and the support of the socialistic democratic party to be its chief purpose."

The socialist, Fourierist, and reform agitation of the pre-Civil War period was, however, absorbed by the abolition movement, which won the applause of the socialists and the laborers the world over. After having freed the chattel slave, the energies of many of the abolitionists were to be devoted to winning freedom for the wage slave, whose situation was conducive to the birth of a socialist movement.

In the post-war period, the Turners re-organized not as a nominally socialist organization but as one which advocated the study of social questions, the development of true democracy, and the equal development of body and mind; its doctrine was " 'everything is for the people, everything should happen through the people.' " From 1866 until 1870, the socialistic National Labor Union flourished, and its political wing was the Labor Reform Party of Wendell Phillips. In 1868, the New York Communist Club joined the followers of Lassalle in order to found the Social Party, which in 1869 became affiliated with the International Workingman's Association through the Marxian General Council of London. During the years from 1870 to 1875, many sections of the old International appeared in the country and formed connections with the trade unions. In 1872, the General Council of the International shifted to New York—and "modern socialism had undoubtedly begun to exist in America." During the 1870's the

socialists urged the formation of labor bureaus, and in 1876 the
Workingman's Party declared one of its principles to be the establishment of bureaus of labor statistics in the state and federal
governments. Massachusetts had had such a bureau since 1870,
and the other states soon established their bureaus which began
to supply agitators with statistics.

After 1873 many changes occurred in the socialist party organizations. The Social Democratic Workingman's Party, formed in
1874, changed to the Socialist Labor Party in 1877. In 1883, a
split between the moderates and the Bakunin extremists caused the
formation of the International Working People's Association. The
International Workmen's Association, composed chiefly of English-
speaking laborers, was organized in 1881.

Of these three revolutionary socialistic parties, the major points
of agreement in 1886 were to seek the overthrow of the existing
economic and social institutions and to institute control by the
people as a whole of production and distribution. They wished also
to abolish all private property except incomes and personal possessions, all idleness, and all relationships of master and servant.
Their major point of disagreement concerned the method to be
used to achieve the new social state. The Socialist Labor Party
subscribed to the legal, evolutionary method; the International
Workmen's Association wished to educate the people but did not
frown upon violent measures; and the International Working
People's Association advocated violence such as assassination and
dynamiting.

Although Marx's *Das Kapital* had not yet been translated into
English by 1886, his ideas had been popularized in pamphlets,
newspapers, and brochures. Victoria Woodhull had published the
first complete English version of *The Communist Manifesto* in
Woodhull and Claflin's Weekly, and she and Stephen Pearl
Andrews—a philosophic anarchist who had been a disciple of Josiah
Warren, a Fourierist, a Swedenborgian, and a state socialist—joined
the International and did it the inestimable damage of associating
socialism with the free-love doctrine in their articles and lectures.
In 1884 Laurence Gronlund, a Philadelphia lawyer, published his
Co-operative Commonwealth, which expounded the Marxian tenets

in a modified form, for Gronlund admitted that he had an Anglo-Saxon dislike of anything extravagant.

The most important publication before Bellamy's *Looking Backward* (1888) was Henry George's *Progress and Poverty* (1877-79) which sold edition after edition and of which Professor Ely wrote in 1886 that it had caused " 'tens of thousands of laborers' " to become acquainted with economic matters and problems. As a result of the popularity of this book, the single tax theory—which was really a form of agrarian socialism—started a movement which for a time had political repercussions and which in 1886 almost won, with the help of the socialists, the mayoralty of New York for George. In this same year, the newspapers were filled with the charges that the Haymarket Riot had been inspired by the socialists—and this, points out Quint in his *Forging of American Socialism,* started a "campaign of 'red-baiting' " which has rarely been equalled. This "first major 'red-scare' " also served the purpose, however, of calling attention to socialist doctrines.

The influence of Hegel and of "muscular Christianity" in America also contributed without doubt to the acceptance of socialist principles—or at least to a knowledge of them. Walt Whitman saw in Hegel the "perfect philosophy" for his concept of the democratic development of the city of friends; and William Torry Harris, Denton J. Snider, Bronson Alcott, and the Reverend Dr. Elisha Mulford popularized Hegel's ideas. Harris and Snider, who had not only studied but translated Hegel's works, founded their *Journal of Speculative Philosophy* in St. Louis, Missouri, in 1867; and in the first issue they made it clear to the reader that the idea of "brittle individualism" had been only one phase of development and that the second phase during which each individual recognized his "substantial side to be the state as such" needed to be "digested and comprehended." Snider also pointed out the dangers of monocracy to democracy, and he advocated civic ownership or state socialism not only as the cure for an ailing democracy but as the final form of expression of the will of the people.

The influence of Hegel and of the English Christian Socialists was further perpetuated by the Rev. Dr. Elisha Mulford, a friend of Frederick D. Maurice, the English Chartist and Hegelian reformer. Mulford published a highly respected periodical *The Nation* and, in 1881, his work *The Republic of God.* In the preface of his book, Mulford paid tribute to Hegel, Maurice, Stahl, and others; and in the book itself he presented his ideas of the nation as a moral organism, of the possibility of achieving the Kingdom of God on earth, and of the need of religion in secular reform.

This work of Mulford—as well as works by Edward H. Hale, Washington Gladden, Jesse Jones, W. D. P. Bliss, and others—was of great importance in the development of the social gospel movement in America. Though the conservative members of this movement did not advocate political socialism as the answer to the problems and threats of industrial capitalism, they did recognize the need of greater social and economic equality and of greater sympathy for the proletariat on the part of the church. They also recognized the role played by a poor environment in the development of depravity, and they encouraged consideration of the cooperative and profit-sharing plans which had been proposed as solutions to the economic injustices and problems of the period. Believing with Blake that religion was politics and politics religion, they also sponsored the application of Christian principles to the material life of the nation.

Through the principles advocated by the various reform, revolt, and religious groups; through the adverse publicity of conservative newspapers; and through the efforts of the nearly one hundred labor papers which existed in 1886, the American public had, therefore, ample opportunity to become at least acquainted with socialist tenets. It is, therefore, not too surprising that Dr. Edward Aveling and his wife Eleanor—the daughter of Karl Marx—should write in 1886—when they had toured the United States and preached the gospel of socialism as far westward as Kansas, that they were surprised by the prevalence of what they termed " 'unconscious socialism' " and by the fact that the "American people . . . were waiting to hear in their own language what socialism was."

6. Bellamy and Socialist Ideas

Though Bellamy stated after the publication of *Looking Backward* that he had never been a member of a labor union, that he had had no more knowledge of socialism than the average news-paper reader, and that he had never been concerned with social and economic problems in his early novels and short stories, an examina-tion of his earliest writings shows that he had very early in life formulated some basic attitudes necessary to a would-be reformer and that in his lyceum addresses and in his editorials and book reviews he had been concerned not only with the political and industrial problems of his era but with the movements, socialistic and non-socialistic, which had sought solutions to these problems. When the basic principles which he advocated in these articles and speeches are considered, it becomes clear that the ideas and principles advocated in *Looking Backward* were the result not only of his reactions to the problems and movements of his age but of his consideration of them over a long period of time.

Bellamy's "early and natural" interest in social and governmental problems and his early formation of the credo and spirit of a re-former are found in his early essays and in his early journal devoted to thoughts about political economy. As early as 1861, Bellamy expressed in his composition "Treason" the theory of the right of the people to revolt against "an unjust, oppressive, and tyrannical government." The youthful Bellamy thought that it was unreason-able to expect men to show allegiance to an oppressive government and that it was reasonable that they have always the right of self-defense against such a government.

In "Does Time Establish a Usurpation" (1863), Bellamy ex-posed his view of the acceptance of usurpation by the "systems of politics usually accepted by men" in these words: "Is it just that a robber or murderer, seizing the property of his victim and enjoy-ing it unmolested for any time, should, after such a time in which justice has failed to overtake him, rightfully possess that property? Evidently not. Society could not stand on such a foundation. Time, though mighty, cannot construct right out of wrong. Because punish-ment is not at once administered, it is not just that it never should be. . . . Time cannot change evil to good, nor make a rightful inheritance out of a usurpation."

As early as 1867 Bellamy began a notebook entitled "Thoughts on Political Economy" in which he wrote that the ideas it contained resulted from "the study of that subject, reflections upon problems, political and social of the present day. All very crude." In this notebook he recorded his ideas—as good as any he had seen elsewhere, he thought!—for reforming the methods of electing the president; for attaining representation of the minorities, since a majority in the legislative body could sometimes represent a minority of the people; and for obtaining suffrage based on intelligence and literacy. That Bellamy was reading John Stuart Mill during this period is evident, for he appended to one of his own plans of reform one by Thomas Hare which he wrote had been cited by Mill.

In these and other youthful essays Bellamy had established the foundation of a reformer's credo, for he had stated the following principles: (1) the people have a right to revolt against an unjust government; (2) a free people have the right to abolish slavery; (3) a situation is not to be accepted as right merely because it exists; (4) the people will accept that which gives them the things they most desire; (5) and the things which hold a people together—an ensign or an idea—must be something that has a common appeal, something that will unite them in brotherhood. Bellamy had also not only evinced the spirit of a reformer in these early essays and notes but had expressed specific ideas relative to the way of reforming the system of electing the president and of obtaining just representation of the will of the people.

The period in which Bellamy first began to consider socialist theories of reform seems to have begun after 1866. His aunt, Mrs. Harriet Packer, stated in a letter to her son William in 1866 that she had received a letter from Ed Sherman in which "he touched upon Politics, showing quite conservative notions for so young a man." Frederick Bellamy—as has already been noticed—stated that Edward had written and talked about German socialism which he had studied at home before he went to Germany, and Bellamy himself wrote in an article after the publication of *Looking Backward* that he had discussed the "how" of remedying the problem of getting the "dirty work" done in an ideal state while he had resided in Germany. Whether he had studied socialism at home or whether he had read about and discussed socialist principles while attending Union College and had merely clarified and enlarged his ideas while in Germany, Bellamy definitely displayed his knowledge of socialist principles in his second lyceum address of 1872.

It was here that Bellamy denounced the competitive industrial system as a "social barbarism" which shamed "humanity before God and the angels." Such a system was inconsistent with "the plainest principles of equity" for it was "founded upon the subjection of men," since some men were permitted to reap profits from the labors of those they controlled. The solution to the inequalities and the enslavement of men created by private enterprise was socialism, of which he spoke in these words: "Why has the name Socialist by which is designated a believer in this renovation of Society, who denies that the world ought to be administered any longer in the interests of darkness and chaos become a byword and a name of reproach? Verily it is a sad reflection that to have faith in the enfranchisement of mankind from sordid yoke, to lend a hand to breaking up of the golden calf before which the world bows down is synonymous in the minds of most men with ignorant presumption and fanatical Atheism. . . . Worse than all this, there are good men who apparently think the preservation of the present social order to be identical with the interests of Christianity. . . ."

Bellamy also expressed his belief as to what the adoption of basic socialist principles would mean to the world in the following words: "Is it then . . . absurd to dream of the reign of justice on earth, chimerical to anticipate an era when, by equality in the distribution of the fruits of labor, every man at the price of moderate exertion shall be as secure of abundance and comfort, of the means of education and recreation as he is today secure in his political rights and independence? . . . There is then enough in the world to support all in abundance if it were equally divided. If the burdens as well as the pleasures of life were apportioned equally among all, then should none labor beyond moderation, and none be utterly idle. This is a social condition which justice demands. . . ."

Although Bellamy had stated two of the basic theories upon which his ideal state was to rest—equality of labor and of income— he ended his oration with the following statement: "If you expect from me . . . a theory of Socialism, if you expect a minute description of that new world of whose peace and liberty and happiness

I have told you, you will be disappointed. It is an undiscovered country, no community of men has ever essayed its elysian climes, no human foot step has ever trod its shores. The faith of humanity points to its existence. But I know that it exists, and we must find it. . . ."

Though it was many years before Bellamy presented in *Looking Backward* his "minute description" of the new world socialism might make possible, he was to wonder, when he re-read his lyceum address after the publication of his first Utopian novel, why he had not formulated his ideal state decades sooner. If he had re-read also his editorials and book reviews published in the *Springfield Union* in the 1870's, he would doubtless have wondered why he had stated after the publication of *Looking Backward* that he had had only the average newspaper reader's knowledge of socialism when he had written the book. He would certainly have found this statement to be inconsistent with the knowledge of the brands of socialism being promulgated which he displayed, for example, in his review of William B. Greene's *Socialistic, Communistic, Mutualistic, and Financial Fragments* when he wrote: "The views advanced are of the school known as 'advanced.' They savor of the teachings of Stephen Pearl Andrews and Mrs. Woodhull, being for the most part vindications of the doctrine of 'individual sovereignty,' of which free love is one of the developments, Mr. Greene being a disciple of the modified form of that faith. But even for those who eschew the writer's opinions, as we most emphatically do, his writings contain valuable suggestions."

Many of Bellamy's other editorials and book reviews and some of his early fiction show not only his knowledge and consideration of socialist principles but his consideration of the widening and changing role of the government, the problems created by wealth, and the solutions proposed to solve the conflict between labor and capital.

In his editorials dealing with the role of the federal government, Bellamy observed that the Civil War had nullified once and for all the doctrine of states' rights and that the tendency of the government was to become more and more concerned and to legislate about "social questions" rather than political ones. He also called attention to the expansion of the government in other countries into the realm of state ownership—a step toward socialism. In his discussion in 1873 of the ownership of the telegraph by the British government and of the bill—then in the House of Commons—advocating the purchase of the railroads, Bellamy expressed his doubts as to whether government operation of these facilities would be feasible in the United States because of the less dense population to be served and the greater tracts of land to be traversed. That he thought that ownership by the nation of the telegraph and of the railroads was worthy of consideration is indicated by the fact that in his magazine reviews he called attention to such articles as "Government Purchase of Railways" in the British *Quarterly Review* and "The Despot of Today" in *Old and New.* Of the last-mentioned article he said that it classed the Western Union and the New York Associated Press as tyrants of the press.

In 1875 Bellamy observed that municipal ownership of gas and water plants and of housing units had proved successful in Birmingham, England, for the public enjoyed excellent service at a cheaper rate. In another editorial in which he discussed the exorbitant rates of interest charged by pawnbrokers, Bellamy advocated that this business be taken out of private hands and be handled by banks under government supervision like those of France, Russia, Italy, Holland, Germany, and Belgium. The government, he stated, would not necessarily have to go into the lending business; it would merely license these institutions and insure fair rates of interest. In these editorials, Bellamy was airing policies which, after the publication of *Looking Backward,* he was to support as being preliminary steps toward the achievement of state socialism: government control and municipal ownership.

Aside from his consideration of the developing role of the government and his advocacy of municipal ownership, Bellamy evinced his concern about the psychological, moral, economic, and political aspects of ownership of wealth. In his journal of 1872 Bellamy recorded his ponderings about the reasons men sought to amass fortunes, and he concluded that they sought wealth because of the prestige and the power it gave them. He also remarked that if property and inheritance—the backbone of the property system—

were abolished, men would still seek, if not money, power and prestige. He also wrote in one of his editorials of this period that, though property was one of the foundation stones of civilization, its "uses and limitations" afforded "a fair and a fairly opened field of inquiry, a most difficult one, also, to be surveyed."

Bellamy regarded the amassing of large fortunes as the burglarizing of society. He stated that he agreed with Ruskin that the luxury of the rich did not supply any benefits to the community; and, if it did, one would have to gauge its value with a "moral view" and note the destruction of the personal and social virtues which were its result. Unseemly extravagance, luxury, and "self-indulgence" were, he thought, morally, socially, and economically injurious. Socially, the great fortunes and the luxurious living of their possessors embittered the poor, created class divisions, and fanned the flames already "burning so hotly in the hearts of many labor reformers and their followers." Economically, distribution (or consumption of produce) supported nobody, for one who was only a consumer and not a producer contributed nothing to the subsistence or the wealth of the nation. Many of the great fortunes of the day were being held, he wrote, by those who had not earned them—and they did nothing but enjoy them.

Bellamy also expressed his concern about "human distinctions of *meum* and *tuum*" in two of his short stories, "Hooking Watermelons" (1877) and "Extra-Hazardous" (1877). He evinced also his realization of the financial distress of the injured and therefore unemployed laborers in his short story "Jane Hicks." That he was sympathetic with the problems of the laborer is also shown by notations in his Hawaiian Notebooks which indicate his intention to write a story illustrating the ideas of "liberty, equality, fraternity and the rights of labor." He intended to introduce a cynical philosopher whose constant refrain was to be "the depravity and moral worthlessness of the poor" who "desire dishonesty, cheating, and incapacity."

In the great disparities in the wealth of the people and in the mass movement from the town and country to the city which resulted in rented rather than owned property, Bellamy saw threats to the welfare of the nation. It was necessary, he wrote in an editorial, that each citizen have a "stake of his own well fixed in his country's soil," for, if he did not, he would not be concerned about his "country's real and permanent interests." The public spirit of the citizenry depended, therefore, on the "minute division and the widely multiplied ownership of its real estate"; and he cited the Swiss pride, independence, and public spirit which resulted, he averred, from the fact that in Switzerland 465,000 of the 485,000 homes were occupied by owners.

Monopolization of the property of the nation by the few not only endangered the public spirit of the citizens but exerted a subversive and corrupting influence upon the government, a morally corruptive effect upon business, and a divisive effect upon the nation, for it led to the conflict between capital and labor and to panics, depressions, and revolts. Bellamy's earliest fictional portrayal of the tyranny of wealth is contained in *The Duke of Stockbridge* (1879) in which the Shays' Rebellion is pictured as being brought about by an unjust use of property and by the governing of the country by a plutocracy. The plutocrats have set aside democratic institutions; and the common people have no social equality, no freedom from bondage to the rich, and no economic or cultural equality. The commoners frequently lament that they have fought the Revolution only to exchange the rule of the king of England for the tyrannous rule of the rich. Though legislation is eventually passed to rectify the conditions leading to the Shays' Rebellion, the same situation soon reappears, for the rich control the legislators or hire the lawyers who befuddle them.

The attitude of the plutocrats toward the rebels is comparable to that of the Gilded Age toward the strikers when militias were summoned to quell them. In this novel Bellamy portrayed conditions quite similar to those of his own period, which was also notable for its conflict between the haves and the have-nots, or between capital and labor.

In his *Union* editorials Bellamy invariably regarded the conflict between capital and labor as resulting not only from the great disparities of wealth but from "too much human nature." Man's individuality—his selfishness, irritability, and suspicion—prevented his better self from managing his common intercourse in a manner which would contribute to "the common happiness and rights." It also caused him to ignore his debt to society—his labor—which every man, no matter what his capacity, had to pay. Both the capitalists and the laborers, asserted Bellamy, repudiated their debt and injured the social body when they were in conflict. In the face of the needs of the whole of society, private rights—such as the right to strike or to close the factory—had necessarily to be limited; and this was just, for no man's property or rights freed him from moral responsibility or from governmental limitations if the good of the whole commonwealth were at stake. Unjust usage of property and the treatment of men as commodities upon the market rested, Bellamy thought, upon "miry and sandy" ground—and both of them created volcanic arguments which could lead to the destruction and not to the reconstruction of the nation.

The general solution to the conflict of labor and capital was—since moral reconstruction would take too long—to turn man's "self-ishness into a more manly and humane channel" and to use it "in the common interests of those who work and those who pay." The specific methods which Bellamy advocated in his editorials and book reviews as being capable of accomplishing this end were co-operative production and profit sharing, both of which had been tried by various companies and organizations in England and the United States.

Co-operative enterprise or profit sharing, thought Bellamy, would not only instill a sense of personal proprietorship in the employee but follow the trend of the "business system of the age," which was "a wonderful example of the principles of co-operation and mutual insurance. . . . This solidarity of interest and mutual dependence is doubtless infinitely better than the isolation, the individualism, which in the progress of civilization it has replaced." Bellamy also observed that "the political application of the principle" had resulted in democracy and that the "industrial application" of it would resolve the conflict between capital and labor. In regard to its application, he wrote: "We expect to be laughed at for our advice, as quite too green in the science of human nature. Well, we have studied this some, and not always hopefully. But, if human common sense and good feeling cannot be relied on for as much of a contribution as this to the general salvation, we should like to ask, in all soberness, 'What is human nature worth?' If it, after all, is only an oppressive force as a working power and a conciliatory spirit for merely polite and complimentary usages of society then we shall have to fall back on Hobbes' dictum, that a state of war is the natural and necessary state of man, and everyone will have to turn his house and himself into a castle, with the guns all shotted and pointed outward." Man, thought Bellamy, had murdered and been "murdered quite long enough in the interest of dividends" and the time had come to consider the interests of humanity.

Though Bellamy observed that profit sharing or co-operative industry, which would employ the selfish instincts of men, was to be advocated only as a "stepping stone to something more worthy of all concerned," he also argued that it was a remedy far superior to any proposed by the International and was, in fact, one which would mitigate the threat of "international demagoguism" and of "communist violence."

Bellamy's contempt for the socialist plans for the improvement of society was also recorded in his Hawaiian Notebook in his tentative scheme for a story about a Utopia which would "show up notions about reforming all the world" and making everybody happy through charity and "Communistic Ideas." Later he wrote that Eliot Carson, who had become a reformer because he had become tied to humanity by his children, had been helped by his "former disgust with the various socialist schemes" when he had considered what "could be radically done for society, reorganization." To be disgusted with such schemes presupposes a knowledge of them—and that Bellamy was aware of the work of Ruskin, Maurice, Kingsley, the Russian socialists, Joseph Arch, Charles Bradlaugh, and the Marxists is proved by the many editorials and book reviews in which he mentioned one or the other. In one of these editorials, he noted the collapse of the International which, only three years before, had been the subject of "prodigious interest" and had resulted in "books, magazine articles, and newspaper leaders, minatory, explanatory, denunciatory, which . . . would make a pile rivalling the pyramid of Cheops."

In 1873 Bellamy stated that he was interested in finding a scheme which would solve the problems of the age but which would also be more sagacious and sincere than that of the Internationalists. During this same period in an article in which he described the feudalism of industrial control, he stated: "It is a dream of socialism to introduce democracy into the industrial world also, but whether it be realizable, experience only can show." In 1877 he called attention in an editorial to a paper called *The Striker* which advocated government ownership of the railroads and the telegraphy, and he noted that the journal declared "communism to be simply Christianity reduced to practice."

In this same year Bellamy wrote in an editorial entitled "Communism Boiled Down": "The cure-all for our labor and capital frictions and smash-ups seems then, to be this, to put into the hands of the government all the carrying, transfer, exchange, productive industry of the country, its manufactures, agriculture, trade, and its entire use of capital; permitting no private employment of this for personal profits, distributing the income from all this industry so carried on, to the millions of workers, by a scale of meritorious value, as operatives toward the universal prosperity; perhaps allowing a house and a garden to the citizen for private comfort and so much personal property as he might like, under a strict prohibition of using any of it for his own gain. Now go to, ye dreamers, and find the material for a government equal to such an administration of this or any country, in intelligence or honesty. Here we should have a civil service to stagger the immortals! No such material exists on the face of the globe. And if it did, how are we going to get this machine on the track and set it running? Well may the answer come back—'we don't know!' You might as well fly from the haystack to the moon. For a man to neglect his business and his family to study up such a scheme as this, is lunacy and something worse. Yet, we are told, the number of these students is on the increase, in Massachusetts."

In these succinct though doubtful and critical statements of socialist principles are to be found the ones which Bellamy had stated in his lyceum address and which, with slight modifications, were to serve as the backbone of the society presented in *Looking*

Backward. Furthermore, one finds in these statements his preoccupation with the problem of the "how" which he was to seek to solve in his two Utopian novels—and also the basic criticisms which were to be made by his readers of the ideal state which he presented in these novels.

Though there can be no doubt that Bellamy had long thought about the socialist principles being advocated during his period and that he had early adopted some of them as solutions to the problems of his age, there can also be no questioning of his sincerity when he wrote that he had been disgusted by some of the socialist or communist plans which had been proposed as remedies. Bellamy's philosophy of solidarity, his respect for and love of democratic institutions, and his code of ethics would not permit him to sanction any revolt which, because it sponsored group conflict and violence, would widen and not close the breech which existed between men; which would ignore or destroy the democratic principles which were the foundation of the government; or which would show a lack of respect for religious principles. Bellamy also rejected Marxism because, as a prudent man who believed that any change should be the result of much meditation, he felt that sufficient thought had not been given to the planning of the government which was to follow the uprising of the proletariat.

A review of Bellamy's early writings shows, therefore, that Bellamy had noted the expanding powers of the central government and the movement at home and abroad toward governmental or municipal ownership of public facilities. In his thinking about political economy, he had concluded that it had to be based on moral principles, that it had to consider the welfare of all classes, that true wealth of a nation depended upon production, and that there was a close connection between production and consumption. In considering the solution to the conflict between capital and labor, he had decided that the answer lay in co-operation which was in accord with the tendency of the business world, with his philosophy of solidarity, and with his religious principles. In his lyceum address of 1872 and in his editorials relating to socialism, Bellamy had succinctly stated the principles which were to be those of his ideal state and had also expressed critically the problems he was to seek to solve in order to achieve a plan that would be more specific and more peaceful than that of the radical revolutionaries. Long before he began to write his first Utopian novel, Bellamy had amassed, therefore, a body of knowledge which was to supply material for the building of his ideal state, and he had formed attitudes toward the problems of his day and toward the purpose of life which were to make inevitable the type of social order which he would depict in *Looking Backward*.

7. Plans for a Utopia

That Bellamy would cast his plan for a better state and his criticisms of his own era into the form of a Utopian novel was also almost inevitable because of the specific conclusions he had reached about the value of novels of social criticism which were satiric in nature; because of his acquaintance with the Utopian novels of his era and of the past; and because he had long planned, as his journal entries show, to write a Utopian novel.

The fiction of Bellamy's period reflected the confusion and the turbulence of the era, for, from 1870 to 1891, two hundred and fifty volumes of economic fiction were published. Of this number, only thirty appeared before *Looking Backward*; and of all of them it may fairly be said that none of them could compare with Bellamy's penetrating analysis and criticism of the situation which he presented in *Looking Backward* or with the novels and the articles of the muckrakers who were to follow him and continue his work. From 1860 to 1887, eleven Utopian novels and three non-fiction books were published which presented outlines for a new social order. After the publication of *Looking Backward*, a host of Utopian novels appeared which either criticized adversely or defended and extended the ideal state which Bellamy had outlined.

In his book reviews of the novels of social criticism which sought to reveal the political corruption of the age, Bellamy revealed a changing attitude toward the value of satire. In his comments relative to *The Gilded Age* by Charles D. Warner and Mark Twain and to *The Story of Sevenoaks* by Dr. J. G. Holland, Bellamy showed his acceptance of social, religious, and political satire as a means of attacking the vices of the epoch. In his review of Bailey's *They All*

Do It (1877), he evinced, however, a change of opinion which perhaps shows why he chose to present an optimistic and pleasing picture of the development of man and society in *Looking Backward* and to reveal the weaknesses of the civilization of his day in a comparative way. In this review, he wrote: "Whether the effect on the mind of much reading of such social satires as these sketches be healthy, is, however, open to doubt. They strip men and women of every illusion of sentiment or nobility, and exhibit the bare and ugly commonness and vulgarity of human character and nature in a merciless light. Such books as this must tend to increase the already excessive cynicism for which the American people are noted."

Although five Utopian novels were published in the 1880's in the United States before *Looking Backward* (1888), there is no concrete evidence that Bellamy had read any of them. That he was, however, acquainted with other Utopian works is proved by his references to E. Bulwer-Lytton's *The Coming Race*, Edward E. Hale's *Sybaris*, Fénelon's *Télémaque*, Plato's *Republic*, Bacon's *Atlantis*, Hawthorne's *Blithedale Romance*, and to other novels, such as those of Hugo and Rabelais, which presented pictures of ideal states. Bellamy had also read E. Maitland's *By and By*, which he considered interesting despite his feeling that the material might have been more effectively presented if the author had not chosen the Utopian form.

Despite Bellamy's criticism of Maitland's presentation of his criticisms and remedies of the problems of his era in a Utopian novel, Bellamy's journal entries show that he had been entertaining for a number of years the idea of writing a Utopian story. In the 1870's he made notes for a long "prose poem" which was to revolve about a future revolt of men caused by their refusal to "live and labor merely to prolong a life" they despised. During this same period, he recorded an idea for a Utopia of insects. In this story, a humanitarian, who had sorrowfully observed the death of insects in autumn from freezing, was to build a great heated structure which was to be open to flies, gnats, mosquitoes, and all other insects. Because of the comments Bellamy made in some of his editorials of this period, it is possible that he intended this story to be a satire upon the excessive sentimentality of some humanitarians who sought to preserve in some cases some of the human insects who should have been hanged by the neck for their crimes. Since Bellamy did, however, regard the flowers as brothers and sisters, he may have intended to indulge in some sentimental fancy of his own in this story.

During the 1870's and the 1880's Bellamy recorded notes for a story based on stirpiculture, a subject much in the news and one about which Bellamy had written in his editorials in the *Union*. In the first plan for the story recorded in the Hawaiian Notebook of 1878, the plot was to be based upon the mental conflict of a young man who loved but could not wed because of the ideas of stirpiculture. In the other notes for this same work, Bellamy recorded the idea of breeding superior souls which he was to touch upon in "To Whom This May Come" and a plan for a future society in which the state would regulate, with an "enlightened sort of stock raising," all procreation of the race. In this society people were to be mated according to their sensitivities and sensibilities so as to propagate better, more receptive souls. Reflections of these ideas are also to be seen in his outline for the story of "Coming Man" in which Bellamy planned to picture a race of people whose speech had been replaced by mind-reading and whose ears were attuned only to music. In "To Whom This May Come," he did at long last picture such a race.

In the 1880's Bellamy outlined a plot for a Utopia called Autonounce, in which the highest officials of the state were to be chosen by lot from those made eligible because of their outstanding service. This method was adopted to discourage emulation, self-seeking, and pride in office. All lesser officials were also selected in this fashion so that they would not feel indebted to higher officials for their positions.

In the Utopian scheme entitled "A Reorganization of Society to Extirpate Sorrow" Bellamy recorded a plan whereby all children— the chief cause of all the sorrows engendered by parental love— were to be reared by the state. This arrangement would loosen all family ties and would result in "a vast increase of intellectual and artistic sympathy and in cultivation of the sense of the universal life in God."

Still another story of the future involved documents found under a cornerstone and a man born a hundred years before his time—an old "broken down fellow who lives and dreams in the future." In this story Bellamy planned to reveal "different chapters" of the future and to depict the effect foreseeing the future would have upon the selection of labor, men's motives, their attitude toward death, their mental development, their general habits, and their united action. Many of these ideas were later incorporated in "The Blindman's World."

Other Bellamy schemes included the writing of a short story portraying a world in which "everything went backward, and they punished people for what they intended and not for what they had done." Another story was to be concerned with an "imagined vision of the world of Types" and another was to be a "take-off on prohibition" which would describe the state of things "when all bad habits have been corrected by law." Among the things to be banned were coffee, tea, late hours, "all love except matrimonial," and "foolish conversations."

The most interesting of all the proposed Utopias, however, is that in which Bellamy intended to portray the impossibility of making everybody happy through communist ideas!—for Bellamy in *Looking Backward* was to seek to lead people to accept the possibility of just that.

When Bellamy finally wrote his long-proposed Utopian novel, he was exceedingly well prepared for the task of presenting an outline of a new form of society and of criticizing the old. His home town, Chicopee Falls, had presented in miniature a picture of the industrial scene with which he could become intimately acquainted; and his travels in Europe had shown him the end product of the industrial situation which was developing in his own country. His religious background had inculcated in him a strong feeling about the need of religion and ethics in the life of man and in the society which surrounded him, and his mother had made him aware of the virtue of self-sacrifice and of the necessity of a high aim in life. His private studies and reading had made him a student of economics, his legal training had given him an understanding of the laws and the foundations of governments, and his early interest in socialism had caused him to accept and reject certain fundamental principles of reform. His career as an editorial writer and publisher had made him conversant with national affairs, current ideas, and reform movements; and his early literary work had developed his ability to express his ideas and to employ techniques fitted to problem literature.

Bellamy's religion of solidarity gave him a philosophy which had as its basic principle the brotherhood of man and which stressed the potentialities of the impersonal in man as well as the importance of the individuality. Though Bellamy's desire to solve the mystery of life and of himself, as well as his love of books and meditation, had tempted him to withdraw from the world into a hermitage, his marriage brought him back to the stream of humanity. When he became a father who had given "hostages to society," he felt compelled to create a world that would be a happy, secure one for his children to live in. All of the life of Bellamy seemed, therefore, to be a series of educative influences which were to prepare him for the day when he would draft his outline for a new world.

CHAPTER IV

THE REFORMER:

LOOKING BACKWARD, NATIONALISM, *EQUALITY*

1. The Writing of *Looking Backward*

When Bellamy began writing *Looking Backward,* he intended to write a fantastic "tale of social felicity" but not to contribute to reform literature. To prevent its seeming incongruous and to give himself imaginative leeway, Bellamy placed the action of the story in the year 3000 A.D. He envisioned not an ideal nation but an ideal world which had its capital in Berne, Switzerland, and the immediate scene of the action of the story was Asheville, North Carolina.

The opening scene of the novel presented a gala picture of an annual muster day in the year 3000—the day when men of age were taken into the industrial army, and those whose service had ended were mustered out. The analogy between the use of an army for war and destruction and its employment for peace and production had been toyed with by Bellamy for many years after it had been suggested to him by European universal military training. As he began to consider the way the people of his Utopia could use this army to dispose of the problem of labor and to avoid the evils of a classified and competitive society, Bellamy recognized that he had not only a rhetorical analogy for national industrial service but also a basic principle and a working model for the organization of a better state.

When he apprehended that he had discovered the corner-stone of a new state, Bellamy changed the whole purpose of his novel. His aim now became that of reasoning out a definite scheme for an economic, political organization which would guarantee the material welfare of the citizens by giving them an economic equality which would supplement and also guarantee their political equality. He wished also to portray the result such an organization would have upon the moral, social, and intellectual life of the nation. As a

"Edward Bellamy was born on March 26, 1850,
in the two-story brick residence of his father . . ."

". . . The Bellamy family moved to the large white frame house shaded by maple trees and surrounded by a large yard where Bellamy was to live the remainder of his life."

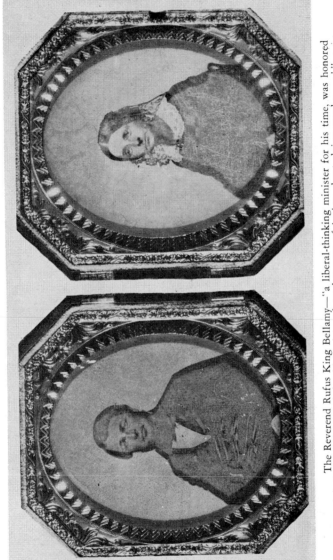

The Reverend Rufus King Bellamy—"a liberal-thinking minister for his time, was honored . . . and especially loved for his quiet and modest way of 'going about doing good . . .'"

"Maria Putnam Bellamy, though less popular because she was more austere and reserved than her jolly, effervescent husband, was no less kind to her fellowmen."

"Edward's life was influenced not only by his mother's attitude toward a high purpose in life and by her piety but by her favoritism and her interests."

"Edward married on May 30, 1882 . . . one of the most important dates in his life . . . for his marriage and subsequent fatherhood were to complete his education . . ."

"Bellamy's emotions outflanked his prejudices against matrimony" and he married Emma Sanderson "who was very much in love" with him.

" . . . because his children Marion and Paul would have no security in the world of his day, Bellamy ceased to be a sentimentalist in his study and became a practical reformer who sought to outline and then to establish an ideal world."

"By the time Bellamy was reading the last pages of the proof of *Equality*, his health was so poor that he had to alternate periods of rest with those of work."

result of this change of objectives, he deleted most of the imaginative material about the customs, the social and political institutions, and the many mechanical contrivances of the year 3000, for he did not wish to divert the reader from his scheme of industrial organization.

The method which he used to achieve his purpose was that which he had employed in his short stories: "to trace the logical consequences of certain assumed conditions." His process of presentation is comparable to that which his brother Charles had outlined in *The Way Out* (1884): "My argument for each of these changes is intended to start from a probable and indefensible wrong in our present arrangement of society. Wherever there is a wrong there must be a right, and as soon as the former is clearly distinguished, the latter is revealed ever opposite." Because Edward Bellamy employed this method of opposing the solution with the evil it eradicated, or vice versa, *Looking Backward* became as much a criticism of the Gilded Age as a picture of its cure—the ideal state.

In *Looking Backward* the iniquities of the old order and the beatitudes of the new society are presented through the eyes of the rich young Bostonian Julian West, who, born in the nineteenth century, awakens from a hypnotic sleep to find himself in the year 2000. Julian soon discovers that the anarchic warfare of the competitive period has been replaced by fraternal co-operation and that the brutalities of social life have been transposed into the consideration and kindliness that had once been reserved for only the family circle. The social and cultural divisions of the nineteenth century have disappeared, for, since all the people are economically as well as politically equal, they have equal opportunities for self-improvement. Since all people are employed in the industrial army, unemployment and poverty have also disappeared.

Julian also discovers that the democratic form of government, which in the nineteenth century had become an oligarchy or a plutocracy, has become a true democracy of, by, and for the people. Wealth no longer has the power to corrupt the government, and its officials are incorruptible because they have no need of money. The dangers of monopolies are no longer existent, for there is now one great monopoly, the state; and, since all the citizens are joint stockholders in this monopoly, they are no longer lethargic, indifferent citizens—it is to their selfish interests to watch the government and to produce to their capacity, for their incomes depend upon their production. Furthermore, the ruthless exploitation of the natural resources of the nation by the few had terminated with the reclamation of their heritages by the people who guard them jealously for themselves and for their descendants.

Though the ideal society which wins the acclaim of the plutocratic Julian is basically a form of Christian, democratic, state socialism, Bellamy adopted the name of Nationalism for his ideal government—and this for cogent reasons. He did not wish for prejudice against the term "socialism" to hinder either the sale of his novel or the acceptance of its ideas. He wrote to Howells: "Every sensible man will admit there is a big deal in a name, especially in making first impressions. In the radicalness of the opinions I have expressed, I may seem to out-socialize the socialists, yet the word socialist is one I never could well stomach. In the first place it is a foreign word in itself, and equally foreign in all its suggestions. It smells to the average American of petroleum, suggests the red flag, and with all manner of sexual novelties, and an abusive tone about God and religion, which in this country we at least treat with respect. For the rest, *socialist* is as genuine slang as those choice phrases *society man, society woman,* etc. It is, so far as the real meaning of the word is concerned, as proper to call a lady of fashion a socialist as to call a man interested in industrial reforms by that name; whatever German and French reformers may choose to call themselves, socialist is not a good name for a party to succeed with in America. No such party can or ought to succeed that is not wholly and enthusiastically American and patriotic in spirit and suggestions."

Although Bellamy stated that he had reluctantly presented his ideas for the new order in the form of a Utopian novel, he was also well aware of the intrinsic value of this method of presentation. He hoped that it would induce "more to give it a reading," and he felt that it would test the logic of his ideas. To Bellamy the true test of a false or an absurd idea was to try to fit it into a story—and, furthermore, he wrote, all the world would criticize the logic of a story but not that of a philosophical essay.

The novel form was certainly best suited to his subject not only because, as he pointed out in *Looking Backward,* the romance of Julian West sugar-coated the pill, but because—in an age which had witnessed the first "red scare"—he could with greater impunity criticize the existing order and suggest socialist remedies for its maladies. Although he could reach a greater audience with a novel, he was also not so likely to endanger himself since a writer of imaginative fiction would not be taken so seriously by those immediately and materially concerned that they would try to suppress him or his novel.

The novel form also allowed Bellamy greater latitude in imaginative portrayals of the effect the basic principles would have upon the form of the future society, and it permitted his manner of presentation to appeal more subtly to the emotions and to the reason of the reader. Furthermore, the novel form was a congenial working medium to Bellamy who had already used it primarily for the promulgation of his ideas and who had already developed the dialogue technique for this purpose in sections of *Dr. Heidenhoff's Process* and of *Miss Ludington's Sister.* Though Bellamy employed devices in *Looking Backward* which he had used before, it is technically by far the best novel he wrote because of the skill with which he handled the dialogue and maintained the point of view.

2. Publication, Success of *Looking Backward*

When Mr. Benjamin Ticknor of Boston was considering the publication of *Looking Backward,* Bellamy wrote to him saying: "If you tackled it, how soon could you bring it out? I am particularly desirous that it should see the light as quickly as possible. Now is the accepted time, it appears to me, for a publication touching on social and industrial questions to obtain a hearing."

The Ticknor firm published the novel in January, 1888, and shortly thereafter Houghton Mifflin purchased the company. When Houghton Mifflin made new plates for the novel, the emended edition—prepared by Bellamy in 1888 for Rabbi Solomon Schindler's German translation—was used; and this second edition was in

Bellamy's hand by September, 1889. Of the changes made in the new edition, Bellamy said that they involved only improvements in statements—"some slight emendations"—but no changes in ideas.

As Bellamy had indicated in his letter to Ticknor, the public was ready for such a publication—and this readiness was one factor which contributed to the fabulous success of *Looking Backward*. Panics, depressions, and bloody conflicts between capital and labor had created discontent. The middle class saw itself being crowded from the business world by the large corporations and monopolies and forced to become clerks instead of employers. The farmers and the laborers had founded or joined organizations—many of which sponsored socialist principles—to combat the conditions oppressing them. Because of the conditions which confronted the public and because of the pronouncements of the various reform agitators, the people were beginning to think that men had never received their just share of what by right belonged to them, that the competitive system did not produce the best type of individual, and that even its creation of individuality in the majority was doubtful. Americans felt that the democratic system, since it had seemingly broken down, was not perfect and that it might, therefore, be replaced by a better system—if one could be found. The solution would have, however, to be one which would not be opposed to the morality, the peacefulness, and the democratic principles of the American people. To many people, the solution which fulfilled these requirements seemed to be co-operative production and distribution which had been advocated and tried by many organizations.

When Dr. and Mrs. Aveling had surveyed the American scene in 1886, they had been surprised not only by the "unconscious socialism" of the people but by the fact that no major American writer had turned his hand to write a novel based on the national economic situation—and they had forecast that one day the "*Uncle Tom's Cabin* of Capitalism" would be written. Laurence Gronlund had also pointed out that there was a great need not only for a book about the leading tenets of socialism but for one which would present socialist doctrines to the people of "judgment and culture." To fulfill this purpose, the book would have to be written in readable English, and its contents would have to be adapted to American phenomena and principles by a writer possessing the American bias for the practical.

Looking Backward seemingly fulfilled not only the prophecies of the Avelings but the specifications of Gronlund. That it formulated an appeal to the waiting and unconscious socialists was confirmed in 1890 by Robert Lindblom when he wrote that the book "reflected and put in order the thoughts and aspirations of the present era." Bellamy himself, in accounting for the popularity of his book, stated that a novel of propaganda produced an effect "precisely in proportion as it is a bare anticipation in expression of what everybody was thinking and about to say. . . ." He was also not surprised, he wrote, by the effect the book had had upon others, for he had been aware of its effect upon him. As he wrote Looking Backward, he became convinced of the adequacy of his plan, and "the mighty hope" that resulted had produced strong emotions in him: "Knowing that 'as face answereth to face in water, so the heart of man to man,' I could not doubt that the hope that moved me must needs, in like manner, move all who should come even in part to share it." Bellamy had also written in one of his journals that "a hungry man can imagine a feast far better than a full one." His own hunger for a full life and his dissatisfaction with the state of the world had helped him imagine and create a society which would answer and express the needs in the hearts of his countrymen.

Furthermore, Bellamy—as a book reviewer, an editorial writer, and a voracious reader—was not only aware of the problems of his day but conscious of the type of book he would have to write if it were to have public appeal: it had to be one which would be a pleasantly told moral tale which would have no "uncomfortable depths" in which the reader would flounder. The style, the contents, and the whole manner of presentation of the ideal society not only fulfilled these specifications—as well as those made by Gronlund—but contributed to the success of Looking Backward. The simple, lucid prose of the novel made it easy to read; the Socratic dialogue made the development of the ideas easy to follow; and the lack of professional terminology facilitated not only the understanding by the uninformed reader of the tenets presented but also his acceptance of them since they were not directly presented as socialist in nature. The thread of romance, the use of hypnosis, and the inventions of the new era added savor to what might otherwise have been dry fare.

In presenting his picture of the ideal world, Bellamy skillfully showed how it was the opposite of conditions familiar to every reader and how it had evolved from those very situations—consolidation of industry and the machine age—which were the cause of discontentment. Instead of mere negation—denouncing or exposing existing conditions and merely opposing them—Bellamy proposed an ethical, economic system which could be erected peacefully through the process of legal evolution upon the democratic and industrial systems already in existence. Because his plan was constructive and because Bellamy's legally trained and logical mind presented almost irrefutable arguments to support the ideas he developed and the criticisms he made, the book had an air of practicality which stirred hope in the hearts of those who read it. Furthermore, Bellamy did not view the world from one particular slant; he regarded it from a social, moral, political, economic, and psychological viewpoint; because he was whole-viewed, his plan lacked the grotesque element which results from seeing only a part of the whole truth.

Bellamy also very sagely omitted the picture of *how* the ideal state was to be achieved, and he humorously explained the reason for this omission in an interview: " 'When you want to induce a bachelor to enter matrimony you don't go on with a lot of particulars about the marriage license and the gloves and the ceremony— you just show him the girl and let him fall in love with her and the rest takes care of itself.' " What Bellamy did present of the legal, bloodless evolution of the new state was such as would quiet the fears aroused in the hearts of the people by the Haymarket Riot and by the newspaper editorials and articles about the anarchists and the communists. Not only, however, was there no conflict depicted or advocated between the rich and the poor, the laborer and the capitalist, but there was no castigation of the rich. The rich, like the poor, were portrayed as being not only the result but also the victims of the competitive system.

The success of *Looking Backward* is attributable, however, not only to the readiness of the reading public and to the internal qualities of the book but also to the favorable reviews, to the adverse criticisms, and to the sponsorship it received from many important people and organizations. The first long appreciative review was written by Sylvester Baxter for the *Boston Herald,* but the most important, favorable review was that written by William Dean Howells for *Harper's.* Cyrus Willard wrote in the *Boston Globe* that the novel had altered his thinking about the possibilities of co-operation, and Hamilton W. Mabie, an author and the associate editor of the *Christian Union,* wrote to Bellamy to express his pleasure in the book and to assure him that it could not fail to do good. Laurence Gronlund not only wrote Bellamy that the novel should be as reliable a weapon for agitation as *Uncle Tom's Cabin* had been but directed his agents to stop selling his own *Co-operative Commonwealth* to labor organizations and to sell them *Looking Backward* instead.

Further success of Bellamy's Utopian novel was assured when it was espoused by representatives of various groups which helped to increase its popularity and its sales and to promulgate its ideas. The various groups who used it to sponsor their own objectives were the Theosophists, the Woman's Temperance Union, the National Council of Women, the socialists, the Christian Socialists, religious groups, the Grangers, sundry labor unions, the Farmer's Alliance, the Nationalist clubs, and the Populists. Many private individuals gave away copies of the book, and magazines and newspapers distributed it as premiums for new subscriptions. As Thomas W. Higginson wrote, *Looking Backward* created "a band of young proselytes who, instead of believing that what . . . [Bellamy] says is too good to be true, believe that it is too good not to be true; and are ready to proclaim its teachings as at least a temporary gospel of good news."

To the Theosophists, *Looking Backward* was the working out in a social scheme of the principle of universal brotherhood advocated by their colorful leader Madame Helen P. Blavatsky. Madame Blavatsky herself endorsed the book in her London publication, and similar endorsements appeared in *The Path* and in *The Key to*

Theosophy. Her disciples were also active in the Boston Nationalist Club, for its roster of members included the following Theosophists: Cyrus Willard, Henry Willard Austin, Arthur B. Griggs, George D. Ayers, John S. Cobb, Sylvester Baxter, and George Ransom Bridge.

When Frances B. Willard—staunch advocate of temperance and women's rights—read the novel, she wrote to Lillian Whiting, a friend employed by Ticknor: "Have been reading Edward Bellamy's 'Looking Backward' and think it's a revelation and an Evangel. Who and where is he? Please tell me or if you've written of him refer me to it. What manner of man is he in private?" Three weeks later, having received no reply, Miss Willard again wrote to her friend: "Some of us think that Edward Bellamy must be Edwardina —i.e., we believe a big-hearted, big-brained woman wrote the book. Won't you please find out?"

Miss Willard publicized the book to her friends, took the credit for introducing it to students at Oxford University, and recommended it to her many audiences. In her address to a meeting of the Knights of Labor held in Chicago, she recommended it as containing a plan of collectivism which would solve the problems of the times. She also spoke cordially of the novel in her address to the National Woman's Christian Temperance Union.

In a letter to John Lloyd Thomas, secretary of the Prohibition Party, Bellamy related his discussion with Miss Willard about the presence of wine in the ideal state, and he refused to make the changes in *Looking Backward* which would have pleased Thomas and his party. Bellamy used the arguments which must have been so successful in his conference with Miss Willard; he pointed out that the "industrial question . . . [was] destined to be the great issue before" the country and that it was greater than all the minor problems it included. If the industrial problem were solved and if poverty and ignorance were abolished as a result, many of the minor social problems such as intemperance might also disappear. Bellamy stated, however, that whether this was true or not, it was for the citizens of the future state to decide the question of temperance for themselves. He did, however, invite Thomas and his party to broaden their too-narrow platform by climbing on the Nationalist bandwagon and adopting the principle of human brotherhood as it applied to industry.

Such publications as the *Labor Standard,* the *Dawn* of the Christian Socialists, the liberal *Arena* of B. O. Flower, and the *Lend-a-Hand* of the Reverend Edward E. Hale publicized the novel and advised that it be read. Other publications such as *The Coming Nation, The Ladies' Home Journal,* the *Indianapolis Leader,* the *People's Health Journal,* and the newspapers published by the Farmer's Alliance offered the novel free or at a greatly reduced charge to new subscribers. The Grangers dispersed five hundred copies of the novel at their picnic in 1890 at William's Grove, Pennsylvania, and such private individuals as John Brisben Walker and Miss Faith Chevaillier (a rich protégée of Wendell Phillips and the first woman member of a Nationalist Club) purchased and gave the book to their friends and acquaintances.

Aside from the publicity provided by these groups, a body of adverse critical articles appeared which served to make the novel a source of controversy. It is no wonder, therefore, that by the time *Equality* (1897) was published, 400,000 copies of the book had been sold in the United States alone, or that by July 1, 1939, 532,329 copies had been distributed. In England from 1890 to 1935, an estimated 235,400 copies of the book were sold—but these figures do not include the sales of the William Reeves Company which established the Bellamy Library of thirty-two titles related to the subject of *Looking Backward* and also issued three or four editions of the novel itself. The novel was rapidly translated into German, French, Norwegian, and Italian and was published either in serial or book form or both. *Looking Backward* had with astounding rapidity become one of the world's best sellers.

The novel's influence, however, was to be no less amazing than its popularity, for it was to supply the incentive for the founding of Nationalist clubs and to stimulate the Christian Socialist and the social gospel movements. Eventually *Looking Backward* and the immediate program of the Nationalist clubs were to supply material for the platform of the People's Party. Its influence also contributed to the publication of many newspapers as well as many social-problem and Utopian novels. Because of its widespread influence, *Looking Backward* was to play an important role in the formation of American liberal thought.

3.   Nationalism

The effect of *Looking Backward* upon the public which led to the spontaneous formation of Nationalist or Bellamy clubs throughout the United States and in Europe was to bring the retiring, home-loving Edward Bellamy from his Chicopee Falls retreat to the position of one of the outstanding reform leaders of his day. The club movement and the critical articles launched against the policies of the Nationalists were to force Bellamy to defend, define, and refine the ideas and social plans which he had advocated in *Looking Backward*. As a result, he was to become a public speaker, an inveterate letter writer, a contributor to magazines and newspapers of articles supporting or stating his principles, and the publisher of a weekly magazine *The New Nation*. This phase of Bellamy's life was to be of particular significance not only because of its importance as a period in which his ideas were spread from coast to coast but because of its influence upon the ideas which were to be expressed in his last novel *Equality* which was to be completed after he had retired from the *The New Nation* and the political fray.

This period of Bellamy's life is also significant in that it witnessed the opening of his personality. Though he was always innately kind, he had covered his true self with a coat of thistles. As a result he had been noted among his colleagues of the *Union* for his cynicism, his sarcasm, and his capacity for wounding the sensibilities of others. Bellamy may have affected coldness and cynicism to cover his timidity and sensitivity, or, like Eliot Carson, he may have felt frustrated because he had not achieved the idealistic aspirations of his youth and because he had not found the world ready to accept his ideas. That he felt that his era would not accept some of the principles in which he believed is made clear by the fact that he started a notebook in which he intended to record ideas which would not stand publication—for the Philistines, he wrote, would not approve.

After the publication of *Looking Backward,* those who had known him during his *Union* days remarked that Bellamy had shed his habit of personal raillery and had become genial, earnest, and sympathetic in his conversations with others. This change in Bellamy was doubtless attributable to the fact that he not only had learned to give and accept love but had become successful in a way which would not only help the world but permit him to advocate openly the ideas in which he firmly and wholeheartedly believed. His success and fame did not, however, change "the natural man" in him which was not "socially inclined" and which was essentially modest. Caring little for the general chatter of social gatherings at any time, Bellamy refused to be lionized or to attend social functions in his honor when he became a popular author.

Bellamy had time, however, to talk with the tramps who appeared at the back door of his Chicopee Falls home. He was interested in their plight, he listened to their stories, and he gave them his clothing and his wife's freshly baked cakes and pies. As his wife has said (as she doubtless thought of the frequent disappearance of the family dessert), "He was a great man—but he was also a 'character.' "

Bellamy did not, however, regard himself as a great man, and his modesty seems to have stemmed from a deep-rooted opinion of himself. He wrote: "If I should gain a victory or write a book, I should not think more of myself but less of the victory. My opinion of myself is the fixed element of my calculations. This way of looking at things saves one from vanity, from being puffed up." The fact that he was a great man is proved, however, by his unstinted giving not only of the small fortune he received from the sale of *Looking Backward* but of his meagre energy to the reform movement through which he hoped to create a better world for posterity.

The Nationalist movement, which resulted from the publication of *Looking Backward,* in which Bellamy was to play an important role, followed two stages in its development. During the first stage, 1888-1891, the clubs which were organized devoted themselves primarily to a moral crusade—to propaganda and education. During the second period, 1891-1896, the Nationalists entered the field of political action, first with their own local party ticket and then as important supporters of the People's Party, or the Populists.

The first Nationalist Club was founded in Boston as a consequence of letters written to Bellamy by Sylvester Baxter, Cyrus Willard, Captain Charles E. Bowers, and General A. F. Devereux. In June, 1888, Willard wrote Bellamy that he wished to found a club for the propagation of the ideas of *Looking Backward*, and he asked Bellamy what he thought of this proposal. On July 4, Bellamy informed Willard that he had received a similar suggestion from Baxter, and he suggested that the two men work together to form a club, for that seemed "a proper measure." To Bellamy it was also particularly "fitting that Boston should lead off in this movement." Since it was the place where the Tea Party had occurred and where the anti-slavery movement had centered, Boston seemed also the proper location for the organization of the third movement for the liberation of the people.

In July, Bellamy congratulated Willard and Baxter for their attempt to convert the "cultured and conservative class," for, he said—in words reminiscent of what Gronlund had said about converting this class—that that was the "special end for which *Looking Backward* was written." As will be seen, this was to be the principle of selection which was to make the Bellamy movement an influential and a distinctively middle-class affair.

By August, 1888, the plans for the formation of the club were under way, but its organization was postponed by Bellamy's inability to be in Boston, by Baxter's trip to Germany, and by Willard's preoccupation with business. In the meantime, Captain Charles E. Bowers and General A. F. Devereux wrote to Bellamy on September 7, 1888, about their movement to found a club which was to be the first organization of its kind. On September 18, this club, called the Boston Bellamy Club, set forth its objective as being "the elevation of man" through the dissemination of the "views . . . set forth in *Looking Backward*." Twenty-seven charter members affixed their signatures to this declaration.

In October, Bowers, Devereux, Baxter, and Willard held a meeting and as a result the two groups decided to coalesce. The first joint meeting was called in December to form a "permanent organization to further the Nationalization of industry." At this meeting held in Captain Bower's office at 61 State Street, a committee of five—Cyrus Willard, General Devereux, Sylvester Baxter, the Reverend W. D. P. Bliss, and Captain Bowers—was appointed to present a plan for the club.

When the group met on December 6, the constitution of the club was presented and adopted, and a nominating committee was appointed. On December 15 Bellamy attended the meeting, received an enthusiastic welcome, and was elected first vice-president of the club. Other officers were: Captain Bowers, president; General Devereux, second vice-president; Cyrus Willard, secretary; Ralph Cracknall, assistant secretary; Sylvester Baxter, treasurer; and Charles M. Saulson, financial secretary. The first regular meeting of the new club was held on January 8, 1889, at Tremont House with about fifty members present. The declaration of principles of the constitution and the statement of objectives were at this time presented and adopted.

The principles adopted by the Boston Bellamy Club, used in their constitutions by clubs which sprang up all over the country, were, therefore, the unifying factors of groups which otherwise had no "central organization." Because of the nation-wide acceptance of these principles, they are quoted in full:

> The principle of the Brotherhood of Humanity is one of the eternal truths that govern the world's progress on lines which distinguish human nature from brute nature.
>
> The principle of competition is simply the application of the brutal law of the survival of the strongest and the most cunning.
>
> Therefore, so long as competition continues to be the ruling factor in our industrial system, the highest development of the individual cannot be reached, the loftiest aims of humanity cannot be realized.
>
> No truth can avail unless practically applied. Therefore, those who seek the welfare of man must endeavor to suppress the system founded on the brute principle of competition and put in its place another based on the nobler principle of association.
>
> But in striving to apply this nobler and wiser principle to the complex conditions of modern life, we advocate no sudden or ill considered changes; we make no war upon individuals; we do not censure those who have accumulated immense fortunes simply by

carrying to a logical end the false principles upon which business is now based.

The combinations, trusts, and syndicates of which the people at present complain demonstrate the practicability of our basic principle of association. We merely seek to push this principle a little further and have all industries operated in the interest of all the nation—the people organized—the organic unity of the whole people.

The present industrial system proves itself wrong by the immense wrongs it produces; it proves itself absurd by the immense waste of energy and material which is admitted to be its concomitant. Against this system we raise our protest: for the abolition of the slavery it has wrought and would perpetuate, we pledge our best efforts.

The immediate objective of the club was to educate the people—through lectures, books, and articles—in the reform measures and ideas advocated by *Looking Backward*. The club members were particularly well prepared for this purpose for they included Colonel T. W. Higginson, famous abolitionist orator and writer; the Reverend Edward E. Hale, philanthropic divine and novelist; Frances Willard; Mary A. Livermore, editor and suffragette; Anne Whitney, famous American sculptress; Henry Austin, poet; Cyrus Willard and Sylvester Baxter, journalists; William Dean Howells; and John Storer Cobb, one of the original founders of the New York Theosophical Society.

In February, 1889, the publication committee of the club which consisted of Baxter, the Reverend Hale, and Anne Whitney—and which had the warm support of Colonel Higginson—decided to recommend the publication of a magazine and of a series of pamphlets. The Nationalist Education Association, with Bellamy as president, was therefore incorporated under the laws of Massachusetts to enable the publication of the monthly magazine *The Nationalist* which made its first appearance in May, 1889, and which ceased publication because of financial difficulties in April, 1891. During this same period, the club distributed 25,000 pamphlets as part of its propaganda work.

The Nationalist published articles relating specifically and generally to the Nationalist tenets and reform measures and to politics and industry. The list of contributors included the names of many people well known at that time: Abby Morton Diaz, Laurence Gronlund, T. W. Higginson, John Orvis, Rabbi Schindler, Thaddeus Wakeman, the Reverend C. A. Cressy, and the Reverend Hale. One of the features of the journal of particular interest to any student of the movement is a section devoted to the national news of the movement which was written by Cyrus Willard.

In December, 1889, the Boston Nationalists celebrated the anniversary of the club with a meeting at Tremont Temple which they hoped would win money for, and widen the reputation of, the cause. Bellamy, despite the fact that he was suffering so severely from dyspepsia that he was considering a trip to Cuba or the Bahamas for his health, addressed the assembled group on the purposes and principles of Nationalism.

Though Bellamy was deluged with invitations to speak and to make lecture tours, his poor health and his principles limited his acceptance of engagements. He felt that he could do better work for the cause with "simple conversation with" his fellow men, and he was convinced that he did not "want to lecture on the subject for money." The speeches that he did give in his own immediate locality took a toll from his energy, but they doubtless contributed to the growth of the movement for he was a capable and interesting speaker. He himself told of his ability to hold an audience when he related that he had given a lecture at the barn-studio on Cape Ann of Ross Turner, the artist, to an audience seated on planks supported by boxes. "I talked for an hour," said Bellamy, "and not a man fell off his bench."

By the second anniversary of the Nationalist Club, two thousand people were present to hear Bellamy speak about the methods to be used in nationalizing industry. Such an attendance was, however, to be expected, for the clubs had grown rapidly in the East and had mushroomed in the West after April, 1889. The list of some of the different club members is of interest in that it reveals the respectability of the movement. The New York club contained such members as Stuart Merrill, the writer; Thaddeus Wakeman; Professor Thomas Davidson; Professor Daniel de Leon; Jonathan Sturgis, author; John Lovell, publisher; and Lucien Saniel, one of the original founders of the Paris *Temps*. The clubs in such

places as Hartford, Connecticut, and Chicago had such members
as Mrs. Emily P. Collins and Miss Frances E. Burr, founders of
the Hartford Equal Rights Club, and Jesse Cox and Clarence
Darrow. A survey of the membership of the clubs in Cincinnati,
Washington, Brooklyn, Minneapolis, St. Louis, Philadelphia, Baltimore, and San Francisco revealed that the members were for the
most part not manual laborers but lawyers, newspaper men, artists,
doctors, and business men. After reviewing these membership
lists, it is easily understood why it was said that Nationalism had
put "the silk hat on socialism."

Indeed, it had been the intention of the leaders of the Nationalist
movement to select the members slowly in order "to secure those
who can give of work or money or influence to the cause." The
members were to be "composed as much as possible of men who
had been successful in the fierce competitive struggle," of those
who were educated and "conservative in speech," and not of those
who were foreign born, uneducated, or fanatical. Cyrus Willard,
Laurence Gronlund, and William L. Garrison all asserted that the
membership was drawn not from the victims of social wrongs but
from the cultivated and the well-to-do; and Henry Ford verified
their statements when he observed that the clubs were not "for the
debtor and the malcontent." The Nationalist movement was, therefore, not one *of* the proletariat but one *for* the proletariat.

The prior affiliations of many of the discontented intellectuals
who became Nationalists are of interest. Two of them, John Orvis
and Colonel T. W. Higginson, had been Associationists and Abolitionists, respectively. Others, like Mrs. Frances E. Russell, had
been followers of Henry George, or, like Miss Faith Chevaillier,
had been protégés of such reformers and liberals as Wendell Phillips.
Other members of the Nationalist clubs had been—or still were—
members of the Grangers, the socialist parties, the labor unions,
the Greenbacks, and of other reform movements such as those for
temperance or equal rights.

The journalists were well represented not only in the Bellamy
Club of Boston but in many others throughout the country by editors,
writers, and publishers who supported Nationalism. In December,
1889, Cyrus Willard stated that fifty newspapers and magazines

unreservedly supported Nationalism; and in 1890 Mason Green wrote that he could visit the editorial rooms of every leading New York or Boston newspaper and shake hands with a Nationalist. By June, 1890, there were in California seven newspapers which supported—or had been founded to express—Nationalist principles, and other states, as well as England, had their own Nationalist publications.

The attention Nationalism received from the press doubtless contributed to the fact that in 1890 the *North American Review* cited Nationalism and electric lighting as being—after the tariff and the speakership—the subjects which were uppermost in the American mind. The movement had, in fact, gained so much attention that the leaders of the Nationalists began to feel that the educational and propaganda work of the clubs was now unnecessary and that the public was ready for political action to begin.

Edward Bellamy introduced the second stage of the Nationalist movement—that of political action—with the publication of *The New Nation* in January, 1891. Prior to the launching of this weekly paper, however, tentative steps had been taken on the political front when in December, 1889, Cyrus Willard had suggested in an article that every club should become a center of "practical politics" and seek the election of state representatives—for the Nationalists in Massachusetts were trying to gain support for a bill which they had introduced in the legislative session of 1889 which would permit municipal ownership of gas and electric plants. The bill had been defeated in the Senate of the legislature of 1889-1890; but, when the Nationalists renewed the fight in 1890, they succeeded in getting the bill passed in 1891. During the following year, sixteen towns in Massachusetts, as well as several in Ohio, began to establish municipally owned plants. The importance of this development to the Nationalists was great, for Bellamy had proposed that public ownership of utilities be the initial step in the evolution of the ideal state since it would be of great value in educating the people about the benefits of public ownership.

Bellamy's decision to publish *The New Nation* was the result of deliberation and of many circumstances. Although Bellamy had been requested in 1890 by Henry Austin to assume the editorship of *The Nationalist,* Bellamy's doctor refused in May to let him accept this responsibility and ordered him to spend the summer resting. By November Bellamy had written to John Orme, editor of the English Nationalist publication, that he intended "to start a first class weekly periodical devoted to Nationalism, in New York, probably in December," and that he wished Orme to write a weekly letter for it which would relate the news of the English Nationalist movement and of "social solutions."

The reason for Bellamy's decision to publish a periodical of his own was indicated in his letter in December, 1890, to Colonel Higginson in which he informed him that *The Nationalist* was in debt and had been published during its last year only because expenses had been defrayed by donations totalling two thousand dollars. Since this publication—which "had never amounted to very much, but . . . has amounted to something"—was fated to cease publication, Bellamy deemed that the time had come for him to "carry out a project" which he had "long been maturing"—to publish a weekly paper which would be devoted to the "discussion of the industrial and social situation from the moral and economic point of view indicated" by *Looking Backward.* In other words, Bellamy wished to establish an organ of propaganda which would deal more directly than had *The Nationalist* with the problems in which he was principally interested, give greater coverage to the Nationalist movement, and show the ways in which people were trying to solve the industrial and social problems of the time.

Bellamy finally decided, however, not to publish the paper in New York but in Boston. This location, he felt, was one which not only promised more support for his venture but permitted him to be closer to his family. Having made his decision, Bellamy took over the subscription list of *The Nationalist,* opened an office at 15 Winter Street, and organized his staff. He himself served as publisher and editor, and his staff consisted of the following: Mason Green, managing editor; Henry R. Legate, president of the Second Nationalist Club of Boston, assistant editor; and John Ransome Bridge, who joined the staff in 1893, business manager.

Bellamy's managing editor, Mason Green, was a graduate of Amherst College, the author of several books, and a journalist who had had wide experience while working for Samuel Bowles on the *Springfield Republican*. Though Green was disliked by some of the Boston Nationalists who thought that he exercised too much influence upon Bellamy, he was well qualified to assume his position on the staff and to play also the role of propagandist for and representative of the movement. While Bellamy stayed in Boston or in Chicopee Falls, Green traveled to conventions and meetings of the Nationalists and later of the People's Party.

In the first issue of *The New Nation,* Bellamy announced in the "Prospectus" that the purpose of the publication was to "criticize the existing industrial system as radically wrong in morals and preposterous economically" and to "advocate the substitution, therefore, as rapidly as practicable, of the plan of national industrial cooperation, aiming to bring about the economic equality of citizens, which is known as nationalism." To accomplish this purpose, the periodical published news items which illustrated the need of a new social order, articles on the debatable questions and doctrines of Nationalism, and editorials and comments depicting the feasibility of applying Nationalist ideas as a solution to the ills of the social body.

Several of the special features or columns of this twenty-odd page publication are of interest. In "Economic Drift"—a column devoted to events pointing toward eventual nationalization—the items told of increasing public ownership of utilities, of civil service reform measures, and of the growth of business monopolies and combinations. In "Read, Reflect, and Inwardly Digest"—a feature dedicated to the recital of incidents in the news which would not occur in the ideal society—stories of fires which had deprived men of life or of employment, of robberies and forgeries, and of suicide because of poverty were printed. In "News from the Front" information about strikes, their causes, and their places of occurrence was given. Special articles relating the social reform progress in England and in Germany were occasionally submitted by John Orme of England and by "Marcus" and Bruno Schoenlank of Germany.

Bellamy began the most interesting and valuable of all the special features in the third issue of *The New Nation*: his own series of simply written dialogues called "Talks on Nationalism" which appeared from February 14 to October 10, 1891. This series is of particular importance because Bellamy, in the guise of Mr. Smith, the Nationalist, discussed many of the problems of Nationalism as they related to a business man, a minister, an evolutionist, a woman's right advocate, a father, a charity worker, a disciple of Malthus, a banker, a college senior, a prohibitionist, a dress reformer, a farmer, and a tariff reformer. The fundamental doctrines of Nationalism—economic equality, social equality, and brotherhood—were also discussed.

To the reader of *The New Nation*, many of the articles seem extremely repetitious for they deal time and time again with the principle of economic equality, with the problem of the nationalization of the railroads, and with the question of the motivation of the laborer of the new state. Since these subjects were not only fundamental problems but ones to which objections were most frequently raised, it was logical that they would be discussed repeatedly. Bellamy's attitude, however, also contributed to such repetition, for he believed that though the objections had been answered many times there was "no reason why they should not be answered again." It was, he believed, only through repetition and the piling of precept upon precept that the new ideas could be made to "overcome the old on so large a scale as" the Nationalists intended they should. Many of these same discussions and arguments which appeared so often in *The New Nation* were used advantageously by Bellamy once more in *Equality*.

Specifically and politically, Bellamy advocated in *The New Nation* as an immediate program for the Nationalists the following: reform of the civil service; immediate government ownership of coal mines, express service, telephone and telegraph companies, and railroads. He also sponsored referendum and recall; equal and compulsory education; and all reforms which tended toward more equalitarian, humane, and fraternal relationships. Bellamy also made a conscious effort in *The New Nation* to bring into closer accord the various reform groups and labor organizations so that their combined influence could procure legislative action which would ultimately secure the evolutionary reforms deemed necessary.

In accordance with this avowed purpose which he had stated in the "Prospectus" of promoting the unification of reform movements, Bellamy's *New Nation* shortly after it began publication became a supporter of the People's Party and published in every issue the platform of the party, as well as news of the party's meetings and progress. The political phase of the Nationalist movement was, therefore, closely associated with the People's Party, for, though the Nationalists were to remain independent supporters of the movement, it was through this third party that Bellamy hoped to inaugurate the policies which would lead to the development of his ideal state.

It was also during the year 1891 that the first state Nationalist party ticket was presented in Rhode Island. Though the Rhode Island candidates were not elected, they did poll one per cent of the votes—and this despite the fact that the ticket had been presented on the eve of the election and that only twenty-five dollars had been spent on the campaign. Though California and Michigan had nominated Nationalists for Congress and several states had placed Nationalists in the field for state legislatures in the fall of 1890, the Rhode Island ticket of 1891 was more important to the Nationalists, for it signified to them that "the baby was born"— that the Nationalist movement was taking form as a political power.

In April, 1891, *The New Nation* revealed that the Nationalists had received an invitation to join the People's Party and to send their representatives to the convention for formation of the party, which was to be held in Cincinnati on May 19, 1891. When the Nationalist delegates appeared at this convention, they were warmly received; and the platform adopted by the People's Party was without doubt the result of the influence of *Looking Backward* and the Nationalist movement.

As Bellamy himself had noted, the region in which his novel had been most popular—the trans-Mississippi states, the Pacific Coast, and the Middle West—was also the area in which the People's Party had its strength. *The Nationalist* had also stated that Nationalism had had a wide influence upon specific groups—the Farmer's

Alliance, the Grangers, the Knights of Labor, Woman Suffrage, and sundry labor unions—which were represented in the People's Party. In 1891 the *St. Louis Dispatch* stated that the activities of the Nationalists at the convention and the study of *Looking Backward* by the farmers to whom the book had been recommended by the Alliance and the Grangers had influenced the platform which the Populists adopted.

Ignatius Donnelly, national lecturer for the Grangers who was also chairman of the Cincinnati platform committee, greeted the Nationalist delegates to the convention with these words: "Edward Bellamy—whom not to know is to argue one's self unknown." Since Ignatius Donnelly wrote most of the platform which was adopted by the Omaha convention in July, 1892, his statement is particularly important. Further evidence of the influence of the Nationalists upon the third party is to be found in the statement of Howells that Bellamy "virtually founded the Populist Party" whose platform owed much to the ideas of *Looking Backward*.

Bellamy also regarded the Cincinnati-Omaha platform as being Nationalist in spirit as well as in objectives since it advocated the extension of the powers of the federal government; government ownership of railroad, telegraph, and telegraph companies; government postal savings banks; and popular election of United States senators. Because of these objectives of the party, Bellamy averred that it offered "the largest opportunity yet presented in the history of our movement [Nationalism] to commend it to the masses of the country. If we fail to take the utmost possible advantage of it, we shall make a fatal mistake."

Bellamy carefully defined, however, what he meant by taking "the utmost possible advantage" of the People's Party when he outlined the role he wished the Bellamy clubs to play in the third party movement: "We do not believe that the nationalistic clubs, as organizations, should turn themselves into campaign clubs. The clubs stand for more advanced principles than any party is likely at once to take up, and it would be unwise policy for them as clubs to engage in any line of work which would compromise the completeness of their doctrine. But individually and as citizens, we hope and believe that nationalists generally will be found in sympathy with the new party."

Bellamy himself as a publisher, individual, and citizen became active in the People's Party; he attended the organizing dinner of the party in Massachusetts; and he addressed the public meeting of the movement at Faneuil Hall, Boston, on October 17, 1891. In his address he discussed the corruptive influence of wealth and the party platform in its particulars. He commended the Populists generally because of their intention of carrying popular government into industry, which, he said, was a necessity if the republican form of government were to survive. Bellamy also analyzed the party platform at a rally at Lynn, Massachusetts, in October, 1891, and he addressed a convention of the party at Faneuil Hall on March 30, 1892. When the representatives for the Omaha convention were selected at this meeting, the following Nationalists were chosen as delegates: Bellamy, Legate, Green, Austin, and Huntington.

Bellamy was expected to address the ratification meeting of the party ticket held on October 13, 1892, in Tremont Temple, but he was unable to attend the meeting because of illness. A letter from him was read to the three thousand people present in which he stated that the People's Party was a means not only of attaining the American dream of a true republic of equality, fraternity, liberty, and justice but of saving the republic from the rule of industry. On the party ticket Bellamy was listed as a presidential elector at large.

During the early days of the Populist movement, Bellamy gave more public speeches than ever before although he also refused to appear at the World's Fair Labor Congress despite Henry D. Lloyd's insistence that he do so. Eltweed Pomeroy also urged him to make a lecture tour in order to enlist the support of the middle class and to help—though not ostensibly so—the Populist Party in this way. Bellamy's refusal to participate in these plans and to accept other invitations to speak was due to his poor health and to his wife's insistence that he take care of himself.

When the Populists convened in Omaha, the Nationalists held a separate meeting in order to establish a committee for propaganda work. The group planned to select a Nationalist from each state to act on a national committee which would circulate petitions demanding legislation authorizing the purchase by the federal government of the telegraph and telephone facilities of the nation. Mason Green acted as general secretary and R. S. Luscomb as corresponding secretary for this committee which tried as late as 1893 to perfect the national organization. From 1893 until 1898, the Nationalists had, however, their "Bureau of Nationalist Literature" in Philadelphia which distributed Bellamy's speeches, *Looking Backward*, and Professor Frank Parson's "Public Ownership of Monopolies" and his "Philosophy of Mutualism." By October of 1897 the bureau had distributed over 104,000 copies of its publications which had been paid for by public donations. The bureau closed in March, 1898, when B. Franklin Hunter, who had managed it, resigned from his position in the post-office to join the Ruskin Colony.

In the election of 1892, the Populist presidential candidate, General James B. Weaver of Iowa, received 1,065,191 votes; he had carried six states and had won twenty-two electoral college votes. The Populists were the first third party since the Civil War to win electoral votes, and this became a matter of concern to both the Democrats and the Republicans. The old parties were also perturbed by the fact that the third party had elected three governors, three state senators, and seventeen representatives.

In the 1893 election in Massachusetts, the Populist vote trebled, and Bellamy indignantly recorded in *The New Nation* the story of the conspiracy of silence which led to articles in the Boston papers telling of the decline rather than the growth of the third party. The regulation dispatches from the polls had contained no space for the recording of the Populist votes—and these forms had been prepared by the Western Union Company and the New England Press Association. Bellamy charged that the same blanket of silence had covered the increases in the Populist vote in Virginia, Ohio, Colorado, Nebraska, and Iowa.

In the 1894 Congressional election, the Populist vote showed a forty per cent increase—but *The New Nation* was no longer in existence to record the fact. The depression of 1893 had affected the subscriptions, and Bellamy's health had become so poor that he had been forced to send his articles to the paper by mail. Because of these financial and personal difficulties and because Bellamy felt that *The New Nation* had played its role, he decided to stop publishing the paper and to devote himself to a more worthwhile contribution to the cause.

In summarizing the role that *The New Nation* had played, Bellamy stated that it had saved Nationalism from the danger it had run in 1891 of becoming "dissipated into a vague and foggy philanthropy" and had made of it a coherent doctrine with an immediate campaign to be waged for the realization of the ideal state. The role the journal had played for the cause was no longer necessary, for Nationalism had gained "its thousand standard bearers," and the Nationalists had become "the advance guard of a national party" which had adopted the *immediate* program of the Nationalists for its platform. Because of these gains, wrote Bellamy, he was retiring to "take up other lines of work promising, possibly a larger service to the cause than he would have been able to render by continuing the publication of" *The New Nation*. Bellamy had begun to write his novel *Equality* which was to show the results of his statements in *The New Nation* about the theory and practice of Nationalism and the manifold results of economic equality.

Bellamy's reliance upon the success of the People's Party was unfortunate for its platform was demolished when the Republicans and the Democrats took planks from it for their own platforms. In 1896 the Populists joined the Democrats, and William J. Bryan ran on the issue of "free silver" for President of the United States. Mark Hanna's machine supported McKinley, who became President, and Nationalism and Populism met their death blow. The first battle between big business and the people had ended, and the industrialists consolidated their power during the Spanish-American War.

Bellamy could, however, have been justly proud of the role *Looking Backward* had played as a spokesman and as an inspiration for the confused and discontented Americans. Because it had presented in concrete terms a synthesis of the ideologies prevalent during its period; because of its practical application of the theories it presented; because of the Christian and democratic principles of its plan; and because of its method of presentation, as well as the

timeliness of its publication, the novel became a guide to the people
and to the reform groups who were seeking to remedy conditions.
Although *Looking Backward* and the immediate program of the
Nationalists served as a basis for the formation of the People's
Party, the influence of the novel and of the Bellamy clubs was not
limited to the third party alone; *Looking Backward* had also a definite influence—both at home and abroad—upon socialism, Marxian
communism, religious groups, and literature—but this is a story
it will take another book to tell.

4. *Equality*

When *Looking Backward* had achieved popularity and influence,
Bellamy declared that "what was left out of it . . . loomed up as
so much more important than what it contained." This statement
was true because of the serious criticisms of its ideologies which
Bellamy regarded "with greater interest, if not greater pleasure, than
the congratulatory notices." Bellamy's interest in the comments of
his critics was due to his firm belief "that the next phase of industry
and society . . . will be a plan of national cooperation, and that this
plan cannot be permanently based upon any other principle than
universal industrial service with equality of material conditions."
He recognized, however, "that the details of such a cooperative organization may be greatly varied consistently with these principles."
Though he had advanced in his first Utopian novel "a series of
details of such an organization" which did not seem unreasonable
to him, he had been "far from considering them as necessarily the
best devices possible," and he had been "accordingly on the lookout
for valuable criticisms and suggestions."

Bellamy was not, however, so much interested in the criticisms
of the "minor details in the book" as in those which attacked the
major aspects of his plan. Professor Charles Secrétan of Lausanne,
Switzerland, in his *Etudes Sociales—Mon Utopie* (c. 1891) had asked
—as had many of Bellamy's other critics—how the tools of the
nation were to be secured by the state; how the indolence of the
worker was to be prevented or overcome; how the officials would
be made responsible, effective, and unselfish; how the owners would
be remunerated for their lost property; and how the freedom of

the individual would be guaranteed. Many of the attacks had centered about the principle of economic equality; others about the organization of the industrial army; and others, delivered by the Malthusians, about the possibility of starvation as a result of unlimited reproduction because of the lack of parental economic responsibility for children. Others—intrigued by his plan or highly critical of it—demanded that Bellamy outline the route to the achievement of his ideal state. Bellamy answered his critics in his speeches, in his letters, and in his articles published in sundry periodicals and in *The New Nation;* and, in so doing, he was preparing the answers that he was to give to all his critics in *Equality.*

Bellamy's notebooks contain many entries relative to the objectives and the contents of the sequel to *Looking Backward,* for Bellamy had realized not too long after its publication that a sequel was a necessary certainty. One of the most detailed plans reveals his intention of using the Eliot Carson story as a Nationalist story. In his outline Eliot, a man sceptical of "radical social reforms," gets married, has a child, and becomes convinced of his "utter oneness with the race." Carson, who defines Nationalism as the people's "only and sure deliverance," discusses his ideas with his college friend, the narrator; and the two of them attend a socialist meeting at which Carson tells the group its errors. The story, wrote Bellamy, was also to portray the misery and brutality of poverty and the sordidness and triviality of social life. With these pictures he hoped to "give an ever thrilling interest to the dryest [sic] details of the remedies. But of course they must not be dry." He planned also to have no "thread of love" but much talk of the "sacredness of a woman" in the novel.

By 1893, according to Mason Green, Bellamy had settled upon a story for his sequel: that of the Great Revival, which would portray the achievement of the ideal state. After he had worked on the novel for a time, he discarded this story as unsatisfactory since it could not include all that he wished to say about the "details and workings of his Utopia," or all that he desired to state in answer to his critics sceptical about economic equality. Bellamy, therefore, changed his plan and reverted to the plot of *Looking Backward* so that he could "cut deeper" and not merely "spend his time surveying convenient routes to his new country."

On November 7, 1893, Bellamy wrote to Howells: "My book is very little as yet, and, as you have noticed, one's book is prettiest when in the cradle, although not even then so pretty as before it is born at all. If I publish a poor book, I ought to be stoned. The responsibility upon us, who have won the ear of the public, to plead the cause of the voiceless masses is beyond limit. You have stood up to it nobly in your Altruria, but the trouble is the better a man does the better he has got to do. 'There is no discharge in that war.' "

Bellamy realized that he was reaching the end of his life while he was writing *Equality,* and, though he had two other books he desired to write, he was forced to regard *Equality* as "his will in the field of economics for the benefit of the coming generations." Each day, despite his failing health, he did his stint of work; and occasionally, when Green left his job in Vermont as editor of *The Rutland Herald* to come to visit Bellamy, the two went to nearby Springfield for a game of billiards. While they played, they discussed the economic wastes of competition.

By the time Bellamy was reading the last pages of the proof of *Equality,* his health was so poor that he had to alternate periods of rest with those of work. When he had completed his final revisions and the book had appeared on the market in the early summer of 1897, Bellamy opined that his often forced labor and his exhaustion of his last reserve of energy had been justified by the result—for to him *Equality* was the best novel that he had written.

The book was, however, considered unsuccessful—and, in comparison to the popularity of *Looking Backward,* it was. Judging from its own record of sales in a period in which the selling of ten thousand copies ranked a book as a best seller, *Equality* was also a success. By September 10, 1897, D. Appleton and Company had sold 14,000 copies of the work, and by December 1, 1897—only six months after publication—it had sold 21,044 copies. By 1905, 41,000 copies had been distributed.

The reception of *Equality* in England, where it had also been published in June, 1897, was "anything but gracious." Most of the American and the English reviewers concurred in bewailing the lack of dramatic interest of the novel and, in many instances, in declaring that it was really not fiction but a philosophical essay. What Bellamy had himself written in 1873 about a serial entitled *The True Reformer* was echoed by the reviewers of *Equality* and might justly have been written about it: "Whether in this novel there is too much politics for the story, or too much story for the politics, we don't feel quite sure, but one or the other is certainly the case, for the whole effect is not good."

Others, however, hailed the book enthusiastically despite its lack of dramatic interest. C. F. Bailey and Thomas Reynolds of London wrote to Bellamy of their enthusiasm, and Frances Willard pronounced the novel to be a "whole body of divinity" for those believing in the right of the people to manage their corporate affairs. B. O. Flower, editor of *The Arena,* wrote that he had read *Equality* with "intense delight" and that he approved of the emendations of the social plans which would insure the maintenance of democratic government. He was also favorably impressed by the stand Bellamy had taken relative to "woman, her rights, her development, and her dress." The reading of *Equality,* wrote Flower, had dispelled his apprehension that socialism would "sound the knell of the freedom necessary to intellectual growth and independence."

Despite the enthusiasm of these readers, it must be admitted that *Looking Backward*—because of its plot, its material, and its style— was far more likely to be popular and influential with the general reader than its sequel. The plot of *Looking Backward* added spice to the content because of the unusual experiences of Julian West who, after a long sleep induced by mesmerism, awakens to find himself in a new world. In it he sees many things which startle him, one of which is Edith Leete, whom he loves and wins, who turns out to be the descendant of his fiancée of his former life. In the last section of the novel the reader is dejected because Julian returns to his old world—and is then delighted when he learns that the return is only a nightmare. Until the end of the novel, therefore, the plot provides suspense because of Julian's situation. In *Equality* Julian is already engaged to marry the girl he loves, and the author —happily enough so far as he was concerned—was freed from the love plot and could let Julian spend his time discussing, viewing, or hearing discussed the ideas and social innovations of the year 2000.

Although *Looking Backward* was principally concerned with presenting the ideal state and with contrasting it to the old order, the dialogues were short, sprightly, and spontaneous. The first novel also contained many striking, original analogies such as that of the coach and society, that of the rosebush and man's perfectibility, and that of the covered streets of the year 2000 and the umbrella of the nineteenth century. These comparisons not only intrigued and impressed the reader but helped him grasp the points which Bellamy wished to make. In *Equality,* however, the discussions seem more contrived, duller, and longer; and some of the material is presented as being from histories or literature of that past. "The Parable of the Water Tank"—excellent as it is and valuable as it was when it was used in pamphlet form as propaganda by the labor unions—is really a lengthy, summarizing interjection; and without much doubt it was, as Green suggested, part of the first and rejected *Equality* manuscript. Of all the sections of *Equality,* the most tedious one, however, is that devoted to the presentation of the failures of the profit system, for Bellamy takes the reader into a school room to hear a stilted discussion by robot-like students.

The differences in the style and the presentation of material in *Equality* must be attributed not only to the exhausted plot but to the purpose of Bellamy in writing the book. In *Looking Backward* Bellamy was primarily concerned with portraying the ideal state, but in *Equality* he sought to accomplish multiple things—to show the route to the ideal state, to change some of the details of the new order, and to answer the critics. When one reads the discussions about the economic wastes of private enterprise, the place of religion in the ideal state, and the answers to the arguments of the critics, one has to admire the skill with which Bellamy lucidly presented such complex ideas in narrative form, as well as the adroitness with which he displayed the effect economic equality had upon almost every aspect of life in the new order.

From the viewpoint of the complexity of the ideas and the arguments presented and the skill with which these are united by the theme of economic equality, *Equality* is—as Bellamy thought it was —far superior to *Looking Backward. Equality* may, however, be called a novel only by grace of the fact that it has an infinitesimal thread of romance running through the book and that it has its setting in a visionary world of the future. To the readers who purchased the book because they wished to read something like *Looking Backward, Equality* must have been disappointing.

Equality showed, in summary, Bellamy's progression toward a more popular and democratic form of government in that he instituted popular elections by employing referendum; made the people legislators by giving them initiative; and gave them power over their agents by instituting recall. He also took great care to portray that the democratic principles of his government had had their conception during the period of the American Revolution and that his ideal state was only the result of an evolution of these ideas—and one which would restore, extend, and preserve the democratic equalities. He also demonstrated fully and carefully that economic equality was the basis upon which the whole of the economic, political, intellectual, and ethical life of the nation rested and that without it none of the other democratic equalities could be achieved or maintained. In *Equality,* therefore, Bellamy carefully defined his democracy, its safeguards, and its necessities, and he showed that his views stemmed from the American radicalism which had led to the establishment of a government of, by, and for the people.

The role of Christian principles in the formation and in the objectives of the ideal state was also so fully presented in *Equality* that no critic could say that Bellamy's Utopia lacked Christianity or that its author was indifferent about the spiritual development of man. In his picture of the religion of the year 2000 which permitted variety in unity and which needed no established church nor ordained ministers, Bellamy reflected not only his rebellion against Calvinism, creeds, and authority but his acceptance of the religious movements of his day. In his statements relative to the part this religion played in unifying the new social order, Bellamy also disclosed the influence of his own religion of solidarity. When he made it the concern of each individual of the new state to determine the principles of his religious faith, Bellamy not only made it requisite that each man would search for his beliefs but gave him

Bellamy's own quest: the discovery of man's relation to the finite
and the infinite.

In order to satisfy his critics, the people interested in his plan,
and his own conception of the ability the reformer should have
in being able to direct the steps to secure a new world, Bellamy
presented in *Equality* a coherent plan of the steps to be taken in
evolving an industrial democracy. He also answered in "The Book
of the Blind" the doubts of his critics as to whether originality and
independence of thought and action would exist in the new order.
He presented also his arguments to those who feared that overpopulation and starvation would be inevitable, that people would lack
the incentive to work, and that liberty would exist in name only.
For those who upheld private enterprise, he presented his most
sustained, scientific, and damning indictment of capitalism from
the standpoint of its economic, political, ideological, scientific, and
moral effects. It was also in this novel that Bellamy presented the
new code of sexual ethics, the picture of agricultural life of the
nation, the new fashion and the freedom from fashion in clothing,
the new role of women, the types of homes and their furnishings,
and the sources and kinds of food that the people of the new order
consumed.

Though all of the characters of *Looking Backward* are generous,
charming, frank, and intelligent, they are little more than that. It
was not, however, necessary that they should be otherwise, for they
were merely used to form a situation which centered about the education of Julian West in the ways of the new world. Except that
Julian is a young man of the upper class of Boston society and
one who had been irritated by, and far from sympathetic with, the
labor problems of his day, very little is known about him. The
facts given are pertinent, however, for they make him the type of
citizen that it would be most difficult to convert to the ideas of the
new state—and the very type of citizen which Bellamy wished to
convert!

West's mental and spiritual reactions to his strange environment
are excellently delineated: at first he is overwhelmed by what has
happened to him, then he becomes interested in what he discovers
in the new society, and finally he is converted. After hearing the

Reverend Barton's sermon, Julian is filled with penitence because of his former indifference to social problems; and he feels that, since he had contributed nothing to the attainment of the new state, he has no right to enjoy its felicities. After his return in a nightmare to the world of the nineteenth century, his conversion is complete, for not only does he recoil from all he finds in Boston but he attempts to convert his old friends to the ideas of the year 2000. Not only does this section of the story show that Julian's education has been successful but it presents one of Bellamy's most forceful indictments of his own era. Presented in newspaper headlines in a fashion which reminds one of John Dos Passos' *U.S.A.*, a preliminary picture of nineteenth century society is given which reinforces the criticisms made of it throughout the book and which paves the way also for the attitude Julian is to have toward the maleficent things he sees as he walks through Boston.

Many of the characters of *Looking Backward*—Julian West, Edith Leete, the Reverend Barton, and Dr. Leete—appear in *Equality*, but there is no development of their characters though there are some changes in their usage. Edith becomes one of Julian's educators in *Equality* in that she supplants her father from time to time in the discussions; she is, however, far from being a domineering female, for she refers Julian to her father and does not pretend to be all knowing. She it is who also demonstrates to Julian not only the character of the emancipated woman but the modesty with which women wear their new clothing and the enjoyment they find in their roles as agricultural or industrial workers. The Reverend Barton, who in *Looking Backward* is only the man who delivers a powerful sermon, makes a personal appearance in *Equality* to discuss with Julian the role of the church in the revolutionary period, the new religion, and the absence of an organized church in the ideal society.

Though it is not unusual for the characters of Utopian or ideological novels to be little more than name-tags to the ideas they express, this type of character is of interest in the study of Bellamy because it fits the pattern of his characters of his other short stories and novels. From his first short story to his last novel, Bellamy showed his preoccupation with the exposition of an idea or with the presentation of the reactions of certain types of people under the pressure of certain situations—and this situation, refreshingly enough, usually did not evolve from the mere fact that boy had met girl. The stories in which Bellamy employed love as a significant part of the plot are concerned primarily with some situation that is its outgrowth as in *Dr. Heidenhoff's Process, Miss Ludington's Sister,* "That Letter," "Pott's Painless Cure," or "Lost." When one reviews, therefore, the stories and the novels of Bellamy, one sees that the total preoccupation with ideas in his last two novels was the proper end of the literary career of a man who had all his life enjoyed the savoring of ideas and the investigation of the reactions of men placed in certain situations and who had unceasingly desired to discover what man's relationship to the finite and to the infinite was or should be.

Although the lack of emotional appeal of *Equality* without doubt contributed to its relatively poor reception, there were also other factors which must have affected its sale. The audience which had read *Looking Backward* doubtless felt—as had George Bernard Shaw—that Bellamy had said all that he had to say in it. Others who had read and discussed it in the late 1880's and in the early 1890's found themselves in a more prosperous economic situation in 1897 and were, therefore, less interested in reforming the social order. The war of 1898, which was in the making at the time of the novel's publication, also diverted the attention of the people from internal to external affairs and policies. Furthermore, many people had probably been disillusioned by the seeming failure of the Populist cause, and, having expended their energies in one reaction, they were disinterested in further reform efforts.

5. Bellamy's Last Days

Bellamy had himself been disheartened by the fate of the Populist Party, but he did not cease to hope that a successful political party would some day evolve which would support his social principles. In 1896 he wrote to his friend Henry D. Lloyd: "The questions you raise in your letters are of course what we are all thinking of. While we are left practically without a party, it is a good riddance, seeing that the organization has fallen in bad hands.

. . . Meanwhile, the past campaign has, unless I greatly err, done much to break up the political soil, cause discontent and prepare the people for the radical doctrine. As to what the radical reformers should now do, I agree with you, first, that there is no need of haste so far as any public action is concerned. We shall know far better where we are a few months later. Would it not be a good idea to put this conference off which you speak of till next summer (unless events otherwise indicate) and spend the intervening time in securing the attendance or endorsement of a sufficient number of persons of large reputation, to command public attention and respect for its action? I believe there are enough persons of that sort to be obtained and they can be obtained by judicious action. A manifesto put forth by such a conference stating our full doctrine—keeping nothing back—and advancing a complete set of propositions as first steps, would I believe, strongly impress the country and furnish the basis for any political organization that might then or later be decided on. Everything, of course, would depend on the weight of the names behind such a manifesto. I have been running over a list in my mind, and you would think of many more. But the one thing needful is that this manifesto should explicitly declare for full nationalization of the productive and distributive machinery of our government. We do not want any more fooling; and the country is ready for plain talk."

Not only *Equality* was to continue to break the ground and pave the way for future political action, for the dying Bellamy was planning not only another book but a resurrection of *The New Nation*. Mason Green wrote that after *Equality* had been completed Bellamy had sketched a brochure on psychology, and he cited the "Religion of Solidarity" as an example of Bellamy's lasting interest in this subject. It is possible that Arthur Morgan is correct in supposing that Bellamy intended to sum up the ideas of this early essay in book form, but it is more probable that Bellamy was planning the book which in his journal he had described as being a medley "of personal reminiscences, and philosophical reflections." This description adequately describes the later version of the Eliot Carson story, and also the big book Bellamy planned to call *Man, Woman, and Child* which was to employ the Carson story. Whatever his plans, Bellamy thought that this book—if he could but live to complete it—would be the greatest work of his career.

Bellamy, who had thought of reviving *The New Nation,* became the president of the board of directors of a paper of the same title which was published in Denver, Colorado, by Myron Reed. The first issue of the paper, which appeared June 2, 1898, was devoted to a discussion of social democracy and equality of opportunity—and it contained the obituary of Edward Bellamy.

The reasons for the early demise of Bellamy, who was only in his late forties at the time of his death, were many. Although he had resolved as a youth to develop his body and although as an adult he had emphasized the necessity of physical well being in his editorials, journals, conversations, and Utopian novels, he was as indifferent to his own health as he was to his clothing—and this in spite of the fact that he had ample reason to realize the importance of vigilance. His mother had married Rufus King Bellamy when she thought her life expectancy to be limited to a year, for she was ill with the tuberculosis which was to cause the death of her son Packer in 1868—and that of Edward in 1898. Edward, who had always been frail, had suffered his first serious pulmonary illness after having slept in damp blankets in a wet tent during a camping trip in the Maine woods in 1874. The cold that he had contracted and the severe illness that followed damaged his lungs, and for a time he thought that he had "got his death."

Though Bellamy seemingly recovered from this bout, he was never strong; and he suffered continuously from ulcerated teeth; from chronic dyspepsia; and, before the trip to the Sandwich Islands, from fainting attacks. Because of his dyspepsia, Bellamy never ate correctly, and he was advised to use whiskey for both his stomach and his pulmonary difficulties. When the family gathered at meal time, Bellamy served the food and then requested the maid to bring him two eggs and a glass of milk; that would be his meal. When dinner guests were present and the conversation was stimulating, Bellamy would excitedly pace back and forth in the dining room while talking to his guests—who wondered whether or not they were to continue eating.

Although whiskey had been prescribed for his ailments, Bellamy had enjoyed his potations before his illness for in his journal of 1873 he had made the following notation: "Giving up liquor as I did in February was a mighty good thing for my disposition." Although he had enjoyed his self-indulgence, he also received a certain satisfaction from self-denial, for he wrote: "He enjoyed the exercise of a capricious self-control and pleasure of tyranny over his own mind. He would often for pure wantonness of power refuse to entertain a pleasing thought or turn aside from an indulgence; when the struggle was hard, the more he enjoyed it. He enjoyed nothing so much as to drink steadily for a month and then stop suddenly and see his appetite squirm."

In his journal of 1873 he also recorded the joyous flights of the intoxicated mind, as well as the pathos of inebriation: "The glamour with which drunkenness overspreads the world is a magic like moonlight. The beauty and charm of all things are enhanced even as they are to one who is filled with a great joy. The drunkard is at loss to account for the change which has clothed a prospect before dull, prosaic, barren, with the golden haze of Indian Summer and imparted a poetic suggestiveness, a richness and satisfying quality to things he before thinks mean, and wearisome, stale, and unprofitable. In his mind he knows that he is subject to an illusion, that he is admiring a mirage that will vanish away so soon as the fumes of intoxication dissipate. There is on this account something pathetic in the very experience of exhilaration to the intellectual temperament. It is only the other sort who do not analyze nor think beyond their present experience to whom intoxication is unmixed pleasure."

To Bellamy, an introspective man absorbed by his own mental and physical reactions, such self-examination and analysis were a means to self-knowledge and to an understanding of others. To himself, Bellamy was a microcosm of the world, and he felt that if he understood the microcosm he would comprehend the universe. For this reason, he found a "ghastly interest" in the "spectacle of his own mental and moral decay." In disintegration he saw the "unravelling of creation"—the other side of human nature that was co-existent with the upper side.

Because of his introspective and sensitive nature, Bellamy's frail physique and his addiction to the bottle contributed to his literary work and to the development of his religion of solidarity. His delicate health contributed to the evolution of his religion because it further sensitized him to the "perception of harmony and beauty." In his "Hawaiian Notebook," Bellamy wrote what his character Edgerton of *Six to One* also discovered to be true: "It is noticeable that a slight sickness, not acute, but leaving one languid, brings the soul wonderfully into the impersonal mood and makes it long for absorption into the grand omnipotency of the universe by death, as it does not in time of vigor." He also discovered as a result of his illness in 1874 that his conception of man's relationship to the universe had prepared him to meet death with equanimity—almost with indifference; and this experience reaffirmed his beliefs.

Bellamy's editorials, book reviews, short stories, and novels also reflect the influence of his poor health. In *Six to One* Edgerton, the newspaper editor who is ill, is without doubt a portrait of Bellamy about the time he was forced to leave the *Union* because he was on the verge of a nervous breakdown. In "Two Days' Solitary Imprisonment" the central character is a sensitive, imaginative man who is suffering from influenza. In his editorials and book reviews, Bellamy repeatedly expressed his concern about problems of health as they were affected by diet, housing, and sanitation. In his Utopian novels, he attempted to improve the health of the nation by rectifying the conditions he had inveighed against in these articles, for—despite, or perhaps because of, his own disregard for his health—he realized that health was as important as a sound philosophy in preparing people to face and meet the problems of life.

The influence of Bellamy's drinking is also to be found in his short stories and novels, as well as in his journal entries. In a memorandum in one of his journals, Bellamy developed a plan for a novel which was to depict the humor of the temperance movement, the impertinence of reformers in general, the position of women in the movement, and the fallacy of thinking that any man who enjoyed taking a drink was doomed to become a dipsomaniac. He intended for this book to be also a "philosophical exposition of delights of drunkenness." Although Bellamy never portrayed any of these delights in his short stories, he did portray the far more socially acceptable picture of the undesirable personal and social effects of drinking in "That Letter" and in "Taking a Mean Advantage." The influence of his own personal habits contributed also to his permitting liquor to exist in the ideal state and to his expressing his antagonism toward sumptuary laws in his Utopian novels.

In 1890 Bellamy, who had suffered more severe stomach distress than was usual, was assured by an examining physician in New York that there was nothing organically wrong with him and that all he needed was rest and a proper diet. After having observed his diet and regular habits and after having rested for a time at the Packer farm near Westerly, Bellamy felt reassured about his condition. In September, however, his daughter Marion contracted the whooping cough, and Bellamy caught the disease from her. From that time on he never ceased to cough—the old lesion caused by the illness of 1874 had been reopened. That he was well aware of the fact that he had tuberculosis may be deduced from the page in one of his journals upon which he recorded his timing of his coughing attacks and the quality of his expectorations.

In 1897 after he had read the proofs of *Equality,* the ailing and exhausted Bellamy went to his brother's cottage at Blandford in the Berkshire Hills of western Massachusetts to recuperate. Since he had consistently refused to consult a doctor despite the fact that he was declining rapidly, Charles and Frederick brought a specialist to see him. Bellamy submitted to a physical examination, and, as a result of the consultation which followed, it was decided that he should go to the Rocky Mountain area for the climate there might have a salutory effect upon the tuberculosis.

In August, 1897, Bellamy and his immediate family went to Denver, Colorado, but the rigorous regimen of physical exercises which the doctors prescribed for him counteracted the benefits the high altitude might have offered him. During the days when he was confined to his bed, Bellamy did not relinquish his work nor refuse to talk with people who were interested in his ideas. One of his visitors at this time was young Benjamin Lindsey who was introduced by the proprietor of Bellamy's hotel. When Bellamy heard of Lindsey's interest in his ideas, his eyes brightened, and he told the boy that it was to the youth of the nation that he wished "to pass on the charge." Many years later after Lindsey had become famous as a judge and as a reformer of juvenile laws, he stated that Bellamy had been the "social and economic guide" of his life, and he described the Bellamy he had met in Denver as having been "worn and wasted" but as having had nonetheless a "particular dash."

In April, 1898, Charles and Frederick made the long trip to Denver from the East to bring Edward back to his home in Chicopee Falls. Happy to be back in the home which he had always so greatly loved, Edward busied himself with the selection of his stories for the collective, posthumous edition *The Blindman's World*. He also intended to revise and publish some of his hitherto unpublished stories, but the sands of his life had run out before this task was accomplished.

During the last days of his life, Bellamy permitted no one to care for his wasted body but his devoted wife who spent hours with him in his tightly closed room—for Bellamy feared that his children would hear the wracking coughs and the groans which he sometimes emitted. One evening while Mrs. Bellamy was sitting beside her husband's bed, she remarked, "We'll soon have been married sixteen years."

She was comforted and made happy when Bellamy replied, "Yes, sixteen years—and I love you more now than ever before."

A few hours before he died on May 22, 1898, Bellamy softly said to his wife, "After all, dying is only moving into the next room."

The emaciated body of the sensitive, reticent, proud, sincere Edward Bellamy was cremated by his request, and the ashes were interred in the family burial plot on the rolling hills of the cemetery of Chicopee. The spirit of Bellamy lived on, however, in the impersonal form of the ideas he had promulgated and in the pictures he had drawn for the contemplation of the world of an ideal government which would create a social order in which men could develop themselves and discover, perhaps, the Great Mystery.

CHAPTER V

BASIC AIMS AND PRINCIPLES

1. Pragmatic, Evolutionary Reform Principles

American citizens of the last quarter of the nineteenth century could regard with pride their country's material progress; but the reform and labor movements, the bloody strikes, and the critical literature of this period testified to dissatisfaction, confusion, and fear that their country might have been making rapid strides on the wrong road. The people were bewildered—just as they were to be in the 1920's, the 1930's and the 1950's—because too many problems seemed insoluble, too many promises were not only unfulfilled but belied, and too many of the essentials of democratic living appeared to have been irretrievably lost in a chaotic world in which the only certainties appeared to be uncertainty and insecurity.

This chaotic situation—which had been created by too-rapid expansion, speculation, mass production, and cut-throat competition —appeared to many to be remediable, and their suggested solutions were numerous and varied. To Horace Bushnell and his disciple, the Rev. Washington Gladden, the salvation of society depended upon the institution of brotherly love as a guiding force in the affairs of men. To Laurence Gronlund, the answer lay in the replacement of private enterprise with collective ownership of production and distribution and in the restoration of solidarity.

To W. G. Sumner, the evolution of society was to take care of itself, for all men had to do was to apply the policy of *laisser-faire,* and all, as Spencer had suggested, would be well. Lester Ward, however, believed that men could and should control the process of evolution and establish a rational social order which would destroy the out-moded practice of free competition. Richard Ely and his disciples recognized that economics had to become ethical and that political economists not only had to be students of actual conditions but had to be humanitarian and pragmatic in their recommendations. To sundry others, such as the prohibitionists or the advocates of civil service, partial reform measures seemed the solution to all the ills of the era.

Bellamy disagreed with Sumner and with reformers who sought to rectify the situation with partial reform measures, for he was more closely allied in his thinking with Bushnell, Gladden, and Ward. To Bellamy—who saw more clearly and more penetratingly than most of his contemporaries the true source of the confusion and the subsequent difficulties—it appeared that men, in creating machinery, mass production, and private enterprise, had unleashed indifferent, amoral Frankensteins which were destroying their liberty, security, independence, dignity, morality, equality, and solidarity as well as their opportunity for the development of their best qualities.

The answer to this situation, Bellamy realized, could not be a return to the days of truly free competition and of individual production, for that would "involve a turning backward of the entire system of modern material progress." To him, this material progress, as well as the economic problems attending it, was the result of the capitalistic, industrial system which had, through a process of evolution, tended to consolidate and hence to destroy competition.

The scientific answer, therefore, had to be one which would promote the evolution of the system in a fashion which would insure that the results of the progress achieved would be beneficent rather than maleficent for the majority of the citizens. The solution also had to leave no "unaccounted for residuum," for, if it did, it would be "no solution at all." Politically, the remedy had to be one which would not only retain the principles of the Declaration of Independence but give them a new significance. To insure the welfare of society, the solution had to contain also the democratic principle of the right of the people to revolt against an inadequate government, and it would have to institute the Jeffersonian principle which stressed the importance of religion, morality, and education to the attainment of good government and the happiness of man. In order to achieve co-operation and solidarity and to attain the spiritual and social qualities necessary for the attainment of social harmony and unity, the solution had to provide the means for developing enthusiasm for humanity and a spirit of self-sacrifice in man.

When he sought his scientific solution to the problems of his era, Bellamy's working method was that of the pragmatist, for he believed what the "Declaration of Principles" of the Nationalists was to state: "No truth can avail unless practically applied." Because of the knowledge his studies and his years as a journalist had given him of the economic, social, and political affairs of the nation, Bellamy saw that the actualities of American life contrasted greatly with the basic democratic aims and principles upon which the American government and social order had been founded. Seeing the wide gap that existed, he set himself the task of finding new and practical instruments which would preserve and develop democratic principles, solve the industrial problems, and function in a fashion that would make men superior to the material things which loomed more important than men and held them in thraldom.

When Bellamy considered the hitherto sacrosanct political institutions erected by his forefathers as a practical and workable means of achieving the ideals of the Declaration of Independence, he, as a pragmatic evolutionist, saw that the government must not be considered as a static but as a living and necessarily changing organism which could be modified to fit the society it was to serve, the tasks it had to perform, and the pressures it had to sustain. Democracy had made possible the collective force of the people to insure the protection and welfare of the people—but it had also made it possible for the rich and the privileged classes to wield power, to distort the application of the principles, and to halt the evolutionary process.

Because of this inherent weakness, the government, which had worked so well for a predominantly agrarian community, had been distorted by the corrupt, rapacious plutocracy produced by the industrial revolution. In their search for material gain, the plutocrats had used the government, robbed it, and caused it to fail as the preserver and the guardian of the rights, liberties, and properties of the citizenry. Other factors which had, however, contributed to their success had been the indifference of an increasingly large propertyless population toward government affairs and the prevalent immoralities and false standards of value of the general public. In order to re-establish the lost democratic principles and to protect them from ever again being so set aside, not only did the power of wealth have to be harnessed or destroyed but the people had to be aroused to a "vivid interest" in the administration of the government by giving it "interests that vitally" concerned "the everyday life of the people." The solution, therefore, had to be one which would combine the citizen's "practical interests with his politics" so that he would give the same attention to the latter that he had "always bestowed upon the former."

To preserve democracy, therefore, the new government which would evolve from the old one had to be a positive institution which would stimulate men rather than a negative one which would suppress them. This government also had to be so constructed that it could be used to prevent moral and political corruption and to restore the lost liberties and equalities—social, political, and economic—by reinforcing them with extended rights and privileges which would make the government not only one of and for an alerted people but one upon which they would have to rely for all subsistence.

When he searched for a type of government which would fulfill these prerequisites, Bellamy found the germs of the ideas for its principles and its form in the situations and principles already existing and "in partial operation in contemporary industry, politics, and society"; and his avowed aim was to promote a beneficial evolution of these in order to achieve the new order. He insisted, therefore, that though others might call themselves revolutionists, he was an evolutionist who was seeking merely to instigate a counter-revolution against the subversive group which had corrupted the government for individual, monetary gains.

Among these already existing tendencies of his time, Bellamy noticed that of the government to assume responsibility for the material and social welfare of the citizens; and it seemed to him that this was a development which had logically evolved from the democratic idea. From the period when the "democratic idea gained ascendancy," it had been but a question of time before the "obvious interests of the majority of the people" would "lead to the democratization of the national economic system to accord with the political system." Bellamy believed that, had it not been for the abolition movement and the Civil War, an industrial democracy would have been achieved as a result of the significant and picturesque socialistic movements of the 1840's which had contained the spirit of such a movement if not its form.

After the Civil War, the consolidating organizations of laborers and capitalists had indicated the feasibility of organizing production and distribution on a scale not before deemed possible. As Bellamy surveyed the centralization of the industrial world of his era, he saw a "stream of tendencies through ever larger experiments in concentration and combination toward the ultimate complete integration of the nation for economic as well as for political purposes." Since the economic reasons for this consolidation had been proved valid and workable by industry, Bellamy accepted this tendency as the "basic principle of association."

Because of the advocacy by reform groups both before and after the Civil War of measures tending toward democratization of industry and because of the evolution of the principles of economic democracy from those upon which political democracy had been founded, industrial democracy would be portrayed as having had long roots in the history of American thought and as having stemmed from the form of the government—as well as from the inadequacies of that form—upon which the nation had been founded. Because of the tendency of the industrial world toward combination, it could also be argued, wrote Bellamy, that the basic principles of this new government—those of association and co-operation—had already been proved to be economically and industrially feasible.

In the society that would evolve as the result of instituting industrial democracy, the Bill of Rights and the Declaration of Independence would have a new meaning in the life of every citizen, for each would be truly free and equal for the first time in the history of the world. The educational and cultural advantages, the economic security, and the re-established liberties, opportunities, and moralities of this new society would provide an interested, enlightened, and aspiring citizenry which would be desirous and capable of preserving democracy, of furthering its evolutionary development, and of preventing its being jeopardized by demagogues. Because of the culture, the morality, and the leisure of this new society, men would be enabled to live in harmony and to develop their minds and souls.

2. Basic Attitudes Toward Life

Like St. Simon and Auguste Comte, Bellamy dreamed that what was essentially an economic reconstruction of the government would result, therefore, in the development of a nobler, happier, healthier citizenry. This hopeful desire to achieve a morally, intellectually, and physically sane society was prompted by Bellamy's philosophy of life and religion and by his attitudes toward leisure, perfectibility, individuality, and social equality and freedom—and, because of these, by his reactions to the problems and conditions of his own era.

Henry James and William Dean Howells had presented the American male as being primarily concerned with business affairs and as condescendingly leaving cultural and intellectual pursuits to the females who had the leisure for such luxuries. Unlike most of these males, Bellamy rebelled at this enslavement of men to the monotonous treadmill of the commercial world because of its destruction of morality and its stultifying effects upon the intellect. To Bellamy, the options offered by the society of his day to the citizens were to starve the mind and secure luxury for the body or to starve the body and obtain leisure for the culture which was the luxury of the mind and soul. Though Bellamy realized poignantly the necessity of scrambling madly to obtain the material things essential to the maintenance of life itself, he felt that man's involvement in the struggle permitted him to have little time for the "real life" or to obtain more than a little of human happiness. If material comfort were secured, it would, in the end, be unsatisfactory, for the acquirement of intellectual wealth was the sole abiding satisfaction and the only one which could make men feel that they had a "grasp of the universe." Consequently, the problem was to find deliverance for man from his thraldom to materialism by a reform which would procure for him the economic security, the leisure, and the educational opportunities which would enable him to "seek to be more" through the pursuit of wisdom and knowledge.

Bellamy's criticism of the life of his era and his consequent aim in reforming it were determined by his belief that the primary purposes of living were the quest of the soul and the development of the intellect. He believed that if material progress did not bring inward peace and enlargement of the mind of man and that if it did not tend to develop in him a more constant sense of sympathy with others, the steamships and the telegraph would be the mere playthings of a soulless humanity. Despite his emphasis on the need to develop the soul, Bellamy thought, however, that the world, because of the influence of the theologians, had been too long concerned with the problem of "happy dying." He welcomed, therefore, the effect of positivism which had directed attention to the "more practical problems of happy living."

Although Bellamy realized that the search for happiness was the motivator of all man's actions, he regarded only those actions which contributed to the happiness of others and which resulted from the play of the impersonal in the actor as contributing to the happiness of the individual and to his attainment of virtue. The man, therefore, who would be able to achieve the development which would result in both individual and general happiness would be neither the worldling nor the ascetic but the individual capable of both renunciation and enjoyment—the man in whom individuality and impersonality would be given proper places in life.

In reality, man was—to Bellamy—a base composition of physical functions, brutal passions, and selfish ambitions; but he had also the ability to become transfigured because of his assimilation of the ideal, and in this lay his salvation. To Bellamy, civilization had been the clothing of the real with the ideal, a process which had depended upon the suppression of the individuality and the development of the impersonality. If this process continued, man would become more preoccupied with the spiritual and the infinite and less concerned with the transitory and the perishable. When the passions of individuality which had led to man's unhappiness were redirected so that they were employed for the general achievement and elevation of humanity, man would become both happy and virtuous—and the ideal man would be achieved.

The ideal man Bellamy envisioned would be neither the "Indian Buddhist in ecstatic contemplation seeking to merge himself in God in disregard of his actual status as individual" nor the "self-seeker in the insanity of individualism concentrating his being in microscopic activities (equally microscopic whether they concern fagots or empires, since they are pursued in the spirit of individualism)." He would be "he whose spirit dwells among the stars and in all time, but whose hands are as deft with the most menial as with the mightiest tasks through which this soul of solidarity can find expression; who turns his hands with equal readiness to the founding of empires and to the washing of beggars' feet, holding all tasks in equal honor, since with him the infinite motive overshadows the deed itself."

Because Bellamy's social order was to free men from their perpetual concern with the material ends of life, was to provide them the economic security and the leisure necessary for a contemplative, creative life, and was to promote their desire to produce works for the use or the enjoyment of others, he believed that it would contribute to the perfection of man; for, as his early writings show, Bellamy had great faith in man's perfectibility. No idea was more common to all ages of men, stated Bellamy in a speech in the early 1870's, than the belief that the world had before it an era of perfection; all that was necessary to achieve this Golden Age was the eradication of the physical, social, and political obstacles which had hindered the development of the good in man. If men believed that the tendency of evolution was toward the higher and the better, they had to sponsor whatever tended toward the "fullest expression of humanity" and the freest unfolding of it. The achievement of perfection was also to be dependent, however, upon man's love of God and of his fellowmen and upon his obedience to the moral law.

Bellamy's faith in the possibility of man's achieving perfection was enhanced by his belief that human attributes had not been the same in all ages; by his faith in human common sense and good feelings; and by his recognition of man's ability, through the exercise of his intelligence and his will, to guide evolution and to become, if not a creator, a modifier of creation. In one of his journals, Bellamy had written: "When shall men draw the line between the creative power and modifying power which men certainly possess in full measure? For instance, God creates a child. My influence profoundly affects its character and fate. If I do not create, my function is at least equal in importance to creation." This belief in man's ability to modify and to guide the course of evolution was confirmed for Bellamy by Spencer in *The Principles of Sociology;* for, wrote Bellamy in a book review of 1877, Spencer had forecast a "completer perfection" for man and had shown his "gradual development by the influence of his environment upon his faculties, the co-working of the external with the internal forces."

Bellamy also believed that a pessimistic view of man's future was unwarranted since he had made throughout the centuries much moral progress. Those who were pessimistic about the future of man were, said Bellamy, those who had regarded only the bright side of the past. Bellamy also rejected this "Cassandra vein of melancholy" because he felt that to accept it would be not only to give credence to the idea of man's innate depravity and to condemn human nature but to endorse Hobbes' theory that a state of war was the natural and necessary condition of mankind.

Bellamy asserted in *Looking Backward* that human nature would not have to be changed before it could attain perfection; and he argued that when the conditions of human life, and, consequently, the motivating forces of human action had been changed, then, and only then, would the innate good in man be given an opportunity to develop. When the conditions of society—or the state of war— which had not only made men act basely but had led them to think that human nature was essentially base had been rectified, men would see that they were like the sickly rosebush which, transplanted from the swamp to the warm dry earth, grew and thrived. In his articles in *The New Nation,* Bellamy further emphasized the relationship of environment and the character of man by indicating that, if it was scientifically foolish to expect a healthy man to retain his health while living in a contagious, infected physical environment, it was just as ridiculous to expect moral perfection without providing ethically salutary surroundings. The moral reconstruction of man depended, therefore, upon external conditions which would cooperate with the forces to be developed within and which would not exercise a vicious influence destructive of piety and morality. In this new environment men would be freed from their forced mental and physical absorption in scheming and working for mere survival; and they could, therefore, enter upon a new phase of spiritual development. Subsequent growth would be made possible by the great objective of the new social order—the promotion of man's spiritual, intellectual, and physical development.

That men already possessed the good qualities necessary for this development and this new society Bellamy did not doubt, for it seemed to him that they evinced within their own homes and circles of friends unselfishness, generosity, and brotherly kindness. In the business world, however, because of the rapacity and the apprehensions it fostered, these qualities were suppressed and were replaced by fear, coldness, suspicion, and selfishness. The immoral and brutal conditions of the industrial order produced immoral and brutal types who were regarded often as the fittest because they survived by adapting themselves to the conditions of the struggle. If such conditions continued to exist and if such types were considered to be the best, social damnation and not social perfection would inevitably result. The solution was, therefore, to replace the general environment of the commercial world with one that would minimize the inherent suspicion of man and his fear that he was being used for the profit of someone else.

The inauguration of the new order which would develop the innate good in men would not have to depend upon man's achievement of perfection; it could be introduced, asserted Bellamy, as soon as men showed a desire and a capacity for the new conditions. Though Bellamy expected this improved environment to contribute to the perfection of mankind, he evidently did not expect it alone to be sufficient, for he provided, as supplementary aids, a religious revival, a moral code, an educational program, a system of euthenics, and a policy that emphasized and instilled faith in man's ability to grow. In *Equality*, Bellamy stressed that the whole of the new social order would contribute to the desired development because it would knit together human interests and arouse in mankind the recognition of "the fact that the welfare of each individual of the race can only be advanced by promotion of the welfare of all. . . . And, without the sense of the identity of social interests, of the solidarity of mankind, which nationalism inevitably must develop, anything like a universal spiritual growth would be impossible."

Although Bellamy wished to achieve social solidarity and harmony, he did not want to attain it by developing an unsavory, unindividualistic but perfected mankind; he desired also the development of individuality, and he argued that this would be assured by the leisure, the intellectual opportunities, and the personal liberty which would be provided by the new state. His concern about the problem of the use of leisure and the development of individuality had been—as his *Union* articles and his journal entries show—an old one. After the publication of *Looking Backward,* he was to be forced, however, to review his ideas because of the charge of his critics that the life of the year 2000 would result in suppression, not development, of individualism.

In an early journal entry concerning leisure, Bellamy had noted that it would be useless to employ any more labor-saving devices until men knew how to employ their leisure; and, in his *Union* editorials, he constantly urged the unemployed to use their time in exercising their mental faculties and in developing their latent souls by reading, attending church functions, and participating in discussion groups. In these articles Bellamy also criticized the "fret, worry, and hurry" of the American way of life; and he chided the Americans for taking their business home with them in the evenings and for being unable to enjoy their leisure as the French and Germans did.

Hoping that Americans would eventually develop a social life that would emphasize other than material ends, Bellamy welcomed the few signs apparent in his time that his fellow citizens regarded the possession of time and money as providing an opportunity for "cultivating the finer susceptibilities . . ., for opening up new avenues of feeling removed from every sordid strain."

Because of these attitudes of Bellamy, all citizens of the new era were to be better off than the characters of Bellamy's unpublished stories such as Mr. Stanley, who had worked until sixty-five in order to secure leisure for his studious pursuits, or Henry Buddington, who had taken a vacation after fifteen years of hard work only because he hoped that he would be enabled to work harder when it was over. In the ideal state, men would work merely to secure the leisure necessary for their intellectual and spiritual enjoyments and pursuits which alone meant life—and the social order would provide public amusements, public discussions, adult education, and an amplified social life to make such a development possible. Citizens without artistic or scholarly interests could enjoy travel, social relaxation with friends, and the development of their personal idiosyncrasies and tastes.

In order to insure all men the opportunity of pursuing their individual interests, there was to be no regulation of the usage of leisure in the ideal state. To so regiment the lives of men would be to ignore, thought Bellamy, the right of personal freedom of the individual in self-regarding matters; to deny the needs of the greatly differing tastes and temperaments; and to institute a soul-killing uniformity. To regulate men's diversions or interests by artificial devices—laws, custom, or fashion—and not to depend upon the law of the spiritual life for their regulation would be, thought Bellamy, destructive of rational and truthful self-discipline. If the development of reasonable and conscientious self-control were shirked, character would be vitiated and trustworthy moral discrimination would be undeveloped in the individual. So long, therefore, as man's habits and interests did not interfere with his ability to work or lead to the abuse of others, he was to be free to do as he pleased.

The lives of all men would be regimented, however, by the stipulation that they would have to work; this regulation was necessary, explained Bellamy, for the creation of an organized society which would provide men with the freedom, the security, and the leisure necessary for their individual development. Bellamy organized the method of the selection of the work to be done by the individual, however, so that it too would contribute to the development and the utilization of man's innate abilities. In this way, the felicity of man, which depended upon his personal freedom to pursue his own ideal in life and to develop his inherent capacities, was doubly insured.

When Bellamy's critics—General Walker, W. T. Harris, and A. D. Vinton—argued, however, that his envisioned social order would suppress the development of the individuality, Bellamy replied that their charge was applicable only to the effects of the old social order. That Bellamy should make such a reply was inevitable, for long before the publication of *Looking Backward* he had expressed in his *Union* editorials his scorn of the rule of fashion which made people act like sheep, and he had warned of the dangers of pressures which enforced conformity in taste, conduct, and opinions.

In the specific replies to these critics which Bellamy presented in his articles and in *Equality*, Bellamy charged that the lack of individuality of the nineteenth century had been due to the fact that only a few of the people had had enough education to be able to recognize their aptitudes or, if they did know them, enough money to develop them and open the way for a career. People who had had character and ideas had had to be subservient to their employers, for their livelihood had depended upon their not insulting their superiors' sense of what was right or true. Men—even the teachers and the preachers who could have been expected to be individualists —had been made cowards and hypocrites in a society based upon economic inequality; and, as a result, individuality had been crushed because of men's subjection to circumstances and to others. The only individuality expressed had been that of the rapacious, greedy vultures who had preyed upon their fellows.

Bellamy asserted that his social state would develop not only "robust and unfettered" individualities but ideal ones. The specific innovations of the new order which would contribute to this growth were: (1) economic equality, which would permit all to rise to their own highest possible level by equalizing education and opportunity and by freeing men from dependence upon, and, therefore, subjection to, others; (2) the idea of the necessity of the development of the innate abilities of all for the good of the state; and (3) the honors and the awards which would stimulate the individual's interest not only in his progress but in his service to others. Generally, the whole social environment would help men not only to be themselves but to become their best selves, for the ideal individuality would not be that of the vulture who preyed upon others but that of the eagle who soared to the heights and lifted mankind upward because of his devotion and service.

Economic equality, which was to be so important to the development of the individuality, was also to close the ranks of a society which had hitherto been divided into the classes of the educated and the uneducated because the inequality of wealth had resulted in unequal opportunities. Such class divisions had been destructive of social solidarity and had prevented the realization of the democratic ideals of social equality, of equality of opportunity, and of the right of personal liberty. In *Looking Backward* Bellamy portrayed a harmonious society in which all were equally rich and in which, consequently, all had the personal liberty and the social freedom to develop their unequal abilities, to rise on the basis of merit, and to develop their individualities. This society, instead of mocking the ancient dream of men of attaining a social order based upon liberty, equality, and fraternity, realized their dream—and the result of its being instituted was the disappearance of glaring disparities in dress, physical conditions, education, and social position.

As a result of these changes wrought by the introduction of economic equality, life was more pleasant for all men because their neighbors were companionable and educated and because, since the burden of work was shared by all, no task was deemed dishonorable. No man felt he was superior to another because of his wealth and no one felt himself obliged, because he was dependent upon another, to abase himself and deny that which he believed. No longer apprehensive of the power of another over him and no longer capable of gaining anything from deception, men condemned lying, ostentation, hypocrisy, and subservience to the dictates of fashion. These factors not only contributed to the felicity of the individual but to the achievement of solidarity and morality in the new state, and these made it possible for the brotherhood of man to become the principle of action.

When—in his notes, his speeches, and his articles in *The New Nation*—Bellamy considered the problem of the divisions of society caused by racial and religious differences and prejudices which were threats to the acceptance of the principle of the brotherhood of man and hence to the achievement of social harmony, he expressed his belief that these antagonisms would be overcome by men's recognition of their mutual dependence. Because the economic security of all depended upon the joint efforts of all, the citizens of the new order would become aware of the fact that their distinctions and disagreements were of little importance in comparison to that of their unity of economic interests. Furthermore, when they had been made to realize fully, because of their religion and their education, that they were brothers in their claims and dependence upon each other, they would no longer tolerate class divisions based upon complexions or religious affiliations.

In pointing out the social, political, and personal dangers of such prejudices and class distinctions, Bellamy warned that they divided the community into embittered elements which could only be held together by the iron rule of despotism. If the rich continued to amass power and wealth and to monopolize art, education, and opportunity, the end result would be a mercantile aristocracy and firm class distinctions which would imprison both the rich and the poor. Such stratifications would cut men off from the body of humanity and destroy the sympathy and understanding which not only should exist among men but should unite them in human and not in class sympathy. Bellamy denounced, therefore, the European socialists who considered only the welfare of the proletariat and inculcated hatred for other classes; and he asserted that Nationalism sought to save not only the wage-worker but also the rich man; for all, as brothers and sisters of the human family, were to share equally all the benefits and duties of the new order.

The importance of this classless society to the new order was stressed by Bellamy in the unpublished preface to *Equality* in which he showed that social distinctions had hitherto been the real basis of all social organizations and that they had from the beginning been the primary determinants of every person's life, for his position in society and his wealth had quite frequently been of more importance than his mental, physical, or spiritual endowments in the determination of his earthly destiny. The most significant movement of his day, averred Bellamy, was the world-wide agitation for more egalitarian social arrangements; and he regarded this movement as having resulted from the modern diffusion of knowledge which produced rational people capable of intelligent thinking and of concerted action. The end result of this movement, stated Bellamy, would be an improved morality since equality was the only basis of truly moral relationships.

3.   Aims and Form of the New Government

Like Locke, Jefferson, and the fathers of the American Constitution, Bellamy believed that it was the duty of the government to be concerned with the common good of its members and that the best government was not only that which made the most grass grow but that which furthered the happiness and the morality of its citizenry. Since the obligation of the government to the citizens was a fundamental part of Bellamy's plan, he outlined its duty and purpose in *Looking Backward* and further expanded his ideas as to its organic evolution in subsequent articles and in *Equality*. As has already been noted, Bellamy was concerned not with just the political and economic aspects of the new society but with its ethical and social effects, which he was to describe in great detail, as will be seen in chapters VII and VIII.

The aim of the new government was to be the establishment of a society in which educational, social, and economic equality would be achieved and in which there would not be the class or material conflicts which had resulted from private enterprise. Bellamy believed that Christianity, civilization, and government existed for the purpose of suppressing the inborn qualities of men which made them oppress their fellows, and he agreed with Thomas Huxley that the highest state of civilization to be attained was one in which the struggle to live would be least existent. To Bellamy, the organic evolution of the American government was to lead to a realization that a nation was a union of the people effected for the purpose of using its collective power not only for negative purposes such as war and police action but for positive ones such as the guaranteeing of the common welfare of all.

Bellamy criticized, therefore, the nineteenth century government because it had been primarily concerned with guarding its citizens from the onslaughts of external foes and from inimical or thieving citizens. This negative police action had necessitated innumerable laws, a large military and police force, and a complicated judicial machinery. The government had ignored for the most part, however, the brutal struggle for existence in which all of its citizens were involved; and it had only interposed to supply their needs when individual efforts had proved fruitless. To correct this conception of the role of the government, that of the year 2000 was to be assigned the duty of being primarily engaged with internal affairs and with providing the "highest degree of happiness and welfare" for its citizens. The duty of the state, said Bellamy, was to battle with the collective force of the nation against the internal foes of hunger, cold, thirst, and sickness; and, in this way, the government, by safeguarding the highest rights of every citizen—the rights of life and self-preservation—fulfilled the supreme duty of any state. In order to guarantee the economic basis of life and to give equal protection and opportunity to all its citizens, the government had to become a universal employment bureau and a great insurance company.

To fulfill these duties, Bellamy created a form of government which had as its prerequisites and its foundation the democratic government of the United States. From this democratic government was to evolve a state socialistic government which would replace capitalists and monopolies by becoming itself The Great Capitalist or The Great Monopoly—for all means of production and distribution would be owned and operated by the state. The industrial and the political state would be identical and would form a "systematized, centralized, interlocking organization of the highest efficiency."

The ultimate control of the political and industrial affairs of the nation would be " 'of the people, by the people, for the people' and for all of them equally"; for, explained Bellamy, the people had merely organized in order to control industry as they had once before in order to conduct their own government. They had finally come to realize that "no business is so essentially the public business as the industry and commerce on which the people's livelihood depends, and that to entrust it to private persons to be managed for private profit is a folly similar in kind, though vastly greater in magnitude, to that of surrendering the functions of political government to kings and nobles to be conducted for their personal glorification."

To Bellamy, this industrial government was the application of the democratic and individualistic principle of self-government, "self-help, self-control, and self-regulation" by the people of their common heritage for the joint interests of the community. This common heritage, or social fund, consisted of the land, the machinery, the natural resources, and the social organism which made production possible. To Bellamy, men had no title to the earth and its products or to the results of the power of the social organism except a common one; and he regarded all men, weak or strong, as equal heirs of the social heritage.

When the government had reclaimed this common heritage for the citizens, specific changes were necessarily inaugurated as to what the people might personally own and consider their private property. Each person, as a partner in the nationalized industries, had stock in them which became his at birth and ceased to be his only with his death. From this stock—which he never saw and could not dispose of—he drew an annual dividend which became his private property which he had an inalienable right to use in any way he pleased so long as it was not employed to earn a profit. Whatever he purchased in the way of household effects or personal possessions was inalienably his—but he could own no other private property, not even the house in which he lived.

All of the houses of the year 2000 were owned by the government which rented them to the citizens who selected their dwellings on the basis of their needs, the amount they wished to spend for rent, and the location they desired. Though they had not the right to sublet or to sell these houses, their title to them, said Bellamy, was as permanent as the one owners had had in the nineteenth century. To support this statement, Bellamy argued that in the past a home had not really belonged to the owner when it had been mortgaged and that, if it had been mortgage free, the owner had possessed it only so long as he had paid taxes upon it to the government. Under the new system, however, there was security of ownership, for under no circumstances could a man lose his home or his income from the state; and this was so because his property in the state was comparable to the private entailed estates of England.

No one in the year 2000 could inherit anything from his parents except their personal effects, and even these one was not permitted to sell. Since such inheritances might prove to be more of an inconvenience than a blessing because of lack of storage space or a difference in needs or tastes, it was possible for the inheritors to give them to the state which could then sell them to other citizens. This inability to inherit property of any kind other than personal possessions was necessary for the maintenance of economic equality, for Bellamy regarded inheritance as the cause of many social inequalities, as the sole source of the wealth of many non-productive individuals, and as the backbone of the property system.

Despite this lack of proprietorship and of inheritance, Bellamy maintained that ownership had not been destroyed by the new order but that it had been made a certainty and not the sham it had frequently been in the nineteenth century. Since all men had an equal share in the stock of the country and since each drew from it an equal dividend, the right of man to property was not only vindicated but more firmly established than ever before—and this was particularly true since the basis of his title in the year 2000 was his right to life, for the "modern ethics of wealth . . . deduce the rights of property from the rights of man." If man had a right to live, he had also an inalienable right to the natural resources and products of the nation for his sustenance. Furthermore, Bellamy pointed out, man had not only property but security for life; and this was psychologically, morally, and socially beneficial; for men were freed from worry about economic affairs, they no longer had to fight without scruples for their means of existence, and the divisive and anti-social influence of unequal wealth no longer existed.

Bellamy further defended his definition of private property in his speeches and articles that followed *Looking Backward* and particularly in *Equality* by declaring that instead of abolishing individual ownership the new government had really established it for the first time and that only private capitalism had been destroyed. His most effective argument was that men of the nineteenth century who had owned stock in big corporations had permitted their property to be managed for them and that from these investments they had drawn dividends. This was the system necessitated by state ownership of the productive and distributive facilities of the nation.

In these articles Bellamy also presented his arguments against man's legal right to property and to all that he produced with his own labor. He argued that the legal title to private property had not always entailed a moral right, for it had not always been earned but had frequently been inherited. When it had been earned by the holder, it had often been procured in an evil or an anti-social way. In considering the arguments of his critics that each man had a right to what he actually produced, Bellamy replied that in co-operative labor—whether privately or nationally controlled—it was impossible to determine how much of any man's production was due to his own efforts and ingenuity and how much of it was the result of the social organism or of the social fund. Though he admitted that men's abilities to produce varied, Bellamy asserted that this difference could never entail a moral right for the superior to use their abilities or power to enslave, make use of, or impoverish their inferiors. The only just and equitable method of distributing the produce of the nation was, therefore, to give each man an equal yearly income.

When Bellamy's critics asserted that giving each man an equal share of the wealth of the nation was to institute a paternalistic form of government, Bellamy replied that those who most loudly affixed this term to the duties of the new state were those who had frequently sought the greatest favors from the government—the capitalists. Furthermore, those who used this term did not understand that a government which consisted of the people and was not something apart from nor above them could hardly be a father—for it would be a father unto itself. Paternalism could exist only in a despotic state such as that of the Incas of Peru; and fraternalism, the basis of the new order, could be the outgrowth of only a democratic society. Fraternalism was the only system that would destroy the paternalistic tendencies of the Goulds and the Rockefellers who had been taking in hand the children's business—for plutocracy was "step-paternalism."

Since the duty of the new government was to serve the people by managing their business for them by co-ordinating all the productive and distributive facilities, it had to be strong enough to be effective but not so powerful that it could oppress those whom it represented. The problem which confronted Bellamy was to avoid anarchy and monarchy and to erect a democratic form of government which would be capable of directing the manifold affairs of an industrial democracy and one which would not be so loosely organized and so dilatory in its actions that it could not "preserve order and execute law in turbulent times, over wide regions of disturbance." In the formation of an effective type of government, Bellamy was aided by his early consideration of the merits and demerits of forms of government and of the tendencies of human nature.

Though Bellamy regarded all forms of government as artificial devices comparable to roofs constructed to shelter men from natural conditions and though he had early stated that there was no true form of government since the principles underlying monarchy, aristocracy, and democracy were "all first principles," he declared that he preferred the republican form of government because it permitted the people to overthrow it or to change it if it proved unsatisfactory. A republic, however, maintaining a system of private enterprise was, according to Bellamy, a threat to the continued welfare of the people, for it would eventually evolve into a plutocracy which might be worse in its effects than a monarchy. Under the monarchial system, "hereditary barriers of rank and pride of birth and station" served to mitigate the power of money which "in a republic finds nothing able to stand before it." There was, therefore, thought Bellamy, as much human dignity under one system as the other; for, though it was humiliating to sustain the arrogance and the assumptions of the lords of the realm, it was just as much so "to live by favor of millionaires and 'captains of industry' "—and perhaps it was more humiliating, for the plutocrats were not content with the toadying given the aristocrats; they wanted to pick one's "pocket to boot."

Bellamy did not overlook the fact, however, that both the aristocrats and the plutocrats based their power upon property and that both picked the pockets of their subjects whether under ancient or modern, agrarian or industrial feudalism. He asserted, however, that the plutocracy—since it was not recognized as the governing power and had no vested responsibility—did not have the regard for the welfare of the country that the monarch might have because of his desire to preserve it for his heirs. There was, decided Bellamy, little advantage in the long run in a "nominally democratic over a monarchial or aristocratic system" unless "the political republic be a stepping stone to the industrial republic, unless political equality be used as the means of securing economic equality."

Although Bellamy had remarked in a *Union* editorial that a government should be "entrusted with power enough to protect all its subjects, under all circumstances," he had recognized also that

. such a government might have a tendency to become oppressive. In
avoiding despotism, there was the danger of creating a government
which would not be strong enough to be just—and it seemed to
Bellamy that the tendency of all governments had been to be either
too weak or too powerful. He realized too that a weak government
could in turbulent times result in the establishment of a dictatorship.

In *The Duke of Stockbridge,* Bellamy had shown how, during the
chaotic period of the Shays' Rebellion, the plutocrats of Stockbridge—
who regarded their fellow townsmen as a "team of horses" they had
been driving and the rebellion as a runaway of the team which had
resulted in jolting the drivers from their seats—turned to Captain
Perez, the leader of the local mob, to protect their lives and property
and to establish the peace necessary to conduct their business. To
gain their ends, they cajoled and flattered Perez and commanded
their women to capture his fancy. As a result of the importance
Perez had in village affairs, he realized that "his fate was in his own
hands"; no one could foresee "the end of the epoch of revolution
and anarchy upon which the state" had entered. To Perez, "these
were times when the sword carved out fortunes and the successful
soldier might command the most brilliant rewards." In this picture,
Bellamy, who was a student of history and of the French Revolution
in particular, showed his awareness of the political, economical, and
psychological factors which could produce a totalitarian state.

As a result of his considerations of the dangers and the potentialities of the various forms of government, Bellamy wished his new
state to be characterized by neither imbecilic weakness, or anarchy,
nor by despotism, or monarchy; to his view, to have either of these
forms would be to regress, in the case of the monarchy, to the days
before the American Revolution, or, in the case of anarchy, to the
original state of nature. In one of his early lyceum talks, Bellamy
had declared that anarchy was the natural state which civilized society struggled to avoid since it meant death to society. Many years
later an echo of this statement appeared in his criticism of William
Morris' *News from Nowhere* when Bellamy wrote that the pleas of
the anarchists for a "system" with no government was a contradiction since no system could be achieved without it. Anarchy, said
Bellamy, differed from Nationalism in that the latter recognized that

no matter what degree of moral excellence communities achieved, they needed a "great deal of system . . . to co-ordinate their efforts so as to obtain the best economic results."

Bellamy wanted the government of the new order to provide, therefore, an organization which would institute a true democracy and be able to "protect its citizens, under all circumstances." Like Gronlund, he also wished his government to be primarily concerned with the governing of things and not of men; and he hoped that under its supervision the citizens would have more political and personal liberty than they had ever before enjoyed. It was also to be less complex than that of the nineteenth century since it would be established upon a foundation of principles so basic that they would simplify the task of governing and hence obviate the necessity of maintaining an army, a navy, a large police force, a large judicial staff, and revenue officials.

3. Democratic, Ethical, Economic Bases of the Government

In *Looking Backward,* Bellamy compared the government of the nineteenth century to a pyramid which, resting on its apex, was held in this unnatural position by props and guy-ropes in the form of thousands of complex laws. In the year 2000, the government had been rescued from this unnatural position and was resting upon its natural, democratic, ethical, and economic base. This transposition had been achieved by two innovations—economic equality and the industrial army. Economic equality, the cornerstone of the new state, was not only the foundation upon which all the freedoms and equalities of the democratic government rested, but it was also the means by which the government fulfilled its duty of providing the right to life and the security of the citizenry. The industrial army was organized to supply the means of providing this material equality and was to be the pledge of its achievement. Bellamy defended these two institutions by showing that they—as well as the resulting government—had democratic, ethical, and economic bases; and that economic equality in particular was the evolutionary result and the fulfillment of the republic born as a result, generally, of mankind's ageless fight for freedom and, specifically, of the Declaration of Independence.

Like Lord Acton and Vernon Parrington, Bellamy regarded all history as being the record of man's struggle for freedom. In each instance in which men had fought against king, priest, or master for political, religious, or personal liberty, Bellamy saw a step made toward the evolution of the true democracy of man. To him the logical result of the general diffusion of learning, of Luther's contest with the church and his triumph at the Diet of Worms, and of the English rebellions against priest, king, and nobility had been the Declaration of Independence and the American Revolution which had instituted the first phase of modern democracy.

Bellamy divided the history of this modern, American democracy into two periods: the negative phase, in which it was merely a political substitute for monarchy and was really a pseudo-republic doomed to degenerate into a plutocracy; and the positive phase, in which the republican form of government evolved into democratic state socialism. He also divided the history of the struggle for freedom in the United States into three periods: the American Revolution, which won political freedom from England and political equality for the people; the Civil War, which freed the chattel slave; and the Nationalistic or socialistic revolution, which emancipated all citizens from economic and industrial slavery, instituted economic equality as well as political democracy, and ended the rule of the rich in wealth in order to begin that of those rich in intellect and merit.

The negative phase of the development of democracy had been caused by the fact that the drafters of the Constitution had not carried their idea of the "inalienable equality" of men to its logical conclusion, economic equality. They had failed to do so because they had not foreseen the industrial revolution and its effect upon the distribution of wealth nor the effect this economic inequality would have in distorting the freedoms and rights of men. The result of this lack of clairvoyance had been that the government of the United States had established freedom from England but not the freedom of its citizens from each other; consequently, the rule of the king of England had merely been replaced by that of the rich whose power increased as the wealth of the nation became more concentrated in the hands of the few.

During the industrial revolution and the anarchical economic struggle that ensued, this spirit of mastership had become pronounced and the plutocrats had destroyed the republic by conducting their own revolution. As a result of the destructive forces of the "business-wrecking, law-defying, man-crushing party of the trusts and syndicates," this rich minority had obtained rule over the majority. Because of the power of wealth and because of its unequal distribution, political equality, equality before the law, equality of opportunity and education, personal liberty, and the dignity of man had been destroyed. Because of the control of the churches, the newspapers, and business by the capitalists, freedom of speech and freedom of enterprise had become nonexistent.

In order to restore the original purposes of the true constitution of the United States—the Declaration of Independence—Bellamy proposed to inaugurate the positive period of democracy as a result of a counter-revolution. The objectives of this revolution would be, negatively, to end forever the political, social, and industrial domination and usage of others for profit and, positively, to establish freedom of speech and worship, freedom from fear and want, and equality of ownership and opportunity. Because of these objectives, Bellamy maintained that Thomas Jefferson, if he had been living in the time of this counter-revolution, would have regarded this "movement toward industrial self-government as the people's only escape from plutocracy" and would have seen that it was a "strictly logical and necessary development of the principles laid down in the Declaration of Independence" which "logically contained the entire statement of the doctrine of universal economic equality guaranteed by the nation collectively to its members individually" in its preamble.

This counter-revolution was, therefore, a truly conservative American movement which would restore the original principles of democratic government by rescuing it from the few for the few and by returning it to the people for all the people. Subsequently, the first "rounded, full-orbed, complete" republic—social, industrial, and political—would be achieved. The responsible agents of the people in this government, the self-interested and enlightened public, and the economic equality of the citizens would preserve the society from future oppressions of either economic or political nature. Bellamy regarded the "economic democracy" of this state as all important, for it was "the corollary and necessary supplement of political democracy, without which the latter must forever fail to secure to a people the equalities and liberties which it promises."

By economic equality Bellamy meant that each citizen who worked or who was mentally or physically incapable of working would draw as his dividend on his stock in the government which was issued to him at birth an annual income which would be equal to that of every other citizen in equal circumstances. The citizen's chief title to this allotment from the social fund to which he contributed with his labor in the industrial army was his being a member of humanity.

In *Looking Backward,* the method Bellamy devised for the distribution of the annual stipend was a credit-card system comparable to the ration books issued to the citizens of the United States during World War II. In *Equality,* however, the credit-card system was discarded for a system whereby each citizen received at the beginning of each year a deposit to his account in the national bank; upon this account he wrote vouchers in payment for his purchases of commodities or services.

In order to achieve the sum of the annual deposit, an estimate was made of the cost of all the provisions and services that were expected to be necessary for the nation; this estimate was then transferred into the sum which it would cost and the total cost was then divided by the total population. The amount, therefore, which was credited to each individual represented his aliquot share of the commodities and services available for the year. Since production and distribution had achieved stability and since there were no wars and very little foreign commerce, the only things that could diminish the supply were internal, natural calamities such as drought. The government policy, however, was to maintain a surplus of staples so that the citizens would rarely suffer severely from a production shortage.

Although one of the fundamental laws of the state required all able citizens to contribute to the social fund with their labor, no regulations existed as to the spending of the annual income. Total expenditure of the income was encouraged, however, by the fact that, at the end of each year, any unspent amount was returned to the coffers of the state in order to prevent hoarding and to simplify bookkeeping. Accumulation from one year to the next was, however, permitted for an unusual expenditure—such as the publication of a book—but in this case the government had to be notified in advance or the unused surplus would automatically be returned to the general fund. Though no person could be such a spendthrift that he could spend his capital and though the government guaranteed "the nurture, the education, and the comfortable maintenance of every citizen from the cradle to the grave," Bellamy foresaw that there might be citizens who would spend their yearly incomes too quickly and thereby take advantage of others and of the government. To prevent this, he provided that those who persisted in becoming public burdens would be assigned a guardian or become the responsibility of their friends or their families.

The effects of this credit system upon the economic, commercial, and moral aspects of the new society were envisioned by Bellamy as being manifold. Though the term "dollar" was retained as a convenient symbol of value, the form and the value of money and the banking and the credit systems of the nineteenth century became obsolete. Bellamy, who had long considered money to be the root of all evil, hoped that its banishment would restore the Golden Age of morality. He had portrayed, in his *Union* editorials, how the need of money to sustain life and the importance attached to it socially had corrupted morality, brought about social classes, destroyed democracy, and had caused the worship of God to be replaced with that of the Golden Calf. As a result of the mad immoral strife for gain, Christian morality was a code of action to be followed in actual life only if it paid; and men's worst qualities—cruel jealousies, selfishness, and avarice—were developed.

As early as 1873, Bellamy had also condemned the credit system as being economically unsound because it was a private method of issuing the equivalent of money and because it contributed to panics. He pointed out that the necessary corollary of the credit system was faith and that so long as it existed all was well; when doubt appeared, however, panic ensued and a rush on the banks resulted which brought destruction and destitution to businesses and individuals through personal loss as well as through a general paralysis of production and distribution.

In his Utopian novels Bellamy condemned the credit system with its interest charges because it had enabled the few to amass disproportionate amounts of wealth and had thereby paved the way to political, economic, and moral damnation. Because interest as well as rent was enjoyed by the recipient without his working, Bellamy regarded them both as "tributes levied by inaction upon action" which did not contribute to the wealth of the community which depended upon the active production of all of its citizens. Not only had rent, profit, and interest been the sources of the power of the plutocracy, but they had also supplied immoral motivations for production and had actually decreased the production of wealth since they had diminished the consuming power of the public.

With the extermination of the monetary and the credit systems, banking and banks became obsolete and were no longer the heart of the business system. To Bellamy, the banking system had been an evil which had taken hundreds of men from active production, had contributed to the business crises of the nation because of extended credit and bank failures, and had had a debauching influence upon the men who had used it to aggrandize their wealth through ruthless speculation. To Bellamy, the one good that had resulted from the banking system was that it had paved the way for the abolition of currency and had made possible the one bank of the year 2000 which kept the accounts of the citizens.

When Bellamy had presented his policy of economic equality in *Looking Backward,* socialists, economists, and radicals criticized it as being impractical. As Bellamy was to point out to them, the plan of economic equality differed greatly from that of the socialists and the communists who, for the most part, sponsored the sharing of the wealth according to the individual need or contribution. Bellamy rejected such bases for sharing, for his motto was "from all equally, to all equally," and he argued that his method of distribution was the only one that would be morally, economically, and politically satisfactory in a democratic nation. In his articles and his speeches and later in *Equality,* Bellamy defended economic equality on these counts and he also sought parallels in the life of the nine-teenth century to prove the practicality of his plan.

Bellamy, who believed that "the simple formula is the only practicable way of dealing with a large problem," maintained that economic equality would restore democratic government and prin-ciples and that it would enable the government to fulfill its aim and duty: to secure the life of its citizenry and to provide for its common welfare in an impartial and egalitarian manner. Because men already had an equal political voice in the government and an equal right to justice and to protection in time of war, Bellamy argued that they had also to be considered equal in their right to the economic support provided by the government as a result of their equal labor and their equal partnership in the industrial business of the nation. Furthermore, if men were not granted economic equality, their other equalities and liberties might not be achieved. Although instituting economic equality might require a reorganiza-tion of the government, the people had the power to change it so as to enable it to perform its duty—for no limitation could ever be placed upon the power of the people in this respect since it was their government and one which existed for the sole purpose of serving them.

Bellamy also regarded economic equality as the method of safe-guarding the stability and the wise ordering of the government, for he believed that, when the people became dependent for their eco-nomic welfare upon it, they would have an impassioned interest in it and would thenceforth be an alerted citizenry. He also expected that men would realize that no one could hurt another without endangering himself—and that hence each citizen would consider the welfare of the whole. To Bellamy, this consideration of the good of others was the primal principle of democracy and, at the same time, the application of the Golden Rule.

Economic equality was not, however, to be only the source of peace, morality, and plenty; it was to be also the restorer of the dignity of man and of the lost liberties and equalities. Bellamy stated in *Equality*: "The cornerstone of our state is economic equal-ity, and is not that the obvious, necessary, and only adequate pledge of these three birthrights—life, liberty, and happiness? What is life without the material basis, and what is an equal right to life but a right to an equal material basis for it? What is liberty? How can men be free who must ask the right to labor and to live from their fellow-men and seek their bread from the hands of others? How else can any government guarantee liberty to men save by providing them a means of labor and of life coupled with independence; and how could that be done unless the government conducted the economic system upon which employment and maintenance depend? Finally, what is implied in the equal right of all to the pursuit of happiness? What form of happiness, so far as it depends at all on material facts, is not bound up with economic conditions; and how shall an equal opportunity for the pursuit of happiness be guaranteed to all save by a guarantee of economic equality?"

Liberty to the proud, sensitive, aloof Edward Bellamy meant the "right not only to live, but to live in personal independence of one's fellows" and family financially. Such independence was impossible in the nineteenth century when children and wives were dependent upon men who had to bargain against each other and to depend upon others for their work which was controlled by the "Masters of Bread." In such a situation, human dignity was lost; and men became slaves to others and to their own physical needs and were, therefore, unable to stand up straight before God or men. Because of the economic equality of the year 2000 which made all men equal economic partners and both masters and servants of the state, men were truly free, and they could voice their opinions without fear.

Economic equality would, in fact, insure freedom of expression by making it possible for the people to own and control their own newspapers and magazines which were to be free not only from the private censorship Bellamy had condemned in the statement of policy in the *Daily News* but from that of the government. Since the citizens were to spend their incomes as they wished, they could by subscription start a newspaper, hire an editor by reimbursing the state for his lost services, and express any ideas or criticisms they wished despite the fact that the paper was printed in the government printing shops. An individual citizen who wished to criticize public affairs could, at his own expense, publish a book or a pamphlet; and groups of citizens could hire auditoriums from the state for the holding of debates and discussions.

Bellamy placed great importance upon freedom of speech because, as his *Union* editorials show, he had long been firmly convinced that "modern free government is a government by criticism." Believing this, he had urged citizens to study the affairs of the nation diligently so that they could "intelligently choose the course" which seemed best "calculated to advance the national welfare." To enable the citizens to be not only more capable judges but more penetrating critics of political measures, Bellamy had also advocated the teaching of political science in the schools. In *Equality,* Bellamy safeguarded the expression of public opinion and the assertion of the public will by instituting recall, initiative, and referendum.

Besides freedom of speech, freedom of the press, and freedom of public meetings, the citizens of the new era were to be given— because of economic equality—freedom from war, starvation, diseased bodies, cold, ignorance, criminality, and insecurity. Because of economic equality, children and women were freed from financial dependence and men were freed of the financial burden imposed by marriage and fatherhood; and all were free to marry for love only since class distinctions based upon money and education had disappeared.

Economic equality was also to restore to the citizens the equality of opportunity which had once existed in the United States but which had been lost when wealth became the "Open Sesame" to education, social position, and professional and commercial opportunities. The importance of equality of opportunity had been stressed by Bellamy as early as 1876 in an editorial considering whether Americans had more or less freedom than Englishmen or Germans. In this article, Bellamy had concluded that the liberty peculiar to his country was a "social rather than a political liberty" and that "forms of government matter comparatively little" for "the real liberty of the citizen is to be judged by the amount of social freedom he has, freedom to move in society, to rise and fall upon his merits, and to be precluded from no advantage and no employment of his fortune by barriers of caste and social prejudice." America was, said Bellamy, the sole country on the earth in which "men count for what they are, and the

career is open to talent"—and it was "this social democracy, of
which . . . political democracy is only the symbol" which made
America the only "really free country of the world."

The worst enemies of this social freedom, said Bellamy in other
of his editorials, were those who sought to "import social and caste
distinctions into" American society. In *The Duke of Stockbridge,*
Bellamy pictured, however, a society in which social and economic
equality had disappeared as early as the time of the Shays' Rebellion
because of the educational, political, and commercial opportunities
afforded by wealth; and, finally, in *Looking Backward,* he presented
the famous picture of the coach which was ridden by the rich and
drawn by the workers. The rich, determined to remain riders, tried
to keep the pullers contented—but with as little as possible.

Though Bellamy admitted that progress had been made in improving the conditions of the workers in respect to housing, wages,
and working hours, he was also of the opinion that the laborer was
more discontented than ever before because he realized that his
industry and his talent would not suffice to win him independence
in a world in which opportunities were limited if one did not possess
wealth. Young men no longer felt that the world was before them,
for they realized that what awaited them depended upon the class
in which they were born. Furthermore, wrote Bellamy, the obvious
inequalities of conditions were the source of a bitterness and a discontentment which would not exist if everyone were having an
equally difficult struggle or an equally comfortable life.

Bellamy disagreed with other reformers about the methods to be
used to restore equality of opportunity, for most of them merely
advocated giving each man an equal start. To Bellamy, such a proposal was comparable to giving men clubs, matching the opponents
"according to weight so that all" would be "fair play," and then
letting the vicious, destructive battle continue. The results of such
a contest would be morally and socially detrimental, for the man who
won the struggle would have developed ruthless characteristics, and,
when he had won his victory because of them, he would be resting
on the defeated—the mass of the people.

By giving each man economic equality, equal educational opportunity, freedom from social barriers and from the rule of might,

all—even the physically weak—would have an equal opportunity to find a place in society and to rise according to ability and merit; and every individual could do so, if he wished to exert the necessary effort, without depriving his neighbor of his livelihood or injuring him in the struggle for existence. Not only the individual but the whole nation would benefit morally from the cessation of the selfish, cruel, internecine strife—and all would benefit politically and economically from the development and the utilization of talent and from the recognition of, and the leadership given to, the natural aristocracy which would be enabled to lead men toward the achievement of the better life, material and spiritual. This moral, political, and economic enfranchisement of men would have been achieved because of the collective power and wealth of a unified nation, and it could never have been achieved by individual action. In *Looking Backward,* therefore, Bellamy wrote his Declaration of Interdependence as well as of Independence, for he considered not only the relations of the people with their government but their relationship with one another.

The only restrictions that were to be placed upon the freedom and the liberty of people of this new society were the "social obligations resting on all alike" which forced them to respect the rights of others and to labor to support themselves and the incapacitated. The necessity of working was, however, to be considered as a compulsion of nature and not as the club it had been when used by the rich to force the poor to labor for them for profit. "Slavery," wrote Bellamy, "exists where there is compulsory using of men by other men for the benefit of the users"; and it seemed to him that the so-called freedom of contract of the nineteenth century had been merely a hollow term since the laborers had in reality been forced to make their bargains with their employers under the pressure of necessity. For, asserted Bellamy, "if you own the things men must have, you own the men who must have them." Though feudalism had been replaced by democracy in political affairs, it had continued to survive in "its pristine vigor" in the "affairs of industry which touch the welfare of the citizens at all points."

Bellamy also defended his ideal government on the grounds of economic and ethical principles which are closely associated with each other and with the political principles which formed the basis of the ideal government. His aim was to achieve political and social solidarity through an economic but ethical revolution which would make the introduction of the new order possible and which would sustain and reinforce it after it had been established. The underlying principles of his state are, therefore, as tightly interwoven and as interactive as his aims—and this was as it should have been, for Bellamy regarded society as an organism of the whole— and it was for the achievement of a unified, harmonious whole that he sought a solution. Because of the doctrine of evolution, Bellamy believed that man could not be considered as an individual apart from his surroundings, for he was born into an environment from whose effects there could be no escape. The problem, therefore, was to adjust man's conduct to the social organism, the whole, of which he was a part—or to adjust the social organism so that it would further right conduct and the achievement of action that would be for the good of the whole. Ethics, therefore, became a sociological search "for right conduct" which was to be defined as the "stable adjustment of the part to the whole."

In his *Union* editorials and book reviews, Bellamy not only had insisted upon the necessity of ethical principles in any political economic theory but he had also argued that from its beginning political economy had been a science known only to such statesmen as Fleury and Colbert, who had recognized that "economy, saving, pure and simple, was the only political economy, the sole secret of financial science." Bellamy had averred that, despite the progress made in the knowledge of laws of trade or of systems of managing money, "housekeeping, private and national, consists in increasing income and curtailing outgo."

Years later Bellamy wrote in *Equality* that Adam Smith's *Wealth of Nations* bore an ironic title since the book had taught citizens how to get rich at the expense of the majority and had presented only a so-called science of wealth production, for the system it advocated was based upon individual and not concerted action. It seemed to Bellamy that Smith and other political economists of the nineteenth century had made the great blunder of "accepting a set of conditions that were mere barbaric survivals" incapable of being the foundation of a "scientific social order." A political economy based upon the principles they advocated would be, he thought, "a science not of national wealth but of national poverty" because of its advocacy of anti-social practices in economic matters.

To correct the errors of the political economists and to achieve the integrated life of the new social order, political economy had to become, therefore, a consideration of the greatest good for the greatest number; it had to be truly economical from the standpoint of preventing waste and of producing wealth; and it had also to consider not mere things but men. It had also to reinforce the democratic and the Christian principles of the nation and at the same time to be the external aspect of the ethical, democratic ideal which Bellamy defined as "the recognition of the solidarity of the race in the alphabet of the religion of the whole."

The basic principle which Bellamy evolved for the political economy of his ideal state was that of co-operation, which he considered as being not only the only ethical but the sole scientific, economical basis of the production of wealth. To prove the successful application of this principle, Bellamy had only to cite its usage by the monopolies of his day. Ethically, he argued that co-operation was the only moral and Christian basis of society, for it alone would promote brotherhood of man or solidarity.

In order to support the principle of economic equality with economic principles, Bellamy sought to prove that the brotherhood of man could be shown in terms of property and that men had, therefore, an economic and an ethical right to an equal income. The four major arguments—aside from that of man's right to property as it was deduced from his right to life—which he presented were the co-partnership of production of the new state which ethically demanded equal remuneration; the idea of the social heritage; the impossibility of self-support in an organized society; and the social organism as the source of all production.

In the presentation of the argument of co-partnership, Bellamy asserted that when the state controlled and owned all the industries and that when the workers were all members of the national industrial army, the country became a joint stock company in which all had an equal share. Since every man was to serve equally in the labor corps, he had to receive an equal share of the national dividend. Though Bellamy recognized the inequalities of the quality of service which might be rendered, he maintained that if each did his best, he was serving equally. To show that his principle had already been recognized and applied, Bellamy cited the Christian principle which demanded that the strongest serve the weakest and be his brother's keeper and the tendency of the labor unions to recognize that an equal wage for all was the best means of promoting unity of interest. Furthermore, Bellamy argued that it had long been the government's policy in war and in peace to protect equally the weak and the incapable; and the tendency of legislation had been to recognize that man had duties to perform for the good of the whole and that he had of necessity to contribute to the support of the dependent as in the case of his wife and children.

Since the social organism—"the machinery of associated labor and exchange"—made the production of wealth possible among civilized men and since the knowledge and the inventions making this production possible had been the contribution of many men throughout the ages, the social organism was "the indivisible inheritance of all in common" and should, therefore, belong to "society collectively." The intention of state socialism was to rescue the heritage of the people from the hands of the minority who exploited it and to return it to the true heirs, the people, who, weak and strong, would share its benefits equally.

The principle of the social fund, therefore, made it impossible to give a man a wage which was based wholly on the product of his own labor, since he perforce utilized the knowledge and the inventions of the past, which also made it impossible to determine just exactly what infinitesimal part the individual did contribute. This sharing of the social heritage not only made equality of income or wage a necessity but resulted in the establishment of justice and of the idea of brotherhood because man's mutual dependence and his mutual support were made clear.

The moral cornerstone of Bellamy's social order was the brotherhood of man, and the motivating force of the citizen was to be his enthusiasm for humanity. Bellamy not only intended for the nation to become "an economical organism, but a *moral* organism as well";

and he wrote to Colonel T. W. Higginson in December, 1888, that on "this last point" he "would lay extraordinary stress. This is of course necessarily an economical reform, but its most important aspect is that of a moral movement for uplifting, enlarging and ennobling the individual life by making every individual contribute his efforts first and directly to the common or national wealth, and himself dependent for his livelihood upon his equal share in it, so that he is rich as the nation is rich and poor as his fellow citizens are poor and never otherwise. Then all the issues of life will be first from the individual to the nation, then from the nation back to him. As the hand profits not directly by what it seizes nor the mouth by what it devours, but only by sending its booty to the common treasury to be nourished in return by the red blood from the heart, so the members of the coming nation will serve and live, in constant remembrance and realization of their common life and mutual dependence. The great heart will beat in the pulse of the smallest member."

The result of this solidarity of interest which resulted from economic equality, co-operation, interdependence, and enthusiasm for humanity was to be a social order which would be morally, socially, economically, and politically based upon and guided by the precepts of Christ. In one of his unpublished manuscripts, Bellamy wrote that this was "no new scheme. The idea that men being brothers should live together as brothers is as old as the first aspirations of humanity. It is the heart of all religion and the express meaning of Christ. . . . All I have done in *Looking Backward,* all I aim . . . to do is to show certain ways whereby men can realize this ideal."

Because of the attainment of solidarity, patriotism gained a new meaning in the year 2000. The flag became a symbol of the "compact of brotherhood" by which every citizen was "pledged with all his countrymen mutually to safeguard the equal dignity and welfare of each by the might of all." The honor of the flag no longer depended upon its treatment by other nations but upon the condition of the people over whom it waved. "To the old-time patriot there was nothing incongruous in the spectacle of the symbol of national unity floating over cities reeking with foulest oppressions, full of prostitution, beggary, and dens of nameless misery. According to the modern view, the existence of a single instance in any corner of the land where a citizen had been deprived of the full enjoyment of equality would turn the flag into a flaunting lie, and the people would demand with indignation that it should be hauled down and not be raised again till the wrong was remedied."

Bellamy had written to Howells that no reform group could or should succeed in the United States which was not "wholly and enthusiastically American and patriotic in spirit and suggestions." In his article "Looking Forward," Bellamy listed patriotism as one of the necessary characteristics of Nationalism, for it, "so often misdirected, is the grandest and most potent form under which the enthusiasm for humanity has yet shown itself capable of moving great masses, and in its spirit is contained the promise and potency of the world embracing love in which it shall some day merge. Social reforms must follow National lines and will succeed as they are able to adapt themselves to National conditions and sentiments and adapt themselves with National traditions and aspirations."

In summary, it may be said that Bellamy adapted his plan to American democratic governmental principles; to the American respect for religion and dislike of bloody conflict; and to the American dream of plenty for all. To save the republic and to do so by instituting a "republic of property" as well as a "republic of citizenship," Bellamy merely extended the liberties and the equalities set forth in the Constitution to include economic equality. The importance of this cardinal principle as the cornerstone of the new government was perhaps best explained by Bellamy in his letter to Sylvester Baxter: "I am profoundly anxious to impress upon everybody that the principle of *equality* in the provision made for the physical wants of all, *must* be urged in any new social order which is to be free from the characteristic vices and defects of the present system. Once consent, on whatever specious ground, that the principle of inequality in the rate of maintenance for citizens shall be retained, and you retain the root and germ of all the evils we are trying to get rid of, and it is only a question of time when they would be flourishing again. Certainly, *Looking Backward* and the whole system of society which it proposes is based upon equality in the material conditions of citizens, and stands or falls with that idea. Compromise on this point is impossible without giving up all our organization stands for distinctively. There is no argument against equality which will hold water for a moment. There is absolutely no answer to the proposition that the bodily needs of all are the same, and, therefore, under any humane and rational arrangement of society, the provision for them must be the same. Even under the present brutal system, which leaves the means to livelihood to be fought for by men, half the energies of men are called forth by emulation for non-social honors and distinctions. All the good work has always been prompted by this sort of emulation, or by the sense of duty and the natural demand of human faculties for expression in achievement."

CHAPTER VI

THE GOVERNMENT OF INDUSTRIAL DEMOCRACY

1.   An Evolutionary Government

Since Bellamy regarded the social and political evils of his time as being the result of an antiquated property system which had permitted economic inequalities which had enabled the rich to have the power to destroy democracy, he sought to replace private with public ownership and to organize "the machinery of production and distribution, like the political government, as businesses of general concern to be carried on for the public benefit instead of private gain." Since the revolution which was to restore democracy was to be conducted by a democratic people for a democratic purpose, the resulting government had to be collectively controlled; it had also to be a "systematized, centralized, interlocking" organization, for it was to employ all of the citizens in the industrial army and to maintain them by giving them economic equality. When the democratic principle of self-control by the people was extended to include the commercial and industrial affairs of the nation, the industrial and the political state became identical, and industrial democracy was achieved.

When Bellamy presented the outline of the ideal state in *Looking Backward,* he was primarily concerned with drawing a picture, specific and positive, of what might be achieved by such a revolution; for he believed that the ends desired should be ascertained before the process for their achievement could be devised. Though Bellamy presented a plan for the government of the year 2000, he did not intend for it to be considered complete or static, for he believed that the details could be variable and that they could best be formulated by the generation that inaugurated the new government. Bellamy would have denied his own principles had he considered his administrative form of the government to be unalterable, for he was an evolutionist and a pragmatist in his practice of evolving his plan from the proved seeds already existing in his own era, and he was a firm advocate of the principle which insured each generation the right to alter or to rebel against an unsatisfactory government.

Believing in the progress of man toward perfection and in the salient influence a better environment would have upon this progress, Bellamy anticipated a spiritual and intellectual renaissance which would be beyond the expectations of the founders of his ideal state. Because the people of the new order would enthusiastically accept the idea of man's perfectibility and because the society would provide opportunities for the development of mankind physically, mentally, and morally, a race of men would eventually appear who would be dissatisfied with even the ideal state of *Looking Backward*. Indeed, these men would consider it as having been only a "single step in the infinite progression of humanity toward the divine" which had been made possible by the development of the godhood in each man and which would eventually return the race to God. In *Equality* Bellamy more succinctly described the effects of the development of the Greater Self and he forecast the coming of the day when the "spiritual forces" would "fully dominate all things, and questions of physical power" would "cease to be of any importance in human relations." The control and the leadership of humanity would then go to those who "partake most of the Spirit of the Greater Self," and these men would never misuse their power for selfish ends; if they did, it would cease to be power.

2. Principles and Motivation of the Industrial Army

When the nation assumed control of all the productive and distributive facilities of the country and guaranteed to all citizens not only the opportunity to work but economic equality, the state became the sole employer, and the organization of the labor force became a necessity. This organization, the industrial army, which was based upon the rational principle of co-operation, was to be ultimately the foundation upon which all the rest of the social order rested. With this organized industrial force, Bellamy hoped to replace the "unscientific manner" in which the nation went to work with a scientific system of concerted action which would not only produce wealth but solve the labor-wage problem, avoid the wastes of private industry, and perform the "dirty work" of the nation.

When Bellamy formulated the general principles which were to be the basis of the organization and the regulation of the industrial army, he gave great consideration to those concerned with the general necessity of labor, the duty of the citizen to work and of the state to provide employment, the development of natural aptitudes, the purpose of life, and the incentives to labor.

Labor, Bellamy revealed in his early journals and novels, was to be considered as beneficent to both mind and body; it was not only the best cure for ennui but the method by which men could see themselves in something they had created and could thereby come to know themselves. Though Bellamy believed that a full enjoyment of life could be achieved only if men cultivated and developed all their faculties and abilities by employing them in suitable occupations, he did not want them to become so engrossed in their work that they would sacrifice their lives to it. Regarding work as the chief end of living and participating in the monotonous "soulless drudgery" which made modern man a machine could, wrote Bellamy in *Six to One* and in the Eliot Carson story, lead to nervous breakdowns and to impoverished and undeveloped souls. The maxim to be remembered, therefore, was that "we do not live to work but work to live"—and to Bellamy, true living meant "to live the fullest, freest, most developed life we can."

Though Bellamy considered the central and original idea of American civilization to be "labor is honorable to all," he regarded it not only as honorable but as a necessity: labor was a debt that each man owed to society. To fulfill this obligation, it was necessary, wrote Bellamy in a *Union* editorial, that each man contribute enough work to "cover his own maintenance and that of those dependent upon him." If a man lived upon inherited wealth and did not work, he was to be regarded as no better than a pauper, for he was not earning his own living but was being supported by the labor of others.

With these early attitudes toward labor, it was inevitable that Bellamy would develop a principle of enlistment in the labor corps that would be similar to that of the army: it was the duty of every able man to contribute to the protection and welfare of the nation before he could devote himself to his higher duty to himself—the exercise of the intellectual and spiritual faculties which was the main business of existence. Duty, which replaced the contract of the old order, became in the new state not only the basis of production but the cement of society; for all men were united in brotherhood, and they stood shoulder to shoulder in their battle against the common foes of hunger, cold, and nakedness and in their attempt to protect the sick and the aged. The individual had his duty to the state, but the latter had also its obligation: to supply the citizen with work, the means to life. In fulfilling this duty of providing employment for all, the government was fulfilling also its "first and greatest duty," which was to "guarantee the livelihood of the people."

Because of the mass unemployment during Bellamy's era, the duty of the state to supply labor and the right of all men to be employed had been subjects widely discussed. The idea of the duty of the state to supply labor had been stated by Fichte in his *Foundation of Natural Right,* and the plan for the public employment of the unemployed in workshops established by the government had been sponsored by Blanc, Comte, the German socialists, and a Pennsylvania state law. In 1873 in Massachusetts, the mayor of Boston requested that the municipality provide a public building for the employment of the unemployed; and, in 1874, Bellamy wrote in a *Union* editorial that the economy of such a project had already been recognized by private industry, for the Baltimore and Ohio Railroad had been able to repair its tracks during the depression with cheap labor. Furthermore, argued Bellamy, for the government to spend money to provide work that would not be makeshift but necessary would benefit the whole nation as well as the unemployed. Years later, in 1885, the mayor of Springfield introduced a bill in the state legislature which would have permitted, had it been passed, the establishment of municipal industries. The Springfield *Republican* opposed the measure with the argument that the sale of the products of these factories or bakeries would endanger and damage private industry.

Reflections of this argument occurred in Bellamy's articles of 1893 and 1894 in which he suggested that the immediate solution to the problem of the unemployed was government-established and controlled industries which would not compete with privately owned ones since only their employees would be permitted to buy their produce. Further reflection of this idea is to be found in *Equality,* where, in describing the period of transition, Bellamy portrayed the state-owned shops as selling their products only to their employees.

Though each citizen of Bellamy's Utopia had to work and though it was the duty of the nation to provide employment, Bellamy showed his concern about the term of service to be required and about the conditions under which the laborers would work. He attempted to set specific limits to the term of service and to devise a system of determining the daily hours of labor so that the burden carried would be equalized.

The possibility of the limitation of work had long been a part of Bellamy's social thinking, for in his lyceum address of the early 1870's he had stated that because of the discoveries of men and the bounty of nature there would be enough to support all people in abundance if the produce were equally distributed and if all the people worked; if none were idle and if the burdens of life were shared equally, all could work for only a moderate time. This interest in decreasing the period of labor stemmed from Bellamy's attitude toward man's purpose in life which is reflected in the case of Eliot Carson who, at the age of thirty, surveyed his life and discovered that his preoccupation with business had not permitted him to grow morally or intellectually during the last ten years of his life and that he had, therefore, denied his youthful aspirations of self-development. Eliot realized that when men were released from college they were taken into the "world press gang" and that from then on they ceased to use their minds except as tools "to weave woolen, to spin cotton, or keep books, or grind off editorials at so much a column." In Bellamy's unpublished "Almost a Suicide," the Rev. Rakesmith remarked that when he was young he had felt that life culminated before forty and he had been puzzled as to what he would do with the remaining years which seemed to have "the effect of an anti-climax."

In *Looking Backward,* Bellamy provided the answer for Eliot Carson's situation and for the Rev. Rakesmith's quandary when he sought to provide man with the leisure to develop himself by limit-ing the term of service in the industrial army to twenty-four years and to make the years after forty-five the climax of life since they brought complete enfranchisement. Both men and women entered the army at the age of twenty-one and were mustered out at forty-five; after retirement, some might be eligible to recall until fifty-five, as in the case of those drafted to be president or judges. For the most part, however, the retired citizen was to be free to occupy himself as he pleased, for this was the period that all had anticipated as the true beginning of their lives. Bellamy, who had stated in his earlier works that individuality and diversity of interests were most pronounced during middle age and that meditation and speculation were best suited for older persons who were more capable of being subjective, not only echoed these ideas in *Looking Backward* but delineated plans for the continued education and development of the older citizens.

The hours of work performed by the laborers during their term of service in the industrial army were not to be uniform but were to vary according to the hazards, the laboriousness, and the unpleasantness of the task. In this fashion, Bellamy sought to make the most difficult assignments attractive by shortening the hours and to regulate and equalize the working conditions in all industries. If too many flocked into a trade, it was to be regarded as offering conditions that were unfairly easy and hence the hours were to be lengthened; if too many avoided an occupation, it was to be considered too difficult or too unpleasant and the hours of required labor were to be shortened.

If no one volunteered to do exceedingly hazardous or unpleasant work, the government was to proclaim the work dangerous and to ask for volunteers, or it was to assign the task to the general labor corps of the industrial army. Though Bellamy expected young men eager for adventure and the winning of honors and public gratitude to flock to the task, he also pointed out that the country could, if it had to, draft men to do the work, or it could so adjust the working hours that men would select the work as a permanent occupation. Generally, the non-hazardous but unpleasant chores of the nation were to be performed by those in the first three-year period of industrial service, for during this time the members did general work. By thus regulating the type of service performed by the general labor corps and by providing a system for the regulation of the hours of labor in all branches of industry, the state was not only to get the "dirty work" done but it was to equalize the burden carried and make the trades equally attractive—or equally difficult.

In order to make the labor requirements so flexible that they would give free play to any instinct of human nature—except that which aimed at living on the fruits of the labor of others!—Bellamy established not only a system of exemptions from service but also the principles to be followed in the selection of metier. Exemptions from the industrial or the professional service were to be provided in three ways: remission by indemnification, whereby a group could pay the state the sum of the annual income for the special services it wished a citizen, such as an editor, to render it; remission by abnegation, which provided that a citizen who had reached his thirty-third year and had filled half of his required term of service could retire from the industrial army if he would draw thereafter only half of his annual income; and remission of women for child-bearing and child-rearing.

The principle of selection of the citizen's occupation was that a "man's natural endowments, mental and physical, determine what he can work at most profitably to the nation and most satisfactorily to himself." This rule, long a favorite one with Utopians, was in keeping with the Puritan idea of "the call" which Bellamy had written about in one of his *Union* editorials of the 1870's in which he had urged every young man to "obey whatever call he may feel" and had admonished him not to forget to be a man. To illustrate what he meant by the latter, Bellamy cited the cynical Frenchman who had recognized the mistake he had made in his life in the epitaph he had had engraved upon his tomb: "Born a man; died a grocer."

Bellamy, who had had difficulties of his own in finding his proper niche in life and whose youthful certitude of a special destiny had seemingly been belied by feeble accomplishments, was aware of the importance to the individual and to the state of a person's finding his true vocation. In his notes for "The Blindman's World," he had written that if every man knew what he could do and if he had the true measure of his own power, he would enjoy in youth the "calm and restful balance of the faculties known to men only in middle age" and he would not suffer because of the difference between his youthful, lofty aspirations and dreams and his actual achievements. In one of his notebooks, he remarked that "the common weal of solidarity" was not advanced when a person thrust aside another whose work he was not so capable of doing.

Because of these early personal experiences and meditations, Bellamy took care in *Looking Backward* and in *Equality* to specify the means whereby the educational system, the three years of general industrial service, and the Labor Exchange would make it possible for men to select and to prepare for the occupations for which they were best suited. To insure, however, the working of the plan in such a way that it would fulfill the needs of the commonwealth, as well as of the individual, Bellamy stipulated certain limitations to the individual's right of selection.

The social order of the year 2000 encouraged each man to follow his natural bent in the selection of his occupation because it emphasized that by his doing so he would not be wasting his talents and would be fulfilling his duty of rendering his best services. Because all jobs merited equal pay, honor, social standing, and expenditure of energy—so far as it was possible to regulate this by adjusting the daily hours of required labor—there was no advantage to be gained by not choosing the work that most fitted the innate abilities. Bellamy pointed out that in the nineteenth century the social standing, the monetary rewards, and the financial investment in education required by many professions had forced many men to do work they disliked and that this had contributed not only to the individual's unhappiness and maladjustment but to a waste of talent.

Since the satisfaction of the needs of the individual and of the state required that each man discover and develop his multiple abilities, it was the duty, therefore, of the parents, the educators, and the officials of the industrial army to watch the youths of the nation for signs of their interests and abilities and to supply them with ample opportunities to discover them by acquainting them with the many trades and professions. Each youth was to select, on the basis of his abilities, two occupations, for this versatility would make it possible for the nation to shift him to a position that might be vacant, to place him if there were no vacancy in the field of his first choice, and to provide him with suitable employment if one of his occupations were made obsolete by invention.

Though the worker had complete freedom in the selection of his vocation, his ability and his service record determined whether his choices would be granted him when assignments were made, for preference was to be given always to those with the highest grades and the greatest ability. To make this possible, a system of grading was maintained throughout a man's entire educational and industrial career; and those with the best records were given opportunities at all times to volunteer for other industries or for professions for which they felt they were better qualified. If a man had made no choice of a special vocation by the time the three years of service in the general corps of the industrial army had ended, he remained in the general duty unit. Bellamy also stipulated that men who elected to study medicine had to have made their selection before they reached the age of thirty.

In *Looking Backward* Bellamy made vague mention of the fact that it would be possible for men to change their occupations as well as the localities in which they worked; but it was not, however, until he wrote *Equality* that he systematized his plan of selection and exchange by establishing the Labor Exchange which he had specifically mentioned for the first time in his article " 'Looking Backward' Again." Under this plan, the government published—as Cabet had suggested—a statement listing the workers needed in each field of endeavor. After studying this report, the youths filled out—in the June of their third year of unclassified service in the industrial army —a blank on which they stated their preferences as to vocations and localities. The completed blanks were taken to a registrar who stamped upon them the rating of merit achieved by the applicant during his educational and industrial career. This ranking denoted his relative intelligence, his devotion to duty, and his efficiency.

The stamped application was then sent from the local exchange to the central office of the industrial district which gave assignments according to rank to all those who had demanded work in the home area—and it was obligatory that such requests be filled. If, however, there were no vacancies in the vocations of such an applicant's choice, the administration had the right to assign him to a task not on his list if, by doing so, it fulfilled the request as to location of work. The applications which contained no requests as to home assignments were sent to the national board which made assignments according to rank, preference, and the national need. By the first of August, every person was notified of his assignment and he reported for work on Muster Day, October 15.

Though the administration had earnestly sought to supply the needs of each citizen, cases of dissatisfaction as to location or occupation were given special consideration through the Transfer Department. This bureau made it possible for all those wishing to change either their work or their locations to communicate with one another and to arrange exchanges that would be mutually agreeable.

Although Bellamy had planned his industrial army so that men, happy in their selected tasks, would work harder at them and had arranged that their efficiency would lead to public honors and official status so that recognition of merit would provide not only the best leaders but an incentive to effort for all workers, he was condemned by his critics as having concocted an unfeasible plan or one that would result in regimentation. His critics—Émile de Laveleye, General Walker, Secrétan, Maher, and others—thought his plan to be unworkable, for they, believing with Mandeville that only the wants and the poverty of men forced them to work, feared that the comfortable citizens of the year 2000 would lack these incentives.

Though Bellamy had considered the problem of incentives to labor in *Looking Backward,* these criticisms caused him to write many articles defending and enlarging upon his previous statements; these were to contribute to the more extensive consideration of the question of motivation in *Equality.* The attitude that Bellamy assumed toward this problem and the arguments that he presented were based upon conclusions that had resulted from his long consideration of the problem of the motivation of human conduct.

As a young man desirous of dedicating himself to the service of humanity, Bellamy had probed his inner depths to discover whether his desire were prompted by a selfish wish for fame or by the natural urge "to fully expand, exert, and express . . . [himself] in great activities." Philosophically, he realized the folly of desiring the applause of the crowd and he recognized that vanity could lead men.

to make the most of the least accomplishment. He hoped that eventually, as men progressed in wisdom and culture, their desire for public recognition would expire.

In his considerations of the motivations of conduct in his short stories, *Union* editorials, and unpublished journals, Bellamy stated that there was little that needed to be considered "except personal vanity and love of approbation" and that all that was needed to purchase a man was an appeal to this vanity. Because of men's desire for approbation, Bellamy believed that if men and opportunities could be brought together it would be seen that many men would be happy to risk their lives in order to win reputations and that they would perform "all the heroic deeds that mankind in its daily experiences stands in need of. Perhaps when society is more perfectly organized this mutual adaptation will be secured." To Bellamy this "tremendous emulative spirit" represented "a moral and physical motor of millions of horse power" which made the political economist sigh because it was lost so frequently in "pursuits so entirely unproductive" and was not "brought to bear on the useful avocations of humanity"; if it were so applied, "the industrial machinery would fairly whiz."

Bellamy had also noted in his *Union* editorials that the "rage for office and title was increasing" to the extent that men would sacrifice a job with a greater income in order to secure a position with a title which gave them official distinction. Having noted such instances, he concluded, as a journal entry shows, that men did not seek money for its own sake but because of the "power and consequence" it secured and because of the excitement and the enjoyment of the "full swing of energies" its pursuit entailed.

Though Bellamy recognized that greed, selfishness, conceit, and envy were motivators of human action, he did not approve of them as such, for they were divisive characteristics of the individuality. To him, the best motivations were honor, duty, patriotism, and devotion to humanity, for these led men to perform deeds of generosity. In "The Blindman's World" and "To Whom This May Come," he portrayed a superior race of people who were no longer concerned with petty individuality and who were no longer led astray by their vanity to indulge in rivalry, emulation, or competition. Because they no longer knew hatred or jealousy and because all of their motives were known and recognized by all, these fortunate ones had achieved moral health personally and solidarity socially. Bellamy, however, had not forgotten that he was not living in an ideal world of the future when he stated in a *Union* editorial that, since man was basically selfish and since there was not time to change him, the solution of the industrial problem was to make use of his selfish interest by turning it into channels where it would serve the good of all.

The result of these early cogitations is seen in Bellamy's ideal state, for the self-interest of the citizen is used not only as a means of preserving the state but of motivating the worker. The incentives that Bellamy portrayed in his Utopias fall roughly into three categories: the appeal to the natural instincts; the appeal to the impersonal, ethical, or religious feeling of man; and the pressure of indirect and direct discipline.

Recognizing that man was naturally selfish and vain and that his lust for wealth was based upon his desire to achieve comfort, social significance and power and to enjoy effective action, Bellamy decided to utilize these natural characteristics of the individuality despite the fact that in an industrial democracy wealth would no longer be a symbol of success or the objective for which individuals would strive. By replacing wealth as the end sought by the honors, power, and offices—which recognized the achievement that wealth had formerly represented—Bellamy sought to maintain the incentives but to divert them in such a way that they would be used to serve the public. In order to insure this usage of man's selfishness for both the public and the individual good, the highest awards were to be given only for the greatest and most efficient service rendered to mankind. In this way, the individual would profit not only in honors received but in the mitigation of his greedy self-interest which his demanded devotion to humanity would necessitate. Human nature would not be changed or abolished, wrote Bellamy; human instincts would, however, be redirected in a way that would contribute to human felicity and solidarity.

Among the other human instincts that were utilized was that of hunger. Though Bellamy did not say so, the fear of poverty and hunger could still exist in his state as a motivating factor, for men were actually supporting themselves by their own efforts; if they did not work, they would not eat. Bellamy had little fear, however, that men would not labor willingly, for he felt that, since action was the normal condition of men, they would find pleasure in such physical and mental activity. Furthermore, he believed that men found a deep satisfaction in the development of their abilities. To him, the "essential motive in all really good work is satisfaction in work itself."

The highest motives which were to spur men to zealous endeavor included not only a pleasing absorption and interest in the work itself but an ethical sense of duty and an enthusiasm for humanity similar to that inspired by patriotism in time of war. Bellamy regarded the source of such inspired action as being the centrifugal or impersonal aspect of man's duality which created a desire in him to submerge himself in religion, in patriotism, and in deeds of self-sacrifice and heroism. Men ruled by the impersonal—the nobler side of their nature—were the finest of the race, and they needed no emulation to motivate them; their motives were within, and they knew that their measure of service was set by their natural endowments. To them, as to the young Bellamy, emulation seemed "philosophically absurd" and "despicable in a moral aspect by its substitution of envy for admiration." Since all men were not, however, of this caliber, emulation was maintained to supply motivation for inferior natures, though Bellamy hoped that in future ages it would become wholly unnecessary.

To provide a necessary incentive to those who were unresponsive to either the inferior or the superior motivations, Bellamy recommended indirect and direct discipline. The indirect discipline was to be wielded by the mass and by women. Since the welfare of all depended upon each individual's contributing his share of work, the attitude toward the malingerer would be one of such severe disapproval that the worker would strive to avoid public contempt. Women were also to express their disapproval of the failures by denying them their love, for they were pictured as sitting aloft in judgment and as reserving their favors as rewards for the victors. Bellamy seemingly overlooked the fact that there might be women who were not considered as prizes or who were also losers—and that these might be content to accept the love of a slacker!

To insure that all would work whether willingly or not, Bellamy showed in *Looking Backward* that the rebel, or non-worker, automatically cut himself off from society. Because of the efficiency of the officials and of the inspectorate, the slacker would be found out; and the man who refused to work would be sentenced to solitary confinement and to a diet of bread and water until he was willing to do his duty. In later articles he repeated this plan for disciplining the rebels but he added that inefficiency would result in demotion or in longer working hours. He provided also a tribunal of the people which was to judge each case so that the judgment of officials alone would not determine the recalcitrant worker's fate.

In *Equality,* Bellamy reversed, however, his policy; he made no mention of his former disciplinary measures and stated that those unwilling to work would be given seeds and tools and would be permitted to withdraw to reservations similar to those established for the Indians who had also refused to accept civilization; there the rebels could discover their own solution to the problems of existence. This change was made, without much doubt, because of a letter written to him in 1893 by Mrs. Frances E. Russell in which she suggested that his plan of solitary confinement be replaced with one permitting the rebels to "go off upon land not actually in use by the commonwealth and there try the experiment of individualism to their heart's content."

Although such writers as Fourier, E. E. Hale, Cabet, and others had spoken of organized workers as an industrial army, Bellamy's use of the term provoked charges of regimentation from such critics as General Walker, Garrison, and William Morris. Though Bellamy admitted that his creation of the industrial army had been inspired by the European military service system which demanded everyone's contribution of service, complete co-operation, and central oversight and direction, he also asserted that the term was merely a convenience and that the principles underlying the organization were of more importance than the cognomen given it.

In answering the specific charges of his critics that his system would deprive the individual of personal liberty and kill his initiative and sense of responsibility, Bellamy argued that under capitalism or private enterprise regimentation and even slavery had existed and that no more discipline would be pressed upon the worker in the year 2000 than had been imposed upon him in private industry— or in the federal post-office system. Bellamy also asserted that under private enterprise the relationship of hireling and master had been not only coldly impersonal but demoralizing: in the employer, arrogance, harshness, and hardness had been developed; in the employees, self-respect, dignity, and independence of thought and expression had been destroyed.

Though regulating, controlling, assigning, and directing the laborer would be as necessary under one system as another, the effect of industrial democracy would be different because the irresponsible, tyrannical, rapacious capitalist had been replaced by responsible agents of the people and because personal caprice and authority had been replaced by principles and laws. Instead of working for others for their profit, the people would be working for themselves and the good of all—and this under circumstances which would require their being courteously and kindly treated, for it was the duty of the inspectorate to investigate and of the judicial system to try all cases in which the laborer complained of unfair treatment.

Though each person would be required to work, this was not new—for in the nineteenth century men had had to be part of the labor force of the nation if they wished to live. Requiring men to work under circumstances that assured them employment, promotions based upon achievement, work selected on the basis of their abilities, and security for life could not be considered an infringement upon the personal liberty of man—unless upon that of the person who desired to enjoy the "liberty of loafing." To charge that personal freedom would be destroyed by a system that provided men with all these blessings was to argue, said Bellamy, that one did not have the right to require men to work for their living.

3. Organization and Administration

The primary function of the executive branch of the government was the direction of the production and the distribution of the products of the industrial army and its three allied corps: the women's army, the professional army, and the invalid's army.

The women's army was made necessary by the "condition of sex," for Bellamy, at the time he wrote *Looking Backward,* was still harboring the opinions that he had expressed in his *Union* editorials relative to the role of woman as a worker. In 1875, he had discussed the two views of the enfranchisement of women: that of the suffragettes who demanded complete economic independence for their sex as well as equality of the right to work and that of the counter-movement which maintained that woman's independence and ability to work were limited by her physical and mental limitations. In his discussion, Bellamy cited Dr. Azel Ames' *Sex in Industry* which described the permanently injurious effects of industrial work upon the health of women and which advised, noted Bellamy, that women should be employed "only under conditions especially adapted to their needs, and involving an elastic arrangement allowing short periodical vacations and long annual vacations."

Bellamy affected a compromise in *Looking Backward* between the two groups by giving women the complete economic independence from their husbands desired by the suffragettes and by assigning them the lighter tasks—because of their "comparative weakness and uncertainty of their health"—demanded by the anti-suffragettes. Though women were to be permitted to select tasks according to their abilities, they could not pursue a line of work not "completely adapted both as to kind and degree of labor" to their sex; they received also shorter working hours, more frequent vacations, and more daily rest periods. Since Bellamy recognized not only the distinctive physical needs of women but the "distinct individuality of the sex," he provided them with an army of their own which formed an *"imperium in imperio"* similar to the separate tribune for women in Hugo's *Ninety-three.* Women, therefore, had a world of their own with its ambitions, desires, careers, and emulation; and it was one which avoided "unnatural rivalry with men."

In *Equality,* however, Bellamy made no mention of the separate industrial army for women and portrayed them as taking their place in the industrial world on the same basis as men and as being superintendents of factories, machinists, carpenters, iron workers, and farm laborers. This shift in attitude was first to be noticed in an article in *The New Nation* of April, 1891, in which Bellamy stated that all women would be required to do such work as they should elect to do and for which they were adequately prepared. This change in opinion was undoubtedly the result of the impression made upon Bellamy by two famous suffragettes, Frances E. Willard and Mary Livermore, who had not only become active supporters of Bellamy's ideas but had vociferously argued that woman's labor was to be limited only by the training she had and that she was to be trained for any work for which she showed mental or physical capability.

The invalid's corps was created to provide employment for the deaf, the mute, the insane, the blind, and the physically handicapped; for Bellamy, like Campanella, did not believe that physical defects necessarily rendered men incapable of working—if tasks fitted to their strength and their abilities could be found for them. The completely disabled were, however, not to be assigned tasks but were to receive their full incomes.

The professional army consisted of members of the liberal professions—teachers, artists, physicians, and authors—who had been released from the industrial army when they had proved their genius or had successfully fulfilled their professional training and requirements. This army did not include, however, members of the technical professions such as architects and engineers, for these formed the construction guilds which were special units of the industrial army. The legal and clerical professions were also not represented, for, since Bellamy regarded them as being the source of trouble and as not contributing to the harmony, solidarity, and serenity of life, they were non-existent in the year 2000.

The executive branch of the federal government—which was to be concerned primarily with the administration of the industrial army and with the direction of production, distribution, and international trade—was depicted in some detail in *Looking Backward*. Except for the portrayal of the government's development during the transition period and for the addition of devices to insure democratic action and representation, Bellamy let his portrayal of the government remain unchanged in *Equality*. This lack of alteration of a system that was far from being perfected in his first Utopian novel was due to the fact that Bellamy did not intend to introduce new social machinery but to adapt the old order to meet the needs of industrial democracy. Furthermore, Bellamy realized the insignificance of such tentative details, for he believed that the new government would have to be formulated to meet the needs and the problems of the era in which it would develop. Bellamy's plan must be considered, therefore, as being a purely suggestive one.

The administrative head of the federal government in the plan which Bellamy presented in *Looking Backward* was the president of the republic, who was designated as the commander-in-chief of the industrial army, as disciplinarian, and as enforcer of the law. No member of the professional army could qualify for the presidency, since the president was required to have risen through the ranks of the industrial army to the office of chief of department; his merit was, therefore, to have been proved by his career. After having retired from the industrial army and after having had his report as chief of a department approved by the Congress, the potential candidate was required to spend five years out of the service before he could be elected to the presidency. This specification was made to enable him to study the general conditions of the whole industrial situation so that he would be aware of its general needs as well as of those of his former special branch of industry.

The president was elected by the vote of all the *men* in the nation who were *not* in service in the industrial army and of those still in active service in the professional army. This method of election was necessitated by the president's being disciplinarian of the industrial army, for it was hoped that it would free him of obligation to the men in active service. To insure the president's serving the nation for its good, his not acting with an eye toward re-election, and his not having to propitiate any group to secure another term, Bellamy limited his term to five years. When his term expired, the president submitted a report to Congress which convened to receive it; and, if his report were approved, he was appointed by Congress to represent the nation in the International Council, a federation of autonomous nations which regulated international commerce.

The chief executive was aided in the fulfillment of his duties by the Inspectorate and by the President's Council. The Inspectorate, which Bellamy called the right hand of the president, was occupied with the maintenance of discipline, for its task was to receive and to investigate all complaints of imperfection of products, of insolence or inefficiency of officials, and of derelictions of the laborers. The Inspectorate was not to wait, however, for complaints to be filed; it was to conduct a methodical inspection of all branches of the service in order to discover what was wrong before anyone else did.

The President's Council consisted of the ten department heads of the industrial army and the general-in-chief of the women's army, which had its own administrative staff as did the professional army. The ten department heads—also called lieutenant-generals—were required to have risen to their office through all the lower ranks of the industrial army. They were elected department heads by the retired members of the branches or guilds of the service which they were to represent and to administer—for each of these ten officials represented a group of allied industries or guilds which had their own separate bureaus, commanded by generals of the guild.

Though the general-in-chief of the women's army was a member of the Council, she had the power of veto only upon measures which affected the women. The professional army had no representation upon the Council, but the chief executive of the nation acted as the chairman of the board of regents of the professional army and had the "casting vote." This board, elected by the honorary or retired members of the professions, determined the requirements and the policies of the professions and was held responsible to Congress for its actions. The lack of representation of the invalid and professional armies in the Council would seem a weakness, for the production of the invalid's corps would have to be regulated, and the educational system, which was left to the educators, would have to be integrated with the needs of the industrial army since Bellamy held the schools responsible for acquainting all students with the industrial life of the nation and with preparing them for participation in it.

In order to fulfill its duty of regulating production, the administration received the estimates of the needs of the nation from the statistical division of the distributive system as well as the private petitions for products desired by the citizens. When the administration—and Bellamy is not clear as to whether he meant the president or his Council or both—had determined from these statistics what was to be produced, the estimates were sent as mandates to the chiefs of the departments concerned, who, in turn, sent directions for production to the subordinate bureaus or guilds.

These bureaus were headed by the generals of the guilds who had complete control of all operations of industry and who were held responsible to the administration for the work produced. Although the general of each guild was elected from the eligible superintendents, or colonels, by the retired members of his guild, he had the power to appoint superintendents from the candidates with the best records. Bellamy does not state his reasons for introducing appointive powers at this level, but he may have thought the privilege would be used correctly since the general was to be held responsible to his superior officers and since all officials above the rank of assistant foreman depended for promotion not upon their personal records alone but upon those of the men under their guidance.

Officials of lesser rank included the foremen, or captains, who were appointed from the list of eligible assistant foremen, or lieutenants. The lowest official rank was that of the assistant foreman who was appointed from the men who had held their rank for two years in the first class of the first grade of privates. Privates of the industrial army were divided into first, second, and third class, but each class also contained different grades and distinctions. Those who did not quite merit promotion could, therefore, be cited for honorable mention or prizes because of personal excellence; and, in this way, every man in the industrial army was provided with an incentive which was to make him work for either the coveted promotion or honor.

The germinal ideas for this organization of the administrative branch of the government of the year 2000 may have been suggested to Bellamy by the social service reform movement of the nineteenth century in the United States and the social service regulations existing in Sweden and England and by the general staffs of the great European armies. In 1876 in a *Union* editorial Bellamy had taken cognizance of the civil service reform movement when he had advocated changes in the government which would secure less "personal government" and insure that the administration would be sustained by measures and not by men—an objective which he was also to seek to fulfill in his ideal government.

In 1877, in summarizing in an editorial a paper entitled "Swedish Civil Service" by a former minister from the United States to Sweden, Bellamy had pointed out that the Swedish system was based upon educational requirements which stipulated that all lesser officials must have passed a high school examination and that all higher ones must have passed a non-competitive university examination. Though the king had the power to appoint officials to be given confidential duties, all other appointments were to be based wholly upon merit. Once appointed, members of the service could not be removed except by judicial trial; and they were, said Bellamy, "regarded precisely as officers of the Army are in America."

The administration of the government depicted in *Looking Backward* compared, wrote Bellamy in 1891, to the "officers of the general staff of one of the great European armies" with its departments of paymaster-general, commissariat, transportation, engineering and construction, ordnance, and government manufacturing establishments which supplied the army. This general staff had facilities which made it possible for it to know all the resources of the country; and, emphasized Bellamy, the efficiency and the success with which these administrators had fulfilled their duties presented a good argument for his type of government.

The administrative officials were to be divided into the ministerial and the discretionary classes; the discretionary class was to be comprised of those who held important posts, such as the headship of a department, and upon this group discretionary functions would devolve. The ministerial class, which would contain about ninety-nine percent of the officials, would be comparable to underlings of the army and would perform its duties according to routine or prescribed rules. The members of both groups, however, would have risen to their positions through the ranks as a result of their proved fitness for the services required of them. They would also have a soldier's sense of duty and desire for honor, rank, and power—but they were not to seek personal gain.

4. Efficient, Responsible Officials

In his *New Nation* articles Bellamy frequently stated that the most effective criticism of his critics—so far as its effect upon public acceptance of his plan was concerned—was that directed toward the problem of how responsible, efficient, and incorruptible officials could be obtained in the ideal state. Though the principles and aims of the new order had been explicitly stated, their inauguration and their achievement depended upon the officials of the nation—and Bellamy as well as his contemporaries was only too aware of the lack of responsibility and integrity of the governing class and of the corruptibility of parties and of the elective system.

Bellamy maintained, however, that the general principles and the special characteristics of the new social order; the specific stipulations as to merit, manner of election, and tenure; and the type of administration would guarantee the efficiency and the responsibility of the officials. Furthermore, the innovations of the new order which would insure conscientious service on the part of the agents of the people would also correct the basic situations which in the old order had contributed to the inefficiency and corruptibility of the officials and to the lackadaisical attitude of the citizenry toward government affairs.

The effect of the changed social environment, argued Bellamy, would make the selfish, profit-seeking motive of the nineteenth-century politician obsolete and impossible, for there would no longer be classes whose interests would be opposed to those of others. Since money would be non-existent and since all would have economic equality, there would be nothing with which to bribe another— and no reason for a man's succumbing to bribery. Since self-interest could not be separated from the interest of the whole, one could not hurt others without hurting oneself. Furthermore, the likelihood of such an attempt would be diminished by the fact that the public would be vigilant in regard to officials and government policies because its self-interest demanded that it be so. Since the only honors, promotions, power, and social distinctions would be those gained through practiced enthusiasm for humanity, as evinced in concrete services, only those who were recognized as having served humanity well—no matter how selfishly!—would be distinguished by being given public offices.

When Bellamy's critics demanded the whereabouts of the wonderful men that his "complicated machinery of government" would require, Bellamy asserted that unusual governmental genius would not be necessary for the management of his state—and that the wonderful men of their knowledge had been those noted for their "rare qualities of cunning and force" which had been required by the competitive, chaotic conditions of the nineteenth century. Though the new government was a vast machine, it would be relatively simple to operate because it rested on obvious and easily applied principles based on logic; only a fool, wrote Bellamy, could derange it, for it would practically run itself.

Bellamy also pointed out that the administrative duties and, subsequently, the worries of the national officials would be far simpler and less bothersome than those of the business executive of the nineteenth century because the operation of the industrial system—which was the primary concern of the government—would be scientifically organized on the principles of co-operation and co-ordination and because the fluctuations of the markets, the machinations of rival competitors, and bank failures would be non-existent. It was easier, stated Bellamy, for a general in a balloon with a perfect survey of his field to maneuver a million men to victory than for a sergeant in a thicket to manage a platoon.

To assure the proper functioning of the government of the year 2000, the officials needed only to have good common judgment, honesty, and industry. These were the essential qualities, for most of the work to be done was of the type that average minds—if they were working to their best ability—and average executive abilities could easily master and direct. But Bellamy sought to make sure that no average man who had not done his best, and would not continue to do so, would secure office, for, with his merit system, he hoped to secure "the most perfect aristocracy of government by the best" morally and intellectually, since merit would depend upon the value of the service rendered to the community. He actually hoped that in the year 2000 the greatest men and women would hold empire and tenure unselfishly but absolutely; and he expected the wisdom and intelligence of the well-educated citizenry to assure its not being led astray in its judgment of good leadership.

That Bellamy had some qualms as to the ability of the people to divorce themselves from self-interest, to recognize the best leadership, and to know the qualities that were necessary for successful administration of certain offices was shown, however, in the method he established for the election of the officials: limited suffrage. By instituting this tentative system of election, Bellamy tried to insure a lack of self-interest and of entangling alliances on the part of the electors and to assure to the elected official freedom to rule without dependence for preferment upon those most directly under his supervision.

Bellamy reasoned that if the industrial army were permitted to elect its own officers, such an election might result in intrigue, lack of discipline, and injury to the common good. He instituted, therefore, a plan which provided for the election of all officials above the rank of colonel by the alumni of the industrial army. These retired members would have an impersonal interest, so far as discipline was concerned, in the choice of a leader. Since their welfare would suffer if the officials selected were incompetent, they would be personally and vitally interested in choosing a man capable of fulfilling his duties. Because of their own experience which had given them a knowledge of the duties to be performed and therefore of the qualities the official should have, they would be best suited to select the administrator. A further result of this system of election was that all officials above the rank of colonel were stripped of appointive powers, which in the nineteenth century had been the backbone of the patronage system and of the political parties, neither of which existed in the year 2000.

Bellamy had had little to say in *Looking Backward* about tenure of office except for having stipulated the term of service of the president. In *Equality*, however, he sought to make the officials more sensitive to the public will and needs and to insure the mainte-

nance of democracy by instituting a system of recall. Though officials
were to be elected for a set term, this period was to be considered
as a convenience and not as an irrevocable grant of tenure. Officials
who at any moment seemed to fail in serving the public were to
have their power revoked by a vote of their electing body—and,
said Bellamy, public elections could be held a hundred times a year
if necessary!

This change which appeared in *Equality* was due to the influence
of Bellamy's critics and to his awareness of the need to introduce
measures which would insure democratic government. The general
attitudes, however, that he evinced in his Utopian novels toward
suffrage, the party system, and the elective system were the results
of his prior preoccupation with these institutions and of his observations of their effects in the society in which he lived. As early as
1867, Bellamy had not only considered the necessity of reforming the
method of electing the president so as to insure the true expression
of choice of the majority but, more important, had written in his
notebook devoted to thoughts on political economy that zeal had out-
run reason in the bestowal of the privilege of equal suffrage. Man-
hood alone was not a sufficient qualification for the exercise of the
power of voting, thought young Bellamy, for a degree of intelligence
and knowledge should also be required. Bellamy did not wish the
requirements to be so high that they could not be attained by the
majority, but he felt that all voters should be literate.

Though in his early unpublished manuscripts Bellamy had written
of the necessity of political parties in a republic as a method of promoting popular government, he had also deemed a clear comprehen-
sion of the philosophy and ethics of party obligations highly necessary. No man, he thought, owed any allegiance or loyalty to a
political party if his ideas did not coincide with those sponsored by
it; and anyone who voted the party ticket who was not in agreement
with its platform betrayed his country and the purpose of party
organization despite the fact that it had become customary for the
parties to censure deserters as traitors. To Bellamy, unthinking and
forced allegiance to parties was detrimental to progress and to reform;
and the use of party pressure was in sharp contradiction to the liberty
each citizen was supposed to have in his political opinions.

Years later, Bellamy also had much to say in his *Union* editorials about the true workings of suffrage and of the party system. Elections, he wrote, seemed a "wearisome vanity" and a "delusion and a snare"; during the din of arguments, mud-slinging, and profanity of the pre-election period, one felt that the electoral franchise was anything but a blessing. Compensations for this pandemonium were, to the ignorant and the young, recreation and holiday excitement and, to the older, more cultivated person, a feeling of "common intense interest," "a devoted strain of patriotic thought," and mental stimulation. Each person, however, was touched, according to his capacity, "with something of the ennobling feeling of belonging to a great brotherhood of men and a vast commonwealth of interests" and he was given at least "some inkling of what it is to think and act from broad and impersonal views of the general good."

Such mystical benefits were, however, offset by the effect of the party system upon the moral sense and the development of selfishness and greed. Bellamy denounced the avarice, bribery, and corruption of the party system which delivered the country into the hands of un-principled politicians—if not into the bondage of something worse. To these politicians, politics was an enriching business, and their intention was to make by whatever means they could as much money as possible while in office.

A contributing factor to this lack of personal morality was the effect of the party upon its members. Because of "subtle and varied causes" it destroyed the "simplicity of moral issues." By merging himself with his party, the politician or the citizen lost to some extent his individual conscience and was "actuated only by a sort of corporate public conscience, a much less delicate and reliable standard"; not only this, however, but he was prone to be "carried away by the tumultuous influence of a great multitude."

The principles of action of the political parties were, thought Bellamy, "derived from the traditions of dissimulation as formerly produced in diplomacy in an age when diplomats boasted of their cunning and triumphs by the use of the basest means of bribery and deceit." The effect of the rule of such principles led to lying to the public, to the slander and personal abuse of men, to fooling the public in respect to freedom of democratic discussion and action within the parties, and to the killing of such progressive movements as civil service reform which would be destructive to party patronage.

In *Looking Backward*, Bellamy instituted a system of election which destroyed all party interests and political parties; there was only one interest and one great party—that of the whole of the people. He sought also to insure the election of the best officials by making private politics impossible and by making the electors those who were best qualified to act. Though Bellamy was not so outspoken in *Looking Backward* as he had been in his *Union* editorials about his opinions of the party system and the elective system, he doubtless created the system he did because of these. In *Equality*, however, he flatly stated what he had avoided concluding in his *Union* editorials: he charged that the parties were under the control of the rich who contributed large sums to their campaign funds. Party bosses selected the candidates for their own purposes, and the people had only the choice of choosing from not-too-promising candidates who, when elected, would be controlled and used by the plutocrats. Wealth controlled, therefore, the government through the buying of votes and through the control of the party bosses who relied upon the rich for money. The only reformation that would insure the restoration of democracy and the incorruptibility and responsibility of the officials was that which would give all people economic equality and a common interest.

5. The Distribution of Commodities

Since all forms of production were "held in trust by the nation for the people," it necessarily followed that all means of distribution of commodities be maintained by the government which could organize them in a scientific fashion. This centralized distributive control would insure savings to the consumer since the "parasitical middlemen"—the drummers, the advertising agencies, and the wholesalers and retailers—and the corrupt business of adulteration and misrepresentation of the products would no longer exist.

Ethically, this change of distributive methods would be of value to the nation and to the individual. Commerce—which had been so feared by Jefferson as corruptive of government and individuals and which had been condemned by Bellamy as an anti-social influence since it was based upon the principle of self-seeking—was to be placed on a non-profit basis. Individually, men occupied with distribution would be saved from misrepresentation and from tempting the consumer to buy, for their livelihood would no longer depend upon the profit made from a sale. The method of distribution was, therefore, to be in harmony with the basis of the ideal state: mutual benevolence and community of interests.

The physical facilities for the distribution of products consisted of central warehouses, government stores, and delivery service. All products first went to the centrally located warehouses, and only samples of them were displayed in the stores where the potential customers might examine them and read the government labels specifying price, quality, and durability. The clerks who served the customers merely took and recorded the orders, made the charges, and sent the orders to the warehouse in a despatch box by way of pneumatic tubes which connected the corresponding departments of the store and the warehouse.

When the order was received in the warehouse, it was rapidly filled and the material was sent by pneumatic tubes to the city district in which the purchaser lived. By the time the shopper had returned to his residence, the purchase had been delivered. Rural areas were also supplied with the same service, though the warehouse might be twenty miles from the sample store!

Shopping in the ideal world was greatly simplified by the lack of duplication of both products and stores, by the nonexistence of high-pressure salesmanship and advertising, and by the existence of merchandise of unquestionable quality. Because of the tremendous savings made by this system of distribution, shopping was also more economical, for the price paid for a product was virtually the cost of production plus a small charge for the cost of distribution. In comparing the prices of the products of the year 2000 with those of the nineteenth century, Bellamy estimated that one-half or one-third of the price of the product under the old system of distribution had consisted of the costs of rent, salesmen, advertising, accountants, transportation, and repeated handling; though some of these costs still existed, they had been greatly reduced and the savings were passed on to the consumer.

The basic price of the product in the ideal world depended upon the number of hours or upon the arduousness of the labor involved in its production. The factor of scarcity also affected the price of such commodities as fresh vegetables which were out of season or articles which required highly skilled workmanship or which were made of rare materials. High prices for such products did not, however, mean that only the rich could buy them—for all had equal incomes. Since the staples of life were always to be in abundance, their prices were rarely to be affected by scarcity; to assure this, the government maintained a surplus so great that poor crops could not create a shortage. Though Bellamy stated that the price of staples was to decrease continually, he did not explain how this was to be attained.

6. The International Council

Though the products which could not be produced by the United States were imported by the government on the basis of demand, all international trade was conducted by the country's foreign trade bureau and was regulated by the International Council. The foreign trade bureau, which managed both the importation and the exportation of produce, had as its duties the estimating of the amount needed, the sending of the orders to the other countries, and the notifying of other countries of any changes in production. Although Bellamy did not say so, this bureau had also, in all probability, to notify the chiefs of departments of the surplus that would have to be produced if the country were to fulfill its foreign or export obligations. This bureau also had to decide, no doubt, whether the wares to be imported were requisite for the general welfare, since Bellamy stipulated that this was to be the principle of importation.

In *Equality* Bellamy expanded his statements relative to foreign trade in order to show the reasons for its decrease in the year 2000 and the fallacies of the theory of the nineteenth century that such trade brought general prosperity. He also delineated not only the threat that had existed in the nineteenth century of an international plutocratic regime which could have resulted from the wealth and power of the merchant princes but the possibilities that a form of world government could develop in the future from the International Council.

The decrease in foreign trade that had resulted from the establishment of the new order was due to the fact that each industrial democracy had the ambition to be as self-sufficient as possible. As a result of the equalization of culture and of the knowledge of science and the mechanical arts, each country had become more capable of fulfilling this ambition because it was more able to develop its natural resources and its industries; to be unable to do so was considered humiliating. Furthermore, diversified industry was considered beneficial to the citizens since it provided a variety of jobs and had a mind-awakening influence upon the citizenry. Because of these developments and influences, the principle was that each country would trade only enough to supply its people with the essential products that it was incapable of producing.

In the nineteenth century, international trade, which had resulted in the deliberate economic vassalage of the backward countries and of colonies in order to secure foreign markets, had been conducted by private enterprise for profit. The generally accepted theory relative to this foreign trade had been that it brought prosperity to the industrialized country and that it was the result of the natural differences of resources and cultural development existing among countries. Bellamy, however, believed that foreign commerce had had only a deceptive utility for a country generally and that it had enriched only a few specifically. Foreign markets were necessary, wrote Bellamy in 1892, for the unloading of surplus products—because the citizens lacked the equality of wealth necessary to make them consumers. As a result, the shoes and clothing needed by the populace had to be foisted upon Africans and Asians.

The condition of the people who produced the exported wares was worse, Bellamy argued in *Equality,* than it had been before the country entered the world market because competition between countries forced the wages down to the level of those of the lowest-standard-of-living industrialized nation. Furthermore, both the agricultural and the industrial workers became dependent, because of international trade, upon the "delicate balance of a complex set of international adjustments," and their living standards were no longer wholly dependent upon local situations but were affected by those of other countries and their catastrophes. Because the capitalists, who were powerful as a result of their large-scale production, could crush the enterprises of the beginning and weaker industrialists, home industries were frequently not developed, and a country became dependent upon the produce of another nation and upon the terms of trade the powerful capitalist wished to offer. Such a situation, reflected Bellamy, had been the cause of the American Revolution.

Bellamy also pointed out that free trade and protective tariff meant nothing to the people of a country. Free trade was advocated by the industrialist strong enough to enter the world market without fear of competition of others; and the protective tariff was sponsored by the weak and beginning industrialist who wished to build a protective wall around his country in order to have a chance to grow. For the people generally, trade conducted by private enterprise meant exploitation by either the home or the foreign capitalist; and one could be expected to be no more considerate than the other. Because of the wealth and the subsequent power the world traders had amassed, they threatened to establish a world plutocratic empire that would be more powerful than any envisioned by Napoleon or Alexander.

To prevent the evils of international trade, Bellamy instituted, therefore, the International Council, which maintained peaceful relations among the countries by inspecting the products exchanged, by establishing the policies toward backward countries, by enforcing the rule that no product could be sold to another country for more than it would bring on the home market, and by balancing and supervising the settling of the accounts of the nations.

The International Council examined the books of every foreign trade bureau, and it cleared the accounts among nations by a system of debit and credit. If, for example, France owed the United States, the latter might be in debt to England which might be in debt to France; by arranging the credits and the debits among these countries, the International Council avoided an exchange of goods in settlement of the accounts, and only the country left with a balance had to pay its debt. The payment was made whenever the Council ordered it, and it was made in the form of staples that had been listed as acceptable in the preliminary trade agreement.

The questions that arise as a result of the consideration of this plan are many. What arrangements would be made if the country left with a balance did not produce the staples that might have been listed as acceptable payment by the country to which, due to the switch of credits and debits, it was in debt? With this system of settlements, how could the preliminary arrangements provide for settlements, since the country would not know what nation it would have to settle with; and how could it insure production of the necessary surplus of the staple, since it would not know which country's needs were to be met?

Aside from its regulation of foreign trade, the International Council also arranged a credit and debit system which permitted both travel and emigration. Bellamy's dream was that one result of the pecuniary equality, the universal vacations, and the leisure made possible by the new order would be more travel for pleasure and less for business reasons; he therefore planned that any person holding a credit card could travel in any other country. All that was required was that upon arrival in another country, the traveller would take his card to the foreign branch of the International Council and there exchange it for the credit card of the host nation. The amount of the credit given him would of course be charged to the account of the visitor's homeland in favor of the country issuing the temporary credit card.

Migration was arranged by a similar system of international indemnities. If, for example, an American worker twenty-one years old migrated to France, the United States would have lost the investment made in his rearing and education and France would have gained a worker; France, therefore, would have to make an allowance to the United States. If, however, a worker nearing retirement age migrated to France, the United States would have to credit France with an allowance for his support. Indemnities varied, therefore, to suit the case or the status of the migrant.

Though the International Council of the year 2000 had no power or right to interfere with the internal affairs of a nation, it was a federal system of autonomous nations which Bellamy envisioned as developing into a world government, the ultimate form of society and the social ideal to Bellamy. In *Equality,* this world union was pictured as bringing about peace, the cessation of economic strife which had resulted in more fatalities than actual warfare, and the end of the petty rancors and jealousies which had embittered one nation against another. This unification on a world basis was to have resulted from economic equality, fraternal sympathy, and mutual understanding and good will.

Bellamy's dream of one world was an old one, for in 1870 he had stated in a speech that he had written that he did not base his "faith in the good time coming," the federation of the world, upon "the mystical hyperbole of Jewish seers" nor upon any "subjective transcendental philosophies" but upon deductions made from evident social and political trends. Regarding the lack of facilities of communication as a source of the mutual misunderstandings among nations which bred narrow and intense prejudices, Bellamy thought that modern inventions such as the telegraph, steamships, newspapers, and railroads as well as the commercial and cultural relationships they made possible would bring nations "into closest relations of mutual interests." As a result of this intercourse, ignorance of other nations would be dispelled because their mores and habits would be studied. As a result of this study, "a selection . . . of the peculiar excellencies of every nation of the cosmos for the use of humanity" would be compiled.

Politically and socially, this union had received encouragement from the spirit of philanthropy which recognized no boundaries and from the expansion the world over of the idea of the federal system of government which permitted local supervision of local matters and central supervision of matters of common concern. The application of this principle to the world would bring a world federal government into being—and Bellamy optimistically stated that such a union might be effected within a hundred years.

To accomplish this union, the only prerogatives the nations of the world would have to yield would be those the human family had surrendered when a government had been established: the right to do lawless violence to another; the right of the strong to oppress the weak; and the right to squander money and men in warfare. The advantages to be gained would be the salvation of the fruits of industry wasted in war and of the talents of men killed in battle as well as a cessation of the double-dealing diplomacy which had often resulted in war and in the humiliation of one nation by another. When all disputes were settled in a world court by arbitration and when all nations lived in security and peace, the energies wasted in war could be used for the advancement of the common good.

7. Legislation

The role played by the Federal Congress in the government received very little attention in *Looking Backward,* for Bellamy merely stated that it convened every five years for the purpose of receiving and acting upon the report of the retiring president and of electing him, upon approval of his report, to the International Council. The legislature also accepted and evaluated the reports of the retiring chiefs of departments and determined whether they were eligible or not for the presidency. The regents of the professional army also submitted reports to the Congress. Bellamy did not state, however, why these reports were made to the legislature, what powers it had to modify administration policies, or, for that matter, what the qualifications of the legislators were or what groups of citizens elected or selected them.

Bellamy did state most specifically, however, that the legislature rarely passed a law. The Congress which wished to inaugurate a law had only the right to commend that it be passed to the Congress which would convene five years later and which could pass the bill. This, said Bellamy rather unnecessarily, prevented doing things too hastily!

This lack of legislative power and of legislation was made possible by the fact that the social order rested on a basis of fundamental principles which settled once and for all the problems and misunderstandings which had been the cause of the great mass of complex laws of the nineteenth century. Nearly all of the laws of that benighted era had dealt with property and trade problems; in the year 2000, since no private property existed other than personal possessions and salaries and since the government controlled and operated all commercial affairs, such legislation was unnecessary. Despite the fact that little legislation was needed to control things, Bellamy stated that the legislature would have more power over them than over men, since sumptuary laws were spurned and since laws governing the social relations of men were unnecessary, for crime had virtually disappeared.

Bellamy's attitudes toward legislatures and laws were also the result of the criticism he had trained upon those of his own period and of the considerations he had given to reforming them. As early as 1867 he had been concerned with a reform of the legislature which would secure more adequate representation for minority groups. In 1872 he had insisted that the characters of the representatives rather than their ideas be voted upon, for, after all, they were to act upon matters determined by their constituents. In a review in 1876 of an anonymous pamphlet entitled *Lessons of the Century,* Bellamy remarked that the work was radical in its suggestion that the presidency and the legislature be abolished and that they be replaced by a house of deputies which would always be in session and whose members would be subject to recall at the will of the constituents who were also to vote upon all important laws.

The reasons for Bellamy's early interest in the reform of Congress may be found in his criticisms of legislators of his day whom he denounced for having carried the profit principle and the business man's conscience into the legislature. In *The Duke of Stockbridge,* Bellamy showed how the power of wealth influenced the legislature and resulted in the repeal of laws passed in critical periods for the amelioration of the conditions of the people, in the passage of laws beneficial only to special interests, and in the delusion of the legislators by lawyers able to " 'fool 'em so they didn't do a thing.' " The cures, thought Bellamy, of the ills of the legislative body were a higher moral sensibility and a higher and more clarified conscientiousness which would prevent its selling out the people to special interests.

Because of his experience in the legal profession, Bellamy never ceased to castigate the chicanery of lawyers or to criticize the complexity of the laws which not only made lawyers necessary but permitted them to find legal loop-holes to circumvent the achievement of justice. Because of the intricacies of the law and the greed of lawyers for money, rogues and swindlers were made secure; furthermore, the possibilities of postponing trials, of dragging out cases, of demanding costly retrials, and, in the case of murderers, of pleading emotional insanity, gave criminals further protection.

Regarding laws as being of little value unless the people were prepared to accept them, Bellamy stated that the greatest deterrent to effective laws, or an effective enforcement of them, was the popular acceptance of the maxim "every man for himself and the devil take the hindmost" as the general code of action. Without a reform of the social order which so emphasized the profit principle and without one in the hearts of men and of their ethical principles, laws would be futile, no matter how stringent they might be.

After consideration of these early ideas expressed in his novels and his editorials, it is easy to comprehend why Bellamy believed that the brotherly love, the mutual interests, the economic equality, and the use of the Golden Rule as the principle of action in the year 2000 would destroy the need for much legislation as well as the motivations for transgression. In the new era, the laws that existed were to be couched in language that could easily be comprehended by all. Furthermore, there was to be no conflict between the laws and the morality of the people such as had existed in the nineteenth century when the punishment of a thief had seemed unjust and ironical since the whole economic system had been based on the appropriation by a few through fraud or force of the country's natural resources or of the fruits of the labor of others.

Bellamy asserted that crime would become almost non-existent in the new society because the conditions that helped to promote it would have been eradicated. Everyone would have all that he needed; and, because of this, there would be no reason to steal or to feel class hatred, envy, or jealousy; furthermore, this lack of class friction would make it impossible for communist demagogues to inspire the oppressed to acts of violence destructive of the social fabric and of property. Children would no longer be morally deformed by working in factories or by living in homes and districts which bred vice and crime; and adults would have their strong, natural, personal passions bridled by their sense of duty to the community. Even crimes incited by the sexual instinct would have ceased to occur— Bellamy argued in 1891 in his criticism of William Morris' *News*

from Nowhere—for the idea of "sexual proprietorship in one another" would have become obsolete in a society permitting the
absolute autonomy and independence made possible by economic
equality. Bellamy also argued that education and refinement, as
they increased the individual horizon and perspective, would make
not only the aspects of life pertaining to the individuality of less
importance but the calculation of consequences instinctive.

The few criminals who might exist in the year 2000 were to be
regarded as abnormalities or as cases of atavism since the rational
motives for committing crimes no longer existed. These transgressors
were to be treated in hospitals with the compassion and firmness
shown to the kleptomaniacs with whom they were comparable. Laws
governing such cases and jails were, therefore, known in the year
2000 only as institutions which had existed in the past.

Not only were there to be no laws regulating the punishment of
criminals but there were to be none pertaining to personal behavior
in self-regarding matters. Because of the spirit of personal sovereignty, the citizens of the year 2000 would not tolerate the legal
interference with individual practices which had existed in the old
order. This attitude toward sumptuary legislation was a reflection
of the position Bellamy had maintained in his *Union* editorials and in
his plot for a satirical Utopian story which would portray the world
that would result from prohibitory laws. In one of his editorials of
1873, Bellamy had called such legislation "the distinctive hobby of
this generation"; and in 1874 he had accused the advocates of laws
prohibiting the consumption of tea, coffee, and wine of being people
who needed instruction not only in the need of respect for individual
privacy but in the art of minding their own business. Man, wrote
Bellamy, should be his brother's keeper—but this did not mean that
he was to be his brother's jailer!

Bellamy condemned prohibitory legislation as being an unscientific cure of the social ills since it was purely a symptomatic treatment
that was a confession of inability to deal with the basic causes. In
the year 2000 the logical and scientific organization of society would
automatically accomplish the ends so vainly sought by sumptuary
legislation, for the causes would have been exterminated. Because
of the moral, economic, intellectual effects of economic equality, men

would at last have achieved a state of grace which would enable them to live in almost a state of anarchy so far as a lack of punitive and coercive regulations was concerned. This state of anarchy would apply, however, only to the social life of the nation, for a coordinating government of industrial affairs would always be necessary.

In *Equality* Bellamy recognized, as he had not in *Looking Backward,* the need of laws; and the changes that he introduced were foreshadowed by those he had advocated in his articles in *The New Nation.* In these he had recommended the introduction of initiative and referendum which had worked so well in Switzerland and which had been advocated in the United States by the People's Party and by labor organizations as the means of securing more direct popular government and of rescuing the government from politicians and lawyers. By incorporating referendum and initiative as well as recall as the means of regulating legislation and of insuring the maintenance of democratic procedures, Bellamy not only indicated that laws relating to public policies would be necessary but he increased the role played by Congress which in *Looking Backward* had been ludicrously ineffective as a law-making body and had been merely a report-receiving group. The status of the legislature in *Equality* was comparable to that of a congressional committee only, however, for the people proposed most of the bills to it and they voted directly upon all laws of more than routine importance. Since the entire nation was organized so that it could act as one large congress when necessary and since the people directly conducted the affairs of the nation which so vitally concerned them, Bellamy was instituting the true democracy of the New England town meeting. Such participation on the part of the whole population was made possible by modern methods of communication which enabled the government to record and to report the mass vote quickly.

Bellamy not only gave the people a greater voice in the government but, by instituting recall, he greatly curtailed the power of their representatives and made them more responsible and sensitive reflectors and agents of the people. In making these changes, Bellamy decreased the possibility of tyranny and dictatorship which had so worried his critics and men like B. O. Flower when they had considered the plan advocated in *Looking Backward.*

8. The Judicial System

The systematized, economic organization which made it possible
to guarantee social and economic equality for all and thereby to
decrease the number of crimes had also made it possible to reduce
the number of laws, to delegate less power to the legislature, and
to dispense with the study of law as a profession. The effect of
these achievements upon the judicial system was portrayed by Bellamy
in *Looking Backward,* and the outline of the judiciary's functions
and form was left unchanged in *Equality.*

Since the new government had merely evolved from the old, the
general outline of the court system seemingly remained the same;
the major innovations were those which affected the training and
appointment of judges and the methods of trying cases. The Supreme
Court still existed as the guardian of the Constitution, but the members were no longer appointed by the president—they were elected
from judges serving in the minor courts by the retiring judges of
these courts. The judges of the lower courts were, however, appointed by the president for a five-year term. These judges were no
longer required to have been students of the law; they were to be,
however, men and women over the age of forty-five who were
judicious, discreet, and widely informed.

Trials in the new state were few, for those charged with a crime
invariably pleaded guilty, for they knew that, if found guilty, they
would receive, because of having lied, a heavier sentence. Those who
pleaded not guilty were tried by three judges, two of whom were
appointed by the judge who heard the plea of the accused. These
two judges studied and stated the opposite sides of the case, and
they did so without bias since they had none of the economic reasons
for lying or for coloring the facts which had motivated the lawyers
of the nineteenth century. If the judges trying the case could not
agree upon a verdict when all the evidence had been presented, the
case had to be tried again.

The judges of the new order had the task also of serving as
arbitrators in all labor difficulties. When a complaint of unfair
treatment was lodged by a worker against an official, one judge
tried the case; in graver matters, three judges officiated. It was,

wrote Bellamy, the duty of the court to enforce justice and civility in the industrial army.

After the publication of *Looking Backward* and in a *New Nation* article of 1892, Bellamy lambasted the court system of his era as being one that defeated the administration of justice because of the delays in trials caused by the technicalities and legal finesses of the system and because of the high costs of legal procedures which made justice too costly for the poor man. He defended the system outlined in his Utopia by showing that justice would be quickly rendered, that a hearing could be afforded by all, that the case would not be purposefully muddled by the presence of lawyers, and that the efficient and speedy execution of justice would have a sound moral effect. These criticisms of the legal system of his day were those which had been made by a commission appointed to investigate the judiciary of Massachusetts—and which Bellamy had incorporated in one of his *Union* editorials of 1877.

In fact, a review of Bellamy's criticisms of the judiciary system prior to the writing of *Looking Backward* shows that the changes he introduced in it in his novel were not only the result of the form of his ideal state but of his previous observations and criticisms. In 1872 in a *Union* editorial, Bellamy had ascribed the prevalence of lynchings to the inadequacies of the judicial system, and he had warned that faith in it could only be restored by the use of legal methods which would insure a more honest and a more faithful discharge of duties on the part of the ministers of justice. He had argued also that so long as the transgressors of the law could elect the ministers of justice, there could be no safeguard which would insure an independent and pure judiciary; he had recommended, therefore, that the appointment of judges be divorced from politics.

Bellamy also condemned the jury system as being both obsolete and inefficient. In editorials written in 1872, 1873, 1875, he had averred that the jury system which was responsible for the escape of many criminals had been inaugurated originally to save the people from monarchial oppression but that it had become the people's enemy since it could be swayed by the newspapers which not only informed but influenced the opinions of the populace. Bellamy had advocated that either the jury be made more effective—as it had been in England—by no longer being required to render a unanimous but a majority verdict, or that the whole jury system be discarded and replaced by a more efficient method of achieving justice—such as that of letting the judges hearing the case determine the guilt or the innocence of the defendant. Bellamy had recognized, however, that great caution would have to be exercised in the selection of the judges if they were to be delegated such power.

In this last-mentioned reform, Bellamy had suggested the one that he was to introduce in the ideal state—and he had also recognized the weakness which was to characterize the judicial system of the new era, for it was not to rely upon legal precedent but upon the wisdom, integrity, conscientiousness, and impartiality of the judges. Though Bellamy indicated in *Looking Backward* that the minor judges were to be appointed and that they in turn were to elect the superior judges, he made no provision for the dismissal of the inadequate judge. Though he provided for the retrial of a case in which the judges did not reach a unanimous verdict, he also made no specific mention of the possibility of an appeal to a higher court. Though Bellamy may have felt that these were details to be filled in by the generation that would perfect his system, they are weaknesses in his plan which are particularly important to this present generation which has been made aware of the miscarriages of justice in the courts of Hitler and Stalin.

9. The Result of Industrial Democracy: Wealth

Though Bellamy regarded the primary concern of living to be the expansion of the intellectual and spiritual potentialities of men, he believed that this development could be made possible only by achieving a resolution of the economic problems—and these had to be resolved in such a way that the end results would provide the wealth, the moral atmosphere, and the leisure and security necessary for the moral, social, and intellectual development of men. Bellamy had, therefore, the task not only of erecting an ethical social structure which would insure economic advantages but of convincing his critics that industrial democracy would do so.

In *Looking Backward* Bellamy presented the picture of the ideal world of "abundance and comfort" at the price of moderate exertion which he had spoken of as being possible in his lyceum address of the early 1870's, and he incorporated as the bases of this new order many principles and ideas which he had considered in his *Union* editorials. Though he also condemned in his first Utopian novel the industrial order of the nineteenth century as being economically imbecilic because it had not fully developed the monopolistic or co-operative principle, Bellamy was not to depict its economic follies in great detail until he wrote articles for *The New Nation* and his novel *Equality;* in the latter, five chapters are devoted to portraying the stupidities and the maleficent effects of private capitalism.

As his *Union* articles show, Bellamy had long searched for the causes of the business crises which had endangered the life of the nation, and he had eventually formulated his own theory about them. In his editorials of 1875, Bellamy repeatedly denounced the theory that over-production resulted in hard times, for production was actually the source of the nation's wealth. If over-production caused hard times, it was because the needs of the Chinese and Japanese markets had been overestimated or because farming, the source of raw materials, was being neglected for manufacturing. If the neglect of farming were intimately associated with the causes of such financial crises, the solution might be to assign the proper ratio of men to the farms and to the factories and to decrease the number of speculators and middlemen engaged in non-productive activities.

In 1877, Bellamy once more considered the theory that over-production was the cause of poverty and business depressions, and he cited an article by a Mr. Bunce that had been published in the *Popular Science Monthly*. According to this article, machinery and mass production had rendered the industrial age especially liable to over-production in certain departments, and this had led to confusion and depression because, wrote Bellamy, "production and consumption do not have the intimate relation to each other which they had when industrial development was in a ruder stage." The old-time weaver, for example, had woven cloth as he discovered the need for it; and supply and demand had gone hand in hand. Factories had replaced the weaver, and they had unlimited powers of production but "no accurate relation to consumption." Because of this, the "old-fashioned nice and sensitive balance between producer and consumer" had disappeared. Speculation took the helm, and more was produced than there was grain to exchange for it; and, long after the old-fashioned producer would have felt the glut on the market and have ceased producing, "the mills, borrowing money from banks, go on piling up their fabrics, running at a loss, to crush rivals or manipulate the market." This situation was inevitably followed by a crash, unemployment, and a "weary convalescence."

The only solution, asserted Bellamy, was co-operation among producers to limit the production of goods and to relate what was produced to the needs of the community; and this had been done by the Pennsylvania coal barons who—for far different reasons!—had combined to regulate production and stabilize prices. Furthermore, the wisdom of regulatory measures could be proved by the condition of France; in a period in which Germany, England, and the United States were suffering stagnation, France was prosperous—and she was a country of small producers who did not engage in speculative production and one in which the old-fashioned relation of production to consumption had remained undisturbed.

In these editorials Bellamy had evinced his awareness of the relationship of production and wealth, of the necessity of having few middlemen and of assigning men to the work needing to be done, and of the value of controlling production so that equilibrium was maintained between consumption and production. Although all of these ideas were to be used in his Utopian novels, Bellamy was also to portray an increase in consumption, and therefore of production, as a result of dispensing with the profit system and of introducing economic equality.

The strongest defense of the capitalistic system had been its efficiency in the production of wealth; but Bellamy, directing his attack at this argument in his Utopian novels, found it to be the Achilles' heel of private enterprise. He denounced the system as being unscientific, unorganized, unstable, undirected, and inefficient; and he asserted that it resulted in spasmodic and speculative production of wealth for the few and in general poverty for the many. To replace an order which actually prevented production, Bellamy recommended a scientific, stabilized, concerted, directed, integrated industrial system which would produce general wealth by solving the problem of getting "the greatest results out of the national resources of a country and the capital and labor of a people."

Bellamy's fundamental law for the production of wealth was that production was limited by consumption and that economic equality, which made possible the widest and fairest distribution of wealth, increased and stabilized production. To achieve the production of wealth, Bellamy relied upon the effects of co-operation and integrated action; they were, to him, not only the basic factors in the science of wealth production but the source of the freedom, morality, solidarity, and happiness of the social order. Positively, scientifically organized state industries would utilize all of the talents of the citizens and all of the inventions and natural resources; negatively, they would avoid the wastes of private enterprise which were largely the results of middlemen, rent, profit, and interest; the duplication of plants and handling; and the lack of scientific co-ordination between production and consumption.

Production was to be regulated in the year 2000 by the bureau of statistics of the distributive department which kept a record of all sales. On the basis of these figures, plus an allowance made for security, the production of staples was achieved. For the production of novelties, the sale of which fluctuated with the public taste, figures were provided weekly so that production would be barely ahead of consumption. To insure the gratification of special tastes, Bellamy insisted that small minorities were to have the right to petition the administration to produce what they wanted—but the price would depend on the cost of manufacturing the demanded article. The result of the integration of the requirements of the people with the production was that gluts in the market of both merchandise and labor ceased to occur and that the mad search for foreign markets was halted. Business crises and unemployment became, therefore, things of the past.

State-controlled industry also dispensed with profit, interest, rent, middlemen, advertising, complex systems of handling transactions, speculation with the product, the credit system, and the necessity of multiple handling and shipping of the produce. Though the sole motivation of private production had been profit, Bellamy asserted that under such uncertain conditions profits had been necessary to

encourage investments and enterprise. Under the old order each
business had been a veritable fortress which had had its guns trained
on other fortresses—for men had had to battle to succeed, and in the
strife many businesses had become defunct and energies wasted.
Since the investor had risked such fatality, his profits on his investment had had to be more than the current rate of interest; furthermore, they had had to be sufficient to cover the cost of insurance on
the endangered capital. If the investor personally administered the
business, he had had the right to further compensation for his skill,
judgment, and energy. The capitalist, therefore, could not be considered a "moral monster"; he had been also the victim of the com-
plexities, mistakes, risks, and wastes of a business system comparable
to a lottery "in which the blanks greatly outnumbered the prizes."

In the year 2000 the profit motive was replaced by the aim of
general wealth and maintenance for all. With the distribution of the
wealth afforded by economic equality and with the lack of profits,
etc., which had diminished the consuming power of the public, there
would be no limit to the production since consumption would be
unlimited. In making this statement, Bellamy forgot, however, that
production and hence consumption could be limited by the natural
resources and by the efficiency and ability of the industrial army.

Bellamy also asserted that, since production would be unlimited
and since the total labor force would be fruitfully employed, inventions would be utilized for the first time for the benefit of all and
that they too would contribute to the general wealth of the nation.
Under private enterprise, the introduction of new machinery, new
ideas, and new inventions had often inconvenienced the employee
by making him jobless and the employer by necessitating large out-
lays of capital to change his system of production or by making his
product no longer salable. To save himself, the capitalist had frequently purchased the patent right in order to keep an invention or
a product from being made available.

Though inventions had helped to bring about the industrial
order that was to develop into industrial democracy, they had not
benefited the general mass despite the fact that they had greatly
increased man's ability to produce. They had resulted in a glut in
the labor and the produce markets and the result had been unemploy-

ment and lower wages. Furthermore, argued Bellamy, the savings which inventions had made possible in the cost of production—or in the ability to produce more at the same labor cost—had rarely been passed on to the consumer when times were normal in the form of lower prices but had been used to swell the capitalist's profits. Inventions had increased, therefore, the wealth of the minority and had enabled it to gain power more rapidly instead of banishing poverty and improving the social environment—as many Utopians had dreamed they would.

Under industrial democracy, however, this dream of the Utopians that invention and science would bring comfort, peace, and wealth to mankind would be realized. Inventions would be welcomed by everyone since the interest of all was the increase of the common fund and since the directed and integrated character of industry would permit quick and harmless adjustments to new innovations. If a new invention eliminated certain tasks, the laborer would not be unemployed; because of his vocational adaptability, he would merely be shifted to another position. The favorable attitude of the citizenry would also be increased by the fact that, since all of them had had at one time to do the "dirty work" of the nation while in the general labor corps, all would be interested in the perfection of labor-saving devices which would make work of all kinds easier.

The government would, therefore, not only utilize all inventions but encourage inventors by offering them honors and public recognition. A further incentive—and basically a more important one— would be the state's willingness to provide facilities for experimentation with new devices or methods. Since inventions would contribute to the development of man's intellectual and spiritual qualities by providing him with more leisure for meditation and study and by freeing him from the material cares which often destroyed serenity of mind, they would be regarded as essential, for they would be a means of fulfilling the primary aim of the new order.

The wealth of the nation was also to be increased by the fact that, with the cessation of economic warfare, world peace had been established and that nations no longer had to squander wealth in maintaining large armies and navies or in making the materials required by war. The only victories to be celebrated in the year 2000 were those won through co-operative labor over poverty, misery, and immorality—victories which had been impossible when wars were a constant occurrence, for they had not only squandered the resources of the nations but they had halted social progress. Indeed, wrote Bellamy, wars had been used by monarchs to divert the people from attempting to realize their social dreams!

Other wealth-increasing economies of the new order were those made possible by the lack of revenue officials and of large numbers of policemen, judges, sheriffs, lawyers, tramps, and criminals. The labor force was increased and the burden of the community decreased by the use of these men and the invalids in the labor corps and by the eventual decrease—because of the better environment and the practice of eugenics—of the number of those physically and mentally incompetent. The productive capacity of the nation was also increased by the fact that no talents were wasted since all were given an equal education and an equal opportunity to rise according to merit. Further savings which increased the wealth of the nation were also made possible not only by scientific organization of the whole of industry but by the innovation of co-operative kitchens and laundries which diminished the duplication of tools and facilities which had been so necessary but so wasteful under the old order.

In the year 2000 the wealth of the nation was also to be aggrandized by the utilization of all the forces of nature—such as the tides—to supply power and by the preservation of the natural resources. In his *Union* editorials, Bellamy had stated that the waste of forests had resulted in floods and erosion, and he had preached the necessity of the conservation of all natural resources as well as of the chemicals found in sewage. In *Equality*, he showed that reforestation had been one of the earliest programs inaugurated by the new government and that the sewage was returned to the soil in the form of ashes.

Though Bellamy had recognized the unhappy plight of the American farmer in his *Union* editorials and in *The Duke of Stockbridge*, he had made no mention in *Looking Backward* of the effect the new order would have in remedying his economic problems. In his *New Nation* articles, however, he discussed these problems, and this for good reason—*Looking Backward* had become exceedingly popular with the farm revolt groups and in the primarily agricultural regions of the Far and Middle West. To Bellamy, the ageless depressed condition of the farmer was to be attributed to his lack of educational and social facilities; to his isolation, which made combination for political or economic action almost impossible; to his inability to control his working hours; and to the impossibility of his regulating his produce since he could not control nature. Bellamy also wrote in these articles that the situation of the farmer in the 1890's was to be ascribed to the fact that farming remained in the stage of individual operation by small capitalists—a condition entailing economic wastes and disadvantages—when other businesses were being conducted on a large scale by consolidated capital. Because of these factors, Bellamy argued that cheaper transportation rates and/or lower rates of interest would not permanently help the farmer; only syndication or Nationalism would do that—and Bellamy feared that the former would merely substitute the selfishness of the group for that of the individual. No group, Bellamy stated repeatedly, needed Nationalism more than the farmer, for it was his only route to salvation.

In *Equality*, Bellamy included these ideas which he had expressed in his articles relative to the cause and the remedy of the farmer's plight; but he also delineated the social and scientific revolution that had transpired in the year 2000 in farm life. The unequal burden of labor carried by the farmer, which had made farm life disagreeable and which had resulted in the desertion of the land for the factory, had been equalized. Shorter working hours for the farmer had been made possible by shifting relays of men from one part of the country to another to do the heavy seasonal work, and by employing the machinery which had been used on the large bonanza farms of the nineteenth century. The employment of this machinery did not ruin the farmers by making it possible to produce bumper crops which in the nineteenth century had brought ruin to the small farmer by cutting the market price below the cost of production; the farmer as well as the other citizens benefited from the lower prices that resulted.

Productivity was also increased by scientific geoponic methods which were used in the digging of ditches for drainage or for irrigation and in the cultivation of the land in such a way as to

conserve it or to increase its fertility. Intensive cultivation was
employed also in greenhouses so that vegetables were produced for
the winter market—and the picture of the methods employed
suggests the introduction of hydroponics.

Farming, the staple and essential industry of the nation, was
also made more attractive as an occupation because of the centrally
located villages in which the farmers could live and from which they
could commute to their work. Because of this community life and
because of the invention of television and radio—which Bellamy
described as existing—the social and cultural advantages and opportunities prevented farming from being a mind-and a soul-killing
vocation. Far greater in its general effect upon human felicity and
security than these innovations, however, was that of the state-
operated farm which released the farmer once and for all from
slavery to the holder of his mortgage and from his victimization by
the middlemen and the speculators. The farmer was also freed
from his dependence upon the whims of nature, for the state and
not the farmer bore the loss when the weather was not conducive
to the production of crops. Not only the farmer benefited from
these changes, however, for the general public enjoyed the advantages of lower prices for the staples which were made possible by
modernized farming methods, organized farm labor, increased production, and a reserve of staples.

The wealth that was to result from the economies made possible
in all realms of production as a result of the application of the principle of combination and co-operation, which had first been introduced by private enterprise, was to be used to give the citizens the
life abundant. Wealth was not to be used primarily, however, for
individual luxury, although men could live as luxuriously as they
wished—or could afford. The desire for such living would have
been diminished, however, by the cessation of the practice of keeping
up with the Joneses, which had led to personal extravagance, as well
as by the fact that men, as they led more spiritual and intellectual
lives, would have developed more wholesome standards of value
and simpler tastes. Though the people would still wish to have
comfortable homes, they would prefer to spend the surplus wealth
of the nation in the beautification and improvement of the public

buildings and museums and for the promotion of public services and entertainments—for these were the things that all could use or enjoy as they shared their social life with one another. Wealth meant more, however, than public splendor, for the economic equality made possible by co-operative labor was to result also in education, virtue, and liberty, as well as in comfort, security, peace, and Roman holidays.

CHAPTER VII

INTELLECTUAL, SPIRITUAL LIFE

1. Formal Education

Julian West, the Bostonian, plutocratic narrator of *Looking Backward,* told his audience that, since he had but a slight interest in the educational matters of the nineteenth century, he would not describe in detail the school system of the year 2000. West was stating in a roundabout way Bellamy's intention of not giving a detailed picture of this phase of the new social order, and he was not reflecting his creator's true attitude. Not only do Bellamy's early publications in the *Union,* the *Golden Age,* and the *Daily News* reflect his preoccupation with the educational problems of his day but so does his initial lyceum address in which he spoke of education as a "topic which has long occupied my earnest thought" and of the educational reform movement as being an all-important one. In this same address Bellamy described education as being of vital importance politically because the success or failure of the state depended upon whether or not the people had the ability to form intelligent decisions and the morality to prevent their being corrupted. Individually, the happiness of man, his dignity, his ability, his desire to perfect the social order, and his lack of religious superstition and prejudice depended upon his being educated.

Bellamy's criticism of the educational system of his era in the *Union* articles and reviews was directed chiefly at the existing inequalities of education which he regarded as endangering the unity, prosperity, and political future of the nation. Because of the employment of boys at an early age in the factory or on the farm and because of the thousands of immigrants, too many citizens were illiterate for the safety of democracy. The lack of proper education resulted also not only in a too-large group of unskilled workmen but in idleness and crime. The disparities in the educational achievements of men and women—for the females were better educated than the males, since fewer of the former went to work during the

school-age period—contributed to their lack of mutual enjoyment
and understanding and, hence, to the increasing number of New
England's old maids!

As a remedy for the situation, Bellamy advocated compulsory
education which, he observed, had worked successfully in Germany
and in Switzerland. He also suggested that night schools, libraries,
and debating societies be utilized by adults.

In these early articles, Bellamy also suggested reforms in the
administration and curriculum of the school system so as to accomplish more effectively the purpose of education which he deemed to
be the development of intelligence and the inculcation of right
principles and "patriotic goodness." To fulfill these objectives,
the teachers were to discover, waken, and develop the dormant
faculties of their students; and they were to teach them to think
and to encourage independence of thought. Bellamy urged that
good, well-trained teachers be employed; and, to insure this, he
suggested that they be chosen by a board of education comprised of
professional educators and that, once hired, teachers be given complete freedom in their choice of methods. He also recommended that
they discipline children by suspending them from school—for this
method had worked successfully in both Chicago and Chicopee—
and refrain from administering corporal punishment, which he feared
would warp the moral nature of the child by degrading and harden-
ing him.

Bellamy encouraged also the enlargement of the curriculum to
include instruction in the physiology of sex, the laws of health,
political science, and calisthenics. He waged war against educational requirements which smacked of the academic education of the
gentility, for he felt that for many students a slight knowledge of
Latin was not so valuable as training for a trade; as a result of
this attitude, Bellamy urged that the schools also include vocational
training in their programs.

Since Bellamy believed that education was to be concerned with
the development not only of the intellectual and vocational abilities
of the student but of healthy minds and bodies, he advocated that
the schools give attention to the physical and social capabilities of
the students. He pointed out that the highest development of in-

tellect and that the greatest efficiency of the student, or laborer, depended upon his having a healthy mind and a healthy body.

The ideas expressed by Bellamy in these early editorials formed the nucleus of the policies and aims of the educational system portrayed in *Looking Backward;* for, first of all, he instituted compulsory education: from the age of six to twenty-one, all the youths of the nation were to be in school. Since education in the year 2000 was considered to be a life-long process in which only the basic and formal education ended at twenty-one, schools of art, music, technology, and histrionics were to be open at all times to adults interested either in self-development or, if not too old, in preparing for another profession.

A primary duty of the schools of the year 2000 was the discovery of the aptitudes of the students who were to be developed mentally and physically. The schools were also to train them in manual skills and to give them a theoretical knowledge of the agricultural and industrial vocations so as to aid them in making intelligent selections of their occupations. To help accomplish this objective, Bellamy advocated that the schools promote excursions to the various industrial plants.

In his articles in *The New Nation* and in *Equality,* Bellamy repeated the criticisms and suggestions he had first presented in his editorials and in *Looking Backward;* but, in his last novel, he stressed the fact that the ideal state would liberate both schools and teachers from the influence of pressure groups and would, therefore, assure for all teachers the freedom of thought and originality that had been permitted in the nineteenth century only to those teaching dead languages. He insisted also that mediocrity in teaching had become a thing of the past, for the use of radio and television had made it possible for the students of the decentralized and community universities to be instructed by the greatest teachers of their time.

Adult education was also given greater emphasis in *Equality,* for Bellamy wished to stress that education in the most important branches of learning began really only after the age of twenty-one when men were more ardent and effective students. He wished to show also that, after the revolution had established the ideal state, the schools had been opened to the uneducated adults and children who flocked into them in order to prepare themselves to assume their new responsibilities.

The basis of the educational system, wrote Bellamy in *Looking Backward,* was economic equality which made it possible for all to enjoy equal educational opportunities. The social principles upon which the system rested were not only that every man had to be educated if he were to obtain the highest enjoyment of himself but that every citizen had the right to have educated, intelligent people as neighbors and friends and that every child had the right to be born of educated, refined parents.

Though Bellamy touched upon the political, social, and industrial significance of the educational system in *Looking Backward,* he was not to develop this aspect until he wrote *Equality.* In *Equality,* Bellamy described the educational system as being the greatest boom made possible by the new state and he showed how every phase of the individual and national life was affected by it. The relationship of the school and the state was interactive since the success of the latter depended upon the procurement of enlightened and wise citizens, of efficient and productive workmen, of the truly and not the apparently best leaders, and of a unified and homogeneous citizenry. Education increased the solidarity of the nation by decreasing superstition and ignorance and by replacing the divisive religious sectarianism with the broader and more unifying principle of brotherly love. Unification was also assured when society became more cultured and refined, for its members would place less emphasis upon matters pertaining to individuality and would devote more time to intellectual and aesthetic pursuits, which would result in less play of the brutal animal instincts and in a greater development of the impersonal.

2. Health: Physical and Mental

In his discussions of the educational procedures of the new era, Bellamy had shown that physical education was to be stressed until the citizen reached the age of twenty-one but that throughout his life he was to take pride in maintaining his physical fitness. To help him do so, he had been taught physiology, the laws of hygiene, and the science of medicine. As a result of this education, doctors were consulted only for confirmation of the patient's own diagnosis or for the treatment of rare diseases. Because of this emphasis upon physical culture and the laws of health, the educational system was to promote the fulfillment of the main objective of the ideal state: mental, moral, and physical improvement in the condition of man. Not only the educational system was to contribute to the achievement of this aim, however, for the whole character of the social order was to promote its attainment.

In *Looking Backward* Bellamy portrayed a physically and mentally healthy population whose improved condition he ascribed to economic equality and to the conditions of life it made possible. Men no longer began working when they were too young, and when they did work it was not for too long a period or under unsanitary or dangerous conditions. Not only were they performing tasks which they liked and were capable of doing, but they were relieved of the nervous and mental strain of insecurity. The mental strain induced by lack of adaptability to the work done or by anxiety over the possibility of not being able to earn a livelihood, as well as the nervous tensions created by the ceaseless battle for life and security in a highly competitive world, had all disappeared—and so had insanity and suicide!

The health of the nation had also been improved by the studied care given the children, who enjoyed, because of the principle of sexual selection in mating, a better heritage as well as a better environment than had the half-clad, unwanted, brutalized children of the poor of the nineteenth century. Other conditions inimical to the health of the citizens had also been eradicated by the installation of sanitary sewage systems and water mains and by the building of houses which were easily heated and cleaned. Because of the invention of household furnishings which could be easily destroyed when soiled or contaminated, contagious and zymotic diseases had disappeared. The health of the citizens was also improved by the unadulterated and scientifically prepared food provided by the communal kitchens.

In *Equality* Bellamy enlarged upon the effect the emancipation of women had had upon the health of the race by showing that it had exterminated prostitution and therefore syphilis and that, because women were not only healthier but freed from sexual slavery to their husbands, they had fewer but stronger children. Though Bellamy argued with reason that economic independence would free women from the necessity of prostituting themselves, he overlooked the fact that economics had little to do with the presence of nymphomaniacs.

The physical and mental health of the nation was also to be improved by the physical recreation of the citizenry as well as by its cultural and intellectual interests, as will be seen in the next section of this chapter. To Bellamy, recreation was to be considered as important as work or a knowledge of hygiene or physiology in the maintenance of healthy minds and bodies—and he believed that there was little likelihood that a healthy mind could exist without a healthy body. In *Looking Backward* Bellamy portrayed sports as being actively enjoyed by the whole nation. In the new era, there were no professional athletes or teams; instead, there were guild teams which played one another for glory and fun and not for prizes. In *Equality* Bellamy pictured the activities of the citizens in the gymnasiums and beautiful natatoriums which were maintained for the people's pleasure and profit by the state.

As a result of the general improvements of all conditions of life and their effects upon the mental and physical health of the populace, it was almost inevitable that Bellamy would envisage people who would live to eighty or ninety and who at the age of forty, when the most enjoyable period of life was to begin, would be as physically and mentally young as they had been at thirty-five in the nineteenth century.

Though Bellamy was correct in his surmise that an improved environment would increase longevity, he was not aware of the personal and social problems of old age which in this era are commanding and receiving the attention of gerontologists and economists. Since Bellamy also predicted a decline in the birth rate as the general culture increased, a disproportionate number of aged citizens would exist at some period in the history of the development of the ideal state—and what would be the effect upon progress of having the balance of power in the hands of an ultra-conservative or vegetating and distinterested group of citizens?

The optimistic visions of the promotion of health and longevity in the ideal state contrast greatly—as indeed they should if an accession of years means also the development of wisdom—with Bellamy's early pessimistic attitude toward this problem. At the age of fifteen Bellamy had written that no reform in morals or of the state could prevent the eventual extinction of the human race—its blood was already too tainted as the result of vice and its consequent diseases. Since the life span of man from the day of Methuselah had decreased to a mere thirty years, the youthful Bellamy concluded that the experiment of humanity had been tried and that the last scene of the fifth and final act had arrived.

Bellamy as a young adult and man had had, however, many and good reasons to be aware of the blessings of good health—and to be pessimistic about the possibilities of attaining it. He suffered from the curse of a frail body wracked by tuberculosis, abscessed teeth, influenza, and chronic dyspepsia. He had witnessed the poor health of his indomitable but long-suffering mother and the early death of his brother Packer from tuberculosis. In a letter to his wife telling of the debility of his brother Frederick, Bellamy wrote: "If we can hang on to our health we ought not to mind what else happens." As he sat in the window of his Chicopee Falls home and watched the passerby, he would say, when he saw a particularly robust man pass: "I wish I could trade places with him." It was no wonder, therefore, that Bellamy wrote in his journal that "a sound philosophy and a good digestion are triple brass against the ills of the world"— or that his editorials and his Utopian novels reflect his realization of the value of a strong constitution.

A superficial glance at the ideas and criticisms Bellamy expressed in his *Union* editorials relative to the health and, in relation to this subject, the life of a nation, shows that not only these early ideas but also his personal recreational interests influenced the innovations to promote health which were portrayed as being made in the year 2000. To Bellamy, his country was a "nervous, dyspeptic, and bilious nation," and his era was one of nerves. He regarded Americans as crusaders against time who, in their mad rush, took neither the time to eat nor to sleep properly, for they were striving to make their fortunes, build their cities, take their exercise, and fulfill the country's destiny in the shortest time possible. Instead of walking they rode in buggies. As a result, their legs "were withering into spindle-shanks through lack of use," and they were being carried to their graves by torpid livers, apoplexy, and degeneration of the heart.

Bellamy regarded the replacement of farm life by factory life; the prevalence of earning a living by the wits in a highly competitive business world instead of by the hands; the poor food, inadequate ventilation, and poor sewage systems; and the American's inability to enjoy leisure as factors contributing to the physical and mental decline of the nation. To correct these degenerating conditions, Bellamy advised his readers to give more attention to the art of living. The "coming race," wrote Bellamy in 1873, would make the laws of health part of its religion, and its motto would be "healthy minds in healthy bodies." In this future era, both the mind and the body would receive attention—and the latter would no longer be contemned. Indeed, it would be given the respect once awarded it by the Greeks.

Bellamy, who enjoyed active participation in sports, was pleased when he noted an increasing interest on the part of the public in athletics. It seemed to him that this indicated that the Americans, hitherto careless about matters of recreation and health, were paving the way for an "athletic revival" which could lead to the development of better physiques. He also recommended athletics to young men as an antidote to vice; for he noted that depraved, feeble bodies resulted in a morbid, inactive condition which abounded in unhealthful and excessive appetites and desires. In commenting elsewhere upon the interaction of the physical and the psychical, Bellamy stated that it was no strange doctrine to his era when someone asserted that the "influence of the body on the soul is as great as the influence of the soul upon the body."

Bellamy was not, however, particularly pleased when the public interest in athletics led to the organization of professional, commercial teams. In his *Union* editorials, he stated that such professionals teams made spectators instead of participators of the majority of the citizens or students who themselves needed the benefits to be derived from active participation after they had finished work. Making sports an occupation also enabled men to avoid productive labor; and, furthermore, since success in this field frequently depended upon luck or chance, such an occupation was harmful to the character.

To Bellamy, recreation and hobbies—useless or useful—were necessities, if not an imperative duty. When the Rev. Dr. J. S. Holmes of the Baptist Church stated in 1880 at a convention of clergymen that amusements had little place in the lives of Christians who could obtain all the relaxation they needed in praying and communing with God, Bellamy wrote that he was relieved that other ministers had not sympathized with these views—and he entitled his article "The Lord Deliver Us From Such Fools as Brother Holmes."

3.   Art and Literature

Provision was also made for the intellectual and cultural develop- ment of the citizenry, for Bellamy, who believed that man did not live by bread alone and that Americans were too prone to do so, wished above all else to provide an environment conducive to intellectual growth. Aware of the lack of art galleries, libraries, and museums of his own day, Bellamy not only provided these for the citizens of the new era but he fulfilled a dream expressed in a *Union* editorial of creating a world in which useful things were to be made as ornamental and as decorative as pure taste and their purpose would permit.

In *Looking Backward,* the beautiful stores and public buildings were described as being decorated with works of art selected by the people. Bellamy explained in his *New Nation* articles that with this innovation he had intended not only to return art to the people, but to free it from the debauching influence of commercialism. Art, he argued, could be truly great only when it was a part of the life of the community, when it had a religious message, and when it served a public purpose. Furthermore, because of the education and general environment of the year 2000, Bellamy expected the citizens to be capable judges of art, and he anticipated another renaissance as a result of this cultural progress.

Libraries were portrayed in *Looking Backward* as being better

managed than those of the past which had so irritated Bellamy because
of the inaccessibility of the books in them. In the year 2000, books
were no longer railed off or hidden from the people, for they
were permitted to roam and to browse at will. The novels the
reading public took from the shelves were, however, quite different
from those written in 1888, for their plots and stories reflected the
changes that had occurred in the social scene. Wrote Bellamy: "The
storywriters of my day would have deemed the making of bricks
without straw a light task compared with the construction of a
romance from which should be excluded all effects drawn from the
contrasts of wealth and poverty, education and ignorance, coarseness
and refinement, high and low, all motives drawn from social pride
and ambition, the desire of being richer or the fear of being poorer,
together with sordid anxieties of any sort for one's self or others;
a romance in which there should, indeed, be love galore, but love
unfettered by artificial barriers created by differences of station or
possessions, owning no other law but that of the heart." Furthermore, wrote Bellamy in *Equality*, the new literature lacked the
tragic tone of that of the nineteenth century because of man's
changed conception of life. When he had come to believe that all
life was hidden in God, he had found security and had learned to
regard the vicissitudes and accidents of the individuality as trivial
matters and to regard death as but another step in life.

Bellamy also emphasized in *Looking Backward* that the quality
of the literature published had been improved by the new method of
publication which would not permit inequalities and favoritism to
interfere with merit. In the year 2000, every author had the same
facilities for bringing his work to the attention of the public if he
thought he had something worthwhile to say—and if he were willing to make the contingent sacrifices. Mere scribbling was discouraged by the fact that every author had to pay the state the cost
of publication; the state, however, was required to print any book
submitted to it and had, therefore, no privileges of censorship. The
only censorship was that indirectly exerted by the public which was
the sole judge of merit. If an artist were successful enough to earn
enough royalties to pay an indemnity to the state, he was released
from industrial or professional service so long as he could do so.

Newspapers and magazines were published in a similar manner by associations who paid the cost of printing and an indemnity to the state for the service of an editor whom they could fire or hire at will. Since no censorship could be exerted by the government and since the associations were usually formed because of some ideas or criticisms they wished to express, newspapers and magazines became the true means of expression of public opinion which, in the nineteenth century, they had merely pretended to be. In that era, they had been controlled by capitalists who had used them to form public opinion and who had, therefore, forced editors to publish only the ideas or facts that were in agreement with capitalistic interests. The news of the year 2000—which in the nineteenth century had been withheld or distorted by the suppression of facts—was presented directly to the people: because of the invention of television, the public could witness events as they transpired and form its own opinion.

The trenchant criticisms Bellamy trained upon the newspapers of his era were the outgrowth of his experiences and observations as a citizen, an editor, a publisher, and a reformer. He had not, however, reserved his critical comments for his Utopian novels, for in the Eliot Carson story he had classified editors as hirelings of the powerful interests that controlled the newspapers and dictated their editorial policies; an editor, wrote Bellamy, had to sell not only his time but his principles if he expected to earn a living. In sundry *Union* editorials Bellamy had also condemned newspapers on four counts: their abuse and persecution of persons for their own private reasons; their portrayals of crime; their destruction of personal privacy; and their distortion and censorship of the news. In these editorials and others of a later date, Bellamy also expressed, however, positive standards to be attained by the press.

Bellamy charged that newspapers, because of business, social, or political reasons, frequently misused the public confidence by waging war upon private individuals whom they wished to destroy. Instead of respecting and honestly reflecting public opinion, they sought to formulate it for their own selfish purposes. Laws of libel were ineffective against such defamation of character since it was achieved with insinuating and subtle misrepresentations which merely, but effectively, planted prejudices in the minds of the readers. If the newspapers were charged with libelous actions, they defended themselves by asserting that freedom of the press was essential to public safety.

Bellamy also criticized the newspapers for printing lurid descriptions of crimes which could prompt the morbid desire of emulation or have a brutalizing effect upon the reader. By pandering to the worst instincts in men, newspapers became not benefactors of the community but corruptors of it—and this because they recognized no principle but that of gain. Furthermore, when newspapers not only printed stories about criminals but judged them, they were usurping the function of the courts and were swaying the verdicts actually rendered by them.

The most serious abuse practiced by the press was, however, the misstatement of facts; though little direct lying was done, the same effect was achieved by withholding salient data or by suppressing complete stories. Since various papers, because of prejudices or ignorance, published different versions of the same incident, the readers were baffled by the contradictions and did not know what to believe; as a result, said Bellamy, the world was settling down to a state of semi-belief on all subjects and such an attitude was injurious to its ability to be decisive in action. Bellamy thought, however, that if truthful accounts could not be given, it was best to have contradicting stories, for then the reading public had at least an opportunity to try to form an opinion of its own by reading the divergent statements. The reading public could force the press, Bellamy wrote, to alter its methods and to develop a sense of responsibility for truth and justice if it would cease to buy papers which flagrantly distorted the news.

During the period of the People's Party movement, Bellamy received another, more personal lesson in the suppression of news which did not further the interests of the owners of the newspapers; and he then decided that silence was worse than open hostility. In *The New Nation* he reported—as has already been noted in the section of Part I relating to the growth of the Bellamy movement—the distortion of the statistics relative to the votes cast by the Populists; and he also related the treatment given in the newspapers to a meeting in Chicago of an anti-trust convention to which the governors of thirty states had sent representatives. The original *Associated Press* dispatch concerning the meeting had been a column and a half in length but no one knew how much of it had been received in New York, for only three lines of it had reached Boston. As a result, only one reader in a hundred in New England knew that an interstate conference had been held to consider ways and means of breaking the coal monopoly. Because of this policy of suppression, Bellamy concluded that it was imperative that reform groups own and operate their own newspapers.

In his *Union* editorials and in the statement of policy of the *Daily News,* Bellamy had stated his positive standards for a newspaper which was to be free not only from the debauching influence of the public's desire for sensational news but from that of pressure groups. Newspapers, said Bellamy, should be of such caliber that a difference would be made in a man's culture if he did not read them. Since the press had the ability to transform the world into a debating club and to focus its attention simultaneously upon problems, it had to develop a sense of responsibility for truth and cease to sway the convictions of the reader by appeals to his emotions or by distortions of facts. As Frederick Maurice had stated in *The Friendship of Books,* newspapers would serve the public, therefore, only if they supplied people with material for thinking; if they were used, however, as substitutes for thinking, they would destroy both character and intellect.

Bellamy repeated that he, like John Milton, wanted freedom of the press but that he did not want lawlessness or license of the press. He recognized that the newspapers were the standing guard of the republic, for they aroused the public interest and kept the citizenry informed. To be truly effective, however, newspapers had to be free—free from pressure groups and from government censorship. Because of these ideas and his own experiences, Bellamy sought in his Utopia to restore liberty of the press by making magazines and newspapers the true reflectors of public opinion, since they—like his own reform journal, *The New Nation*—were owned and operated by associated groups of citizens. Bellamy wanted the people to think for themselves and to say what they thought—and for this same reason he was to dispense with an organized church which had also tried to teach people what to think.

4. Religion, Morality

Early in his life Bellamy had paid tribute to the power of the prejudices instilled in youth when in one of his journals he had written that though one might seek to flaunt them by not acting in accordance with them, they inevitably asserted themselves and caused a sense of guilt, conflict, and remorse. As might be deduced from this statement and as has been shown in Part I, Bellamy had had his own rebellion against Calvanism and organized religion; despite this rebellion against and this rejection of the creed of his forefathers, he was, however, to maintain throughout his life a sense of values and standards of judgment which were intrinsically those instilled in him by his religious mother and father. Like his ancestor, the famous Rev. Joseph Bellamy, Edward Bellamy sought to restore the true religion; unlike his ancestor, however, he did not have a conventional attitude toward God nor did he believe that any one sect had found the true interpretation.

Regarding the multiplicity of creeds as being responsible for personal as well as social conflicts, Bellamy, when he formed his religion of solidarity and later the church of the ideal state, dispensed with theology and sects but maintained the spirit and morality of Christianity. The highest religion to Bellamy was unselfishness in loving and serving others; and he regarded this love for others as being the result of the impersonal, unifying All-Soul in men which contributed to cohesiveness, sympathy, and understanding. The day would come, hoped Bellamy, when men who lived honest, moral, unselfish lives would no longer be considered heretics if they subscribed to no religious sect.

Bellamy's early awareness of the individual and the social need of religion was expressed in his journal entries which show his despondency and loneliness during the period in which he was groping for a religion which would replace the one he had lost, in his formation of his philosophy of solidarity, and in his statements made in his *Union* editorials and book reviews. Individually, religion explained to man his relationship with the finite and the infinite; and it formed and regulated his ideas, his character, and his spiritual and physical life. If a man's religion were but two faces of the same medal and could not be divorced, all law, all actions, all intellectual and cultural activities had to be based upon them if progress and a civilization which would truly consider and develop the welfare and happiness of humanity were to be achieved.

To Bellamy, any reform made in the social state had to be accomplished not only by scientific discoveries of the natural laws but by the study of the moral truths and by their application as a result of the education of the heart and mind of man. As Bellamy succinctly stated in his review of George MacDonald's *St. George and St. Michael* (a novel of the Civil War in England which portrays how fiercely people fight over ideologies), "it is vain to battle for political liberty and a very little thing to have gained it, unless the soul is free from the bondage of selfishness and sin." The millenium, wrote Bellamy in an editorial in which he quoted the Rev. R. G. Green's *Glimpses of the Coming,* would be brought about by vast moral and spiritual and therefore national and social upheavals which would result in men's having more profound impulses and in their being moved by higher spiritual forces.

The reformation of society, wrote Bellamy in another *Union* editorial, would not be achieved by the cynics, the atheists, nor the agnostics but by those who had faith in God. Criticism or mere dislike of existing wrongs would not achieve reformation; and hatred of evil could start a crusade but, with only this to sustain it, it would not last long. The world could only be "set right by love, and this demands confidence in goodness and trust in God. Positive forces are the saviors of humanity—clear, strong, mighty beliefs in the good time coming, and in the power of Christian truth and grace to bring it about. The doubters and devilers cannot march in the van of this army."

Bellamy, who had always recognized that religion had been a potent force in the shaping of American history, regarded the Great Awakening as having contributed to the American Revolution because it had demolished the intellectual and spiritual barriers that isolated the colonists and had fused the people together in one common enthusiasm. For the first time, stated Bellamy in a *Union* editorial of 1873, the colonists were motivated by one thought, moved by one impulse, and swayed by one mind. In the glow of this enthusiasm, Puritans, Quakers, Lutherans, and Huguenots were able to forget their jealousies and enmities and were united in a "spirit of common nationality." The French and Indian War which followed the Great Awakening had also been a unifying factor, but, wrote Bellamy, in considering the complex question of the proportionate influence of these experiences, it was correct to say that the general effect of the revival was to unify the colonists. In *Equality,* some twenty-four years later, Bellamy was to employ the "Great Revival" as the moral force behind the revolution which was to establish the principle of brotherly love and the Kingdom of God upon the earth.

Aside from these statements recognizing the necessity of religion to the individual, society, and the reformer, one may also find in Bellamy's *Union* editorials and book reviews his condemnation of the moral standards of his era and his knowledge of and interest in the sundry religious movements which were to contribute not only to the type and aims of the ideal state depicted in *Looking Backward* but to the religion that was to be the basis of the social order.

In his jeremiads aimed at the society of his day, Bellamy denounced the popularly accepted principles of action which conflicted with those of Christian morality and created a "moral depression." To Bellamy, it seemed that Mrs. Oliphant in her novel *At His Gates* had correctly indicted the smug and pious Philistines as being the true criminals of society, for their rule of action was that of business: anyone had the right to get the better of another. The trinity of Wall Street, opined Bellamy, was the world, the flesh, and the devil. This lustful worship of material things led to corrupt and piratical business practices, to veniality in the legislatures, to an emphasis upon sensual enjoyments, and to mutual distrust. Though the nation was Christian in name, its mode of life was comparable to that of Greek paganism; and the desire to attain and enjoy epicurean luxuriousness was not only undermining the physical stamina of the nation but destroying the ability or the desire to cultivate and exercise moral standards.

The attitude of the general public was that it was far better to be a knave than a poor fool—and this sinister maxim led to the condoning of the getting of the so-badly-wanted riches by dishonest methods. The desire to be conspicuously successful or wealthy made men prefer notoriety or infamy to the retired life of virtue— and to these the shallow sophistry that the end justified the means was acceptable. The public worshipped the devious smartness that led to success, and devil-may-care audacity won its applause. Smartness, wrote Bellamy, was capable of covering a multitude of sins!

The church, avowed Bellamy, was in part responsible for this laxity of standards of living and judgment, for it was more concerned about religion than about religious practices—and this attitude made religion sheer hypocrisy, for true belief and behavior could not be divorced. The role of the church was to combat the evils of the day; to improve society through the inculcation of positive faith in the capabilities of universal truth and genuine good to lead to improvement; and to instruct people in, and to encourage their following of, the ways of virtue and godliness. The church needed to follow the precepts of Christ by going about doing good and by carrying the principles of good living into the slums; it needed, instead of periodic revivals, to be persevering and stable in its work.

Instead of fulfilling this role, the churches, because of their selfish sectarian interests, were dissipating their energies in destructive religious squabbles and were denouncing as unorthodox such practicing Christians as Dwight Lyman Moody and Professor David Swing. The results of the materialistic standards of society were also reflected in the churches which not only were emphasizing the need of exclusive and finer buildings but were making shrewd real estate investments in selecting the sites for them. A reflection of the public attitude toward wealth was also to be seen in the churches which permitted wealthy but unscrupulous financiers to teach Sunday School classes or to direct the Young Men's Christian Associations.

These inconsistencies were permitted to exist because morality had been divorced from religion and because pandering, pharisaical ministers were submissive to the rule of the rich who supported the churches and their pastors. Because of their dependence upon wealth for their livelihood and for support of the churches, ministers could not be independent enough to tell the people the truth. And ministers, wrote Bellamy, if they were to fulfill their duty to the people, had to be independent. Those who entered the ministry had to be men capable of working with the people, of using their responsibilities for the common benefit, of keeping in close contact with public affairs, and of being courageous enough to do at all times what they thought right.

As Bellamy reviewed and wrote about the current church movements which were to influence his treatment of the church and religion in his Utopian novels, he came to the conclusion that his period was marked by an " 'independent' fever" which manifested itself in religious as well as political tendencies. It seemed to Bellamy that soon everyone would have his own party or his own church, for men seemed bent upon revolting against all traditions and laws and yet to desire, paradoxically, "mutual assistance without mutual deference, mutual co-operation without mutual compliance."

The religious agitation of the age was also distinguished by the fact that rapid changes were occurring in the doctrines of the churches. The most pronounced trend was toward a more philosophical and liberal attitude regarding Christian tenets, rituals, God, Christ, science, and practical Christianity. As Bellamy viewed these changes, he hoped that these tendencies of his time would result in a perfected Christianity.

Bellamy, who advocated that men forget ritualism which could become "rutism" and creeds which were devisive and too all-absorbing, regarded theological schools as institutions which kept dogmas alive. Believing that such doctrines were not sacrosanct nor stationary and that they exercised a perverting influence upon science, created fanatical intolerance, and resulted in the clergy's placing more emphasis upon dogma than upon the moral, social results of religion which could lead to the perfection of society, Bellamy recommended a return to the *Bible* itself as a source of instruction.

The *Bible* itself might be more intelligently interpreted, thought Bellamy, because of the researches and scholarly studies of Max Muller, Deutsch, Dr. Muir, and Whitney who had investigated the myths and legends of the past. In his *Union* editorials Bellamy called the attention of his readers to studies showing the influence

of the Zoroastrians of Persia upon the Hebrew conception of the
devil; to the works of Samuel Lee and George S. Merriam in which
the authors denied the existence of eternal punishment; and to those
of the Rev. John Miller and others who stressed the fact that the idea
of God as a Being of wrath, sternness, and revenge had been too much
emphasized. To Bellamy and to many of the writers he cited, God
was essentially the God of Love; and love of God incited in the true
believer love of one's fellows; to be a Christian, therefore, was
to have born within the soul a new affection for Christ, for God,
and for everything good, which would not be a mere sentiment but
a reigning, motivating love.

Bellamy also noted with interest the effect of Darwin's theory
of evolution upon the churches, and in 1873 he wrote that the aim
of the true student should be to make the unity of science and religion manifest, for both were branches of science—if science
recognized true wisdom and was inspired by the right motives and
if the elements of religion were correctly grasped. Both science
and religion should stand on the same footing, and to find a way
to this basis through "whatever jungles of physical or theological
error" was the great necessity of modern thought. Bellamy reported
that Professor Asa Gray in *Darwinia* and Dr. James Martineau in
Hours of Thought on Sacred Things had concluded that the theory
of evolution did not conflict with Christianity; indeed, the latter had
stated that Darwin's theory gave a more sublime truth to Christianity.

Bellamy was no doubt interested in the resolution of this conflict between religion and science because of his realization of the
dangers of its creating an even greater amount of religious scepticism
and of scientific materialism—for he considered the "gravest problems of human life" to be the scientific materialism and moral
indifference of his age. It was because of his recognition of this
tendency that Bellamy had welcomed Bulwer-Lytton's *Kenelm Chil-
lingly* which delineated the pilgrimage and despair of a man who
had been taught to trust and live by his five senses and who finally
arrived at a "conviction of the deeper reality of the ideal world and
its divine right to rule the real."

Because of these attitudes and interests, Bellamy regarded favorably the writings of such men as Dr. Holland, who wanted a religion

without creeds, or E. Maitland, who in *By and By* had pictured a civilization without an ecclesiastical organization but one which had absorbed the spirit and message of Christ in its general culture. Bellamy felt that the Rev. Minot Judson Savage was wise in advocating that the essentials of Christianity be stressed and the non-essentials ignored and that Dr. James F. Clark spoke with "common sense quite uncommon" in his *Common Sense in Religion* when he stated that men should use their judgment rather than rigid textual interpretations of the *Bible*.

Bellamy was also acquainted with the movements which, like that of Kingsley and Maurice in England, advocated a practiced or muscular Christianity; and in his *Union* editorials and book reviews Bellamy frequently mentioned the novels of the Rev. Edward E. Hale who advocated that everyone lend a hand to help others and who had pictured the church of his ideal society of Sybaris as being interdenominational and as being held responsible for all crimes and poverty. John James Taylor's *Last Series of Christian Aspects of Faith and Duty*, George Merriam's *The Living Faith*, Dr. Bartol's *The Rising Faith*, Frederika MacDonald's novel *Nathaniel Vaughn, Priest and Man*, and Matthew Arnold's *God and the Bible* and his *Last Essays on Church and Religion* were but a few of the books mentioned or reviewed by Bellamy which advocated a practical application in daily living of Christian ethics as a means of improving humanity and its environment. In view of his early opinions relative to the qualities a minister should have and of his later innovations relative to the ministry in his Utopia, it is also not surprising that Bellamy noted that Adirondack Murray had suggested in an article in the *Congregational* that ministers become farmers, or that Bellamy opined that such muscular Christianity would benefit both ministers and farmers.

Though Bellamy mentioned in his *Union* editorials such religious sects as the Millerites, the Comminsites, and the Dentonians and though he expressed the opinion that Swedenborgianism and the Higher Pantheism were subtle and fascinating religious philosophies, he was most interested in the Unitarians and the Evangelical Alliance. To him, the Unitarian movement was the most interesting one in recent American history; and he regarded it as one closely allied with the political, social, and philosophical ideas which had been attracting attention in the world. Anyone who wished to understand the development of American opinions, wrote Bellamy, had to read W. C. Gannett's *Ezra Stiles Gannett* and Frothingham's *Life of Parker*. To Bellamy, it seemed that the Rationalists—Rev. O. B. Frothingham, Ednah D. Cheney, John W. Chadwick, F. E. Abbott, T. W. Higginson, D. A. Wasson, and John Weiss—were trying to substitute a vague belief in the good, the true, and the beautiful for Christianity. Rationalism was, he decided "a religion of irreligion" which evaded definition; if the Rationalists were pressed for a definition, they took refuge in "transcendental mysticism and Emersonian infinities of expression, where they were as safe as needles in a haystack."

The Evangelical Alliance, which proposed the unification of all Christian sects for the sake of the practical work and the greater influence such a union would make possible, had as its motto "Variety in Unity." To Bellamy this slogan not only expressed the social ideal and "the secret of the universal frame of things" but was the perfect basis for the universal church. The principle of variety would permit intellectual liberty in matters of metaphysical interpretation and would, therefore, end the theological efforts to enforce uniformity of belief in matters of dogma. Such uniformity to Bellamy not only was dangerous in that it precluded growth of thought but was impossible to attain in a large body of men; furthermore, he considered that it was not essential to real unity of belief relative to fundamental principles.

Bellamy considered unity in essentials as being necessary, however, if combined, associated, and effective work were to be achieved. Institutions existed, he wrote, to accomplish certain types of work; and the principles and laws which were their bases and which gave them their power were only the means to the desired end. The church, therefore, did not exist to save its doctrines but through them to save the human race and society. The only unity necessary, therefore, was that relating to the vital principles; if men believed in them, it were better that they be lacking in didactic qualities, for such characteristics would kill the spirit of worship and devotion which could be emotionally satisfying and stimulating.

The influence of the American religious scene of his times and his reactions to it, as well as that of Bellamy's philosophy of solidarity—which also determined the tenor of these reactions—may be seen in *Looking Backward* and in *Equality* in his pictures of the role played by the church and the clergy, in the religious principles he adopted, and in the general conditions of the social state.

Though Bellamy portrayed in *Looking Backward* a whole social order based on the principle of the brotherhood of man, he said very little specifically about the actual status of the church. He did state that there were no national churches nor official clergymen and that, instead of attending church, people preferred to listen to sermons broadcast over the radio by "ministers" who were indemnified by their listening public. He also stipulated that people who wished to hold services in public halls could do so if they would pay rent for them to the state.

Though most of Bellamy's readers recognized the basic Christianity of the new order, one newspaper review stated that there was not one word about Christianity in the novel and that the millenium that had come was not Christian for, in fact, religion had had very little to do with the achievement of the results portrayed! Many of his critics—Anna Dawes, William Higgs, Michael Maher, A. G. Sedgwick, and Francis Walker— condemned *Looking Backward* and the society it delineated as being opposed to certain Christian beliefs. It was only through conflict with evil, wrote these critics, that men could develop their souls—and material comfort did not contribute to spiritual growth. Furthermore, the life of ease pictured in Bellamy's Utopia was directly in opposition to the command of God that men must forever earn their bread with the sweat of their brows and to the statement that the poor would always exist.

As a result of this almost ludicrous reaction on the part of these critics, Bellamy—in his letters, his "Talks on Nationalism," and in "Looking Forward"—carefully defined the religion that was the basis of Nationalism and showed that its aims and principles were Christian. In these answers to his critics, he emphasized that the basic principle of Nationalistic religion was the brotherhood of man and that acceptance of this tenet obliged men to assume their responsibilities to one another and to recognize that fraternal co-operation was not only a scientific method of producing wealth but the only moral basis of society. Furthermore, Nationalism followed the mandates of Christ in that it taught men to love their neighbors as themselves; made it the duty of the strong to help the weak; and preached unselfishness, the root and flower of all true religion. Love, said Bellamy, was established as the basis of society.

The establishment of a social order based upon the Golden Rule of Christ would result in His second coming; though this coming would be in the hearts of men, it would lead to the application of His principles to every phase of living. Christ, instead of being defied, would be truly deified. The social order would no longer be a mockery and a continual crucifixion of the Founder of Christianity—and the absence of poverty in it would not be in conflict with His teachings, which were, in this instance, to be interpreted in a relative sense.

To those who wondered if economic reform were necessary for moral salvation, Bellamy replied that moral reformation could not solve a problem that was basically economic; if the moral stigmas of the system could be removed, the economic defects would still remain. Furthermore, Christ would not have sanctioned the maintenance of economic conditions which developed the worst qualities of men, for His had been a message of good will and peace—and He had hoped that these very qualities would lead to the perfection of men.

Bellamy also warned the churches that they had lost prestige during the abolition movement by not supporting it and that, if they wished to survive, they had to drop their nonsense of the commentaries and theological seminaries and begin to preach the true gospel of Christ. He pointed out, however, that since almost every denomination contained a radical group which saw the fallacies of not seeking a broader religion and which recognized the need of practiced Christianity, the future of the church seemed promising. From this radical movement, Bellamy hoped to see the church of the new era evolve—one that would be similar to the Bellamy-inspired "Church of the New Era" in Los Angeles—which would support the true Nationalist religion.

In *Equality,* the Dr. Barton of *Looking Backward* was reintroduced to explain to Julian West the role of the church during the revolutionary period and its condition after it. Dr. Barton condemned the church and the clergy of the nineteenth century for having been the staunchest supporters of the old order; and he made it clear that they had adopted their position because they had been trying to save their monopoly on religion, had been pandering to the interests of the wealthy parishioners who controlled them, and had been more interested in the after-life of their members than in their earthly condition. The church had acted as if the cornerstone of society were property—and, though ministers had preached that the greatest sin was theft, they had blissfully ignored the fact that few people had an ethical right to their property. The church, because of its blind following of tradition, its lack of common sense, its inadequate teaching of the true gospel, its inability to move the hearts of men, and its class interests had brought about its own destruction as an organization.

Not only the actions of the church had contributed to this, however, for the signs of the end of the ecclesiastical system had been evident in the nineteenth century in the "deliquescence of dogmatism," in the obliteration of sectarian lines, in the repudiation of narrow authoritarian interpretations, and in the growing contempt for creeds. As a result of the actions of the church and of these tendencies, institutionalized religion with its ritual and creeds had been replaced in the year 2000 by a wholly spiritual religion which was the fusing and the founding factor of the new social order— and this religion was that which Christ had envisioned when He had talked by the well with the woman of Samaria.

In the year 2000, the ministerial profession no longer existed, for the ministers were laborers or professional men who spoke only because they had something to say—and the people listened only because they had a message worth hearing. Though men could be released from the industrial army by indemnity to become ministers, they had too much respect for their independence of thought and speech to permit themselves to be hampered by catering to the whims of any one group. Not only had the mediocrity and dependence of the clergy become characteristics of the past but so had the occupa-

tional and educational differences which had formerly distinguished
it.

In *Equality* Bellamy attributed the founding of the new order
to the influence of the great humanitarian enthusiasm for humanity
which, with its passionate impulse of brotherly love, had brought
men together. Though this humane movement had not been con-
sciously Godward in its aspirations, it had resulted in the true finding
of God and in a deep understanding of the message of Christ. When
men had experienced mutual love and unselfishness and had welcomed all men as brothers, they had then, and then only, learned
the true significance of "God the Father" and of the words which
expressed the religion of love. " 'If we love one another God
dwelleth in us and his love is perfected in us.' 'He that loveth his
brother dwelleth in the light.' 'If any man say I love God, and hateth
his brother, he is a liar.' 'He that loveth not his brother, abideth in
death.' 'God is love and he that dwelleth in love dwelleth in God.'
'Every one that loveth knoweth God.' 'He that loveth not knoweth
not God.' "

In the year 2000, each man's most engrossing pursuit was his
search "after knowledge concerning the nature and destiny of man
and his relation to the spiritual and material infinity of which he
is a part." This quest was made possible by the release from the
authoritarian ecclesiastical system which had not permitted freedom
of thought, by the eradication of the idea of the innate depravity
of man, by the high educational level the citizenry had achieved,
and by the security and leisure industrial democracy made possible.
Since there was no church to dictate to him, each man was indeed
obliged to discover his own religion; and society as a whole—because
it, like that of "The Blindman's World," did not rely upon the
authority of the past—anticipated gaining greater knowledge of the
soul and of God and believed that there was no limit to what might be
known about man's destiny. The changes made in the ecclesiastical
system were to contribute, therefore, to progress in the science of
the soul and to knowledge of its relation to the eternal and the
infinite; and this, in turn, was to result in an increase of human
happiness.

The implementation of this modern religion based upon the teachings of Christ and of this ideal society founded upon the principle of brotherly love resulted in a new earth of righteousness which replaced the hell that had been the barbarian and wolfish society of the nineteenth century which had forced men to belie their religious principles and to lie, cheat, steal, and hate if they were to live. The institutions of the year 2000, instead of appealing to and developing the brutal, selfish side of human nature (the individuality), fostered the development of unselfishness, sympathy, generosity, and lofty aspiration (the impersonality)—and they did so by giving men economic security and equality, mental enlightenment, liberty, and an ethical industrial and political order based upon the principle of brotherly co-operation. Such a moral condition of life not only made it almost impossible for a man to sin, but it assured the survival of the truly fit, which the competitive social order had not; under the latter, those who had survived had also been those best fitted to live and thrive under existing conditions, but to do so they had had to develop cunning rapacity, pitilessness, and selfishness.

Because of the great contribution Christian principles and economic principles had made in creating a world of moral human intercourse, happiness, and progress, the young men of 2000 no longer found that the practices of the world were in opposition to their Christian ideals and principles. The noble youth with high aspirations of honor, duty, and service no longer found himself mocked and derided when he entered the world; instead, he found ample opportunity to use and to develop his generous enthusiasms until the end of his life.

Bellamy not only sought to save the youth with noble aspirations the disillusioning experience that had been his own but to give to every man in his ideal state his own engrossing problem: the solution of the question of man's relation to the finite and the infinite. As a result of his own religious experiences, his philosophy of solidarity, and his knowledge of the religious movements of his day, Bellamy formed a religion free of rituals, creeds, and superstitions which were socially divisive and intellectually stultifying and one that would be emotionally and practically unifying because of its stress upon love and the duty of man not only to God but to his fellows. In this religion and in the institutions that were based upon it, men were forced to develop the unifying characteristics of Bellamy's religion of solidarity.

In summary, the religion which Bellamy created in his Utopian novels was to be the motivating force in the achievement of the ideal state, which, in turn, was to promote religious ethics by making them the bases of the political, social, economic, and individual life of the nation. The principle of brotherly love—which Bellamy described as being "very like what we mean by the Holy Ghost"—was the foundation upon which the principles of economic equality, co-operative industry, and social and political equality and liberty rested. The most important attribute of the projected state, reiterated Bellamy, was not that it would supply men with material comforts but that it would free them from bondage to the world of the flesh and the devil and lead them to the moral life of the true Kingdom of God in which neither humanity nor Christ would any longer be daily crucified.

To Bellamy—as to Charles Kingsley—religion meant little if it did not lead to the moral world that so many men had dreamed of achieving and if it did not preach liberty, equality, and fraternity. "Think you," wrote Bellamy in one of his journals, "there is any thought dearer to the mind of God than that His children should be brothers?"

CHAPTER VIII

DOMESTIC LIFE IN THE YEAR 2000

1. Status of Women

Though Bellamy's notations in his journals show that he had considered the effects of the development of the impersonality in man upon his personal relationships and that he had hoped that the development of brotherhood among men—which would be "the survival in another form of the parental relation"—would weaken familial ties, he said nothing of these considerations or expectations in his Utopian novels—and this for cogent reasons. During his own epoch, he had witnessed the public reactions to the innovations sponsored by such socialists as John Noyes, Mrs. Victoria Woodhull, and Stephen Pearl Andrews; and without doubt Bellamy wished to escape the odium and the adverse criticism which would certainly attend the introduction of iconoclastic ideas relative to love, marriage, and domestic life. To the literary detective who studies Bellamy's oblique references to the effect of the new order upon marriage in *Equality*, it becomes apparent, however, that Bellamy was implying changes which he did not wish to state too openly.

The slight changes openly portrayed as existing in the relations between the sexes in courtship and in marriage were, said Bellamy, the result of the changed status of women which had resulted primarily from the introduction of economic equality and secondarily from the subsequent social and industrial order. The majority of these changes were also, however, in keeping with those which had been suggested by the various women's rights movements of the period—for these had supplied Bellamy with much material for his editorials in the *Union* and had dovetailed neatly with his positivist ideas of the role of woman as a symbol of humanity and with his desire to give every person an opportunity to express freely his individuality.

Long before the writing of his Utopian novels, Bellamy had neatly summarized his attitude toward women in this statement:

"Woman is divine, women are human." Bellamy, who recognized that Christianity had been perfecting for over a thousand years the idealization of woman, regarded her as divine because she, in giving birth to a child, created a soul. Because she bore the burden of humanity, men instinctively worshipped her because of an instinct of race and not of sex.

Bellamy was not, however, particularly pleased with woman "the human" of his era, for he regarded her as the natural enemy of religious and social progress. Because of their ignorance, their superstitions, and their status as dependents, women were conservative clingers to the *status quo* or to the church and the social institutions which they thought protected them. If a man rebelled or was a philosopher, he had, wrote Bellamy, to hate women and their hampering love. Women, "the priestesses of sham," embodied the social tyranny of convention not only in their conservative support of tradition but in their lives which were stunted and warped by these same conventions.

Bellamy's most sympathetic picture of the hampering effects of convention upon women was given in an unpublished short story delineating the plight of Ethel Damon. Ethel, who had been free to play and romp with her brother Tom, became, as she grew older, increasingly aware of and indignant about the injustice of the distinctions made between the sexes. She realized that the social conventions—"a grand repressive scheme" of restrictions—separated her from life and turned her onto a straight, narrow path which imprisoned and humiliated her and retarded the development of her mind. Tom, as he viewed his sister's situation, was glad that he had not been born a woman because of the "hemmed in, cramped, and precise existence . . . [she] led." And then Bellamy wrote: "If God had depended for volunteers there would have been no women. But He conscripted souls . . . for that duty."

Bellamy had also inveighed against not only the social conventions of the period which forced women to conform to certain set patterns of affected behavior but against an economic dependence which forced them to become huntresses of husbands. In one of his *Union* editorials he suggested that the convention which made it impossible for women to move in society without an escort restricted the enterprising woman. To remedy this situation, he advised either that the public be made to realize that freedom of movement would entail no perils or that a bureau of escorts for hire be established. He also remarked that the public sentiment in matters relating to the protection of women seemed to spring from the feeling that females were weak in mind or too incompetent to take care of themselves and from the attitude among men—whether husbands, fathers, or brothers—that they had proprietary rights over their female relatives or mates. If women would assert their right to be regarded as independent and self-controlling members of the community, it would, wrote Bellamy, free their fathers and brothers from the necessity of shooting their seducers!

Though Bellamy believed that women possessed finer nervous systems than men, he had no illusions as to their supposed female frailties; for, though they might lack the physical strength of men, they possessed more passive courage. This fortitude, which he had pictured in the mother of his short story "The Cold Snap," supported the female mind against the inroads made by carking cares, bereavements, and the hardships of life; and, because of it, few women committed suicide. In a serious emergency, women did not swoon; they yelled, made themselves heard and seen, and were far from touchingly mute in their appeals for male protection. If a woman did faint, she most likely did so purposefully; and satirization of such affected weaknesses, like that of Angela Cushington's *Thoughts on Men and Things,* was to be welcomed. To Bellamy, writers who perpetuated the old Miltonic picture of women as the soft, sweet, attractive sex or who, like Hardy, portrayed them as creatures of much feeling and little thought, were decidedly old-fashioned.

Bellamy, who wished all people to develop their individuality and who had portrayed Ethel Damon as wishing not "to endure anything that looked like ignoring her individuality," was conscious of the need of educated, intelligent, and active women if civilization were to progress. In 1873 in a review of Dr. Bartol's *The Rising Faith,* Bellamy remarked that the author had had much to say about the coming man but had ignored the coming woman. "But the woman, his mother, must come before he can. Without a Mary there would have been no Christ. No individual prophet, but a true womanhood is the desire of all nations and the Messiah of the world."

As a result of these attitudes and opinions, Bellamy was inclined to regard the women's rights movement of his day with interest and sympathy and, because of it, to consider his age as the transition period in the history of the female. In his *Union* editorials he wrote that "the woman question" was the "Proteus of the age, confronting us in every shape, assuming every form as we wrestle with it." When the Woman's Congress convened in New York in 1873, Bellamy recognized the importance of the fact that the women had gravely discussed questions of social improvement and of social science such as dress, co-education, the moral and physical aspects of motherhood, and the rearing of children. It seemed to him that, because of this, the suffrage movement was ceasing to be a purely political issue and was merging into the broader and deeper question of woman's general status in society, a step forward which might have much significance. If suffrage were extended to women, he wrote, it would indicate the readiness of the public "for a great and profound revolution in the status of the sex."

Suffrage or no suffrage, a revolution in the status of women had been going on in the period in which Bellamy lived, for women had been making for themselves a place in the world of affairs—and this despite the opposition of those of both sexes who wished to limit their sphere of activity to the home. The industrial revolution had given women a place in the factory, and from 1870 to 1894, the number of those over sixteen who were employed in industry grew from 364,819 to 1,199,640; and by 1890, the women employed in factories, offices, and stores totaled 1,707,415. Dr. Harriet Hunt and Drs. Emily and Elizabeth Blackwell had pioneered in the medical profession and Antoinette L. Brown Blackwell had first set the example for the 165 women who by 1880 were ministers of the gospel. Lavinia Goodell had been the first woman to be graduated from a law school, and Mrs. Belva A. Lockwood had been the first of her sex to plead a case before the Supreme Court in Washington; by 1880, there were seventy-five women lawyers in the country. Women such as Mary Clemner Ames; "Gail Hamilton," who is mentioned frequently with respect by Bellamy in his editorials; and

Grace Greenwood had followed in the wake of Margaret Fuller and Fanny Wright by entering the journalistic profession.

Bellamy approved of women's participation in the professions, for he considered " 'the ivy' theory of the feminine sphere" to be a subject worthy of satire. Work was an honor and a fulfillment to both men and women, but to the female it could be, wrote Bellamy, the way "to life, liberty, and the pursuit of happiness." Though it might be impossible to see where the coming revolution in the status of women would end, Bellamy believed "that the fullest liberty is a medium in which the natural is sure at last to rise and survive, and the artificial to sink and disappear, and, in this confidence, [we should] demand free play and fair play for all."

Because of these attitudes, Bellamy recommended to his readers books and articles which advised that all women learn a trade or which related the stories of women who had been successful as farmers, inventors, printers, brokers, editors, and lawyers. For the same reasons, he twitted the male students who had forced the dismissal of females from colleges by remarking that the men not only had done something contemptible but had so acted because of their fear that the women might raise the scholastic standards. He also informed the medical profession that the spirit which caused its members to crush any woman who entered the field belonged to the Dark Ages and not to the nineteenth century.

Bellamy displayed also, however, a selfish, masculine view of the woman question when he wrote in his journal a suggestion for the Eliot Carson story to the effect that women should be supported by the state when they married since the necessity of earning a living to support them forced men to neglect nobler pursuits. Women would also benefit, however, from this economic independence, for they would have more liberty and freedom and they would be able to disregard financial matters in their selection of a mate. In 1877, Bellamy also called attention to an article in *The Radical Review* which proposed that the state support women. These plans for the economic enfranchisement of women appealed to Bellamy not only because he wished to free them from their dependence upon others but because he desired to secure the emancipation of men as well so that they would be free to study nature and books and to investigate their relationship to the finite and the infinite.

Years later, after he had published *Looking Backward,* Bellamy as a father showed his emotional concern over the future of women, for he said to Frances Willard in an interview: "I am a married man with a boy of four and a girl three years old. I believe a man must have a daughter of his own before he really learns how to sympathize with women in their difficult relations to life. Now I do not propose that my boy shall get ahead of his little sister in opportunity so far as I can influence the forms of society. I would make women absolutely independent of men to the extent the material values are concerned,—thus sweeping away at one stroke the greatest temptation the physically weaker has to go wrong and the most potent weapon of the physically stronger in putting her at disadvantage and himself to shame."

In his countless reviews of novels dealing with the woman question, Bellamy evinced a deep dissatisfaction with the picture they presented of the coming independent woman who was selfishly ambitious and domineering and who disliked not only household work but the bearing of children. Womanly charm, wrote Bellamy, did not have to be replaced by unsexed women, for such charm could bloom in a factory as well as in a hothouse atmosphere. Furthermore, such forecasts filled the public with trepidation and made the subject of woman's rights an unpopular one. The enfranchised woman should be presented, therefore, in a "winning and propitiating guise"; she should be shown not only to possess strength and ability but to be so feminine that marriage would seem a fitting crown to her life.

Because of Bellamy's attitude toward the purpose of life, his fatherly concern about his daughter's future, his criticism of women, and his knowledge of and attitudes toward the progressive movements of his day, it was inevitable that Edith Leete, the heroine of *Looking Backward,* would be portrayed as a serene, frank, intelligent, feminine—though employed—woman and that women should be portrayed as being emancipated from marriages made for money; from prejudices against their participation in political, professional, and industrial affairs; from prostitution and marital sexual slavery; and from the cramping social conventions of the nineteenth century.

In *Looking Backward,* Bellamy provided, with the creation of the women's industrial army, a sphere for the activities of females which he said allowed for the individuality of the sex but did not seek, as had the reformers of the nineteenth century, to obliterate its differences. The women's industrial army would obviate "unnatural rivalry with men" but it would provide an opportunity for women to lead full, developed lives. The new order was, in fact, a "paradise for women" because it permitted them equal educational opportunities, work which followed their natural bent, and economic freedom. Though women were honored and respected because they bore and nursed children, they were interested in the affairs of the world, were able to be themselves when in the company of men, and were free to enjoy outdoor life.

Though Frances Willard hailed *Looking Backward* as the route to female social salvation, Mary H. Ford and Mrs. Abby Morton Diaz expressed displeasure with the role Bellamy had assigned to women. In a lively article, Miss Ford stated that she wanted—as did Mrs. Diaz—a world for women that would not treat them as females but as human beings capable of participating with men on an equal basis in the affairs of the world. Instead of wanting more time for the amorous dalliance which *Looking Backward* had promised them, women wanted comradeship and the opportunity to prepare for and do anything for which they had ability.

In his articles published before the writing of *Equality,* Bellamy stressed that the problem of the status of women was so involved with other social questions that its only solution was socialism. Nationalism, however, was the only type of socialism which would insure for women the achievement of independence, equality of income and opportunity, and freedom and dignity; for it was the only plan which advocated economic equality. The European socialists who advocated equal pay for equal work would not advance the cause of women, who because of their physical weaknesses and their bearing of children, would be disqualified, therefore, as equal competitors of men. Economic equality was the basis of the salvation of women not only socially, professionally, and economically but sexually; the economic independence of women would end once and for all, asserted Bellamy, not only prostitution but their sexual servility in marriage. Though the English Methodist Church had stricken the word "obey" from the marriage ceremony, only National-ism would eliminate the necessity of obeying—for it was in fact woman's "Declaration of Independence."

Though Bellamy repeated in *Equality* the picture of the enlarged and elevated sphere of female activity which he had first presented in *Looking Backward,* he also portrayed women as the industrial and professional equals of men—as Mary Ford and Mrs. Diaz had suggested—and he included statements as to their general status which reflected themes he had harped upon in his journals and in his *Union* editorials. Women, because of their education, independent economic status, and newly acquired self-confidence, were no longer the upholders of precedent and authority. Because their educations and their social environment were no longer suppressive, they had ceased to be artificial nonentities.

Bellamy also recognized in his last Utopian novel the outstanding female reformers of the late nineteenth century by stating that these few serious, original, and thinking women had foreshadowed those of the year 2000. Of the woman's movement itself, however, he wrote that it had had too limited a program and had been too narrow in its interpretation of the true causes of the enslavement of women to be effective. Instead of "tyrant man" or "man the monster," the whole social system had been responsible for the sorry plight of the female. Since the primary cause had been an economic one, only economic equality and state socialism had been able to emancipate women.

2. Love and Marriage

The notations Bellamy made in his journals both before and after the publication of *Looking Backward* show his consideration of the effect that a reorganization of society could have upon love, courtship, marriage, reproduction, and parental responsibility. In his plan for "A Reorganization of Society to Extirpate Sorrow," Bellamy noted that the sources of grief were "certain affections of men, women, and children"—and that the greatest and most piteous of these was parental love. Since the "cultivation of tenderness" in the parental relationship resulted in an anxiety and sadness which far outweighed any happiness received, Bellamy hoped to eliminate parental love and therefore sorrow by relieving mothers of nearly all care of their children and fathers of intimate relationships with them.

To achieve this impersonal relationship, the children were to be placed at an early age in kindergartens, and thenceforward their education and their discipline were to be regulated by the state, which would confer with the children as they grew older in order to discover their individual interests. Since all economic provisions would be made by the state and since the parents would be relieved of all responsibility, the "chief inducements to devoting fondness" would be lacking. Since parental love existed only because nature needed a way to provide for the rearing of children and since this need was now supplied by the state, such affection, if it existed at all, would be "an effete survival, an aching root of a tooth no longer useful."

As a consequence of the discontinuance of family life or affection, fraternal and parental ties would be loosened; and people, no longer bound by the individualistic, transitory relationships of the family, would be free to develop intellectual and aesthetic sympathies and to cultivate "their sense of the universal life of God." Instead of being concerned with sexuality and with familial affairs, men would sublimate their affections and devote themselves to "nature, the eternal, the ideal" and to the "general advancement and elevation of the human type."

In his notes for a sequel to *Looking Backward,* Bellamy evinced once more his consideration of the problem of decreasing the sorrows of disappointment and bereavement resulting from love. People, he wrote, would not cease to love—they would merely love more rationally; and this rational love would be sufficient to induce marriage in the ideal state, for it was only under barbarous conditions that they had had to be mad with love before they would assume the burden of marriage.

This rational love would not decrease the raptures of the "love passion," for, thought Bellamy, it was doubtful whether those sick with love—"the constitutionally jealous or piners"—received even under the most felicitous conditions as much pleasure from sexual intercourse as the more genial and humane—those "less intensely individual." Furthermore, intense rapture was usually followed by reactions of brutality which were undesirable outgrowths—and the coming race would have no desire to perpetuate "these intense and shudderful emotions whether of pain or pleasure, these sottish hearts" which turned men not into angels but into cannibals.

In his *Union* articles and reviews, Bellamy had also asserted that love was not the great "perverter, disturber, agitator" that the poets had described it as being and that people did not fall in love so easily nor so profoundly as the novelist's characters. Petrarch, said Bellamy, had really experienced the rare love that could make men poets; but this rapture—like all other lofty emotions and ecstasies which were possible—could be attained only by a rare few. For such sensitive persons, marriages without love were dangerous; but for the majority of people, it was possible to marry, to have children, and to keep the faith without ever knowing what real love could be. It was doubtless for this majority, and not for the Petrarchs, that Bellamy suggested that "blighted affections" could be cured by exercise in the fresh air, a good diet, and an interest in nature; recovered, the afflicted one would find that his second love was more sensible and fortunate than his first one had been.

Bellamy regarded sexual harmony as being less essential to a happy marriage than spiritual and intellectual sympathy; and he believed that the importance of the latter was proved by the lust of the lover, despite physical satiation, for a blending of spirits. The reasons for this attitude were perhaps explained by Bellamy in the manuscript of an early short story in which he described the love of Celia for Bob as resulting in an "intense sense of being understood. To a nature like hers whose excessive self-distrustfulness lent to a morbid self-consciousness that gives no peace, there is no relief and luxury at once so novel, so delightful, so beneficial, as the abdication of personal responsibility and the duty of introspection consequent on the feeling that it . . . be all left to the loving eye . . . of another second self. An ecstasy of self-revelation is experienced."

In "To Whom This May Come," Bellamy portrayed the race of the mindreaders who regarded love as a great spiritual ecstasy or "high spiritual communion" which lacked the intense ache of the heart of common man's love for it meant "complete knowledge and understanding." The people of this Pacific island were passionate pilgrims who searched for the persons whose natures were pitched to correspond to their own; when they found their true mates, the recognition was instantaneous and mutual; and, without courtship, each claimed his own.

In his Utopian novels, however, Bellamy wrote remarkably little about love, and he wisely enough did not air his above-stated conceptions of the tender passion. These ideas would doubtless not have been understood by the majority of his readers who were incapable of such mystical interpretations, for they, because of their novel reading as well as their undeveloped capacities, were prone— as Bellamy remarked—to regard the "heart as a sexual organ only." Bellamy did not overtly indicate any major changes in marital or family relationships which would shock or offend the average reader; and, though minor changes which he did institute in the relations of the sexes during courtship and after marriage were shown as being the result of the institution of economic equality and its subsequent effect upon the status of women, they were also the result of his prior attitude toward and his criticisms of existing conditions.

In his early published writings and in his journals, Bellamy had been particularly critical of the hypocrisy and materialism of courtship and he had also had much to say about the burdens and fetters which marriage imposed upon both men and women. Though courtship was ostensibly the prerogative of the male, Bellamy believed that men were actually the victims of the women who used their beauty to shackle them in order to achieve economic security. Girls who desperately needed to find husbands to support them regarded men as horses which, if caught, could be ridden; and they looked upon men's taste for women as an angler regards a fish's taste for worms: as a foolishness of which they might fairly take advantage.

The female pettiness and coquetry which existed when matrimonial designs were afoot were also inveighed against by Bellamy in a review of L. B. Walford's *Mr. Smith;* the moral of the book was,

wrote Bellamy, that the coquette was as contaminated morally as
the women of the *demimonde* were physically. In a journal of the
same period, Bellamy wrote of the love of an "utter woman" who
thought of no concealment of her affections; in fact, she was not
sufficiently sophisticated to enhance her gift of love by bestowing it
in driblets or to employ the coquettish arts which would have
brought the man she loved to his knees. Grace, in the manuscript
entitled "The Medium's Story," rebelled at the convention which
forced women to disguise the depths of their love until after marriage; and the deceits practiced in courtship by both men and women
were entertainingly portrayed in "Pott's Painless Cure."

The problems of courtship were also pondered and discussed
in the Eliot Carson story by the character Edna who felt that a
woman had no right to be aggressive in courtship since she was
perforce an economic burden to the man she married. Edna was
also perturbed by the fact that many women seemed capable of
marrying men they could not admire and were seemingly satisfied if
the men admired them. To this beautiful bluestocking, such an
attitude smacked of the Oriental idea that women were pets and
playthings and that the greatest good which could befall them was
to find good, adoring masters. Such a situation seemed degrading
to Edna to whom the most important aspect of the marital relationship appeared to be the woman's attitude toward her husband.

In other of his writings before *Looking Backward,* Bellamy portrayed marriage as an artistic, economic, and philosophic liability to
men; and he went so far as to depict the advantages to be derived
from a Comtean worship of women which would save men from
marriages which inevitably resulted in wearing and wearying personal relationships and noisy children. Despite his recognition that
marriage was an economic burden and his belief that the basis of
marriage had always been a more practical than sentimental one,
Bellamy inveighed against marriages for either social or financial
aggrandizement. In discussing the case of the loveless marriage of
his character Marion, Bellamy observed that no woman could dream
of the hardships of loveless marital relations before they had been
experienced. Women, if they were not to be a torment to themselves
and to others, should marry those they loved—and so should men

if they sought sympathy, companionship, and helpfulness from their mates. Though Bellamy wrote in his review of Susan Warner's *Diana,* which portrayed the horrors of the surrender of a woman to a man she did not love, that this subject was not a fit one for a novel, he made notes for a story concerning a Millerite girl doomed to marry a man she did not love; and, in *The Duke of Stockbridge,* he related the plight of Peleg Bidwell, who, in order to save his mortgaged property and himself from debtor's prison, surrendered his wife to the lust of Solomon Gleason.

Though Bellamy wished people to marry only because of love and mental and spiritual sympathies, he realized that the rich did not always marry the rich because of economic reasons and that lovers had other responsibilities to consider besides the fulfillment of their desires. In his review of the essays in *The Bazaar Book of the Household,* which advocated that the rich marry the poor and vice versa, Bellamy pointed out that the rich loved and married the rich not only because of money but because of cultural equality. Bellamy, who realized the differences education made in the achievement of true companionship, recognized cultural inequalities as barriers to marriage, but he felt that making an ado over the marriage of people of different religious sects was "an unChristian, unmissionary notion." Far in advance of his time, he also believed that the discriminatory laws against the intermarriage of the Caucausian and the Negro races should be repealed; such matters should and could safely be left to the taste of the individuals concerned.

The exercise of common sense and prudence in the choice of mates was not, however, inconsistent with matrimonial felicity, for, wrote Bellamy, it was "fully as sensible to marry a man for his money as for his mustaches." Since the welfare of a lifetime was concerned and since the "gloss of the early passion gilds at best only the first few months of marriage," practical considerations of comfort and heredity were not to be ignored. For the welfare of the public and that of their progeny, people suffering from hereditary physical or mental diseases should not marry—for no one had the right to bring children into the world unless he felt that life was distinctly a blessing. Furthermore, wrote Bellamy, no man should indulge in narcotics or stimulants until after he had begotten his

children; though he had the individual right to destroy his own body
if he so desired, he had not the right to "transmit a hereditary taint
to posterity."

Because of this attitude toward man's responsibility for the
caliber of the future race, Bellamy became interested in the desire
of the anthropologists and scientists and in the "manifest modern
tendency" to apply the theory of stirpiculture to the human family
in order to develop a higher type of mankind. In the 1870's, Bellamy,
who had rebelled always at the "false delicacy" and "morbid sentiments" which discouraged scientific discussion not only of the physical aspects of marriage but of stirpiculture, wrote an editorial in
which he lauded the farmers who had frankly discussed at a convention "one of the greatest social questions of the time," human
breeding. Though Bellamy quoted the farmer who had advocated
that scientific mating, which had proved so successful with cattle,
should be applied to the human race, he also stated that in his own
opinion humanity would probably never conform to any reasons for
marriage but "sentiment, passion, and policy."

When he had read an article by Charles Darwin in the *Contemporary Review* which contained a proposal for the passing of legislation which would prohibit the marriage of the dumb, the insane,
the deaf, and the tubercular, Bellamy stated that, though the reasons
for such legislation were obvious, he doubted if legal restrictions were
either desirable or practical. To him, it seemed that the best method
would be to create an intelligent and reasonable public opinion which
would encourage "a moral sentiment" on the part of the afflicted
to regard themselves as bound from duty to humanity to be celibates.

One early influence of these considerations of the problems posed
by the stirpiculture movement may be seen in Bellamy's outline for
a story which was to depict a future society in which the state regulated matrimony and procreation for the improvement of humanity.
To achieve this objective, a system which was an enlightened form
of stock-raising and which was based upon the principles of cross-
breeding advanced by the "writers on temperament" was to be
employed.

In *Looking Backward,* these attitudes which Bellamy had expressed in his earlier works are reflected not only in his criticism

of courtship but in the institution of a new equality in wooing and of a sense of moral responsibility for the future of the race. Because of the economic independence of women, it was possible for the woman of the year 2000 to declare her love and yet to retain her womanly modesty. In "A Love Story Reversed," Bellamy fully delineated the new system and portrayed the modesty of the heroine who found the man she wanted, told him of her love, won him for her husband—and found him grateful, for, said he, had she not declared her love he might never have discovered the woman God had intended for him.

As a result of this innovation which dispensed with the artificiality of the relationship between the sexes during courtship and with the coquetry and affectation practiced by women of the nineteenth century, love in the year 2000 was more quickly and frankly acknowledged, and, because of the economic equality that existed, this love was considered the only moral basis of marriage. Marriages in the new order were based, therefore, upon Darwin's theory of natural or sexual selection; and Bellamy expected the result of its practice to be a noted improvement in the "physical, intellectual, and moral character of the race." Because of economic equality, the only advancement a woman could seek in marriage was a more elevated social position—and if her choice of a mate were ruled by this ambition, she would marry perforce one of the best specimens of the race.

The men and the women of the new social order were not wholly free, however, in their selection of mates, for they had been taught to feel the moral responsibility for the future of the race which Bellamy had advocated in his early editorial. This feeling of responsibility was an ethical idea which reinforced their sense of duty to the citizenry of the future; and, as a result of its implementation, people felt obliged to marry only the best and noblest representatives of the race. Bellamy suggested two means by which this moral sentiment could be made effective: firstly, all women were to be reared to regard themselves as the guardians of the world to come and they were to have, because of this, "a sense of religious consecration." Secondly, any woman who betrayed the future welfare of the race by marrying a man who had not acquitted himself creditably as a man and as a worker would defy the opinion of other women—an extremely dangerous and foolhardy thing to do!

Marriages of the year 2000 were depicted as being happy ones despite the fact that careers for women were permitted. With much care Bellamy pointed out that such employment, instead of being detrimental to marital happiness, actually contributed to it; women, released from their dull round of domestic duties, lived broader, happier lives and were, therefore, more capable of making their husbands happy. Since no one had to worry about economic matters, no homes were wrecked because of financial squabbles or difficulties. Because of the additional leisure, people also had more time for the enjoyment of love.

This enjoyment of love was not to be burdened or hampered in the year 2000 by the fear of parenthood and its contingent economic responsibilities, for all children received from the moment of birth a stipend from the state which relieved their parents of financial support. Though they were relieved of this responsibility, parents still had the duty of being good ones and of discovering the innate capabilities of their progeny. Not only did the state realize the necessity of securing good parents, but it believed that no one deserved so much from the world as they did, for "there is no task so unselfish, so necessarily without return, though the heart is well-rewarded, as the nurture of children who are to make the world for one another when we are gone."

Because of his statements which implied that reproduction would not be hampered by the fear of economic responsibilities, Bellamy was criticized by the Malthusians who feared that such a situation would result in unlimited reproduction which would overpopulate the world and eventually lead to its starvation. In his replies to the Malthusians in his articles in *The New Nation*, Bellamy not only continued to extol the values of economic equality but to show its influence upon sexual relationships. He asserted that overpopulation and starvation would not occur in the ideal state for a variety of reasons—and the chief of these was that the rich and the cultivated families of the nineteenth century had not produced numerous offspring. In the year 2000, all people would have the widened thought and interests which could be expected to decrease the sexual impulse;

and the energy and passion which had formerly been expended upon sexuality would be directed toward the general advancement and elevation of the human type and toward an investigation of the finite and the infinite.

Furthermore, argued Bellamy, reproduction would be limited by the economic independence of women who would be liberated from sexual slavery. As a result, women would no longer become mothers unwillingly, and their natural instinct of self-preservation would limit the number of children they would have. If, however, reproduction were not limited by any of these factors, an increase in population would not create a serious problem because of the progress that had been made in the mechanical and scientific means of the production of the essentials of life.

In these articles Bellamy also stressed the fact that the children of the new era would be "cherished as precious jewels, inestimable pledges of the divine love to man" despite the fact that they would be supported by the state. This, argued Bellamy, was the "only sound and proper" plan, for it alone would prevent the ill effects of deprivation, safeguard the children's welfare, and free them from dependence upon the disposition or the ability of the parents to provide for them. During their early and very important formative period, all children would have the equal advantages of environment and culture which were so important to their development and their future welfare.

In *Equality,* Bellamy repeated the arguments he had presented in these articles with the intention of showing his critics that he could argue as well as dream Malthusianism out of existence. He expanded, however, the information relative to the way an increased food supply would prevent catastrophe in the case of a great increase in population; and he also made some notable changes in the sexual code of the year 2000 and in the methods to be used to purify the race.

In his last Utopian novel, Bellamy introduced a scientific bureau which had been established to survey the menus, recipes, and edibles of the world and to seek constantly new sources of food. Because of the increased supply made possible by this survey and by the more effective cultivation of the land, chemical experimentation, and

the new methods of cooking, the people not only ate better than
they ever had but they had an unlimited food supply. Because of
the scientific preparation of all food from vegetables (for all the
inhabitants were humanitarian vegetarians like Bellamy) and the
government control which prevented adulteration of products, the
citizens were not only better but more healthfully fed.

In describing the code of sexual ethics which resulted from the
new status of women and from economic equality, Bellamy stated
that the moral principle upon which it was based was that the first
condition of any ethical action in any relationship was freedom of
the actor. Sexual relationships only became moral, therefore, if the
participants were independent and were not constrained to form or to
maintain an alliance because of economic, social, or personal pressures.

In the nineteenth century, said Bellamy, marriages had really
been primarily an economic contract in which the male had legally
assumed the task of supporting his wife and his children. The whole
moral code had been based upon whether the sexual unions were legal
—and not upon whether they were with persons unfitted to produce
children or whether they were inspired by sordid motives and not
love. On the other hand, women who had indulged in illicit sexual
relationships had been considered unchaste and abandoned no matter how great their motivating love had been; men, however, had
fared better because of the double moral code. In brief, women
alone in the nineteenth century had been forbidden to observe the
laws written on the heart or to follow the instinctive morality of love.

This situation was rectified in the year 2000, for only one
standard of conduct was to be observed; and this was not the slave
code imposed upon women, for all men and women were to face
each other with "attitudes of absolute equality and mutual independence." Mothers were no longer to be faced with the necessity of
teaching their daughters to protect themselves from their own
generous instincts, and no one could acquire any sexual proprietorship that could be asserted or maintained against the will of another.
Each person was to have, therefore, "absolute sexual autonomy and
independence" as a result of economic equality and the new moral
standards that were the bases of sexual unions. Because of this new
relationship in marriage, women no longer assumed the names of

their husbands when they married; and the children they bore took, according to sex, the surname of the mother or the father.

In view of the fact that Bellamy's wife and his daughter, Marion Earnshaw, state that Bellamy wrote a chapter for *Equality* which he refrained from publishing because he felt the women of his era were not ready to accept the message it contained, it is significant that an idea of the sexual code may be obtained only by putting together the scattered references to it. It is also significant that, despite his statements relative to sexual autonomy and his plan for the naming of children, Bellamy made no provision for divorce and that he did not indicate that any changes would result in the home life of the ideal state or in the facilities supplied for the rearing of the children. The omissions of specific statements about the actual practices and results of his moral sexual code were probably due to his desire not to injure the acceptance of *Equality* by including these ideas which he knew would not be acceptable to the majority of his readers, and particularly to women.

The suggestive phrases that Bellamy did include in *Equality* make it possible to surmise that his ideas were similar to those expressed by his brother Charles in *An Experiment in Marriage* (1889), a Utopian novel which presented a society similar to that of *Looking Backward* in that state socialism and economic equality were its basic principles. Charles' novel is, however, primarily concerned with the delineation of the type of marriage which would result not only from such a social state but from an acceptance of an idea which Edward had used frequently in his early published works: the idea of the changes in men's personalities which make their lives divisible into many stages and their souls multiple.

In Charles' Utopia, women married only for love; when a marriage was no longer held together by that bond, the marriage was quickly and easily dissolved and the partners were free to marry again. As men and women developed, they had at different periods of their growth different needs—and this system of marriage would provide their having the proper mates during all the different periods of development. When men were completely developed— or when they had run the gamut from seeking sensuality to intellectuality in their mates—it was probable that they would then find their permanent and perfect mates who would please them mentally, spiritually, and physically. To give the inhabitants of this Utopia complete freedom in the exercise of the principle of sexual selection, the children were reared by the state—just as Edward had suggested that they should be in his plan for a reorganization of society for the extirpation of human sorrow.

In *Equality,* Bellamy also expanded his ideas of the method of race purification, but the plan he introduced was one that he had mentioned in one of his *Union* editorials as being the only means of eradicating crime. Under this plan, the vicious and the criminal of the ideal state were treated as morally insane and were confined and prevented from marrying; as a result, there was no inherited depravity or base congenital instincts. In view of the sexual code outlined in this book, it is interesting to note that Bellamy stated that crimes of passion and jealousy were nonexistent because they had been the result of the barbarian attitude of sexual proprietorship.

3. Houses and Their Furnishings

Although Bellamy had had exceedingly little to say about family life within the home in either *Looking Backward* or *Equality,* he presented in the latter quite a detailed description of the effects public services, new inventions, new styles of architecture, economic equality, and the organization of the labor force of the nation would have upon the type and location of the homes and upon the life of the women who had hitherto been preoccupied with their management. In the reasons he gave for many of the innovations introduced in *Equality* and in the results he expected from them, Bellamy once again reflected the influence of his reading, his epoch, and his desire to teach people the art of happy, healthful living.

In his *Union* articles, Bellamy expressed his concern with the problem of healthful and safe methods of heating houses, and he repeatedly stated that scientists might better devote their energies to such problems than to speculations about the efficacy of prayers or the origin of life. He anticipated that by 1900, houses would be supplied with heat from a central supply station and that their inhabitants would no longer be exposed to the dangers of explosions, asphyxiation, poor ventilation, fires, and too dry heat.

Bellamy not only criticized the lack of "solid and true" building and the use of shoddy materials but he announced to the world at large that the selfishness and the ignorance of the builders which led to false economies in the building of houses and office buildings were responsible for the great fires which in Boston and in Chicago had destroyed both life and property. Architecture, "the science of sham," needed to reform and to devote all its scientific knowledge and common sense to the art of planning houses, for, said Bellamy, nothing—not even politics or theology—was more closely connected with the well-being of the average man than his house. Because of this opinion, Bellamy heralded the publication of books for the laymen which dealt with the problem of sanitary drainage of houses and towns, for he hoped that the enlightened householder would force his workmen and the town authorities to employ the best methods for the preservation of health.

Bellamy also did a little architectural dreaming of his own, for he wrote in his notebook that it would be convenient to have a house built on a pivot like an office chair so it could be turned at will to change the prospect or to catch the sun. A lover of nature, he had a balcony built on the rear of the second story of his house so that he might sit as if amid the boughs of the over-hanging apple trees of his backyard. Because of this personal enjoyment of nature, it is not surprising that he advocated that cities be planned for the health and happiness of their citizens and that parks be provided for them. When he reviewed Sir Arthur Helps' *Social Pressure,* Bellamy noted that the prominent theme of the book was that rural life should be so improved that it would have the advantages of the city and that the cities be so planned as to give the people as many as possible of the advantages of rural life.

As a result of these early considerations of the problems of housing and city planning, Bellamy portrayed in *Looking Backward* a Boston of the year 2000 that was a city of broad streets, open squares, parks filled with fountains and statuary, beautiful public buildings, and houses set in broad gardens or yards. Since the houses were heated and the public conveyances were operated by electricity, the city lacked the noise and the dirt of that of the nineteenth century which, in his nightmare, Julian West compared to an inferno.

Bellamy not only attempted to give the city some of the advantages of rural life; he also gave to the rural communities many of the benefits hitherto enjoyed only by the urbanites. In *Looking Backward,* he showed how the invention of radio and television made life in the country richer and more attractive since musical and theatrical events were made accessible. In his articles in *The New Nation* and also in *Equality,* Bellamy pointed out that the rapid transit system would permit people to live in the country and to commute to their work and that the whole tendency of the new order would be to check the growth of cities. Bellamy argued that the national organization of the industrial system of the country would result in a decentralization of both population and industry because the cities—which had been convenient for the exchange of both labor and commodities—would no longer be needed. The growth of cities would also be checked by the fact that people could afford equally good living quarters and could live where they wanted to live; as a result of this economic situation, many people would leave the city because they would prefer the charms of the countryside.

Bellamy had had little to say in *Looking Backward* about the type of house in which the citizens would live; he had merely portrayed the people as selecting their homes on the basis of their individual needs and tastes and as paying the state a stipulated rent for the well-built dwellings they occupied. In his articles in *The New Nation* and in *Equality,* Bellamy stressed that both the homes and the industrial buildings would be so planned, located, and built that the health and safety of the citizens would be assured.

In the more detailed picture of the houses of the new era which he gave in his last Utopian novel, the interiors were of hard surfaces which could be sluiced with water without injury. The furnishings— carpets, bedding, dishes, and draperies—were made of paper; and instead of being cleaned or washed when they were soiled, they were replaced. The result of these innovations, said the hygienists of the year 2000, had been the eradication of the germs of contagious diseases which had contributed more than any other change to the health of the nation. Bellamy, himself a victim of a highly contagious disease, was showing, in this matter, his awareness of the need of hygienic furnishings which would minimize the dangers of contagion as well as his knowledge of the development in Japan and in the United States of paper fabrics which could be used for clothing and furniture.

The homes of the new world were no longer filled with the rattle of pots and pans, the crash of breaking dishes, or with the unpleasant odor—detested by Bellamy—of the laundry. Women were no longer sacrificed to the "cooking stove, broom and scrubbing brush," for Bellamy—who had written in 1874 that he heartily sympathized with Mrs. Abby Morton Diaz's pleas in *The Schoolmaster's Trunk* that women be liberated from "the demon of housework" so as to have time for the cultivation of the life intellectual—had inaugurated public kitchens, dining halls, and laundries as a means of their enfranchisement.

Aside from freeing women from domestic drudgery, Bellamy expected co-operative housekeeping to have social and economic advantages. In his articles written from 1874 to 1881, he had considered these aspects of such a system and had decided that eating in common would develop *esprit de corps,* check the tendency to form cliques, and increase social pleasures. Aside from these social benefits, the system would be economical, for the duplication of fires, stoves, pots, rent, and labor increased the costs of individual preparation of food. Years later in *Equality,* Bellamy also observed that co-operative cooking would provide the nation with scientifically prepared foods which would be not only more edible but more healthful—and in this instance he showed his ignorance of the quality of most institutional cooking.

Though members of the general labor corps would have to perform menial tasks in the state-owned kitchens, dining halls, and laundries, no stigma was to be attached to their so doing in a nation in which all work was considered honorable and in which the fundamental principle was that all in turn were to serve others. The waiters in the public dining halls were, for example, the social equals economically and culturally of those whom they served; and there was, therefore, no possibility of their being treated as servants or as inferiors.

Bellamy, who had had much to say in his *Union* editorials about the caste pretensions based upon laziness and the use of the words "master" and "servant," had, in his new social order, dispensed with the need of servants. He did, however, provide a system whereby help could be secured from the general industrial corps when an emergency such as sickness or extensive cleaning and renovation arose; all the citizen who needed aid had to do in such a case was to make application at a special bureau for it and pay the nation for the service that was then secured.

Bellamy's plan aroused a great interest among women of the nineteenth century, and in "A Vital Domestic Problem" he outlined a method whereby the women could begin to organize public kitchens, laundries, and co-operative agencies for cleaning. He pointed out to the women of his time that municipal ownership of public services was the first great step toward a household reform which would result in making a woman the true mistress of her home and not the "first slave" in it.

4. Clothing and Fashion

Bellamy sought not only to free women from domestic duties which curtailed the expression or the development of their individualities but to liberate them also from their subservience to the rule of fashion and from their restrictive, unhygienic clothing which was so fashionable during his period. Though Bellamy himself was so indifferent to the clothing he wore that his wife usually had to see that it was inspected and refurbished before he appeared in public, he was aware of the social and hygienic importance of the reforms being advocated in his day relative to women's clothing, and he was not unaware of the psychological, social, and economic reasons behind the rule of fashion.

In his *Union* editorials and book reviews of the 1870's as well as in his journal of the same period, Bellamy took cognizance of the reforms in women's apparel advocated by Dr. Mary Walker, Mrs. Amelia Bloomer, the Boston reform group, and the Woman's Anti-Fashion Convention which had met at Vineland. His statements show that he considered as sound the suggestions that clothing made of paper be worn as a hygienic measure and that corsets—which squeezed the life out of the girls and mixed up "their blessed inside anatomies"—be discarded. Bellamy also endorsed the reformers who inveighed against shoes that caused unnatural postures, too-tight garters which injured the circulatory system, bustles that caused unnatural sitting positions, and dresses which dragged the ground or were too tight for comfort. Such clothing, wrote Bellamy, increased the physical incapacity of women, prevented their enjoying vigorous outdoor exercise, and created mistaken social ideas of proper female decorum. Such concealing, distorting apparel also prevented a man from knowing "what is what" when he was selecting a wife—but then, concluded Bellamy, "if he can't find out in the course of courtship, he deserves to be sold."

To Bellamy, the fashions of the day were purgatories of elegance and the rule of fashion was an outrage to a "human nature which revels in variety." He realized, however, that the yoke of fashion bound women because they liked to array themselves "like lilies of the field" and to discuss—no matter what their intellectual levels— the latest fashions from Paris. He resented, however, their voluntary submission to the dictates of fashion which made them act as if they had no individual tastes to be asserted, no individual necessities to be considered, and no aesthetic instincts to be outraged. Bellamy admitted, however, that women were the victims of the fashion mongers, clothing manufacturers, and retailers who conspired to change and popularize fashions in order to increase production, sales, and profits.

Bellamy did not believe that an edict or a prohibition would achieve reform in dress, nor did he feel that the answer to its reformation had been found in the masculine attire advocated by the radical Bloomer group or in the unattractive garments created by Dr. Walker. He did deem a reform in women's clothing to be inevitable because he felt that costumes needed to be adjusted to the need or to the climatic conditions and that they needed to have the variety and the comfort which a touch of the Oriental, Greek, or Roman style would give them.

In *Looking Backward,* Bellamy vaguely presented the garb of the new era as being so little changed that Julian West was puzzled only by a few aspects of men's attire and was able to note only that women's clothing was no longer dehumanizing to the female figure but accentuated its graces. Though Bellamy had not included a description of the future dress because—as he had written in an "Old Folks' Party"—no "prophetical accuracy in dress" was possible, his lack of prophecy disappointed his public as well as his publisher's readers, as Bellamy's letter to Benjamin Ticknor shows: "Concerning the dress of the twentieth century, one guess would be as good as another as to how it might differ from ours. It is only because I believe that as to their social and industrial usages one guess may not be as good as another, that I have ventured to write about them at all."

When Bellamy's critics maintained that the fashions of the year 2000 would lack individuality, freedom, and variety since they would be determined by an arbitrary edict of the state—as they had been in Cabet's colony—Bellamy replied in his articles in *The New Nation* that only under capitalism had the Goddess of Fashion really ruled. Under private enterprise, the senseless and arbitrary rule of fashion—and the just as senseless changes in fashion—had been encouraged by the manufacturers of dresses, by designers, by fashion journals, and by the retailers—all of whom had profited economically thereby at the expense of the consumer. Under Nationalism which would sponsor a completely democratic society, there would be no regulation of costume, for not only would the people refuse to submit to such tyrannical rule but they would also recognize that fashion was the result of the caste system and of tradition. Any regulation of fashion would be that of the individual, who would select the clothing that was the most attractive and sensible to his tastes and needs. As to the type of clothing the women would wear, Bellamy admitted in these articles that his vision was limited but that he was certain that they would be wearing more rational apparel.

Because of the desire of his readers and the comments of his critics, Bellamy pictured in *Equality* the specific effect of the social order upon the rule of fashion and the clothing of the year 2000. The reign of fashion had been terminated in the ideal state because economic equality had killed not only all uniformity but the need for ostentation and rivalry in dress or for keeping up with the Joneses. As a result, no individual tried to imitate or outdo another; he dressed to suit his tastes and needs. Women, though they still sought to be attractive, gave less time to their ornamentation; but men, since their bank accounts no longer sufficed to make them sufficiently attractive, had to give more thought and time to sartorial splendor. No jewelry and no cosmetics were used by the people, for jewelry—like fashionable, expensive clothing—had lost its monetary value and with that its social value; cosmetics were no longer needed because the women were radiantly healthy because of the active lives they led.

Employing the idea of paper clothing which he had mentioned in his *Union* articles and the suggestions as to reforms made in his early journal entries, as well as those sponsored by the women reformers, Bellamy created a costume for the inhabitants of the year 2000 which revealed to Julian West, when he first saw the heroine Edith Leete dressed in trousers, the difference not only between the costumes but between the mental attitudes toward sex of his own epoch and those of the new era: he blushed with shame at his own thoughts when he gazed at Edith. This description of Julian's reactions may well have been Bellamy's memory of his own when he had been confronted in his home by an invading group of women reformers dressed in masculine attire.

Recovered from his embarrassing reactions, Julian West saw for the first time the artistic possibilities of masculine attire for women. He realized that it was a natural and convenient mode of dress since the bodily formation of the two sexes was essentially the same. Furthermore, this costume did not disguise and cripple women's figures, nor did it hamper their movements the way the "old bags" of the nineteenth century had.

In this social order in which individual preference was the rule in all self-pertaining matters, women were not restricted to this type of apparel; they could wear instead the costume of any age, of any country, or of any design they wished to create. All that was required was that they take their request to the national clothing manufacturers who would speedily produce at the reasonable cost of from ten to twenty cents a seamless garment made of paper fabric. Those not wishing to create their own costumes could, however, obtain any of the generally popular styles at the stores.

The advantages of paper clothing were that, because it was remarkably cheap, germ infested or soiled garments could be discarded and sent—like the household furnishings—back to the factories to be reused. Because the need of washing was abolished, lighter colors in clothing became fashionable. Because of the different methods of processing that had been invented, the paper fabric was as beautiful as textiles and was also impervious to water and to cold. Since it could also be made as hard as iron, shoes as well as hats were made of it. Hats, however, were worn only as protection against rain or snow, for the people preferred to be bareheaded; men had discovered that the heavy headdress of the nineteenth century had caused their baldness.

Although laundries ceased to have significance as one of the public services offered by the state because of these innovations made in the type of fabric used for clothing, the public enjoyed gratuitous water, light, news broadcasts, musical and theatrical performances, postal and telephonic services, rapid transit lines, libraries, and excellent roads. Beautiful natatoriums were also open to the public night and day—as were all of the public buildings, for part of the population worked by night and the other by day. Whenever they worked and wherever they lived, the people of the year 2000 were able to enjoy equally well, and according to their personal tastes and capabilities, all the facilities, comforts, and amusements which made for happy, healthful living.

5. Result of the Social, Economic Life

When the politicians dubbed the Nationalists "the salvation army," Bellamy wrote that he accepted the title, for he wished to "offer men salvation from the earthly hell of poverty, with the physical wretchedness, the mental darkness, and the morally degrading surroundings which it implies."

Bellamy, who was remarkably whole-viewed, realized that man would have to be emancipated from materialism by having his physical needs satisfied; then and then only would he have the security and the peace of mind which would permit him to devote himself to the intellectual and spiritual life which Bellamy craved for himself and which he therefore sought to give to all men. He realized that he would be deemed the promoter of "a mere sensuous paradise" despite the fact that he had repeatedly stated that his ideal state (which was based upon the ethics of Christ and upon the unselfishness Bellamy considered to be the heart and root of all religions) was to result in a stupendous change in moral conditions. This "moral beauty" which was to result from this "paradise of order, equity, and felicity" would lead to a spiritual and intellectual renaissance and to a second creation of man; and this was the only objective of the revolution which Bellamy considered truly significant.

To achieve this moral and intellectual rebirth, Bellamy sought therefore to create an industrial, political, and social order which would not lead men into temptation but would help them to lead happy, moral, healthful lives; give them an opportunity to develop their minds and their talents; permit them to express their ideas freely; and provide an opportunity for the full play of their personal tastes and desires. To provide the religious basis of this new order, Bellamy sought to replace the dry, dead husks of theology with the broader and deeper spiritual values which would make man realize that love of his fellowman was love of God and that he who sinned against his neighbors also sinned against Him. Of this New Eden, the people of "The Parable of the Water Tank" in *Equality* spoke thusly: " 'And there was no more any thirst in that land, neither any that was ahungered, nor naked, nor cold, nor in any manner of want; and every man said unto his fellow 'My brother,' and every woman said unto her companion, 'My sister,' for so were they with one another as brethren and sisters which do dwell together in unity. And the blessing of God rested upon that land forever.' "

To those whose hearts were kindled by the reading of *Looking Backward* to seek the promised land, the novel was unsatisfactory, for it did not show them the route. In *Equality,* however, Bellamy provided a map to the land of at least the Nationalist dreamers.

CHAPTER IX

THE ROUTE TO THE IDEAL STATE

1. Evolution, Not Revolution

In *Looking Backward,* Bellamy had been principally concerned with the presentation of a mirage of the ideal state which would entice the panacea-hungry citizenry to accept the principles of state socialism; and he had had, therefore, comparatively little to say about the methods to be used to attain the new society. When a reporter had asked him why he had not portrayed the means of its attainment, Bellamy humorously and succinctly replied that one did not persuade a man to marry by showing him all the difficulties marriage entailed; one merely showed him a beautiful woman and let him fall in love. In this analogy and in other of his statements, Bellamy revealed his belief that men must have a clear idea of *what* is desired before they can discuss *how* to obtain it. To Bellamy, the "discussion of means logically follows not precedes the discussion of ends."

As one of his manuscript fragments shows, Bellamy also believed that the omission of the details of the means employed during the transition period to achieve the new order had been a "wise policy"; for their inclusion would have focused the attention and the criticism of the reader upon the process rather than upon the achieved state— and it was the latter which he wished to present as meritorious of consideration and as practicable. By assuming that the ideal state was established and by indicating thusly that it was attainable, he hoped to strengthen the impression his portrayal would make.

For these reasons, Bellamy had been content to give merely a general indication of the course the transition from the old to the new state would follow by showing that the new order had peacefully evolved from tendencies toward consolidation which had been discernible in the nineteenth century industrial world and which had culminated in the "universal partnership of the people." The culmination of these tendencies had been occasioned by the enthusiasm of the people who, having been taught that such an evolution was the sole means of their salvation, had instigated a popular but bloodless uprising which had peacefully established the new society. Those impressed by or critical of Bellamy's picture of the new social order were not, however, satisfied by this sanguine and too general depiction of a "moral and material transformation"; and the omission of the details of the transition period became, said Bellamy, the source of the "most common criticism." Those who considered the blueprint of the new society favorably wanted another which would point the way to its achievement; critics who were unfavorable in their attitude declared that Bellamy had not described the steps because none could be found to "a mere place in the clouds"; and others declared that had he detailed the process, he would have "scared his ladies so much that they'd have read no farther."

As a result of the comments of his critics and the demands of his followers, Bellamy early faced the fact that he must outline specific steps in the transition toward the new state. Because he realized that it would "not do too long to put the people off with generalities when they begin to ask what to do," he began to tell them—in his articles published in *The New Nation* and *The Nationalist* and in his speeches—what specific measures were to be taken to achieve the ideal state. He also noted in his journal that a "book explanatory of means" was to follow *Looking Backward;* and, in a notation relative to the contents of this sequel, he wrote that the "Penultimate Chapter" was to be an "account of how to get there. The transition."

In *Equality* Bellamy fulfilled his intentions of pointing the way to the attainment of the new order, for he depicted "why and how the Revolution came, the moral and economic causes which compelled and justified it, and finally the steps by which it began and proceeded and the economic measures by which the transition from the old to the new order were effected without disastrous confusion."

That Bellamy would plan a method of transition which would not result in bloody conflicts or in disturbing confusion was foreordained because of his character; his religion of solidarity; and his attitudes toward revolution and evolution, democracy, and the methods of change to be employed in a democracy. Basically a speculative man and not one of action, Bellamy's course of action had to be one that was the result of long consideration as well as one that could be acceptable as rational and prudent and as consistent with his desire to unify humanity. Bellamy could not favor what he termed " 'hasty or ill-considered measures' " which would breed division and hatred and, thereby, increase rather than decrease the petty individualities of men; he could only favor methods which would make men more impersonal, more capable of unselfishness, and more devoted to the good of the whole.

As a student of history, Bellamy had learned of the futility of bloody uprisings from his reading about the French and American revolutions and the Shays' Rebellion. In *The Duke of Stockbridge,* he had depicted the inadequacy of the American Revolution, for its characters discover that they have exchanged bondage to the king for slavery to the wealthy; they decide, therefore, that they must take matters in their own hands and fight for their rights. The result of this decision is the Shays' Rebellion; and, though the rebels succeed in getting the legislature to pass some laws to ameliorate their condition, the same situation that had caused the rebellion soon reoccurs. Years later Bellamy wrote of the reasons for the failure of all such revolutions, French or American: "There have been innumerable revolutions great and little in human affairs, but as compared with the coming revolution, they have been merely superficial in their effects, for they have left untouched the fundamental fact on which the social organization through all the mutations of history has continued to stand—that is, the division of mankind into rich and poor, masters and servants, superiors and dependents. Nearly all institutions are either founded on this great underlying fact or have been conformed to it."

Though Bellamy thought that the American Revolution and the founding fathers had failed in instituting complete democracy because they had not established its only true basis, economic equality, he stressed that the democratic form of government which they had succeeded in establishing was the only foundation upon which the new social order could be built. As he time and time again reiterated, industrial democracy was to be but the further development of government of, for, and by the people. His evolutionary aim was to preserve what had been gained by the writers of the Constitution and to restore what had been lost during the rule of plutocracy.

As a speculative man who disliked change for the mere sake of change and as one who believed wholeheartedly in democratic processes, Bellamy was necessarily a believer in conservative methods of reconstruction. In his first lyceum talk of the early 1870's, Bellamy had warned that "all innovations and changes" which would lead to the "assumption of the power of the people" had to be adopted by them only after great deliberation, for the foundations of society could not be tampered with with impunity. The remedies of political demagogues would not contribute to the "symmetry and stability" of the social order, nor would any reforms—wrote Bellamy in his editorials of 1872 and 1876—forced "by illegal means beyond the convictions of the people" be effective "in a government like our own, where the people make and unmake constitutions and laws, so soon as the people are convinced that they are just." The defects in the Constitution and the government had to be "remedied one at a time, by partial amendments, and whenever possible it is desirable that precedent and custom should rather be allowed to work gradual modifications than that there should be too many formal changes."

Bellamy believed that "forward, not backward, is the law of life and work" and he realized that "one age cannot wear another's garments"—but he also wished men to preserve with careful, discriminatory action the good elements of democracy, Christianity, and the industrial revolution and, by an evolutionary process, to evolve from them a new social order. To make certain that men would democratically and with intelligent deliberation select and enforce their own institutions, Bellamy sought not only to incite them to do so but to enlighten them so that their action or choice would be morally, economically, legally, and democratically sound. The key words, therefore, of his evolutionary revolution were education, religion, and democracy; and the sequence of events leading to the culmination of the revolutionary movement was divided into two periods: the preparatory, or incoherent, period and the rational, or coherent, period.

2. The Incoherent Period: Preparation

Bellamy regarded the American Revolution as the event which had begun the general incoherent period, for it had paved the way for a more specific preparatory period by instituting a political democracy which, because it lacked economic equality, had contained the seeds of its own death. For a time after the Revolution, a certain economic equality had existed and the ample free land of the nation had guaranteed freedom and economic independence for all— for the price of labor. As was inevitable, and as both Plato and De Tocqueville had anticipated, the concentration of wealth in the hands of the few had become marked in a relatively short time. As early as the 1840's, thoughtful Americans, wrote Bellamy, not only had recognized the threat of plutocracy but had proposed a cooperative social order as the remedy. The Abolition Movement and the Civil War had halted, however, the formation of such a state, and the war itself had enthroned the capitalist class. By 1873, Americans had realized that the concentration of wealth had made America the land of millionaires whose weath and power were in conflict with the basic democratic idea of the equal right to life, liberty, and happiness. Subsequently, it appeared to many that democracy had failed since the nation had ceased to be the land of free competition, of equal opportunities, of social equality, and of government by all the people for all the people.

The general situation from the year of the panic of 1873 had contained, therefore, the immediate political, economic, and moral compelling causes and justifications of the movement which had led to the instituting of industrial democracy. The general discontent and the ills of the body politic not only had made men seek a cure but had also forced them to realize eventually that political democracy would not suffice as the remedy for the social and economic difficulties and that the solution might be the formation of a cooperative society. Before this solution had been popularly accepted, however, the citizens had been aroused from their lethargy by depressions, labor unions, reform movements, and propaganda.

Specifically, the year 1873 had ushered in a period which had witnessed, within twenty-three years, six distinct business crises which had brought low wages, unemployment, many business failures, poor living conditions, and insecurity to the people. During this period, the government, controlled by the plutocrats through their lobbyists, had turned the wealth of the country over to the capitalists through franchises, subsidies, land grants, and special privileges. Because of the disappearance of democratic equalities; the mutual suspicion, fear, hatred, and hostility which had followed the institution of corporate management; and the use of the militia to quell labor uprisings, class divisions had resulted which had destroyed the social unity of the nation.

The most subjected class, the laborers, had been the first to feel the turn of the screw; and they had, therefore, been the first not only to question the right of existence of the social order but to organize to defend themselves against capitalism. Though Bellamy considered the labor organizations as having been portents of things to come and as having introduced the first, incoherent phase of the revolution which was to result in the popular acceptance of industrial democracy, he felt that they had not accomplished anything truly constructive or durable since their bases of organization and their aims had been too narrow in scope. Instead of rebelling against private enterprise as a system, the laborers, like the farmers, had merely sought to ameliorate their own conditions.

The most valuable contribution made by the labor unions had been the thousands of strikes during the 1860's, the 1870's, and the 1880's which had not only aroused the world to an awareness of the industrial problem but had focused its attention upon it. Because of the sacrifices the laborers had made in their battles to secure their rights, they had convinced many people of their dire need and of their earnestness. The failure of labor as well as farm organizations in securing lasting improvements had also convinced the members of both groups that capitalism could not be resisted and that no return could be made to the pre-Civil War days of free competition. As a result, they had realized that another solution to their problems had to be found.

The other reform groups—the prohibitionists, the suffragettes, and the anti-monopolists—had been as short-sighted as the laborers and the farmers; for they too had expected to ameliorate the general situation with their specific but partial reform measures. Though they had failed to discover the basic cause of the maladjustment, the economic system, their failure had been a good discipline, for it had taught them the futility of attacking mere manifestations.

To supply the atmosphere that would promote the birth of order from this chaos of difficulties and panaceas, Bellamy relied upon specific education of the people and upon awakening in them a religious enthusiasm of brotherly love; for education would show the people *what* to do, and their religious fervor would show them *how* to do it. Believing that before any change could be successfully made, the economic, moral, and intellectual conditions had to be ripe for it, Bellamy averred that, if these conditions existed, the course of the revolution would run smoothly and it would not be an abortive affair.

The fact that Bellamy, long before he became a reformer, had noticed the difficulties of the reformers and had criticized their methods gave him a conception of the proper tactics to be used to educate and win people and a knowledge of the obstacles to be overcome before success could be achieved by any reform movement. In his *Union* articles, Bellamy had pointed out that reformers not only were too likely to have their own peculiar nostrums which, like quack medicine, were expected to cure all ills, but were also too prone to be excessively vehement, vindictive, and sentimental. Because of these qualities and their lack of wisdom, they alienated the interest and the sympathy of the public. Decades later, in *Looking Backward,* Bellamy stated that the anarchists had deprived even the best of the social reformers of a hearing because they had not understood the peace-loving character of the American people and had sought to reform through fear and conflict.

After the publication of *Looking Backward,* Bellamy outlined in articles and letters the methods that reformers should employ; and in these suggestions there is more than a reflection of the opinions he had expressed in his *Union* articles. The reformers who would succeed in swaying the people to accept the ideal state would not be men who were "blatant, blasphemous demagogues" but ones whom the people would instinctively trust. To achieve this trust, they had to be men of education and position comparable to those who had led the people in 1776. To be able to win the support of the thinking, law-abiding masses of the American people, they had, however, to make their appeal in simple direct language and in a straightforward, quiet, earnest manner. If they were to move the people to action, they had also to be capable of interpreting and, therefore, of swaying the human heart.

Bellamy also advised that the reformer's definition of aim should be so simple and so inclusive that it would be understood and accepted by all men as something which basically concerned them. The two ends that every man wished to achieve, wrote Bellamy, were "to provide for himself, then for his wife and babies." The task, therefore, of the reformer was not only to convince men that an industrial democracy would lead to improved social conditions which would facilitate the fulfillment of these personal goals, but to inspire them with so much faith and hope in this type of government that their fear and dread of change would be overcome.

In order to convince men of the necessity of the revolution and to incite them to action that would promote it, the reformer— wrote Bellamy in *Equality*—would have to overcome their ignorant prejudices, their false conceptions, and the inertia which was the result of their hopelessness. Among these ideas and attitudes which had to be changed before the people would be intellectually and morally ready for the introduction of the first practical steps which would inaugurate the coherent period was, first and foremost, the idea that man was innately depraved and that this depravity would make the achievement of the ideal state impossible. Men had to be taught, therefore, to regard the human race as innately good and as capable of further developing—under the influence of a changed and more healthful environment—the social, generous instincts which it already possessed.

Because of the mistaken belief of the people in the value of free competition, their fear that a change in systems would result only in new evils, and their deeply rooted dislike of change itself, the reformer would have to re-teach the principles of democracy and then prove that free competition and democracy had both been destroyed by combination and by the plutocracy. The new state was then to be presented as the evolutionary, logical development of democracy and as the restorer of the lost democratic equalities and liberties. In order to give them hope, to fire their imaginations, and to mitigate their fear, the reformer was also to present concrete pictures not only of the character of the coming revolution but of the significance of the new state morally, socially, and economically to the people and to their descendants. To give the people righteous cause for creating the revolution, the reformer was to remind them that they had the political, moral, and economic right to change the system of government and to discard the property system of their forefathers. They were also to be taught that, if the revolution were to be success-ful, the new government would have to rest upon the fundamental principle of economic equality.

Bellamy also pointed out in *Equality* that the reformer would not find it easy to make his appeal to the public, for the newspapers, the ministers, and the teachers—who were controlled by the capital-istic interests—could not be relied upon for assistance. In order to reach the public, the literary reform group would have to "create, arouse, and direct" public opinion through books and tracts; and all the reformers would have to welcome opposition, since this would keep the issue before the public and open the way for discussion and debate. Though, wrote Bellamy, such methods might be derided by radical revolutionary socialists, they would be effective in their appeal to the "sober and morally minded masses."

The reformer would also have to be prepared to answer the attacks the capitalists would level at his plan for the reorganization of society; but, asserted Bellamy, this would not be too difficult since most of their arguments could be turned against the very system they supposedly defended. Among these arguments which were to be refuted—and which Bellamy himself answered in *Equality*—were those that charged that it would be impossible to find capable leaders for the new order; that industrial democracy would destroy indi-viduality, independence of thought, and originality; that there would be no incentive to work; that the government would be not only corrupt but tyrannical; and that the new order would lead to over-population.

During the incoherent period, the reformers were to favor com-pulsory education and the improvement of the educational facilities and standards; for, wrote Bellamy, it was essential that the citizens of the future be prepared for their new roles. In or out of school, the people were to be taught to think and to be encouraged to adopt new ideas only after much cogitation. Bellamy believed that nothing was to be feared and that much was to be gained by the development of independent and logical thought; for he was certain that when intelligent, educated people seriously considered the merits of his plan they would become convinced of the necessity of exchanging the chaotic system of private enterprise for industrial democracy. Furthermore, Bellamy realized the futility of beginning the revolution before the citizens knew just exactly what they wanted; to begin it before this rational decision had been made would be to act prematurely and to promote what would inevitably be merely a superficial or a short-lived change.

While the formal and the informal educational programs prepared the people intellectually to accept the revolution, they were to be prepared religiously and emotionally for the action they were to take by a "Great Revival." This revival was to fill men with the religious enthusiasm of brotherly love, inspire them to free themselves from the bondage of selfishness and sin, teach them that man was not innately depraved, and enable them to unite in a true fraternity. When men had hope and love in their hearts and when they were ready to renounce the anti-Christian, individualistic life of the barbarian, their hearts would be captured and their imaginations would be fired by the possibility of achieving social salvation by applying the Golden Rule of Christ to the economic, social, and political life of the nation.

Bellamy regarded this "Great Revival"—which provided the religious and emotional force that would cause men to change the structure of the state—as the culmination of the humanitarian movement which throughout the nineteenth century had evinced itself in literary, industrial, educational, and philanthropic reform movements. This humanitarianism had softened and prepared the heart of man by prompting the growth of "the spirit of tenderness and sympathy for human misery," and it had intellectually prepared him by instilling in him an idea of his responsibility for the welfare of others.

Bellamy stressed that the moral, religious, emotional preparation for the revolutionary period was more important than the intellectual preparation; for a state based upon ethical principles could not be achieved without it—and without an ethical basis, the new order would fail. The fundamental principle which men had to accept and which they had to strive to fulfill through the revolution was that which Christ had stated when he had "declared that the golden rule of equal and best treatment for all was the only right principle on which people could live together"—and this principle would be instilled by the "Great Revival." Men, Bellamy had believed for a long, long time, did not accomplish things through laws but through heart work; to him, the world could be set right only by love, belief in God and His goodness, and by faith—faith not only in the future but in the power of Christian truth and goodness to bring it about.

3. The Coherent Period: Political Action

When the educational work of the reformers and the reformation wrought by the "Great Revival" had intellectually and morally prepared the citizens to accept a radical reorganization of the economic system and to live according to the ethical precepts of the new society, the time had at last arrived for the coherent period of Bellamy's program to be introduced. At this time—the 1880's—a political party had emerged to lead the people in the fight against the plutocracy for the restoration of democracy. This party sought to nationalize industry, to realize the ideal of a nation as an association of people, and to raise patriotism to a rational level by making the fatherland something that kept people alive and did not merely demand that they die for it. Because of these general aims, the party was called the National party.

The general policy of this party toward the revolutionary methods to be used to attain the ideal state was to discourage precipitant or violent actions and to retain the old order until the new had been established by legal, logical, peaceful procedures. As a result of this attitude, the practical action it inaugurated was so conservative that there was no marked change in the character of the nation except for the appearance of a new spirit and intelligence which led to the gradual introduction of a logical and self-conscious evolutionary program.

In 1896 the platform of the Nationalists was adopted by one of the great national parties, which, however, did not directly nor openly attack capitalism. The revolutionists used what Bellamy termed a flanking movement; for their tactics forced the enemy to desert his position because it was no longer tenable. As will be seen, this method—which had long before been proposed by Louis Blanc—was to employ state-controlled industry as a means of ousting private industry. Because of these specific methods and the general spirit of the revolutionary party and because of the moral readiness and the popular demand for change, the revolution led to no violent overthrow of the government.

In his speeches and articles and later in *Equality*, Bellamy described the procedure used by the revolutionary party as being one of "progressive nationalization of industry" on two levels, local and national. The local level included the municipalization of public service facilities such as those which provided light, heat, water, coal, gas, and transportation. The effective working and the cheaper rates that resulted from municipal ownership and management were good object lessons to the people of the benefits to be derived from the new order.

The level of a nation-wide nationalization included at first all newly discovered natural resources, the liquor distribution business, and the quasi-public services or those involved in inter-state commerce such as railroads, the express service, the communication systems, the coal mining industry, the iron and steel industries, and the life insurance companies. The nation assumed control of these businesses first because they were so closely associated with the public welfare, because they were so powerful that they interfered with the operation of the government in some fashion detrimental to the good of the whole, or because they were already so highly systematized and organized that they could be placed under government control without difficulty.

The general business of the nation was nationalized when necessity—either business difficulties or exploitation of the people—warranted such action. Among the first that were nationalized were those industries which supplied the citizens with the necessities of life, and the order of procedure was for the government first to regulate and then to assume management and ownership of them. The land was nationalized last, however, since it was the basis of property, banks, and mortgages; and to have nationalized it first—as Henry George had suggested—would have been, thought Bellamy, a foolish action which would have antagonized too many interests at the very beginning of the period of conversion.

The next vital step toward the nationalization of industry was taken by the government when it established industries which not only were to employ the unemployed but were also to produce the necessities of life for their employees. As the number of these industries increased, they formed the nucleus of the government factories which produced the articles sold at cost in the government stores established for the civil service workers, who were paid with a special script usable as a medium of exchange only in these distribution centers.

In order to supply these stores and to give further employment to the unemployed, the government began to farm the idle land and to run the unused factories. At this early stage of the transition period, the state compensated the owners of these unprofitable holdings with an income based upon the value of their properties so they were happy to surrender them. During this period, idle merchant ships and fishing fleets were also used by the government for exporting to other countries the excess products of the state farms and factories, for importing the necessary raw materials for the state industries, and for securing the sea food desired by the government employees. It was also at this time that the government established public laundries, dining halls, and household service agencies.

The laborers in the nationalized industries were regarded as government employees and were placed under a merit system. New employees were, however, assigned tasks on the basis of the results of a non-competitive examination; and no employee, whether old or new, was discharged without a hearing before the tribunal. The policy of the government toward its employees was to create safer and better working conditions for them, to regulate their hours of labor, to remunerate them fairly, and to provide them with pensions and disability insurance. The security, health, dignity, safety, and happiness of these workers—who formed the nucleus of what was to be the industrial army—provided favorable examples of the benefits to be derived from the institution of industrial democracy.

Because of the satisfactory life of these government employees and because of the immense savings they enjoyed, other people were eager to share their benefits. The government, therefore, permitted all who wished to do so to become its employees or to turn their lands or factories over to the nation. The prevalence of the usage of government script—as the payroll of the nation increased—brought about the collapse of the financial system and the end of the value of money. As a result, all who wished to live had to enter the national service, for their money could purchase nothing.

When all of the citizens had become members of the industrial army and when all of the industries and the land had come under state control, economic equality was instituted with the sanction of the people—and the last step of the revolution had occurred. Economic equality, "the keystone of the arch of the social fabric," was fittingly and necessarily the last thing to be put in place.

The spirit of the revolutionists, wrote Bellamy in "Looking Forward," had contributed more to the success of the revolution than the methods they had employed. Since a vindictive, intolerant spirit would have made even the best methods ineffectual, the revolutionists had had to be tolerant and charitable, to avoid alienating people by denouncing them, and to maintain the confidence of all by avoiding riots and bloodshed. Throughout the revolutionary process, they had kept their reforms in line with the nation's democratic and religious ideals and had remembered that they were seeking to help all classes of people.

The revolution had been an exceedingly peaceful affair, said Bellamy in *Equality,* not only because of these attributes of the leaders but because of the educational program and the religious reformation which had won the acceptance of the people of the ends sought by the revolution and had softened their hearts. There had been no conflict between the people and the capitalists, for such an overwhelming majority of the citizens had supported the revolutionary program that the industrialists had recognized the futility of trying to resist its will with armed warfare. Furthermore, some of the capitalists themselves had been converted to the ideas of the new state because of their logical and moral bases—and when he made this statement Bellamy was without doubt thinking of Henry Demarest Lloyd, the Chicago millionaire.

The people, instead of shooting the former plutocrats, forgave them for their past sins, for they realized that the capitalists had not only served a purpose in the development of industry but had supplied in industrial combination the object lesson for and the idea of state socialism. The teachers, ministers, and authors who had opposed the revolution were also magnanimously forgiven, and they became loud in their praise of the new order. The people, like those Bellamy had portrayed in *The Duke of Stockbridge,* had decided to "let bygones be bygones"—for the day of brotherly love had come to pass and the lion could lie down with the lamb.

If, wrote Bellamy in *Equality,* the capitalists had capitulated before they did, very little change would have been made in the character of the revolution. If they had suddenly and *en masse* surrendered their businesses to the state, the government would merely have commandeered all the food supplies of the nation—as it did in times of flood disasters—and would have rationed supplies to the people from the national storehouses while the period of reorganization was taking place. In such an event, no more confusion would have resulted than that which was ordinarily occasioned by a panic.

Because of the trends of his time, Bellamy was so optimistic about the rapidity with which the revolution would come that he feared it might arrive before the people were properly prepared for it. He said that he had first set the date for the establishment of the new order at the year 3000 but, when he had created the plan for the industrial army, he had become certain that by the year 2000 the ideal state would have become an old story. In *Looking Backward,* he had stated, therefore, that the revolution had been completed in the early part of the century that had followed the beginning of the incoherent period.

When the *Boston Transcript* published a review criticizing Bellamy's having allowed such a short time for the revolutionary process, Bellamy asserted in his reply that the time allotted was right; for, he argued, many unexpected changes had occurred in less time because the moral and economic conditions had been ripe for them. To Bellamy, the world-wide insurrection of the workers, the readiness of men and women to revolt against a form of life which mocked religion, and the criticisms of economic scientists all indicated that a social transformation was approaching. That the people should choose industrial democracy as the solution to their problems was not surprising, for this form of the ideal society had behind it "a long stream of influence."

When Bellamy's letter to the *Boston Transcript* created a very favorable impression upon the readers, Bellamy urged his publishers to include it in the reprints being made of *Looking Backward*. In his articles published in *The Nationalist* and *The New Nation*, he also continued to reiterate his belief that the revolution could be completed in half a century; and he denounced, for psychological reasons, those who spoke of the revolution as requiring hundreds of years. Such statements had to be stopped, said Bellamy, for they were more demoralizing than opposition to the whole plan. Furthermore, those who spoke in this fashion failed to "appreciate the portentous rapidity with which the present competitive system, grown topheavy by the enormous modern development of business, is falling to pieces and creating an imperative demand for an adequate substitute."

In 1893 Bellamy wrote that he regarded the Columbian World's Fair as historically appropriate, for it exhibited the best that the despotic industrial system had accomplished at the very moment that it was being replaced by an industrial democracy. Four years later, despite all the reverses the reform movement had received, Bellamy maintained in *Equality* that the revolution had been completed in the early part of the 1900's and that it had been achieved not only in the United States but in the democratic, advanced countries of the world. Bellamy doubtless remained optimistic because he knew that his work was being carried on by such men as those who were seeking to re-establish *The New Nation*.

Bellamy did not claim, however, that as soon as the new government had been established all had run perfectly or smoothly. It had taken many years for the new system to adjust itself, but in from two to ten years the citizens had been overwhelmed by its efficiency in the production of wealth. Since the economic efficiency of any community depended primarily upon its personnel, it had not been until the first generation born under the new order had come to maturity and could show the results of the intellectual, moral, and industrial training it had received that the people had seen the true results of industrial democracy.

4.   On the Route?

For reasons which Bellamy recognized, the downfall of private enterprise and the establishment of industrial democracy as a result of the chaotic conditions and trends toward combination did not occur in the United States. The idea of the value of "rugged individualism" was too strongly entrenched in the minds of the people of the nineteenth century to be so quickly or so easily replaced. Better living conditions; the increased wages; the powerful unions; the narrow bases of reform groups; the people's lack of faith in, and fear of, change; and a press so powerful that it could destroy with headlines and cartoons the career of a man like John Altgeld also halted the progress toward Bellamy's state. When the evils of capitalism were mitigated by reform measures, the life of private enterprise was prolonged—as Bellamy foretold it would be.

Nothing can justly be said in criticism of Bellamy's plan for the achievement of his ideal state, for his methods of intellectual preparation were proved effective by the Fabians of England, whose educational program and measure-by-measure political progress toward their goal contributed to the achievement of the English socialist state. Furthermore, the wisdom of Bellamy's insistence upon an evolutionary revolution founded upon an already democratic state and inspired by an unselfish love of mankind is portrayed by the Russia of today. As Dostoevsky showed in *Crime and Punishment* and Turgenev in *Fathers and Sons,* the influx of ideas from Western Europe about rational systems of society led to a disregard of traditions and ethical principles. As a result, writes Heinz von Homeyer in his novel *The Radiant Mountain* (1957), the Marxist state, though it taught men to be subservient to the common good, rejected the brotherly love of Christ and created, therefore, a world ridden with hatred and materialism which enslaves and tortures man in the name of mankind and progress. Such a development would not, however, have surprised Bellamy; for he preached that no society based upon hatred, violence, class conflict, and denial of God could produce good. Furthermore, Bellamy would not have been surprised could he have read an article published in the 1930's by Louis Boudin, American communist, in which he asserted that the influence of Bellamy's ideas had been responsible for "retarding the growth of . . . [Marxism] during its entire existence of some forty-odd years" in the United States.

If Bellamy could return to the world of today—the era in which the ideal state was to have been attained—he would doubtless observe many tendencies which might indicate that his country was still "on the way" toward the year 2000—or that it needed to reconsider some of the ideas he had stressed. Bellamy—like Norman Cousins, Dr. Albert Schweitzer, and Leo Cherne—would note that the world of today stands at the parting of the ways: it may direct itself toward a technological Garden of Eden in which men may continue to live creatively, or it may wander down the path leading to degeneration— if not annihilation—of the human race. If men co-operatively, un- selfishly, and ethically develop and direct the usage of automation and—more important—of atomic energy so that they serve the common good, they may create an era in which they will have the economic security, the leisure, and the educational opportunities to grow intellectually and spiritually.

To Bellamy, this world of the Second Industrial Revolution would be regarded as introducing an era to be known eventually as the Epoch of Bigness—bigness in business, in government, in unions. He would observe too that the United States—already in its third great period of mergers—was entering a period in which automation, tax benefits, increasing costs of production, and research would continue to throw the advantages to bigger and bigger business combinations. As a result, he would warn that the problems to be posed by a rapidly changing and expanding economy, by greater leisure and longer life spans, by the educational requirements of a changing society, and by an ever-diminishing opportunity for un- skilled labor or for the small businessman could be solved only by co-operative planning by the government, industry, and unions.

Bellamy would forecast, however, that such co-operative planning could be achieved. Like William Whyte in *The Organization Man* and Roger Burlingame in *The American Conscience,* he would assert that "rugged individualism" and "free competitive enterprise" have ceased to be typical of American life and have been replaced by organization, co-operative enterprise, and government control. Labor and capital sit amiably around the conference table today to solve mutual problems; the proletariat has been absorbed by the middle class which has accepted the responsibility of the government for the common good in all areas of life; and big business, no longer managed by a captain of industry but by a group or by hired managers, has realized that its welfare depends upon that of the society which it serves and upon which it relies for consumption and investment of capital.

And yet, despite all of these trends toward the year 2000, Bellamy, like Arnold J. Toynbee in *An Historian's Approach to Religion,* would remind the world that progress depends upon spiritual insight and upon unselfishness—the development of the impersonal. And he would doubtless warn that unless men begin rapidly to practice the Christianity they profess, to return to the spiritual values lost in an excess of materialism, and to retrieve their faith in man's ability to solve the problems created by the machine and by atomic energy, mankind will be doomed. Instead of co-operatively creating a world in which men may grow intellectually and spiritually, they will foster in their blind selfishness a world for "soulless men" to die in.

ANNOTATIONS

Since these notes are not intended for the general reader but for the students of Bellamy who might be concerned with sources and verification, they are presented in the following fashion: each subdivision of the entry for each chapter refers to the material upon which the content of the section was based. All material, unless otherwise stipulated or placed under *OA* (other authors), was written by Edward Bellamy. All articles appearing in the *Springfield Union*, the Springfield *Daily News*, and *The New Nation* which are cited as being written by Bellamy were identified as his work by the author of this study. Where the term "editorial comment" is used, an article attributed to Bellamy has appeared without a title and has been used as a filler for the editorial page.

All references to *Looking Backward* are to the Modern Library edition, and all those to *Equality* are to the D. Appleton and Company edition of 1933.

The following abbreviations have been used in referring to different sources:

AJ: *Appleton's Journal.*
AM: *Atlantic Monthly.*
BF: Bellamy Family, in reference to the journals, letters, and telegrams still possessed by Mrs. Marion Earnshaw, 75 Avon Place, Springfield, Mass.
BW: *Blindman's World,* collection of Bellamy's short stories.
CM: *Century Magazine.*
CR: *Contemporary Review.*
DHP: *Dr. Heidenhoff's Process,* early novel by Bellamy.
DOS: *Duke of Stockbridge,* early historical novel by Bellamy.
E: *Equality,* Bellamy's second and last Utopian novel.
EB: Edward Bellamy.
GA: *Golden Age,* periodical published by Tilton.
HL: Houghton Library, Harvard University, where Bellamy papers are deposited.
LB: *Looking Backward,* Bellamy's first Utopian novel.
LHJ: *Ladies' Home Journal.*
MLS: *Miss Ludington's Sister,* early novel by Bellamy.
N: *Nationalist,* publication of the Nationalists in Boston.
NAR: *North American Review.*
NN: *New Nation,* weekly published by Bellamy.
OA: Other authors.
OP: Other publications containing works by Bellamy.
SA: *Sunday Afternoon.*
SDN: Springfield *Daily News.*
STO: *Six to One,* earliest novel written by Bellamy.
SU: *Springfield Union.*
TWH: Thomas Wentworth Higginson or his MSS, Houghton Library, Harvard.
WDH: William Dean Howells or his MSS, Houghton Library, Harvard.

ANNOTATIONS

CHAPTER I. THE YOUNG PHILOSOPHER

I. The Boy of Chicopee

MSS: HL, *Notebook*: XI, 23; *Folders*: XIX, *re* Hugh, 11, 12-24, 1-2; VII, "A Law for the Republic of San Domingo," 1; III, "Considerations upon Divorce," 1-13; VII, "The Force of Flattery"; I, Lyceum Addresses. *Letters*: Maria Putnam Bellamy to Ethel Clark, 11/30/7?, 1-4; Maria Putnam Bellamy to Mrs. E. H. Gorham; May Packer Brockway to Arthur Morgan, 4/11/40, 4/29/40, 5/4/40; Paul Bellamy to Arthur Morgan, 5/8/40, 4.

OP: "Overworked Children in our Mills," SU, 6/5/73; "A Providence," CM, XII, 3(7/76), 375-6; EB in "Interview", *Free Press Telegram*, BF.

OA: [Clark W. Bryan] "Editor's Portfolio," *Good Housekeeping*, X, 4 (12/21/89), 95. Arthur Morgan, *EB*, 25, 41. Mason Green, *EB*ms, HL, 12-13, 6.

II. Union College, Then Europe

MSS: HL, *Notebook*: I, 28-29; XI, 12,80; XV, 1-6; *Folders*: VII, "Necessary Self Education"; XXIX, "Almost a Suicide," 10; XIX, *re* Hugh, 17-22; I, "I am now come . . ."; XI, "In the winter of 1860 . . ." and "It was in the summer of 1860. . . ." *Letters*: EB to Delta Kappa Epsilon, August or September, 1887, 2; Isaac Landt to EB, 1; Rufus and Maria Bellamy to EB, Frederick, and Charles, 7/16/68. *Speech* of Frederick Bellamy to Boston Bellamy Club, 3/29/16, 1-2.

BF: Notebook about EB.

OP: "Pott's Painless Cure," BW, 160 ff. "How I Wrote 'Looking Backward' ", LHJ, XI, 5(4/94), 2; "Literary Notices", SU, 2/14/77, 9/28/72; 12/22/75; "Mental Stimulants," SU, 11/28/73; "Children's Books," SU, 10/11/75; "What Reading for the Young," 8/15/77; Editorial Comment, 11/23/77; "Out Door Life in Summer," SU, 5/23/77; "Home, Sweet Home," SU, 9/27/73.

OA: A. Morgan, *EB*, 44; Green, *EB*ms, HL, 22; "General Gossip," *Current Literature*, IV, 3/90, 185.

III. Religious Experiences

MSS: HL, *Notebook*: I, 4-5, 11-12, 30-32, 36-39; II, 53, 54, 57-58, 217-8; III and IV, autobiographical Eliot Carson story contained in these notebooks very valuable for information relative to Bellamy's religious experiences; III, 2, 3, 67-76, 180-183, 178, 206; VI, 23-24; XIV, 74-75; B, 14. *Folders*: XIX, *re* Hugh, 25-30, 33.

SU: "How the Alliance Has Met the Two Great Enemies of Protestantism," 10/11/75; "Literary Notices," 5/21/74.

OA: Green, *EB*ms, HL, 9, 28-29.

IV. Religion of Solidarity

MSS: HL, *Notebooks*: I, 47, 57; II, 48, 52-53, 60, 62, 74; III, 11-12, 13, 53, 184-185, 185-186, 193-194; IV, 3, 24, 27, 35-36, 47, 48, 169, 176, 200; V, 7, 10-11, 12, 15-16; VII, 53, 11; XI, 9, 84; XII, 16, 43; XIV, 72, 94, 104; B, 1-13; C, 25-28. *Folders*: XIV, "The very fact that . . . ," 1-27, 30, 35-37, 39; XXVII, "Spring Feeling," 1-2, 10-11, 15; XXXV, "Positive Romance"; IX, "The Dual Life," a, 6-7, 10-11, 1-6; XVI, "We rarely think until we come to die . . . ," 1-2; "They seem to come forth . . . ," 2; "Vagaries," 3; XIII, "Joseph Clairbourne"; XXVII, "The man who was noble and generous . . . "; XX, "To Whom It May Come," 57.

OP: *STO*, 31-32, 38-39, 54-55, 57, 80-81, 92, 116, 121, 124; *BW*: "An Echo of Antietam," 21-33, 42, 44, 55-58; "Cold Snap", 92; "Deserted," 239; "Positive Romance," 300-301, 304, 306; "Lost," 333; "Blindman's World," 17. *MLS*, 29-30, 31-32. "A Tale of the South Pacific," *Good Company*, V, 7 (1/80), 11-15. Letter to John Peck, *N*, II, 2(1/90). *Religion of Solidarity,* ed. by A. Morgan. *SU:* "Winter Occupations," 12/26/75; "Literary Notices," 6/11/74, 9/16/75; "The Holiday Season," 12/22/75.

OA: Green, *EB*ms, HL, 197; Morgan, *Philosophy of EB,* 6; Morgan, *EB,* 201, 138-139.

CHAPTER II. LAWYER AND WRITER

I. The Lawyer

MSS: HL, *Notebooks*: XI, 13, 15.

NN: "A Friendly Criticism," I, 41 (11/7/91), 645.

OA: Green, *EB*ms, HL, 23.

II. Journalist

MSS: HL, *Notebooks*: I, 25; XI, 17; XIV, 5; XV, 17. *Letters*: Wm. Packer to EB, 9/71, 1-6; Maria P. Bellamy to EB, 5/14/72; Rufus Bellamy to EB, 4/12/72, 2-3, 5/31/72; Frederick Bellamy to EB, 3/4/72, 2; Maria and Rufus Bellamy to EB, 5/31/72, 4; EB to Charles Bellamy, 1/15/78, 2-3, EB to Maria and Rufus Bellamy, 4/4/78.

SU: "New Books," 6/17/73, 7/2/73.

OA: Green, *EB*ms, HL, 30. Allen Nevins, *The Evening Post: A Century of Journalism,* 364-73. SU, "City Items," 1/14/78, 3/2/78, 4/4/78.

III. Bellamy's Minor Fiction

MSS: HL, *Letters:* EB to Horace Scudder, 8/25/90; Dewitt Seligman to EB, 11/27/86; EB to WDH, 8/26/86, 3/22/84, 3/18/84, 4/7/84, 8/7/84; Sylvester Baxter to EB, 2/19/89; Horace Scudder to EB, 9/11/93; G. P. Putnam's Sons to EB, 11/2/89.

OA: Sylvester Baxter, "The Author of 'Looking Backward'," *New England Magazine,* Vns., 92-98 (September, 1889). Robert L. Shurter, "The Literary Work of Edward Bellamy," *American Literature,* V, 229 ff (1933). Katherine Woods, "Edward Bellamy, Author and Economist," *Bookman,* VII, 398 (July, 1898). Arthur Morgan, *Edward Bellamy* (New York, 1944), 64, 70, 200, 202, 203. A. Morgan, *The Philosophy of Edward Bellamy* (New York, 1945), 7-34, 34-68. Joseph Schiffman, "Introduction," *Edward Bellamy: Selected Writings on Religion and Society* (New York, 1955), XXI-XXVIII. William D. Howells, "Edward Bellamy," *The Blindman's World* (Boston, 1898), VI-VII; [Clark W. Bryan] "Editor's Portfolio," *Good Housekeeping,* X, 4 (December 21, 1889), 96.

IV. Themes: The Impersonal, the Individuality

MSS: HL, *Folders:* XXXIX, "Woman Worship" (this ms. contains ideas about woman worship).

STO: pp. 80, 55, 81, 99, 25, 65.

DOS: pp. 44-45.

BW: "To Whom This May Come," 411, 398-410; "The Cold Snap," 92; "An Echo of Antietam," 146; "A Positive Romance," 300-301; "Pott's Painless Cure," 163-167; "A Love Story Reversed," 192-236; "Two Days' Solitary Imprisonment," 104-128; "Hooking Watermelons," 274-275.

OP: "Jane Hicks," *Good Company,* IV (1878), 250; "A Mid-Night Drama," *Appleton's Journal,* III, 14 (August, 1877), 162-166; "That Letter," *Good Company* (September, 1880), 14-23; "Extra-Hazardous," *Appleton's Journal,* III, 17 (November, 1877), 440.

OA: A. W. Levi, "EB, Utopian," *Ethics* (1/45), 132; C. A. Madison, "EB, Social Dreamer," *New England Quarterly* (9/42), 447; Louis Filler, *Crusaders for American Liberalism,* 26; Granville Hicks, *The Great Tradition,* 140; A. Morgan, "An Early American Social Revolt," *Survey Graphic,* XXIX, 12 (12/40), 618-619.

V. Themes: Sin, Man's Development

MSS: HL, *Notebooks:* A, 1-12; I, 2; II, 72, 80-81, 83-84, 95-96, 44; IV, 67-68, 19-20, 14-17; V, 2-3, 5. *Folders:* XXIV, "Almost a Suicide," 27 ff; XXVII, "unreasonableness of the difference a man makes. . . . "

SU: "Puzzles in Morals," 6/1/75, cols. 4-5, 4; "Toward a Solution," 8/1/77, col. 7, 4.

BW: "The Old Folks' Party," 63-64, 66, 72; "Lost," 331-334; "A Summer Evening's Dream," 129-156; "The Blindman's World," 26, 28-29, 13, 26.

DHP: 119-120,121,122.

MLS: 31, 38, 252-253.

VI. Bellamy's Aim in Writing

MSS: HL, *Letter:* EB to TWH, TWHms, 12/20/86. *Notebooks:* A, 1-12; I, 30-32, 57; II, 12, 13, 14, 35-36, 86-87.

SU: "Recent Miracles," 8/11/74; "Spiritualism and Science," 7/14/74; "Literary Notices," 5/24/73, 9/22/77, 2/20/75.

BW: "Two Days' Solitary Imprisonment," 106.

OP: "How I Wrote 'LB'," LHJ, XI (4/94), 2.

VII. The Publisher

MSS: HL, WDH, Letter of EB, 8/21/84.

SDN: 8/11/81, col. 4, p. 2.

OA: [Clark W. Bryan] *The Paper World,* quoted in obituary of C. J. Bellamy, C. J. Bellamy Clippings, Connecticut Valley Historical Association, Springfield, Mass.

CHAPTER III. WHY A FATHER WROTE A UTOPIAN NOVEL

I. Marriage and Fatherhood

MSS: HL, *Notebooks:* II, 28-29, 44-46, 69-72, 78-80, 97-100, 101; VII, 28-29, 16-17; XI, 29, 62; XIV, 118; C, 7; A, 7. *Letters:* EB to Emma Sanderson, 1/9/81; EB to Mrs. EB, 5/3/84, 5/19/87, 9/23/86, 1; Mrs. EB to Ethel Clarke, 12/13/85, 3; Mrs. Mary Gorham Spratt to Arthur Morgan, 6/3/39, 2. *Others:* "Papers Concerning Emma A. Sanderson, Guardianship," 9/1/74, 3; A. Morgan's "Mrs. E. Bellamy's Reminiscences," 12.

BF: Journal of EB, 1874, as read to author. Letter of EB to Mrs. EB, 3/24/84, 2.

OP: "Principles and Purposes of Nationalism," 10.

OA: Robert Lindblom, *Nationalism . . . ,* 6.

II. Economic Revolution

MSS: HL, *Folders:* I, First and Second Lyceum Addresses; XVII, "The Gypsies," 13.

SU: "Literary Notices," 10/9/76, 9/22/77, 11/20/75, 1/27/76; Editorial Comment, 8/15/77, 8/20/73; "The Experiment Not Finished," 10/14/76; "Was It Worth It," 10/24/74; "Home Types of Wickedness," 10/21/75; "Serbonian Bogs," 4/7/74; "Moralities in Politics," 11/17/76; "A Republic without Virtue," 6/5/74; "The Shame and Salvation of Popular Government," 3/4/73; "Drifting," 1/27/77; "Overgrown Fortunes a Social Injury," 6/17/73.

DS: 108, 34.

LB: 38-41, footnote 108-109, 189, 199, 223, 225-227, 229-230, 230-231, 233, 264, 234-235.

N: EB's speech to Free Religion Association quoted in John R. Bridge, "The Changes of Fifty Years," I, 6 (10/89), 227. "Looking Forward," II, 1 (12/89), 14.

NN: "The Shadow of the Man on Horseback," II, 46 (11/12/92), 675; "Letter [of EB] to the People's Party Ratification Meeting," II, 43 (10/92), 644-5; "The Millionaire or the Republic Must Go," II, 3 (1/6/92), 32-3; "The America of Today not the America of Yesterday," III, 14 (4/8/93), 178-9; EB's speech quoted in "The Cradle of Liberty Rocked at Faneuil Hall," I, 38 (10/17/91), 606; "The Blight of Wealth Centers," I, 9 (3/28/91), 133; "The Reign of the Hucksters," II, 1 (1/2/92), 5.

SDN: "Tea Table Talk," 9/24/80.

E: "Preface," X; 17-19, 21, 27, 69, 96, 99-100, 103-106, 162, 189, 200, 243, 251-52, 254-55, 259, 269, 278-9, 323-4, 352.

OP: "Principles and Purposes of Nationalism," 3-4; "Plutocracy or Nationalism—Which?", EB's Tremont Temple Address, 5/31/89, 6-7.

OA: A. M. Schlesinger, *Political and Social History of the United States,* 281-296; A. W. Levi, "EB, Utopian," 134; L. Gronlund, *Co-operative Commonwealth,* 59; "Attitude of the Press," N, III, 1 (8/90), 39-40.

III. The Laborer

GA: "National Education," II, 13 (3/30/72), 2.

SU: "The Cheap Labor Problem," 6/4/71; "The Anti-Chinese Uprising in California," 4/8/76; "The State of the Labor Market," 2/7/74.

SDN: "Tea Table Talk," 10/26/80, 3.

OP: "The Programme of the Nationalists," *Forum,* XVII (3/94), 81.

OA: M. Josephson, *The Robber Barons,* 159-163; Edward Hamilton, Rev. O. P. Gifford, *et al.,* "Destitution in Boston with Striking

Illustrations and Practical Suggestions," *Arena*, II, 12 (10/90), 745; Rev. C. A. Cressy, "New Industrial System," N, III, 3 (10/90), 162; Collins G. Burnham, "The City of Chicopee," *New England Quarterly*, XVIII ns (5/98); Dr. Frank Draper, "The Homes of the Poor in Our Cities," Report of Massachusetts State Board of Health, Boston, 1873, p. 429; J. Dorfman, *Thorsten Veblen and His America*, 15; L. Gronlund, *The Co-operative Commonwealth*, 46-47, 81; John A. Kouwenhoven, ed., "America on the Move," *Harper's*, CCI, 1205 (10/50), 120; Wm. G. Moody, *Land and Labor*, quoted in J. R. Bridge, "The Changes of Fifty Years," N, I, 6 (10/89), 228-9; Thaddeus B. Wakeman, "The Decline of the Farmer," N, I, 7 (11/89), 234-5; E. B. Lytton, *The Coming Race*, 291; L. Symes and C. Travers, *Rebel America*, 134; R. Ely, *The Labor Movement in America*, 499; Stanley Stevens, *Primer of Political Economy*, quoted by Joseph Cook in *Boston Monday Lectures* (1880), 32.

IV. Reform Movements

MSS: HL, *Folders*: I, First Lyceum Talk, 4-5.

SU: Editorial Comment, 8/22/77; "Two Types of Reformers," 9/25/73; "Some Good Words Spoiled," 6/22/76; "What the Grangers Say of Themselves," 2/7/74; "The Patrons of Husbandry," 2/10/74; "Who Has Got to Pay," 7/25/77.

OP: "Programme of the Nationalists," *Forum*, XVII (3/94), 83.

OA: Allan Seagar, *They Worked for a Better World*, 78; F. J. Turner, *The Frontier in American History*, 267 ff; R. Ely, *The Labor Movement in America*, 61-62, 168, 171-4, 176-9, 180-181, 182-183, 185, 187-88; J. Dorfman, *Thorsten Veblen and His America*, 15; Levi, "EB, Utopian," 133-134; Symes and Travers, *Rebel America*, 158.

V. Socialism

OA: J. F. Hudson, "The Anthracite Coal Pool," NAR, CXLIV, 362 (1/87), 54; T. W. Higginson, "Step by Step," N, I, 4 (9/89), 146; A. Lincoln, quoted in Nationalist Pamphlet, by T. W. Gilruth, Kansas City, Mo., January, 1890, 2; R. Ely, *Labor Movement in America*, 208-294; R. Ely, *Recent American Socialism*, 21-24, 31-32; H. A. James, *Communism in America*, 59-60; J. Macy, *Socialism in America*, 51, 60-63; Symes and Travers, *Rebel America*, 134-179, 120, 123, 180-181, Aveling quoted, 169.

VI. Bellamy and Socialism

MSS: HL, *Notebooks*: I, 32-34; VII, 53; XII, 21; "Thoughts on Political Economy" notebook (1867), 1. *Folders*: I, First Lyceum Talk, 8-9; Second Lyceum Talk, 3-14; VII, "Treason," 2; "Ensigns," 1; "Does Time Establish a Usurpation," 1-2; VIII, "How Many Men

Make a Man," 25. *Letters*: Mrs. Harriet Putnam Packer to Wm. Packer, 10/25/66, 4; **EB** to **WDH**, **WDH**, 6/17/88, 3.

GA: "Railroad Disasters," II, 2 (3/16/72), 2.

SU: "Literary Notices," 6/5/75, 10/16/72, 5/7/73, 12/23/74, 12/2/73; Editorial Comments, 11/8/72, 2/8/73, 12/3/75, 2/22/77, 11/16/74, 8/28/77, 7/29/72; "The Poor Man's Banker," 2/23/75; "Luxury and Extravagance," 7/7/73; "Rents and Ownership," 9/25/75; "Towards a Solution," 8/4/77; "Puzzles in Morals," 6/1/75; "Ethics of Strikes," 4/15/73; "Communist Hopes and Follies," 6/28/73; "Vanderbilt's Way," 8/1/77; "In the Right Direction," 1/4/73; "What the Grangers Say of Themselves," 2/7/74; "The Patrons of Husbandry," 2/10/74; "Why Co-operation Does Not Always Succeed," 12/13/77; "Co-operation at the South," 8/18/73; "Two Types of Reformers," 9/25/73; "More English Lectures," 4/22/73; "The Order of Enoch: a New Phase of Mormonism," 4/19/74; "Collapse of the International," 9/26/74; "A Reign of Terror Ended," 3/17/77; "Feudalism of Modern Times," 11/3/73; "Communism Boiled Down," 8/3/77; "Forefather's Day," 12/22/77; "How Can Confidence Be Restored," 2/10/74.

OP: "How I Wrote 'Looking Backward,'" LHJ, 2.

OA: *Boston Journal,* 5/23/98, Bellamy Clipping File, HL.   Green, *EB*ms, HL, 10-11.

VII. Plans for a Utopia

MSS: HL, *Notebooks*: II, 78; IV, 75-77; VI, 17-18, 31-34; XII, 20, 40, 45; XIV, 39, 97, 113-116, 117, 106, 25, 144, 129-130; XV, 55; C, 58-59.

SU: "Literary Notices," 12/20/73, 10/21/75, 9/29/77, 10/2/73.

OA: W. F. Taylor, *The Economic Novel in America,* 59; Vernon L. Parrington, Jr., *American Dreams, A Study of American Utopias.*

CHAPTER IV. THE REFORMER: *Looking Backward,* Nationalism, and *Equality*

I. Writing of *Looking Backward*

MSS: HL, *Folders*: XXI, "To Whom This May Come," fragment with famous statement relative to crucifixion of humanity on back of page; *Letters*: EB to WDH, WDH, 6/17/88, 1-2; Mason Green, postal card to EB.

OP: "How I Came to Write 'Looking Backward,'" N, 1, 1 (5/89), 1-3; "How I Wrote 'Looking Backward,'" LHJ, 2.

OA: Green, *EB*ms, HL, 56, 60.

II. Publication, Success of *Looking Backward*

MSS: HL, *Notebooks:* IV, 24a. *Letters:* EB to Benjamin Ticknor, 8/11/87, quoted by Green, *EB*ms, 61; EB to Benjamin Ticknor, 10/1/87; EB's contract with Rabbi S. Schindler, 11/26/88, 1; EB to Houghton Mifflin, 7/23/89, 12, 9/9/89, 1, 7/23/89, 2, 6/17/89; Frances Willard to Lillian Whiting, 5/15/88, 6/4/88; EB to John Lloyd Thomas, 2-8; E. L. Huntington to EB, 8/24/89, 2; John B. Walker to EB, 8/7/87, 3; Miss Faith Chevallier to Mrs. Marion Earnshaw; Ferris Greenslet to Arthur Morgan, 8/14/89; George Routledge and Sons to Arthur Morgan, 10/19/?; William Reeves to A. Morgan, 12/15/38.

OP: "Progress of Nationalism in the United States," NAR, CLIV, 426 (6/92), 746; "Principles and Purposes of Nationalism", 10; "How I Came to Write 'Looking Backward,'" N, I, 1 (5/89), 2; "Literary Notices," SU, 6/17/76.

OA: Green, *EB*ms., HL, 98, 63; Symes and Travers, *Rebel America,* 180 (quote of Dr. Aveling); Gronlund, *Co-operative Commonwealth,* 9-10; Robert Lindblom, "Nationalism," 5; S. W. Foss, "Can We Popularize Absolute Justice," N, I, 3 (7/89), 74-75; Files of clippings of reviews, HL; T. W. Higginson, "Step by Step," N, I, 4 (9/89), 145; Cyrus Willard, *Autobiography* Ms, HL, 12-13 ("The Nationalist," *Lucifer,* IV, 23 [7/15/89], 1140, quoted); "We Trust This Is Not Sound Theosophy," NN, II, 50 (10/10/92), 723; Frances Willard, "An Interview with EB," *Our Day,* IV, 24 (12/89), 540; Frances E. Willard, "The Coming Brotherhood," 10-11; Morgan, *EB,* 260-275.

III. Nationalism

MMS: HL, *Notebooks:* I, 56; C, 6. *Letters:* EB to WDH, 11/7/93, 2; Franklin Hunter to EB, 4/15/94, 5/12/94, 4/3/95, 9/16/95, 10/26/97, 3/23/98; EB to Mrs. EB, n.d.; EB to TWH, 1/5/89, 12/21/90; Hamlin Garland to A. E. Morgan, 2/40; Sidney Reeves to Emma Bellamy, 6/22/34; Sylvester Baxter to EB, 2/19/89; EB to Houghton Mifflin, 10/17/89, 1-2; Henry D. Lloyd to Samuel Bowles, 3/15/93; Eltweed Pomeroy to EB, 2/18/94.

BF: EB to Mrs. EB, February, 1893—letter written on the back of a form letter used by the Nationalist committee of propaganda.

NN: "Prospectus," I, 1 (12/21/91), 13; "Objections to National Ownership of the Railroads," III, 17 (4/29/93), 213-214; "Reason to Thank God . . . ," III, 42 (10/21/93), 466; "The New Party and the Nationalists," I, 18 (5/30/91), 277-278; "A Word of Explanation," III, 30 (7/29/93), 360; "Announcement," IV, 4 (2/3/94), 5.

OP: "Progress of Nationalism in the United States," NAR, 746, 747, 750-751, 752; "Nationalism—Principles and Purposes," 6-10; "First

Steps Toward Nationalism," *Forum*, X (10/90), 174-184; Letter of EB to John Orme, "Correspondence," *Nationalization News*, 12/90.

OA: [Clark W. Bryan] "Editor's Portfolio," *Good Housekeeping*, 95-96; John R. Bridges, "Editorial Note," N, II, 1 (12/89), 33; C. Willard, *Autobiography*, ms, HL, 21; Edward Page Mitchell, *Memoirs of an Editor*, 436-438; Green *EBms*, HL, 27, 139, 278-9; Mary Packer Brockway, "Impressions of Background of EB," ms, HL, 6/30/39, 1-2; C. Willard, "The Nationalist Club of Boston," N, I, 1 (5/89), 16-20; "Nationalism File," constitutions and published Nationalist speeches, John Crerar Library, Chicago; "Declaration of Principles," Nationalist Club, 1889; "Our Anniversary," "Editorial Notes," N, II, 1 (12/89), 35; "News of the Movement," N, I, 4 (8/89), 127; "Nationalism at the Boston Anniversaries," "Editorial Notices," N, I, 3 (7/89), 86; "The Second Anniversary of Nationalism," NN, I, 19 (6/6/91), 303; "What Is Nationalism, A Paper Read before the San Francisco Nationalists," 11/4/89, 4; F. I. Vassault, "Nationalism in California," *Overland Monthly*, XVns (6/90), 660-661; "News of the Movement," N, I, 1 (5/89), 23-24, I, 6 (10/89), 225; II, 2 (1/90), 75. Stanbury Norse, "Nationalism and Politics," N, quoted in J. T. George, "EB and the Nationalist Movement," MS, Amherst, 1938, 97; C. Willard, "A Retrospect," N, II, 1 (12/89), 38-39; L. Gronlund, "Nationalism," *Arena*, I, 2 (1/90), 153-154; W. L. Garrison, "The Mask of Tyranny," *Arena*, I, 5 (4/90), 553; J. A. Martin, "A Co-operative Commonwealth," N, I, 6 (10/89), 204-8; "Reviews," N, I, 2 (6/89), 2; "Announcement of an Excellent Publication," NN, I, 12 (4/18/91), 182; "Nationalist Publications," NN, I, 36 (10/31/91), 565; John Orme, "Labor and Nationalism in Great Britain," NN, I, 4 (2/21/91), 63-64; *North American Review*, quoted by J. Foster Briscoe, ed., "Attitude of the Press," N, II, 4 (3/90), 143; C. Willard, "A Practical Suggestion for Nationalist Clubs," N, II, 1 (12/89), 56. J. T. George, "EB and the Nationalist Movement," ms., 110-115; "Well Done Rhode Island," NN, 1, 7 (3/14/91), 108; "A Fine Infant," NN, I, 11 (4/11/91), 172; *St. Louis Dispatch* quoted in "The Significance of the Party," NN, I, 34 (9/19/91), 539; "The Senator from Alaska" [Fred R. Martin], *Fool's Gold*, 185; Wm. D. Howells, *Literature and Life*, 294; C. E. Russell, *Bare Hands and Stone Walls*, 74-77; "The Cradle of Liberty Rocked," NN, I, 38 (10/17/91), 606-8; "A Rousing Meeting at Lynn," NN, I, 40 (10/31/91), 636; "Faneuil Hall Ablaze," NN, II, 15 (4/9/92), 230-4; "Nationalism in Politics," NN, II, 43 (10/22/92), 643-5; "Massachusetts at It Again," NN, II, 38 (9/17/92), 582; "Nationalists in Counsel," NN, II, 30 (7/23/92), 469; "An Attempt to Fool the Public," NN, III, 47 (11/25/93), 507; Sadler, "One Book's Influence," 538, 540.

IV. *Equality*

MSS: HL, *Notebooks*: VII, 2, 15-16, 17-19, 22-26, 61-62; XV, 53. *Letters*: EB to WDH, WDH, 11/7/93, 1-2; D. Appleton and Company to EB or to Mrs. EB, 9/10/97, 12/1/97, 10/17/39; Frances Willard to EB, 9/13/97; B. O. Flower to EB, 8/9/97, 1-2; Thomas Reynolds to EB, 8/97; C. F. Bailey to EB, 9/11/97, 1-2.

OP: *Equality*, VII; " 'Looking Backward' Again," NAR, CL, 400 (3/90), 351-2; "Several Stock Objections to Nationalism Objected To," NN (11/28/91), 697-9; Letters of EB (12/15/93, 1/28/94) quoted in Green, *EB*ms, 182, 183; "Literary Notices," SU, 4/8/73.

OA: Green, *EB*ms, 115-6, 182, 183, 184, 188; A. G. Sedgwick, "Bellamy's Utopia," *Nation*, LXV, 1678 (8/26/97), 170; "Equality," *Saturday Review* (London), LXXXIV, 2176 (7/10/97), 45; C. R. Henderson, "Fact and Fiction in Social Study," *The Dial*, XXIII, 266 (7/16/97), 49.

V. Last Days

MSS: HL, *Notebooks*: I, 17-18, 44; II, 55-56, 73, 74; IV, 13; VI, 16, 18-19; VII, 28-29; B, 18-19. *Folders*: X, "How is it that the greater . . . "; "Mem.", 1; XXIX, "Almost a Suicide," 27-29. *Letters*: EB to Wm. D. Lloyd, 12/96, 1; Judge B. Lindsey to Mrs. EB, 9/11/39, 2; EB to Richard Watson Geldes, 1/11/98, 1; Maria Bellamy to EB, 12/20/71, 1-2.

BF: Letter of Mrs. Rufus King Bellamy to EB, 9/15/90, 1-2; EB to Mrs. EB, 3/10/90, 1, 3/12/90, 1; Excerpts from journals of EB in Notebook of Mrs. Marion B. Earnshaw.

OA: Green, *EB*ms, 54-55, 205; Morgan, EB, 70; "Edward Bellamy," *The American Fabian*, reprinted in *EB Speaks Again*, 21; *New Nation* (Denver), I, 1 (6/2/98), 1.

CHAPTER V. BASIC AIMS AND PRINCIPLES

I. Pragmatic, Evolutionary Principles of Reform

Editorial Comment, SU, 12/10/77; "Progress of Nationalism in the United States," NAR, 10/92, 742-6; " 'Looking Backward' Again," NAR, 3/90, 354; "What Nationalism Means," CR, 7/10, 16; "Plutocracy or Nationalism—Which?", Nationalist Extra No. 1, 7; "Extension of Municipal Functions the Cure for Municipal Misrule," NN, 4/9/92, 226; LB, 107; E, 333.

II. Basic Attitudes Toward Life

MSS: HL, *Notebooks*: I, 54; II, 33-34, 52-53, 69; III, 27; IV, 20, 31; VII, 42-43, 43-45, 50-51, 62; XI, 1, 5, 6, 16a-17, 33, 35, 36, 47-49,

55, 85; XII, 46; XIV, 21, 118, 128. *Folders*: V, "This scheme of a future so bright . . . "; XXXVII, Unused Preface of E, 1-5; XVII, "A faith in the good time coming," 1-14; XII, "Liberty of the Press," 35; VI, "Religion"; XX, "Superfluity of Naughtiness," 2, *re* Mr. Stanley, 2; XIV, *re* Henry Buddington and Eliot Carson, 1-6; XI, "It was in the summer . . .," 1; "The Troubadors," 1; II, "Civilization and Barbarism," 1.

BF: Journal of EB.

N: Letter of EB, quoted in "True Individuality," "Editorial Notes," 7/89, 88; "Principles and Purposes of Nationalism," 490, 174-180.

NN: "Talks on Nationalism," 2/28/91, 69; 3/14/91, 111; 4/4/91, 151; 5/19/91, 239; 7/11/91, 379. "The New Nation," 1/31/91, 10-11; "Mr. Foulke on Individualism," 3/11/93, 131; "Why We Cannot Agree with the Tribune," 5/16/91, 247-48; "Nationalism and Persecution of the Jews," 5/30/91, 277; "Fallacies of a Fallacy," 6/25/91, 401-402; "The Divine Basis," 8/1/91, 427; "Socialism Abroad," 11/14/91, 663; "Human Sympathy Compared with Class Sympathy," 12/5/91, 711; "Nationalism and Anarchy," 12/12/91, 727; "The Coming American Aristocracy," 1/16/92, 36; "Is Nationalism Reconcilable with a Wage System," 3/12/92, 161; "Edward Bellamy's Speech," 5/19/92, 232-233; "Why the Social Conscience in Advance of the Individual Conscience," 12/16/93, 531; "Nationalists Are Color Blind," 10/3/91, 567; "The Divine Basis," 8/1/91, 427.

SDN: "An Epauletted Snob," 11/13/80.

SU: "Literary Notices": 2/5/73; 2/22/73; 4/22/73; 4/29/73; 5/29/73; 9/4/73; 10/23/73; 11/5/73; 12/6/73; 10/16/73; 9/11/75; 11/20/75; 3/3/76; 4/29/76; 4/9/76; 11/25/76; 4/21/77. "Opportunity of the Workmen and the Church," 12/4/73; "Out of the Fashion—Out of the World," 5/10/73; "A Sensible City Fashion," 2/19/74; "Wrestling with a Holiday," 4/3/74; "Civilization and Cultivation," 5/21/74; "The Uses of Leisure," 7/7/74; "Dull Times a Blessing in Disguise," 6/13/74; "How Can Confidence Be Restored," 2/10/74; "The Unfitness of Things," 5/11/75; "Treasures for the Taking," 7/10/75; "Burning The Candle at Both Ends," 4/8/76; "Hard Times and Suicide," 5/2/76; "America the Only Land of Freedom," 7/8/76; "Forewarned—Forearmed," 10/4/76; "Amusements," 12/19/76; "The Jewish Sensation," 6/20/77; "Shall We Call Them Servants," 9/26/77.

LB: 1-6, 45, 75, 76-77, 94, 95, 124-125, 159-160, 165, 179-181, 198, 214, 230-234, 234-236, 238, 256, 267-268, 271.

E: 133, 155-156, 159-160, 272, 380, 391-393, 399-402; Introduction, VI.

DOS: 13, 18.

STO: 45-46.

OP: "Programme of the Nationalists," *Forum,* 3/94, 83-84; "How I Wrote 'Looking Backward,'" LHJ, 4/94, 2.

"Hooking Watermelons," BW, 269; "Extra-Hazardous," AJ, 436, 439-440; "An Old Folks' Party," BW, 78.

III. Aims and Form of the New Government

MSS: HL, *Notebooks:* I, 34; XV, 22; XVII, 82, 124, 127; *Folders:* XXIII, "An Iowa subscriber . . . ," 2.

NN: "Talks on Nationalism," 2/14/91, 37; 4/11/91, 176. "Must Man Be Master or Servant," 8/27/92, 543; "Edward Bellamy's Speech," 4/9/92, 232; "Nationalism Logically Implied in Individualism," 2/13/92, 98; "Why Every Workingman Should Be a Nationalist," 4/15/93, 275; "Some Account of Eugen Richter's Anti-Socialist Romance," 6/6/92, 275; "Socialism and Nationalism," 1/27/94. "A Confusion of Ideas," 2/21/91, 62; "Talks on Nationalism," 3/21/91, 127; "The Congregationalist on Nationalism," 10/31/91, 630; "Edward Bellamy's Speech," 4/19/92, 232-233; "Why Every Workingman Should Be a Nationalist," 4/15/93, 193.

OP: "Programme of the Nationalists," *Forum,* 3/94, 84; "What 'Nationalism' Means," CR, 7/90, 18; "Brief Summary of the Industrial Plan of Nationalism . . . " , *Dawn,* 9/89, 3; "The Old Faith and the New," SU, 12/22/73. "Plutocracy or Nationalism—Which?", Nationalist Extra No. 1, 9, 11-12; "What 'Nationalism' Means," CR, 7/90, 8-9.

LB: 41-42, 44-45, 92-93, 163, 169.

E: 9-10, 27, 56-58, 73-79, 107, 108, 109-113, 117-121, 203, 330, 331, 407, 408-409.

OA: E. E. Hale, "The Best Government," N, 6/89, 39-40; Charles Bellamy, *The Way Out,* 1-3.

IV. Democratic, Ethical, Economic Bases of the Government

MSS: HL, *Notebooks:* I, 5; IV, 49; VII, 12-13, 14, 48, 65; XIV, 15-16; XV, 55-57, 58. *Folders:* I, First and Second Lyceum Addresses; II, "Political Views," XIII, "What Is This Sanctuary of Self"; XC, "father, you're a great . . . "

HL, TWH: Letter of EB, 12/28/88, to TWH, 4-6.

HL, WDH: Letter of EB, 6/17/88, to WDH, 1-2.

N: "Looking Forward," 13/89, 2-4; Letter of EB to Lord John Peck, 2/90; "Principles and Purposes of Nationalism," 4/90, 174-180. Letter of EB quoted, "What is Nationalism," 5/89, 11-12.

NN: "Edward Bellamy's Speech," 4/8/92, 232; "Has the Republic Failed," 8/27/92, 544; "Mr. Bellamy's Letter," 3/21/91, 118; "The

Millionaire or the Republic Must Go," 1/6/92, 32-33; Editorial
Comment, 10/17/91, 597; "The Nationalist the True Conservative
Party," 1/28/93, 49; "The Globe 'Away Off,'" 2/20/92, 115;
"Spots on the Sun," 3/8/91, 142; "The Co-operative Common-
wealth," 5/2/91, 224; "Several Questions Answered," 7/11/91, 374;
"Why Every Workingman Should Be a Nationalist," 4/15/93, 193;
"Nationalism and the European System of Pensioning Workmen,"
8/22/91, 472; "Scientific Basis of Economic Equality," 6/18/92,
388-389; "Mr. Gladden Attacks The Principle of Economic Equality,"
4/29/93, 215-216; "More Talks About 'Individualism' and Common
Sense," 4/1/93, 167; "Why Should Not the Functions of Government 'Include Support of the People,'" 4/15/93, 192; "Two Ways of
Looking at It and the Right Way," 4/1/95, 166; "The Social Conscience in Advance of the Individual Conscience," 12/6/73, 531;
"Economic Equality," 4/8/93, 177; "Fourth of July, 1992," 7/9/92,
436; "The Root of the Present Social Discontent," 7/8/91, 389-390;
"Plenty of Room at the Top," 8/6/92, 500; "Just What We Maintain," 3/14/91, 110; "One of the A, B, C's," 9/19/91, 536 "The
Only Respect in which a Republic is Better than a Monarchy,"
1/28/93, 52; "News from Nowhere," 2/14/91, 47; "A System without Government of Any Sort," 10/21/93. "The Divine Basis,"
8/1/91, 427; "The Old Patriotism and the New," 7/8/93, 333-334;
"Property Is Power," 4/14/91, 190; "Not Too Soon," 12/9/93,
523; "Talks on Nationalism," 6/20/91, 329; 4/4/91, 159; 8/1/91,
425-426; 7/25/91, 409-410; 4/18/91, 192; 3/7/91, 85; 5/2/91,
224; "The New Nation," 1/31/91, 11.

SU: "Luxury and Extravagance," 7/7/73; "Science and Sentiment,"
   12/29/75; "America the Only Land of Freedom," 7/8/76; "Everything for Money," 10/25/73; "Wealth and Sensual Pleasures,"
   2/24/73; "Riches and Rottenness," 11/14/77; "Latest from the
   Black Hills," 5/2/77; "How and How Far Panics Can Be Prevented,"
   10/3/73; "Springfield Shylocks," 1/5/73; "Morbid Criticism,"
   2/2/75; "Industrial Feudalism of Modern Times," 11/3/73.

LB: 2, 12-13; 17; 36; 68; 69; 70; 72; 82; 104-105; 107;
   114; 125; 133-134; 149; 163-164; 169; 170; 175; 192-193; 194;
   213-214; 214-215; 216; 224; 229; 237-9; 272.

E: 1; 5; 14; 16; 17; 18-19; 20; 22-23; 24; 27; 29; 33; 30-31; 73-
   79; 72-73; 78; 79-82; 83-86; 88-91; 93; 98-101; 107-108; 104-
   106; 117; 113; 101; 153; 155-180; 175-176; 190; 191-192; 194;
   195; 268-269; 273-275; 279-280; 288; 306; 316 ff; 332-333; 342;
   356-357; 372; 384; 387-390; 394-395; 397; 400; 406-407; 407-408.

DOS: 13; 18; 26; 77; 179; 237; 302; 344.

OP: "Introduction," *Fabian Essays,* XII-XVIII; "Christmas in the Year
   2000," LHJ, 1/95, 6; "Progress of Nationalism in the United States,"
   NAR, 6/92, 742; "Programme of the Nationalists," *Forum,* 3/94,
   81, 85, 91, 85-86.

CHAPTER VI. THE GOVERNMENT OF INDUSTRIAL DEMOCRACY

I. An Evolutionary Government

MSS: HL, Morgan MSS, Rev. Robert Bisbee, "The Bellamy Revival" MS, 3.

NN: "Socialism and Nationalism," 1/27/94, 38; "Some Account of Eugen Richter's Anti-Socialist Romance," 6/3/93, 275.

OP: "Programme of the Nationalists," *Forum,* 3/94, 84-85; " 'Looking Backward' Again," NAR, 3/90, 351-352; "Brief Summary . . . ," *Dawn,* 9/89, 3.

LB: 114, 194, 237-239.

E: VII-IX; 153.

II. Principles and Motivation of the Industrial Army

MSS: HL, EB: *Notebooks,* I, 32-34, 53-54; II, 14-17, 40-41; III, 198-199; IV, 4, 28; XI, 1, 28, 31; XIV, 110, 135-136; XV, 36; XVII, 51; C, 11-12, 35. *Folders:* I, Second Lyceum Address, 1-5; VI, "Religion," 1; VII, "The Force of Flattery," 1; XIV, *re* Henry Buddington, 8; XIX, "An Essay at Autobiography," 19-24; XXIX, "Almost a Suicide," 10-11, 17-18. *Letters:* Charles E. Buell to EB, 7/21/89, 1-5; Mrs. Frances E. Russell to EB, 10/30/93, 1-3.

SU: "Literary Notices," 10/2/75, 3/27/74; "The Tramp," 11/17/74; "Shall We Call Them Servants," 9/26/77; "Earning Before Spending," 11/15/73; "The Ethics of Strikes," 4/15/73; "The Policy of Public Works in Dull Times," 11/21/74; "From the College into the World," 7/11/74; Editorial Comment, 7/27/75; "The Rage for Office and Title," 10/2/73; "Von Moltke's Criticism of Our Army," 8/3/75.

NN: "Talks on Nationalism," 4/25/91, 208-209; 3/14/91, 111; 2/14/91, 37; 6/27/91, 346. "Nationalism in a Nut Shell," 10/10/91, 590; letter of EB quoted in "The Great Principle Involved at Homestead," 8/20/92, 532; Comment, 7/30/92, 48; "The Right to Labor. 'Work for the Unemployed,' " 1/2/92, 18-19; "The Solution and the Only One of Unemployed Problem," 9/9/93, 418; "Should the State or Municipality Provide Work for Its Unemployed" (Interview of EB reprinted from *Boston Traveler*), 11/11/93, 493-494; "What Ought to Be Done for the Unemployed," 12/16/93, 530; "The Co-operative Solution of the Unemployed Problem More Fully Set Forth," 1/20/94, 25, 27; "City Industries," 2/14/93, 38; "A Hot Weather Argument for Nationalism," 7/4/93, 358; "A Continuance of Our Friendly Debate with Professor Secretan," 11/21/91, 678; "Some Account of Eugen Richter's Anti-Socialistic Romance," 6/3/93, 275; "The Philosophy of Competition," 4/23/92, 259; "Herbert Spencer's Attack on Evolution," 4/4/91, 157; "More

Talks about 'Individualism' and Common Sense," 4/1/93, 167; "The Question of Incentives Once More," 4/18/91, 185, 189; "Cut Bait or Fish," 3/14/91, 110.

N: EB quoted, "Attitudes of the Press," 3/90, 144.

STO: 5-11.

BW: "Old Folks' Party," 71-72; "Pott's Painless Cure," 167, 174; "Hooking Watermelons"; "An Echo of Antietam," 46; "The Blindman's World," 24; "To Whom This May Come," 403.

OP: "Christmas in the Year 2000," LHJ, 1/95, 6; " 'Looking Backward' Again," NAR, 3/90, 353, 354, 357; "How I Wrote 'Looking Backward,' " LHJ, 4/94, 2; "What 'Nationalism' Means," CR, 7/90, 2, 4, 5; "Brief Summary . . . , " *Dawn,* 9/89, 3; "A Solution for Unemployment Devised in 1893, for the Present Crisis," *Golden Book,* 6/33, 48-49; "Taking a Mean Advantage," SA, 3/79, 270.

LB: 45-50; 50-51; 52; 53; 54-56; 73-76; 96-103; 108-109; 137; 148; 158-160; 166; 168; 209-210; 219; 264.

E: 35-39; 67; 90; 41-43; 248-250; 381; 390; 394-398.

OA: Morgan, *EB,* 88-89; General F. A. Walker, "Bellamy and the New Nationalist Party," AM, 2/90, 248-262; Sylvester Baxter, "What Is Nationalism," N, 5/89, 12.

III. Organization and Administration

SU: Editorial Comment, 12/4/72; "Sex in Industry," 5/12/75: "Literary Notices," 12/4/75, 2/10/76; "Medical Education in the United States," 11/8/75; "A Reform Worth Having," 7/13/76; "The Swedish Civil Service," 11/1/77; "About These Cabinet Appointments," 2/26/77.

NN: "Talks on Nationalism," 4/18/91; "Consumption and Rheumatism," 12/19/91, 750; "Several Questions Answered," 7/11/91, 499; "Practical Questions about Railroad Nationalization," 9/2/93, 410.

OP: "Brief Summary . . .," *Dawn,* 9/89, 3; "What 'Nationalism' Means," CR, 7/90, 13.

OA: Mary A. Livermore, "Co-operative Housekeeping," *Chautauquan,* 4/86, 396-99; "Frances E. Willard a Nationalist," NN, 4/14/91, 102.

LB: 55-56; 96; 100-101; 104-105; 112-113; 114; 131-132; 147-149; 152-157; 166-170; 209-211.

E: 43-44; 77; 228-229; 283-284; 368.

IV. Efficient, Responsible Officials

MSS: HL, *Notebook* VI, 18; *Notebook,* "Thoughts on Political Economy," 1-4, 10-14; *Folders:* II, "Political Views," 2; XV, "It is the duty . . . , " 1, 2-3, 3-4; XIII, "Joseph Claibourne."

SU: Editorial Comments, 12/8/76, 11/2/76, 10/23/76, 4/18/76;
"New Books," 7/12/73; "Useful Wishes and Useful Work,"
7/23/74; "A Reform Worth Having," 7/13/76; "The Logic of the
Situation," 3/10/77; "The Swedish Civil Service," 11/21/77; "The
Compensation of Elections," 10/28/73; "Taking the Election,"
11/15/76; "The Shame and Salvation of Popular Government,"
3/4/73; "The Head and Tail Changing Places," 4/3/74; "Morality
and Politics," 11/17/76; "How the French Vote," 10/17/77.

NN: "Well Done, Mr. Andrews, but Look at Home," 6/4/92, 353-
354; "Some Points of Nationalism Argued Out," 8/29/91, 486-487;
"Shall Public Business Be Conducted by Public Employees," 11/7/91,
647; "Nationalism and Civil Service Reform," 12/18/91, 743-744;
"Elections Under Nationalism," 11/11/92, 673; "Ask Me Something Harder," 8/6/92, 500; "The Defects of Self-Interest as a
Motive," 12/19/91, 741-742; "A Picture of Labor," 10/24/91, 616.

SDN: "Bribery at New York," 11/3/80.

LB: 45-46; 52-53; 147; 149; 151-152; 154; 156; 157.

E: 11-13; 104; 202-203; 256-257; 274-276; 367; 314; 390; 398; 400;
404-405.

OP: "Brief Summary . . . , " Dawn, 9/89, 3.

V. Distribution of Commodities

MSS: HL, Folder XVIII, "New York City, April, 1872," 2.

SU: "Luxury and Extravagance," 7/7/73; "Why Co-operation Does
Not Always Succeed," 12/12/77; "Drummers," 12/7/72; "Some
Common Adulteries," 5/9/77.

NN: "The Value of a Public Brand," 9/16/93, 427.

OP: "Brief Summary . . . , ." Dawn, 8/89, 3.

LB: 21-22; 66-67; 69; 83-85; 114; 146; 149; 150-151; 256-259.

VI. The International Council

MSS: HL, Notebook VII, 66, 57-58; Folder XVII, "A Faith in the
good time coming . . . , " 3-4, 5-15.

NN: "A Nationalist Text from Calvin's City," 11/12/92, 674-675.
"Talk on Nationalism," 7/18/91, 394; "Immigration and Nationalism," 4/25/91, 205.

LB: 112-113; 114-115; 116.

E: 212-213; 214-221; 257-258; 276-278; 280-281.

N: "Principles and Purposes of Nationalism," 4/90, 174-180.

VII. Legislation

MSS: HL, *Notebooks:* IV, 58; XI, 13-15, 36-40; "Thoughts on Political Economy," 5, 15-17; "Hawaiian Notebook," 38. *Folder* XXVII, "The philosopher cannot condemn criminals . . . "

SU: Editorial Comments, 11/20/72, 10/29/74, 1/27/73; "Literary Notices," 1/20/76, 2/14/77; "Men not Principles," 8/3/72; "Striking Hard Pan," 3/15/73; "The Female Lobbyist at Washington," 5/7/74; "The Case of Boss Tweed," 12/18/72; "The Arrest of Charles Bowles," 12/19/72; "The 'Great Lawyers' of New York," 6/11/74; "The Last Case of Emotional Insanity," 12/20/73; "Emotional Insanity," 1/1/73; "Punishment and Insanity," 1/22/76; "The Lesson of the Fifth Avenue Fire," 1/3/73; "Overworked Children in Our Mills," 6/5/73; "Curiosities of Juvenile Crime," 2/7/74; "Crime and Its Causes," 2/19/74; "The Cause of American Lawlessness," 6/10/73; "The Dark Side of Human Nature," 4/25/74; "Responsibility in Mental Disease," 5/12/74; "A Hard Nut to Crack," 3/23/75; "Prison Reform and the Proposed Means," 2/17/74; "Minding One's Own Business," 4/21/74.

NN: "Will Erotic Crimes Ever Become Unknown?", 8/15/91, 456; "The Truth Shall Make You Free," 3/19/92, 179-180; "Proportional Representation," 7/23/92, 466-467; "Devices to Restore Popular Government," 6/1/92, 372; "An Excellent Book on a Very Different Theme," 7/23/92, 466; "The Referendum in Nebraska," 2/7/91, 121.

OP: "The Plea of Insanity," *Christian Union,* 5/8/72; "Railroad Disasters," GA, 3/16/72, 2.

SDN: "The Ministers and the Divorce Laws," 1/14/81.

MLS: 229.

LB: 152, 155, 157, 168-170, 162-168.

E: 274-75; 363-364; 408; 409.

VIII. The Judicial System

MSS: HL, *Folders:* XII, "Liberty of the Press," 6-7; XVIII, "New York, April 24, 1872," 3-4.

SU: "Judicial Reform," 1/9/77; "The Lynch Law," 12/2/72; Editorial Comment, 12/11/72, 12/19/72; "Trial by Jury," 2/8/73; "An Absurdity of the Jury System," 7/6/75.

NN: "How to Secure Free and Speedy Justice," 7/2/92, 420; "How Rich and Poor Can Be Equalized Before the Law," 7/9/92, 420; "Let Us Have Free Justice," 4/29/93, 214-215.

LB: 165-167, 168, 211.

E: 16-17, 76, 317.

IX. The Result of Industrial Democracy: Wealth

MSS: HL, Notebooks: VI, 1; XIV, 98-99; XV, 36, 50. *Folder* 1,
Second Lyceum Address, 3-14.

SU: "The Condition of Business Prosperity," 8/16/76; "Time Lost
by Slow Travel," 1/4/73; "Economy the Only Political Economy for
Our Government," 12/16/73; "Over Production and Over Trading,"
7/20/75; "The Glut of Asiatic Markets a Cause of the Hard Times,"
7/8/75; "Modern Business Crises, Their Cause and Cure," 6/23/77;
"The Tornado as a Peace Maker," 6/20/77; "Literary Notices,"
2/3/77, 7/18/77, 2/14/77; Editorial Comment, 4/16/77; "The
Rainfall Declining Year by Year," 11/16/76; "Floods and Forests,"
8/3/75; "Forest Culture," 8/30/73; "Woodman, Spare That Tree,"
7/7/73; "The Destruction of American Forests," 1/2/75; "Water,
Water Everywhere and Not a Drop to Drink," 8/16/73; "The
Illinois Farmers in Convention," 4/4/73; "Farmer's Boys," 7/15/72;
"Flow of the Population Cityward," 9/7/75; "Real Independence,"
1/20/77; "The Great Strike in England," 4/30/74; "English Serf-
dom," 5/4/74; "Scientific Farming," 11/3/75; "Good Reading
for Farmers," 8/16/76; "How to Make Farm Life Attractive,"
8/8/77.

NN: "The Root and Cause of All Panics, Crises, and Hard Times and
the Remedy," 8/12/93, 389-390; "How Free Competition Flourishes
in Our Midst," 8/13/92, 517; "Some Facts about Trusts," 3/26/92,
195; Editorial Comment, 2/7/91, 28; 9/10/92, 365; "Talks on
Nationalism," 6/13/91, 313; 8/29/91, 490; "Mr. Edward Atkinson's Little Stove," 4/25/91, 206; "The Accumulation of Wealth,"
7/23/92, 468. "The World's Fair of 1893 and the World's Fair of
AD2000," 5/6/93, 227; "The Shadow of the Man on Horseback,"
11/12/92, 675; "Flood Disasters and Nationalism," 6/11/92, 371;
"National Forests," 12/12/91, 731; "Preserving Our Forests,"
10/10/91, 587; "Nationalist Drift," 2/28/91, 73; "How the American Farmer Is Being Turned into a Peasant," 4/2/92, 210; "The
American Farmer Must Choose Between Becoming a Nationalist
and a Peasant," 10/21/93, 466-467; "Farming Corporations,"
6/11/92, 372; "Farmers, Frost and Nationalism," 9/19/91, 535.

OP: "Plutocracy or Nationalism—Which," Nationalist Extra I, 2, 8;
"Brief Summary . . . , " *Dawn,* 8/89, 3; "Looking Forward," N,
12/89, 1; "Principles and Purposes of Nationalism," N, 4/90, 10-11;
"Railroad Disasters," GA, 3/16/72, 3.

DOS: 9, 14.

LB: 30, 41, 44, 85, 94, 146, 147-48; 149-150, 184-185, 187-188, 188-
189, 191-197, 198, 233, 257, 260.

E: 30, 31-32, 33-34, 41, 51, 85, 94, 96, 97, 158-159, 160, 164, 165,
168, 170, 171, 175-176, 176-177, 180, 183, 185, 188, 193-194, 216-

221, 222-227, 230-243, 248-249, 276, 297, 300, 301, 302, 303, 304, 309, 312, 313, 324-325.

OA: Walter L. Cheney, "The Effect of Our Patent Laws," N, 6/89, 52-54; C. Bellamy, *Breton Mills,* 276; H. G. Wilshire, *The Poor Farmer and Why He Is Poor,* 2-3; "Nationalism . . . Its Aims and Purposes," 2.

CHAPTER VII. INTELLECTUAL, SPIRITUAL LIFE

I. Formal Education

MSS: HL, *Folder* I, First Lyceum Talk, 1-11.

SU: "An American Education," 3/6/75; "A Book on Education," 9/13/75; "Statistics on Children," 7/25/72; Editorial Comment, 10/24/72; "Overworked Children in Our Mills," 6/5/73; "Our Children Must Be Educated," 11/24/74; "Boy Murderers," 2/26/73; "The Society for the Prevention of Cruelty to Children," 12/28/74; "The Foreign Population of Western Massachusetts," 11/22/76; "Centralization in Education," 1/14/73; "Our Unemployed Young Men," 9/19/74; "Ignorance and Loaferism," 2/28/74; "Compulsory Education," 8/8/72; "How Our Girls Are Better Educated Than Our Boys," 11/7/74; "How to Strike," 11/11/73; "The Model Public Library," 8/28/73; "What Our Young Men Should Resolve to Become," 3/17/74; "The True Mission of the Teacher," 9/3/74; "A Much Needed Educative Reform," 8/8/74; "Corporal Punishment in School—An Instructive Experiment," 9/9/73; "More School Superintendents Called For," 7/7/77; "Let Us Be Nonagenarian," 5/6/73; "What Reading for the Young," 8/15/77; "Children's Books," 10/11/75; "Sex in Education," 12/27/73; "Literary Notices," 5/15/75; 1/6/77.

N: "Our Prospective Sovereigns," 7/89, 68-69; EB quoted in "News of the Movement," 7/89, 91; EB quoted in "Attitudes of the Press," 11/89, 273-274.

NN: "Should Every Boy Learn a Trade? . . . , " 9/3/92, 557; "Too Many College Men Already," 10/10/91, 582-583; "Small Help in a Good Education," 4/1/93, 167-168; "Educated Men Need Not Apply," 8/12/93, 287.

OP: "National Education," GA, 3/30/72, 2; "Tea Table Talk," SDN, 11/11/80; Letter of EB published in "School Conference Report on the State of the School" (New York, 1890), 8.

LB: 50, 54, 164, 177-181.

E: 144, 147-152, 246-250, 256, 259, 283-284, 335-336, 361-362, 378, 401, 412.

II. Health, Physical and Mental

MSS: HL, *Notebooks*: IV, 13; XII, 40; *Folder* II, "The Physical Decadence of the Race," 1-4. Letter of EB to Mrs. EB, 8/24/72, given by BF to author of this work.

SU: "Walking," 9/5/77; "Medical Problems of the Day," 6/6/74; "Legs," 11/16/72; "The Modern Increase in the Average Life," 9/4/73; "The Modern Revival of Muscle," 7/17/73; "The Rising Generation," 2/7/77; "Physical Health as a Moral Factor," 7/19/73; "The Pestilence at Memphis," 10/17/73; "New Publications," 8/30/72; "A Domestic Tyrant," 3/14/77; "Some Hints About Ventilation," 11/20/73; "Literary Notices," 10/8/74, 10/17/74, 1/13/74, 1/1/76, 7/10/75, 5/16/73.

STO: 5-9, 11-14, 23.

BW: "Two Days' Solitary Imprisonment," 104; "To Whom This May Come," 403-404, 409.

LB: 160, 182, 210, 219, 227, 238, 265-266.

E: 51, 145, 147-152, 282-285, 412.

III. Art and Literature

MSS: HL, *Notebook* XI, 42-43; *Folder* XII, "Liberty of the Press," 1-32; *Folder* X, "It is often said with pride by newspapermen nowadays . . . , " 1-4. Letter of Mrs. Rufus King Bellamy to EB, Dec. 3, 187?, 2; letter of Mrs. Emma Bellamy, July 25, 1883, to EB.

SU: "Bliss's New Abridged Catalogue," 1/8/76; "Vacations for Tired People," 7/14/77; "Concerning Mountains," 9/9/76; "Vacation Philosophy," 8/2/76; "The Springtime," 5/19/77; "Walking," 9/5/77; "The Book of Flowers," 1/13/74; "Championship," 7/8/75; "Sunday School Songs," 11/11/73; "Where Are They," 11/18/72; "The Useful Should be Ornamental," 1/27/74; "Moral Murder as a Fine Art," 8/20/74; "The National Sin of Calumny," 5/18/75; "A Pleasant but Sad Seduction," 9/9/76; "The Function of the Newspaper," 5/7/74; "Reading Newspapers," 7/14/74; "Literary Notices," 12/1/77, 11/21/77, 12/9/73, 5/4/73, 12/16/73.

NN: "Art and Nationalism," 1/7/93, 3; "Newspapers Under Nationalism," 11/7/91, 468; "Concerning Nationalism, the Daily Press, and the Reform Movement," 6/24/93, 316.

SDN: "The Lord Deliver Us From Such Fools as Brother Holmes," 10/21/80.

LB: 89-91, 129, 130-133, 132, 137-138, 160, 198.

E: 63-64, 68-69, 207, 255-267, 275-76, 348-349.

IV. Religion, Morality

MSS: HL, *Notebooks:* I, 11-12; II, 33-34, 85-86; VII, 48; XI, 22-23, 40-41, 49; *Folder* XXX, "A Positive Romance," 1-55.

HL, TWH: Letter of EB to TWH, 12/28/88, 5.

SU: "The Church of the Future According to Matthew Arnold," 6/8/77; "Puzzles in Morals," 6/1/75; "How They Look at Him," 1/27/77; "Wastes and Burdens of Society," 11/15/77; "Professor David Swing and the Chicago Presbytery," 5/5/74; "Christianity as a National Law," 1/7/74; "Matthew Arnold's New Gospel," 6/7/73; "Religious Sensuousness," 8/22/77; "A Mischievous Divorce," 11/6/75; "Christianity and Civilization," 5/17/73; "Decoration Day," 5/29/74; "Enthusiasm," 7/11/77; "Glimpses of the Coming," 12/12/77; "Touching Things Spiritual," 11/27/77; "Whitefield One of the Founders of the American Nationality," 10/8/73; "Changing the Crop and the Tillage," 3/2/75; "Criminals—Who Are They?", 12/21/72; "Home Types of Wickedness," 10/21/75; "Hypocrisy and Corruption," 1/31/73; "Architectural Morality," 11/14/72; "The Lying Epidemic," 2/14/73; "A Pleasant but Bad Seduction," 9/9/76; "Better a Knave than a Fool," 3/6/75; "These Dreadful Days," 10/26/72; "Look on This Picture and on That," 5/1/75; "The Upbuilding Work of the Church," 4/24/75; "Religious Nonsense and Religious Common Sense," 11/22/73; "Moral and Religious Revivals," 2/21/74; "Religious Service for the Masses," 11/7/72; "A New England Country Parson," 11/14/77; "The Minister a Citizen," 4/10/75; "Liberty Gone to Seed," 12/6/73; "Confessions and Reservations of Religious Belief," 7/11/74; "Ritualism and Rutism," 2/20/75; "Schools of Instruction in Theology," 5/28/73; "Dean Stanley Upon the Religious Outlook," 4/7/77; "Putting on the Screws," 6/23/77; "How the Alliance Has Met Two Great Enemies of Protestantism," 10/11/73; "The Revision of the Bible," 7/3/72; "Why Don't God Kill the Devil," 10/28/73; "Pulpit and Plow," 5/31/73; "The Old Faith and the New," 12/23/73; "Religion and Science," 3/30/75; "Just How Far Evolution Conflicts with Theology," 10/13/77; "Variety in Unity," 10/7/73; "Literary Notices," 7/14/76, 6/4/74, 1/7/74, 5/25/74, 12/16/73, 12/10/74; 5/27/76, 10/21/75, 11/20/75, 10/8/74, 9/23/73, 12/31/74, 5/29/73, 3/12/73, 3/13/75, 3/5/74, 9/23/76, 1/8/76, 10/17/77, 12/6/73, 7/10/75, 7/23/74, 7/13/76, 9/9/76, 1/1/76, 4/29/73, 5/8/75, 6/5/75, 4/15/76, 3/13/75, 5/4/74; Editorial Comments, 1/4/81, 11/11/72.

NN: "Talks on Nationalism," 3/28/91, 143-144; 2/21/91, 53. "A Better Plan Than Young Women Ushers," 8/5/93, 378; "The Churches and Nationalism," 12/5/91, 710; "Christmas Thoughts of a Nationalist," 12/26/91, 757-758; "The Divine Basis," 8/1/91, 427; "Concerning Nationalism, the Churches, and the New Political

Economy," 5/13/91, 243; "Professor Huxley Furnishes Us with an Argument," 6/10/93, 287-288.

OP: "Three Epitaphs," SDN, 3/6/80; "Extra-Hazardous," AJ, 11/77, 440; "Christmas in the Year 2000," LHJ, 1/95, 6; "Letter of EB to Lord John Peck, N, 1/90; "Plutocracy or Nationalism—Which?", Nationalist Extra I, 2; "Looking Forward," N, 12/89, 2.

DOS: 48-49, 71, 138, 225.

LB: 165, 222-223, 225-239, 254-55, 264, 267, 270.

E: 27, 114, 245, 251-52, 255-256, 258-269, 272-273, 335, 338, 341, 344-45, 382-386, 394-395.

OA: Katherine P. Woods, "Edward Bellamy: Author and Economist," *Bookman,* 7/89, 401; Anna Dawes, "Mr. Bellamy and Christianity," *Andover Review,* 4/91, 413-414; William Higgs, "Bellamy: Objections to His Utopia," *New Englander and Yale Review,* 3/90, 233; A. G. Sedgwick, "Bellamy's Utopia," *The Nation,* 8/26/97, 170-171; F. A. Walker, "Bellamy and the New Nationalist Party," AM, 2/90, 258; Michael Maher, "Socialist's Dream," *The Month,* 1/91, 184-185; Bellamy Clippings, HL, EB's MSS, December, 1889.

CHAPTER VIII. DOMESTIC LIFE IN THE YEAR 2000

I. Status of Women

MSS: HL, *Notebooks*: B, 3-4; II, 101, 26, 6; IV, 18, 26; VI, 31-34, 41; VII, 43-44, 39-41, 46-48; XI, 14, 23; XIV, 49, 112. *Folders*: XV, "The very fact . . . , " back of p. 23; XXV, *re* Celia and Bob, p. beginning "made Bob's . . . "; XXIV, "Woman Worship," 9, 23, 25; XXX, "A Positive Romance," 4;XXXII, "The girl who wished she were a boy . . .," 1-14, 15 (back of page), 9; XXI, "To Whom This May Come," fragment beginning "We become out of patience with our friends . . . "; page beginning, "that when the friend is a woman . . .," 35, 39, 44.

BF: Journal of EB.

SU: "A Brilliant Literary Occasion," 8/11/74; "The Escort Question," 4/14/74; "Suicide in New York," 1/8/73; "The Psychology of Spencer," 10/18/73; "Women Before the Law," 2/26/74; "The Woman's Congress," 10/17/73; "The Present Status of the 'Woman Movement,'" 10/15/73; "Work for Women," 3/15/73; "Who Shall Be the City Physician," 1/17/73; "An Annual Farce," 3/31/77; "Mrs. Woodhull on Free Love," 2/5/72; "The New Magazines," 11/17/77; Editorial Comments, 8/21/77, 4/11/73, 6/5/75, 3/24/73; "Literary Notices," 9/24/74, 8/6/73, 7/12/72, 6/13/77, 12/31/74, 9/20/72, 7/13/76, 7/29/76, 12/16/76, 12/16/73, 9/9/73, 6/7/74, 3/5/74, 8/21/73, 6/10/73, 5/7/75, 2/3/77, 11/7/74.

NN: "The War for Woman's Independence Must Become Socialistic," 10/28/93, 474; "Hurrah for Women," 10/21/93, 467; "Talks on Nationalism," 4/18/91, 191-192; "The New Nation," 1/31/91, 10-11; "The Only Preventive of Prostitution," 11/28/91, 694; "Our Present Social System 'An Agreement with Death and a Covenant with Hell,'" 4/16/92, 241-242; "Why All Women Should Be Nationalists," 6/4/92, 355; "The Word 'Obey' in the Marriage Ceremony," 6/18/92, 387.

OP: "What 'Nationalism' Means," CR, 7/90, 15; "Woman Suffrage Impractical," GA, 3/11/71, 3; "Tea Table Talk," SDN, 11/13/80; "Woman in the Year 2000," LHJ, 2/91, 3; "Principles and Purposes of Nationalism," N, 4/90, 174-180.

BW: "A Positive Romance," 296, 304-305, 306, 311; "Two Days' Solitary Imprisonment," 128.

MLS: 105.

LB: 95, 208-212, 213, 214, 215-216.

E: 85-86, 131-139, 263-264, 400.

OA: Julia Ward Howe, "Women in the Professions," *Chautauquan,* 5/87, 460-462; Frances Willard, "An Interview with Edward Bellamy," *Our Day,* 18/89, 540-544; Mary H. Ford, "A Feminine Iconoclast," N, 11/89, 352-357; Mrs. Abby Morton Diaz, "The Why and the Wherefore," N, 12/89, 5-10.

II. Love and Marriage

MSS: HL, *Notebook:* C, 14; B, 15-16; III, 60-64, 102-103, 120; IV, 37; VII, 20-21, 43-44; XI, 51, 74, 77; XIV, 29, 35. *Folders:* I, *re* Henry Stanley; X, fragments beginning, "She can not understand how she should . . . " and "The girl living on the outskirts . . . "; XX, "Stolen March," 1, 6; XI, *re* Hardin, Carry, and Marion, 37, 55; XXIX, "Almost a Suicide," XXXIV, "Woman Worship," 12, 17-32; XXXII, "The Medium's Story," 16, 94; XXI, "To Whom This May Come," 38.

BF: Journal of EB.

SU: "Are We a Marrying People," 8/14/73; "The Marrying Age," 12/30/74; "The Marriageable Age," 5/2/74; "A Delicate Question," 8/5/73; "New Books and Magazines," 9/20/72; "Who Should Not Marry," 9/30/73; "Stirpiculture," 10/2/75; "Baby Farming," 4/6/75; "A Victim to American Eating Habits," 11/23/75; "Horseflesh as Food," 7/19/74; "Foods. The Palatable and the Nutritious and the Economical Things to Eat," 10/21/73; "Literary Notices," 8/18/77, 2/6/75, 4/11/73, 1/30/75, 12/16/76, 9/23/76, 11/13/72, 10/27/77, 9/24/74, 12/23/74, 5/24/74, 9/28/72.

NN: "Will the World Be Overpeopled Under Nationalism," 2/3/94, 51; "Talks on Nationalism," 6/6/91, 298, 5/30/91, 281; "The Bogy of Nationalism," 4/16/92, 242; "The New Nation," 1/31/91, 11; "The Latest Colony," 12/12/93, 530; "How Nationalism Will Purify the Filial and Fraternal Ties," 5/30/91, 277; "The Value of a Public Brand," 9/16/93, 427.

BW: "Potts' Painless Cure," 159, 161, 164; "At Pinney's Ranch," 375, 384; "A Love Story Reversed," 192-236.

DOS: 345-346, 368.

STO: 42-43, 44, 98-99.

OP: "Jane Hicks," *Good Company,* IV, 1879, p. 242; "Brief Summary . . . , " *Dawn,* 8/89, 3; "Women in the Year 2000," LHJ, 2/91, 3.

OA: Charles Bellamy, *An Experiment in Marriage,* 134-135, 154, 174-176, 186.

LB: 212-220, 247, 250.

E: 139, 140-143, 252, 286-290, 408, 410-412.

III. Houses and Their Furnishings

MSS: Folder XVI, "Vagaries," 2.

SU: *"Firing Up for Another Winter,"* 10/15/74; "Wholesome Heat and Enough of It," 10/20/74; "Lighting and Warming Our Houses," 1/22/74; "Excessive Economy," 6/5/75; "Architectural Morality," 11/4/72; "Will the Lesson Be Heeded," 11/21/72; "More Elbow Room," 5/5/74; "Sense and Nonsense about Servants," 8/16/73; "Domestic Service," 6/30/77; "Shall We Call Them Servants," 9/26/77; "Literary Notices," 1/2/73; 4/1/76, 9/24/74, 4/29/76, 10/8/74, 1/1/76, 2/18/74, 10/20/73, 9/23/76, 1/4/73, 2/9/74.

NN: "The Zone System with a Local Application," 9/26/91, 551; "The Question of Residence Under Nationalism," 1/14/93, 15-16; "Flood Disaster and Nationalism," 8/15/91, 457-458; "The Livery and the Uniform," 4/22/93, 203.

OP: "Leave the Dampers Open," SDN, 11/18/80; " 'Looking Backward' Again," NAR, 3/90, 359; "Woman as an Inventor," SDN, 12/1/80; "Tea Table Talk," SDN, 1/14/81; "A Vital Domestic Problem," *Good Housekeeping,* 12/21/89, 74-77.

LB: 27, 30, 66, 85-86, 93-95, 116, 126-127, 123-124, 255, 265.

E: 27, 51-53, 94, 192, 288-289, 292-293, 295, 353-355, 369-70, 371, 373.

OA: "Scientific Intelligence: Paper Window Shutters," SU, 1/11/73; Mrs. E. L. H. W., "Home Correspondence," "Woman's Press Association and Mr. Bellamy's Domestic Service Problem," *Good Housekeeping,* 3/29/90, 262.

IV. Clothing and Fashion

MSS: HL, *Notebooks*: III, 85; IX, 38; XIV, 5. *Equality* MS, Chapter VII, 47 (detailed picture of new dress cut from final version). *Letters*: EB to Mrs. EB, 3/27/88, 4; EB to Benjamin Ticknor, quoted in Green *EB*ms, 61.

SU: "New Books and Magazines," 8/20/72; "Dress Reform at Vassar," 2/25/73; "Literary Notices," 9/4/73, 3/17/74, 5/9/74, 12/24/74, 9/29/77; "Practical Dress Reform," 12/19/74; "The Anti-Fashion Convention," 6/23/74; "Dress Reform Agitation at Boston," 3/10/74; "The Fall Fashions," 9/28/73; "The Topic of the Hour," 11/10/74; "The Fashions, Generally and Specifically," 10/16/73; "All on the Outside," 8/26/75; "Woman's Extravagance," 10/25/73.

NN: "Capitalistic Greed Responsible for the Tyranny of Fashion," III, 6 (2/11/93), 82-3; "Chautauqua Dress Reformer," I, 29 (8/15/91), 456.

LB: 6-7, 29.

E: 31, 45-53, 56-57, 58-61, 67, 125-130, 157, 295, 297-8.

OP: "An Old Folks' Party," BW, 65.

OA: Mott, *A History of American Magazines,* 96; Madame E. Fleury-Robinson's article in *Open Court* quoted in "The Icarians," N, III, 3 (10/90), 199.

V. Result of the Social, Economic Life

MSS: HL, *Notebook* VII, 32; *Folder* IV, "The Troubadours," 6.

NN: "We Accept the Title," 7/4/91, 359. "The Divine Basis," 8/1/91, 427.

LB: 130, 183, 224, 225, 233-37.

E: 203, 250.

CHAPTER IX.   THE ROUTE TO THE IDEAL STATE

I. Evolution, Not Revolution

MSS: HL, *Notebooks*: II, 29-30, 99; VII, 2, 62; XV, 2-3, 51. *Folders*: I, First Lyceum Talk, 8-9; XXI, "To Whom This May Come," fragment beginning, "We became out of patience . . . "; XXIV, Notes on LB, 1-3, 4, 5, 7; XXXVII, Unused preface to E, 10-11, 12-13; MS "Positive Romance," 13. Letter of Sidney A. Reeves, 6/3/34 to Mrs. Emma Bellamy.

HL, TWH: Letter of EB to TWH, 6/20/89, 2.

SU: "The Old and the New," 10/23/73; "Woman Suffrage," 11/25/72; "Tinkering the Constitution," 12/5/76; "Literature in Samples," 11/26/75; "Literary Notices," 4/29/76, 3/3/74, 4/21/77.

LB: V, 229-332.

II. The Incoherent Period: Preparation

MSS: HL, *Notebook* IV, 12. *Folders:* I, Second Lyceum Talk, 15; V, fragment, "first and greatest of these . . . "; XXVIII, "Some Mistakes of Social Reformers," 1, 1a, 3; XXXVII, unused preface to E, 5; XXXIII, "The Medium's Story," "It is only a question . . .," 19; XXXVIII, MS of E, Chapter XXV, 6.

HL, WDH: Letter of EB, 11/7/93, to WDH.

HL, TWH: Letter of EB, 12/28/88, to TWH.

SU: "Now Is the Accepted Time," 10/1/73; "Why Not Have Candor in Party Platforms," 9/8/77; "Putting on the Screws," 6/23/77; "Father Trask and His Class," 1/26/75; "A Non Sequitur," 2/15/73; "Some Good Words Spoiled," 6/22/76; "Whitefield One of the Founders of the American Nationality," 10/7/73; "Glimpses of the Coming," 12/12/77; "Enthusiasm," 7/7/77; "Decoration Day," 5/29/74; "Touching Things Spiritual," 11/27/75; "Literary Notices," 2/16/76, 12/16/75, 11/20/75; Editorial Comment, 8/22/77.

NN: "Gould Doing Good Work," 10/10/91, 587; "Worth a Thanksgiving," 11/25/93, 370; "General Significance of the Events at Homestead," 8/6/92, 497-498; "The Mistakes of Reformers," 2/14/91, 44; "Eugen Richter's Anti-Socialist Romance," 6/3/93, 275; "Not Too Soon," 12/9/93, 49. Editorial Comment, 8/5/93, 8/12/93, 385.

OP: "Programme of the Nationalists," *Forum,* 3/94, 83; "Principles and Purposes of Nationalism," N, 4/90, 174-180; "Looking Forward," N, 12/89, 1-4; "Introduction," *Fabian Essays,* XV; " 'Looking Backward' Again," NAR, 3/90, 362; Editorial Comment, SDN, 1/14/81.

LB: 1, 8, 10, 36-41, 206, 207, 229-233, 274.

E: 9-10, 12-16, 21-23, 116, 121, 207-209, 228, 277-278, 286, 305, 309-330, 331-335, 344-345, 380, 382-383, 384-385, 385-386, 402.

OA: Robert Timsol, "Back from Altruria," *Lippincott's Magazine,* 2/98, 278 (EB quoted).

III. The Coherent Period: Political Action

MSS: HL, *Folder* XXVII, *re* Nationalism, "An Iowa Subscriber"; letter of EB, 9/13/89, to Houghton Mifflin.

MS: State Historical Library, Boston: Letter of EB, 4/6/89, to E. Yates.

HL, TWH: Letter of EB to TWH, 12/28/88.
State Historical Library, Boston: Letter of EB, 4/6/89, to E. Yates.

NN: "The 'Piece-Meal' Process," 1/28/91, 695; "Nationalism and the Liquor Question," 6/20/91, 326; "Disastrous Effects of Impure Liquor Which Public Management Would Prevent," 7/2/92, 418; "Talks on Nationalism," 7/11/91, 377-379; "Let Us Have State Life Insurance," 5/21/92, 321-322; "An Opportune Time for the State Life Insurance Company," 6/4/92, 354-355; "The New York Standard Suspends," 9/10/92, 567; "Why Workingmen Should Favor All Propositions for Public Operation of Business," 3/11/93, 129-130; "Is Nationalism Reconcilable with a Wage System," 3/12/91, 161; "The Editor and the Office Boy," 2/7/91, 29; "The Spirit and Logic of Nationalism," 2/27/92, 129; "General Snowden Proposes to Suppress the People," 8/13/92, 514-515; "The World's Fair of 1893 and the World's Fair of AD 2000," 5/6/93, 226.

OP: "How We Shall Get There," *Twentieth Century,* 5/11/89, 167; " 'Looking Backward' Again," NAR, 3/90, 362; "First Steps Toward Nationalism," *Forum,* 10/90, 174-184; "Principles and Purposes of Nationalism," N, 4/90, 174-180; "Progress of Nationalism in the United States," NAR, 6/92, 750, 751; "Programme of Nationalists," *Forum,* 3/94, 87, 88-89; "Looking Forward," N, 12/89, 1-4; "What 'Nationalism' Is," Pacific Nationalist Tract, No. 1, p. 7; "How I Came to Write 'Looking Backward,' " N, 5/1/89, 1-4; Letter of EB quoted in "Editorial Notes," N, 5/89, 21; DOS, 42-43.

LB: 41, 274-275.

E: 42-43, 190, 195, 305, 330-331, 333-347, 350-358, 360-379.

BIBLIOGRAPHY

The following bibliography is divided into two sections: the first section contains the material written by Edward Bellamy, and the second the books, articles, and pamphlets written about him, his period, and Nationalism. The order of presentation of the material of the first section is as follows: the novels, the short stories, the signed articles, letters, and statements; the unsigned articles published in the Springfield *Daily News,* the *Union,* and *The New Nation;* and the unpublished manuscripts, journals, and letters of Bellamy. In listing the last-mentioned material, only the general source has been given, for a listing of the fragments, journals, and letters quoted would consume too much space. The space which might have been utilized for this purpose has instead been used to list for the first time the identified, unsigned articles by Bellamy which have never before been published or listed. Though this bibliography of Bellamy's writings is the most complete that has been compiled, it does not contain all of the articles identified as his since many of them were insignificant or not quoted in this work.

In section two of this bibliography, a selected list of books about Bellamy, the utopian novel, and the nineteenth century American social and political scene is presented. Following this, the anonymous and the signed articles, pamphlets, and unpublished manuscripts which were found helpful are cited.

BIBLIOGRAPHY

SECTION I

THE WORKS OF EDWARD BELLAMY

Novels

Dr. Heidenhoff's Process. New York: D. Appleton and Company, 1880.

The Duke of Stockbridge. Preface by Francis Bellamy. New York: Silver, Burdett and Company, 1900.

Equality. New York: D. Appleton and Company, 1933.

Looking Backward. Preface by Heywood Broun. Modern Library Edition. New York: Random House, n.d.

Miss Ludington's Sister. Boston: James R. Osgood and Company, 1884.

Six to One. New York: G. P. Putnam's Sons, 1878.

Short Stories

The Blindman's World and Other Stories. Preface by William Dean Howells. Boston: Houghton, Mifflin & Co., 1898.

"A Mid-Night Drama," *Appleton's Journal,* III, 14 (August, 1877), pp. 162-166.

"A Positive Romance," *The Blindman's World and Other Stories,* pp. 295-314.

"A Providence," *The Century Magazine,* XII, 3 (July, 1876), pp. 374-379.

"A Summer Evening's Dream," *The Blindman's World and Other Stories,* pp. 129-156.

"A Superfluity of Naughtiness," *Lippincott's Magazine,* XIX, 113 (May, 1877), pp. 564-572.

"A Tale of the South Pacific," *Good Company,* V (1880), pp. 8-15.

"An Echo of Antietam," *The Blindman's World and Other Stories,* pp. 30-58.

"At Pinney's Ranch," *The Blindman's World and Other Stories,* pp. 366-388.

"Deserted," *The Blindman's World and Other Stories,* pp. 237-263.

"Extra-Hazardous," *Appleton's Journal,* III, 17 (November, 1877), pp. 436-441.

"Hooking Watermelons," *The Blindman's World and Other Stories,* pp. 264-295.

"Jane Hicks," *Good Company,* IV (1879), pp. 241-250.

"Lost," *The Blindman's World and Other Stories,* pp. 315-334.

"Pott's Painless Cure," *The Blindman's World and Other Stories,* pp. 157-191.

"Taking a Mean Advantage," *Sunday Afternoon,* III (March, 1879), pp. 265-276.

"That Letter," *Good Company,* VI (September, 1880), pp. 14-23.

"The Blindman's World," *The Blindman's World and Other Stories,* pp. 1-29.

"The Cold Snap," *The Blindman's World and Other Stories,* pp. 89-103.

"The Old Folks' Party," *The Blindman's World and Other Stories,* pp. 59-88.

"To Whom This May Come," *The Blindman's World and Other Stories,* pp. 389-415.

"Two Days' Solitary Imprisonment," *The Blindman's World and Other Stories,* pp. 104-128.

"With the Eyes Shut," *The Blindman's World and Other Stories,* pp. 335-365.

Signed, Published Articles, Letters, Lectures

"The A B C's of the Profit System by the Author of 'Looking Backward' —'The Parable of the Water Tank'," *Golden Book Magazine,* XX (October, 1934), pp. 460-465.

Address to Free Religious Association quoted in J. Ransom Bridge, "The Changes of Fifty Years," *Nationalist,* I, 6 (October, 1889), p. 227.

Address at Faneuil Hall, quoted in "The Cradle of Liberty Rocked at Faneuil Hall," *New Nation,* I, 38 (October 17, 1891), cols. 1-2, p. 608; quoted also in Mason Green, *Edward Bellamy,* p. 281.

Address at Faneuil Hall, quoted in "Edward Bellamy's Speech," *New Nation,* II, 15 (April 19, 1892), cols. 1-2, p. 232, col. 1, p. 233.

"Brief Summary of the Industrial Plan of Nationalism Set Forth in 'Looking Backward' for Class Study," *The Dawn,* I (September, 1889), p. 3.

"Christmas in the Year 2000," *Ladies' Home Journal,* XII (January, 1895), p. 4.

"Correspondence," *The Dawn,* I (May 15, 1889), p. 5.

Edward Bellamy Speaks Again. The Foreword by Lester McBride. Kansas City, Kansas: The Peerage Press, 1937.

"First Steps Toward Nationalism," *Forum,* X (October, 1890), pp. 174-184.

"Fourth of July, 1992," *Boston Globe,* July 4, 1892, reprinted in *The New Nation,* II, 28 (July 9, 1892), col. 1, p. 436; reprinted in *Edward Bellamy Speaks Again,* pp. 205-206.

"How I Came to Write 'Looking Backward'," *The Nationalist,* I, 1 (May, 1889), pp. 1-4.

"How I Wrote 'Looking Backward'," *Ladies' Home Journal,* XI (April, 1894), p. 2.

"How to Employ the Unemployed in Mutual Maintenance. The following outline of the Mutual Maintenance Method of Employing the Unemployed has been prepared by Edward Bellamy upon the lines of an article furnished by him to the *Boston Traveller,* November 8, 1893, and various editorials in the *New Nation.*" Pamphlet, New York Public Library, New York City, pp. 1-4. Reprinted in *Edward Bellamy Speaks Again,* pp. 213-215.

"How We Shall Get There," *Twentieth Century,* II (May 11, 1889), pp. 166-167.

"Introduction," *Socialism: The Fabian Essays.* Boston: Charles E. Brown & Co., 1894.

"Labor, Politics, and Nationalism," *New York Herald,* August 28, 1892, reprinted in *New Nation,* II, 37 (September 10, 1892), cols. 1-2, p. 568.

"A Letter from Edward Bellamy. The Rate of the World's Progress." Boston: Houghton, Mifflin & Co., n.d., pp. 1-2. John Crerar Library. Reprinted in *Looking Backward,* Modern Library Edition, New York, Random House, n.d., pp. 273-276. Originally published in the *Boston Transcript.*

Letter quoted in "The Great Principle Involved at Homestead," *New Nation,* II, 33 (August 20, 1892), col. 2, p. 532.

Letter quoted in "Correspondence," *Nationalization News* (England), December 1, 1890, col. 2, p. 2.

Letter to John Lord Peck, *Nationalist,* II, 2 (January, 1890), back cover.

Letter read to People's Party Ratification Meeting, October 13, 1892, *New Nation,* II, 43 (October 22, 1892), col. 2, p. 644; col. 1, 645.

Letter quoted in "Editorial Notes," *Nationalist,* I, 1 (May, 1889), p. 21.

Letter to Benjamin Ticknor, quoted in Mason Green, *Edward Bellamy,* p. 61.

Letter quoted in Katherine P. Woods, "Edward Bellamy," *The Bookman,* VII, 5 (July, 1898), col. 2, p. 401.

Letters of E. Bellamy quoted in Cyrus Willard (ed.), "News of the Movement," *Nationalist,* I, 3 (July, 1889), p. 91.

Letter to Cooper Union Conference, "School Conference Report on the State of the School" (New York, 1890), pp. 1-8.

Letter of E. Bellamy in reply to Professor Clarke quoted in "True Individuality," "Editorial Notes," *Nationalist,* I, 3 (July, 1889), p. 88.

Letter quoted in Sylvester Baxter, "What is Nationalism," *Nationalist,* I, 1 (May, 1889), pp. 11-12.

Letter quoted in "Mr. Bellamy's Letter," *New Nation,* I, 8 (March 21, 1891), col. 2, p. 118.

" 'Looking Backward' Again," *The North American Review,* CL, 400 (March, 1890), pp. 351-363.

"Looking Forward," *The Nationalist,* II, 1 (December, 1889), pp. 1-4.

"National Education," *Golden Age,* II, 13 (March 30, 1872), cols. 2-3, p. 2.

"A Nationalist View of the Homestead Situation," *Boston Globe,* July 7, 1892, reprinted *New Nation,* II, 29 (July 16, 1872), col. 1, p. 453.

"The Outcome of the Battle of Standards," *Boston Globe,* July 16, 1893, reprinted in *Edward Bellamy Speaks Again,* p. 212.

"A Personal Explanation," *Nationalist,* II, 5 (April, 1890), p. 187.

"Plutocracy or Nationalism—Which?" Address of E. Bellamy at Tremont Temple, May 31, 1889. Nationalist Extra No. 1. Boston: Nationalist Club of Boston, n.d., pp. 1-12.

"Principles and Purposes of Nationalism," "Address at Tremont Temple Boston, on the Nationalist Club's First Anniversary, December 18, 1889." Philadelphia: Published by the Bureau of Nationalist Literature, n.d., pp. 1-12. Reprinted, *The Nationalist,* II, 5 (April, 1890), pp. 174-180.

"Programme of Nationalists," *Forum,* XVII (March, 1894), pp. 81-91.

"Progress of Nationalism in the United States," *North American Review,* CLIV, 426 (June, 1892), pp. 742-752.

"Prospectus," *New Nation,* I, 1 (January 31, 1891), col. 1, p. 13.

"Our Prospective Sovereigns," *The Nationalist,* I, 3 (July, 1889), pp. 68-69.

"The Outcome of the Battle of Standards," *Boston Globe,* July 16, 1893, reprinted, *Edward Bellamy Speaks Again,* pp. 211-212.

"Railroad Disasters," *Golden Age,* II, 2 (March 16, 1872), cols. 2-3, p. 2.

"Several Stock Objections to Nationalism Objected To," *Christian Union,*
reprinted in *New Nation,* I, 44 (November 28, 1891), cols. 1-2,
p. 697, cols. 1-2, p. 698, col. 1, p. 699.

"Should Every Boy Learn a Trade? And How Shall He Find Out What
He Is Best Fitted For?" Contributed by E. Bellamy to symposium in
Boston Herald, August 9, 1892; reprinted, *New Nation,* II, 36 (Sep-
tember 3, 1892), cols. 1-2, p. 1.

"Should the State or Municipality Provide Work For Its Unemployed?"
Boston Traveller, November 14, 1893; reprinted *New Nation,* III,
45 (November 11, 1893), col. 2, p. 493, col. 1, p. 494; (December
16, 1893), cols. 1-2, p. 535.

"A Solution for Unemployment Devised in 1893 for the Present Crisis,"
Golden Book Magazine, XVII, 102 (June, 1933), pp. 548-549.

Talks on Nationalism. Chicago, Illinois: The Peerage Press, 1938.

"A Vital Domestic Problem: Household Service Reform," *Good Housekeeping,* X, 4 (December 21, 1889), pp. 74-77.

"Woman Suffrage," *Golden Age,* I, 2 (March 11, 1871), cols. 2-3, p. 2.

"What Nationalism Is," "Edward Bellamy's Belief," Pacific Nationalist
Tract, No. 1. Oakland, California: Nationalist Club of Oakland, p. 7.

"What 'Nationalism' Means," *Contemporary Review,* LVIII (July, 1890),
pp. 1-18.

"Why Every Workingman Should Be A Nationalist," *Building Trades
Council Souvenir,* reprinted *New Nation,* III, 15 (April 15, 1893),
cols. 1-2, p. 193.

"Woman in the Year 2000," *Ladies' Home Journal,* VIII, 3 (February,
1891), p. 3.

Statements of Edward Bellamy quoted in "Attitude of the Press," *Nationalist,* I, 7 (November, 1889), pp. 273-274.

Statement of Edward Bellamy, quoted in *Boston Commonwealth,* reprinted
in "Attitude of the Press," *Nationalist,* II, 4 (March, 1890), p. 144.

Statements of Edward Bellamy, interview, *Free Press Telegram,* February
28, 18--?, "Author of Looking Backward and His Scheme of Nationalization," Bellamy Family Files, Springfield, Massachusetts.

Statements of Edward Bellamy, interview, *Boston Traveller,* reprinted in
"Should the State or Municipality Provide Work for Its Unemployed,"
New Nation, III, 45 (November 11, 1893), col. 2, p. 493; col. 1,
p. 494.

Unsigned Articles Identified as Edward Bellamy's

"About Three Cabinet Appointments," *Springfield Union,* February 26,
1877, col. 5, p. 2.

"An Absurdity of the Jury System," *Springfield Union*, July 6, 1875, col. 5, p. 4.

"The Accumulation of Wealth," *New Nation*, II, 30 (July 23, 1892), cols. 1-2, p. 468.

"All on the Outside," *Springfield Union*, August 26, 1875, cols. 5-6, p. 4.

"The America of Today Not the America of Yesterday," *New Nation*, III, 14 (April 8, 1873), col. 2, p. 178—col. 1, p. 179.

"America the Only Land of Freedom," *Springfield Union*, July 8, 1876, cols. 5-6, p. 4.

"An American Education," *Springfield Union*, March 6, 1875, col. 5, p. 4.

"The American Farmer Must Choose Between Becoming a Nationalist or a Peasant," *New Nation*, III, 42 (October 21, 1893), col. 2, p. 466.

"American Healtheries Company," *New Nation*, I, 18 (May 30, 1891), cols. 1-2, p. 277.

"Amusements," *Springfield Union*, December 19, 1876, cols. 6-7, p. 4.

"Announcement," *New Nation*, IV, 4 (February 3, 1894), p. 5.

"The Anti-Chinese Uprising in California," *Springfield Union*, April 8, 1876, col. 4, p. 4.

"The Anti-Fashion Convention," *Springfield Union*, June 23, 1874, col. 7, p. 2.

"Architectural Morality," *Springfield Union*, November 14, 1872, cols. 1-2, p. 2.

"Are We a Marrying People," *Springfield Union*, August 14, 1873, cols. 6-7, p. 4.

"The Arrest of Charles Bowles," *Springfield Union*, December 18, 1872, col. 2, p. 2.

"Art and Nationalism," *New Nation*, III, 1 (January 7, 1893), cols. 1-2, p. 3.

"Ask Us Something Harder," *New Nation*, II, 32 (August 6, 1892), col. 2, p. 500.

"Baby Farming," *Springfield Union*, April 16, 1875, col. 5, p. 4.

"Better a Knave Than a Fool," *Springfield Union*, March 6, 1875, col. 5, p. 4.

"A Better Plan Than Young Women Ushers," *New Nation*, III, 31 (August 5, 1893), col. 2, p. 378.

"The Blight of Wealth Centers," *New Nation*, I, 9 (March 28, 1891), cols. 1-2, p. 133.

"Bliss's New Abridged Catalogue," *Springfield Union*, January 8, 1876, col. 7, p. 4.

"The Bogy of Nationalism," *New Nation,* II, 16 (April 16, 1892), cols. 1-2, p. 24.

"The Book of Flowers," *Springfield Union,* January 13, 1874, col. 5, p. 4.

"A Book on Education," *Springfield Union,* September 13, 1873, col. 4, p. 4.

"Boy Murderers," *Springfield Union,* February 26, 1873, cols. 1-2, p. 2.

"Bribery at New York," Springfield *Daily News,* November 3, 1880, col. 3, p. 4.

"A Brilliant Literary Occasion," *Springfield Union,* August 11, 1874, col. 4, p. 4.

"Burning the Candle at Both Ends," *Springfield Union,* April 8, 1876, col. 5, p. 4.

"Capitalistic Greed Responsible for the Tyranny of Fashion," *New Nation,* III, 6 (February 11, 1893), col. 2, p. 82—cols. 1-2, p. 83.

"The Case of Boss Tweed," *Springfield Union,* December 18, 1872, col. 2, p. 2.

"The Cause of American Lawlessness," *Springfield Union,* June 10, 1873, col. 1, p. 2.

"Centralization in Education," *Springfield Union,* January 14, 1873, col. 1, p. 2.

"Changing the Crop and the Tillage," *Springfield Union,* March 2, 1875, col. 5, p. 4.

"The Chautauqua Dress Reformer," *New Nation,* I, 29 (August 15, 1891), col. 2, p. 456.

"The Cheap Labor Problem," *Springfield Union,* June 4, 1874, cols. 4-5, p. 4.

"Championship," *Springfield Union,* July 8, 1875, cols. 2-3, p. 4.

"Children's Books," *Springfield Union,* October 11, 1875, cols. 5-6, p. 4.

"Children in Factories," *Springfield Union,* July 25, 1872, cols. 1-2, p. 2.

"Christianity as a National Law," *Springfield Union,* January 7, 1874, cols. 4-5, p. 4.

"Christianity and Civilization," *Springfield Union,* May 17, 1873, col. 2, p. 2.

"The Christian Side of Our National Life," *Springfield Union,* January 17, 1874, col. 5, p. 4.

"Christmas Thoughts of a Nationalist," *New Nation,* I, 48 (December 26, 1891), col. 2, p. 757—col. 1, p. 758.

"The Churches and Nationalism," *New Nation,* I, 44 (December 5, 1891), cols. 1-3, p. 710.

"The Church of the Future According to Matthew Arnold," *Springfield Union*, June 8, 1877, cols. 6-7, p. 2.

"City Industries," *New Nation*, I, 3 (February 14, 1893), col. 3, p. 38.

"Civilization and Cultivation," *Springfield Union*, May 21, 1874, col. 4, p. 4.

"The Colony Idea," *New Nation*, II, 3 (February 16, 1892), p. 36.

"Collapse of the International," *Springfield Union*, September 26, 1874, col. 5, p. 4.

"The Coming American Aristocracy," *New Nation*, II, 3 (January 16, 1892), cols. 1-2, p. 36.

"Communism Boiled Down," *Springfield Union*, August 3, 1877, col. 2, p. 2.

"Communist Hopes and Follies," *Springfield Union*, June 28, 1873, col. 1, p. 2.

"The Compensations of Elections," *Springfield Union*, October 28, 1876, cols. 4-5, p. 4.

"Compulsory Education," *Springfield Union*, August 8, 1872, col. 2, p. 2.

"Concerning Nationalism, the Churches, and the New Political Economy," *New Nation*, III, 19 (May 13, 1891), col. 2, p. 243.

"Concerning the Founding of Nationalist Colonies," *New Nation*, III, 38 (September 23, 1893), p. 434.

"Concerning Mountains," *Springfield Union*, August 9, 1876, cols. 4-5, p. 4.

"Concerning Nationalism: the Daily Press and the Reform Movement," *New Nation*, III, 25 (June 24, 1893), cols. 1-2, p. 316.

"The Condition of Business Prosperity," *Springfield Union*, August 16, 1876, col. 5, p. 4.

"Confessions and Revelations of Religious Belief," *Springfield Union*, July 11, 1874, cols. 5-6, p. 4.

"A Confusion of Ideas," *New Nation*, I, 4 (February 21, 1891), col. 2, p. 62.

"The Congregationalist on Nationalism," *New Nation*, I, 40 (October 31, 1891), col. 1, p. 630.

"Consumption and Rheumatism," *New Nation*, I, 47 (December 19, 1891), col. 2, p. 750.

"The Co-operative Commonwealth," *New Nation*, I, 15 (May 2, 1891), col. 3, p. 224.

"Continuance of Our Friendly Debate with Professor Secretan," *New Nation*, I, 43 (November 21, 1891), cols. 1-2, p. 678.

"Co-operation at the South," *Springfield Union,* August 18, 1873, col. 7, p. 2.

"The Co-operative Solution of the Unemployed Problem More Fully Set Forth," *New Nation,* IV, 3 (January 20, 1894), col. 2, p. 25—col. 1, p. 27.

"Corporal Punishment in School—An Instructive Experiment," *Springfield Union,* September 9, 1873, cols. 5-6, p. 4.

"A Courteous Critic Answered," *New Nation,* I, 7 (March 14, 1891), col. 1, p. 110.

"Crime and Its Causes," *Springfield Union,* February 19, 1874, col. 7, p. 4.

"Criminals—Who They Are," *Springfield Union,* December 21, 1873, col. 1, p. 2.

"Curiosities of Juvenile Crime," *Springfield Union,* February 7, 1874, cols. 4-5, p. 4.

"Cut Bait or Fish," *New Nation,* I, 7 (March 14, 1891), col. 2, p. 10.

"The Dark Side of Human Nature," *Springfield Union,* April 25, 1874, cols. 5-6, p. 4.

"Dean Stanley upon the Religious Outlook," *Springfield Union,* April 7, 1877, col. 1, p. 5.

"Death of a Chartist," *New Nation,* II, 33 (August 13, 1892), col. 2, p. 518.

"Decoration Day," *Springfield Union,* May 29, 1874, cols. 5-6, p. 2.

"The Defects of Self-Interest as a Motive," *New Nation,* I, 47 (December 19, 1891), cols. 1-2, p. 742—col. 2, p. 741.

"A Delicate Question," *Springfield Union,* August 5, 1875, cols. 5-6, p. 4.

"The Destruction of American Forests," *Springfield Union,* January 2, 1875, cols. 4-5, p. 4.

"Devices to Restore Popular Government," *New Nation,* II, 24 (June 1, 1892), cols. 1-2, p. 372.

"Disastrous Effects of Impure Liquors which Public Management Would Prevent," *New Nation,* II, 27 (July 2, 1892), col. 2, p. 418.

"The Divine Basis," *New Nation,* I, 27 (August 1, 1891), col. 1, p. 427.

"A Domestic Tyrant," *Springfield Union,* March 14, 1877, cols. 6-7, p. 4.

"Domestic Service," *Springfield Union,* June 30, 1877, cols. 6-7, p. 4.

"Dress Reform Agitation at Boston," *Springfield Union,* March 10, 1874, col. 7, p. 2.

"Dress Reform at Vassar," *Springfield Union,* February 25, 1873, col. 1, p. 2.

"Drifting," *Springfield Union,* January 27, 1877, cols. 6-7, p. 4.

"Drummers," *Springfield Union*, December 7, 1872, col. 2, p. 2.

"Dull Times a Blessing in Disguise," *Springfield Union*, June 13, 1874, cols. 5-6, p. 4.

"Earning Before Spending," *Springfield Union*, November 15, 1873, col. 7, p. 4.

"Economic Equality," *New Nation*, III, 14 (April 8, 1893), col. 1, p. 177.

"Economy the Only Political Economy of Our Government," *Springfield Union*, December 16, 1873, cols. 4-5, p. 1.

"The Editor and the Office Boy," *New Nation*, II, 2 (February 7, 1891), col. 2, p. 29.

[Editorial Comment] *Springfield Union*, 1872: July 29, col. 2, p. 2; October 24, col. 2, p. 2; November 11, col. 2, p. 2; December 4, col. 1, p. 2; December 11, col. 2, p. 2; December 10, col. 2, p. 2; December 19, col. 2, p. 2.

[Editorial Comment] *Springfield Union*, 1873: August 20, col. 7, p. 2; January 4, col. 2, p. 2; January 27, col. 2, p. 2; March 24, col. 1, p. 2; April 11, col. 1, p. 2.

[Editorial Comment] *Springfield Union*, 1874: February 9, col. 2, p. 6; May 13, col. 6, p. 2; October 29, col. 4, p. 4; November 16, col. 1, p. 3.

[Editorial Comment] *Springfield Union*, 1875: July 27, col. 6, p. 4; September 11, col. 5, p. 4.

[Editorial Comment] *Springfield Union*, 1876: April 18, col. 6, p. 4; October 23, col. 2, p. 6; November 2, col. 5, p. 2; December 8, col. 2, p. 4.

[Editorial Comment] *Springfield Union*, 1877: February 22, col. 7, p. 2; March 16, col. 7, p. 2; March 26, col. 7, p. 2; April 16, col. 1, p. 3; June 5, col. 2, p. 7; June 8, col. 7, p. 2; August 15, col. 4, p. 6; August 21, col. 1, p. 3; August 22, col. 7, p. 4; August 22, col. 4, p. 4; November 23, col. 1, p. 3; December 14, col. 2, p. 2.

[Editorial Comment] Springfield *Daily News*, 1881: January 4, col. 1, p. 2.

[Editorial Comment] *New Nation*, I, 1891: 2, February 7, col. 1, p. 28; 4, February 21, p. 60; 38, October 17, col. 1, p. 597; 46, December 12, col. 2, p. 724.

[Editorial Comment] *New Nation*, II, 1892: 37, September 10, col. 2, p. 565; 31, July 30, col. 2, p. 481.

[Editorial Comment] *New Nation*, III, 1893: 31, August 5, col. 1, p. 377; 32, August 12, col. 1, p. 385.

"The Flow of Population City Ward," *Springfield Union*, September 7, 1875, col. 1, p. 5.

"Foods. The Palatable and the Nutritious and the Economical Things to Eat," *Springfield Union*, October 21, 1873, col. 7, p. 5—col. 1, p. 6.

"Forefather's Day," *Springfield Union*, December 22, 1877, col. 6, p. 4.

"The Foreign Population of Western Massachusetts," *Springfield Union*, November 22, 1876, col. 4, p. 4.

"Forest Culture," *Springfield Union*, August 30, 1873, cols. 4-5, p. 4.

"Four Distinctive Principles of Nationalism," *New Nation*, II, 2 (January 9, 1892), pp. 17-18.

"Fourth of July, 1992," *New Nation*, II, 28 (July 9, 1892), col. 1, p. 436.

"A Friendly Criticism," *New Nation*, I, 41 (November 7, 1891), col. 1, p. 645.

"From College into the World; Choosing a Profession," *Springfield Union*, July 11, 1874, cols. 1-2, p. 4.

"The Function of the Newspapers," *Springfield Union*, May 7, 1874, col. 4, p. 4.

"General Significance of the Events at Homestead," *New Nation*, II, 32 (August 6, 1892), col. 2, p. 497—cols. 1-2, p. 498.

"General Snowden Proposes to Suppress the People of the United States 'At the Point of the Bayonet,'" *New Nation*, II, 33 (August 13, 1892), cols. 1-2, p. 515—col. 2, p. 514.

"Glimpses of the Coming," *Springfield Union*, December 12, 1877, cols. 6-7, p. 4.

"The Globe Away Off," *New Nation*, February 20, 1892, col. 2, p. 115.

"The Glut of the Asiatic Markets a Cause of the Hard Times," *Springfield Union*, July 8, 1875, col. 4, p. 4.

"Gould Doing Good Work," *New Nation*, I, 37 (October 10, 1891), col. 2, p. 587.

"The 'Great Lawyers' of New York," *Springfield Union*, June 11, 1874, col. 3-4, p. 4.

"The Great Strike in England," *Springfield Union*, April 30, 1874, col. 4, p. 4.

"A Hard Nut to Crack," *Springfield Union*, March 23, 1875, cols. 4-5, p. 4.

"Hard Times and Suicide," *Springfield Union*, May 2, 1876, cols. 4-5, p. 4.

"Harvest of Smutted Sheaves," *New Nation*, I, 26 (July 25, 1891), col. 1, p. 413.

"Has the Republic Failed," *New Nation*, II, 35 (August 27, 1892), cols. 1-2, p. 544.

"The Head and the Tail Changing Places," *Springfield Union*, April 3, 1874, cols. 5-6, p. 4.

"Herbert Spencer's Attack on Evolution," *New Nation*, I, 10 (April 4, 1891), col. 1, p. 157.

"The Holiday Season," *Springfield Union*, December 22, 1875, col. 5, p. 4.

"Home, Sweet Home," *Springfield Union*, September 27, 1873, col. 5, p. 4.

"Home Types of Wickedness," *Springfield Union*, October 21, 1875, cols. 5-6, p. 4.

"Horseflesh as Food," *Springfield Union*, July 19, 1874, cols. 4-5, p. 4.

"A Hot Weather Argument for Nationalism," *New Nation*, I, 23 (July 4, 1891), cols. 1-2, p. 358.

"How Can Confidence be Restored," *Springfield Union*, February 10, 1874, cols. 3-4, p. 4.

"How and How Far Panics Can Be Prevented," *Springfield Union*, October 3, 1873, cols. 5-6, p. 4.

"How 'Free' Competition Flourishes in Our Midst," *New Nation*, II, 33 (August 13, 1892), cols. 1-2, p. 517.

"How Nationalism Will Purify the Filial and Fraternal Ties," *New Nation*, III, 26 (July 1, 1893), col. 2, p. 523—col. 1, p. 524.

"How Rich and Poor Can Be Equalized Before the Law," *New Nation*, II, 28 (July 9, 1892), cols. 1-2, p. 420.

"How the Alliance Has Met the Two Great Enemies of Protestantism," *Springfield Union*, October 11, 1873, col. 6, p. 4.

"How the American Farmer Is Being Turned into a Peasant," *New Nation*, II, 14 (April 2, 1892), col. 1, p. 210.

"How Our Girls Are Better Educated Than Our Boys," *Springfield Union*, November 7, 1874, col. 6, p. 4.

"How the French Vote," *Springfield Union*, October 17, 1877, cols. 6-7, p. 4.

"How They Look at Him," *Springfield Union*, January 27, 1877, col. 1, p. 5.

"How to Make Farm Life Attractive," *Springfield Union*, August 8, 1877, col. 7, p. 4.

"How to Serve Free and Speedy Justice," *New Nation*, II, 27 (July 2, 1892), col. 1, p. 420.

"How to Strike," *Springfield Union*, November 11, 1873, col. 4, p. 6.

"Human Sympathy, Compared with Class Sympathy," *New Nation*, I, 44 (December, 1891), cols. 1-2, p. 711.

"Hurrah for Women," *New Nation*, III, 42 (October 21, 1893), cols. 1-2, p. 467.

"Hypocrisy and Corruption," *Springfield Union*, January 31, 1873, col. 1, p. 2.

"Ignorance and Loaferism," *Springfield Union*, February 28, 1874, col. 6, p. 4.

"The Illinois Farmers in Convention," *Springfield Union*, April 4, 1873, col. 1, p. 2.

"Immigration and Nationalism," *New Nation*, I, 13 (April 25, 1891), col. 1, p. 205.

"Industrial Feudalism of Modern Times," *Springfield Union*, November 3, 1873, col. 5, p. 4.

"In the Interest of a Clear Use of Terms," *New Nation*, I, 46 (December 12, 1891), p. 726.

"In the Right Direction," *Springfield Union*, January 4, 1873, col. 2, p. 2.

"The Insubordination of Children," *Springfield Union*, May 7, 1877, cols. 5-6, p. 4.

"Is Nationalism Reconcilable with a Wage System," *New Nation*, II, 11 (March 12, 1891), col. 2, p. 161.

"The Jewish Sensation," *Springfield Union*, June 20, 1877, col. 4, p. 6.

"John Ruskin's New Utopia," *Springfield Union*, March 23, 1875, col. 3, p. 4.

"Judicial Reform," *Springfield Union*, January 9, 1877, cols. 4-5, p. 2.

"Just How Far Evolution Conflicts with Theology," *Springfield Union*, October 13, 1877, cols. 5-6, p. 4.

"Just What We Maintain," *New Nation*, I, 7 (March 14, 1891), col. 2, p. 107.

"The Last Case of Emotional Insanity," *Springfield Union*, January 1, 1873, col. 2, p. 2.

"The Latest Colony," *New Nation*, III, 50 (December 16, 1893), p. 530.

"Latest from the Black Hills," *Springfield Union*, May 5, 1877, col. 6, p. 4.

"Lawless Childhood," *Springfield Union*, January 8, 1876, col. 6, p. 4.

"Leave the Dampers Open," Springfield *Daily News*, November 18, 1880, col. 1, p. 2.

"Legs," *Springfield Union*, November 16, 1872, col. 1, p. 2.

"The Lesson of the Fifth Avenue Fire," *Springfield Union*, January 3, 1873, col. 1, p. 2.

"Let Us Be Nonagenarian," *Springfield Union,* May 6, 1873, col. 1, p. 2.

"Let Us Have Free Justice," *New Nation,* III, 17 (April 29, 1893), col. 2, p. 214—col. 1, p. 215.

"Let Us Have State Life Insurance," *New Nation,* II, 21 (May 21, 1892), col. 2, p. 321—cols. 1-2, p. 322.

"Liberty Gone to Seed," *Springfield Union,* December 6, 1873, col. 6, p. 4.

"Lighting and Warming Our Houses," *Springfield Union,* January 22, 1874, cols. 4-5, p. 4.

"Literary Notices," *Springfield Union,* 1872: July 12, cols. 3-4, p. 2; September 28, col. 1, p. 2; September 20, col. 3, p. 2; October 16, col. 4, p. 2; November 8, col. 2, p. 2; November 13, col. 2, p. 2; December 14, col. 2, p. 3; December 11, col. 2, p. 3.

"Literary Notices," *Springfield Union,* 1873: January 2, col. 2, p. 2; January 23, col. 3, p. 2; February 5, col. 3, p. 2; February 22, col. 3, p. 2; February 28, col. 4, p. 2; March 12, cols. 2-3, p. 2; March 21, col. 3, p. 2; April 11, col. 2, p. 2; April 22, col. 3, p. 2; April 29, col. 2, p. 2; May 4, col. 3, p. 2; May 7, col. 2, p. 2; May 16, col. 3, p. 2; May 24, col. 2, p. 2; May 29, col. 3, p. 2; June 10, col. 2, p. 2; June 12, col. 3, p. 2; July 2, col. 2, p. 6; July 4, col. 2, p. 6; July 23, col. 4, p. 6; August 21, cols. 1-2, p. 6; September 4, cols. 1-2, p. 6; September 9, cols. 6-7, p. 7; September 23, col. 1, p. 6; October 2, col. 2, p. 6; October 23, col. 2, p. 6; October 30, col. 1, p. 6; November 13, col. 3, p. 6; November 25, col. 1, p. 6; November 28, col. 1, p. 4; December 2, col. 1, p. 6; December 6, col. 1, p. 6; December 9, col. 3, p. 6; December 12, col. 1, p. 6; December 16, col. 1, p. 6.

"Literary Notices," *Springfield Union,* 1874: January 13, col. 3, p. 6; January 7, col. 2, p. 5; January 17, col. 1, p. 6; February 12, col. 7, p. 5; February 18, cols. 1-2, p. 6; March 5, cols. 2-3, p. 6; March 5, col. 1, p. 6; March 17, col. 1, p. 6; March 24, col. 1, p. 6; March 27, col. 1, p. 6; April 3, col. 1, p. 6; April 9, col. 1, p. 6; April 30, col. 4, p. 6; May 14, col. 2, p. 6; May 21, col. 1, p. 6; May 25, col. 1, p. 6; June 4, col. 2, p. 6; June 7, col. 1, p. 6; June 11, col. 1, p. 6; June 16, col. 1, p. 5; July 23, col. 6, p. 4; September 10, col. 7, p. 5; September 24, col. 1, p. 6; October 8, cols. 3-4, p. 6; October 17, col. 1, p. 6; November 9, col. 1, p. 6; November 19, col. 1, p. 6; November 24, col. 1, p. 6; December 3, col. 7, p. 5; December 10, cols. 1-2-3, p. 6; December 17, col. 2, p. 6; December 23, col. 2, p. 6; December 31, cols. 1-2, p. 6.

"Literary Notices," *Springfield Union,* 1875: January 3, col. 1, p. 6; January 14, col. 1, p. 6; January 30, col. 1-3, p. 6; February 6, col. 2, p. 6; February 8, col. 2, p. 6; February 18, col. 2, p. 6; February 27, col. 4, p. 6; March 13, col. 1, p. 6; March 27, col. 1, p. 6; April 22, col. 2, p. 5; April 24, col. 1, p. 6; May 8, cols. 1-2, p. 6; May 15, col. 1, p. 6; May 22, col. 1, p. 6; May 29, col. 1, p. 6; June 5, cols. 1-4, p. 6; June 12, col. 2, p. 2; July 6, col. 1, p. 6; July 10, cols. 1-2, p. 6; August 3, col. 1, p. 6; August 21, col. 2, p. 6; August 28, col. 6, p. 4; September 16, col. 1, p. 6; September 23, col. 1, p. 6; October 2, col. 1, p. 6; October 21, col. 1, p. 6; November 6, cols. 2-3, p. 5; November 20, col. 1, p. 6; Decem-cember 3, col. 2, p. 6; December 4, col. 1, p. 6; December 11, col. 3, p. 6; December 16, col. 2, p. 5; December 21, col. 3, p. 2; December 22, col. 1, p. 6; December 25, col. 1, p. 5.

"Literary Notices," *Springfield Union,* 1876: January 1, cols. 1-2, p. 6; January 8, col. 2, p. 6; January 20, col. 2, p. 6; January 27, cols. 1-2, p. 6; February 3, col. 2, p. 6; February 10, col. 2, p. 6; February 16, col. 3, p. 6; February 20, col. 7, p. 5; February 22, col. 3, p. 4; March 2, col. 1, p. 6; March 9, col. 2, p. 6; March 18, col. 1, p. 6; April 1, col. 1, p. 6; April 15, cols. 1-4, p. 6; April 29, col. 1, p. 6; April 29, col. 2, p. 6; May 27, col. 3, p. 6; June 1, cols. 1-2, p. 6; June 17, col. 1, p. 6; June 29, col. 1, p. 6; July 13, col. 2, p. 3; July 29, col. 1, p. 6; August 5, cols. 1-2, p. 6; September 8, col. 2, p. 6; September 16, col. 2, p. 6; September 23, cols. 1-2, p. 6; September 20, col. 1, p. 6; October 9, col. 1, p. 6; October 11, col. 2, p. 6; October 17, col. 3, p. 6; October 18, col. 1, p. 6; November 25, col. 1, p. 6; December 16, cols. 1-2, p. 6.

"Literary Notices," *Springfield Union,* 1877: January 6, col. 3, p. 6; February 3, col. 1, p. 6; February 14, cols. 6-7, p. 5; February 24, col. 7, p. 5; March 10, cols. 1-2, p. 6; March 28, col. 2, p. 6; April 21, col. 1, p. 6; May 23, cols. 1-2, p. 6; June 2, cols. 1-2, p. 6; June 13, col. 1, p. 6; June 30, col. 1, p. 6; July 18, col. 1, p. 6; July 21, col. 1, p. 6; August 18, cols. 1-2, p. 6; August 22, cols. 1-3, p. 6; September 22, cols. 1-3, p. 6; September 29, cols. 1-3, p. 6; October 17, cols. 1-2, p. 6; October 20, col. 2, p. 6; October 27, col. 2, p. 6; November 7, cols. 1-2-3, p. 6; November 21, col. 1, p. 5; December 1, col. 1, p. 6; December 8, col. 1, p. 6; December 16, cols. 1-2, p. 6.

"Literature in Samples," *Springfield Union,* November 26, 1875, col. 4, p. 4.

"The Livery and the Uniform," *New Nation*, III, 16 (April 22, 1893), col. 2, p. 203.

"Living by Sight and Living by Faith," *Springfield Union*, September 30, 1873, col. 5, p. 4.

"The Logic of the Situation," *Springfield Union*, March 10, 1877, cols. 5-6, p. 4.

"Look on This Picture and on That," *Springfield Union*, May 1, 1875, col. 6, p. 4.

"The Lord Deliver Us from Such Fools as Brother Holmes," Springfield *Daily News*, October 21, 1880, cols. 1-2, p. 4.

"Luxury and Extravagance," *Springfield Union*, July 7, 1873, cols. 5-6, p. 4.

"The Lying Epidemic," *Springfield Union*, February 14, 1873, col. 1, p. 2.

"Lynch Law," *Springfield Union*, December 2, 1872, col. 1, p. 2.

"The Marriageable Age," *Springfield Union*, May 2, 1874, col. 4, p. 6.

"The Marrying Age," *Springfield Union*, December 30, 1874, col. 5, p. 4.

"Matthew Arnold's New Gospel," *Springfield Union*, June 7, 1873, col. 1, p. 2.

"Medical Education in the United States," *Springfield Union*, November 8, 1875, col. 6, p. 4.

"Medical Problems of the Day," *Springfield Union*, June 6, 1874, col. 6, p. 4.

"Men Not Principles," *Springfield Union*, August 3, 1872, col. 1, p. 2.

"Mental Stimulants," *Springfield Union*, November 28, 1873, cols. 3-4, p. 4.

"The Millionaire or the Republican Must Go," *New Nation*, II, 3 (January 6, 1892), pp. 32-33.

"Minding One's Own Business," *Springfield Union*, April 21, 1874, col. 5, p. 4.

"The Minister a Citizen," *Springfield Union*, April 10, 1875, cols. 6-7, p. 4.

"The Ministers and the Divorce Laws," Springfield *Daily News*, January 17, 1881, col. 1, p. 2.

"Misapplied Charity," *Springfield Union*, February 17, 1874, col. 5, p. 4.

"A Mischievous Divorce," *Springfield Union*, November 6, 1875, col. 6, p. 4.

"The Mistakes of Reformers," *New Nation*, I, 3 (February 14, 1891), col. 2, p. 44.

"The Model Public Library," *Springfield Union*, August 28, 1873, cols. 4-5, p. 4.

"Modern Business Crises: Their Cause and Cure," *Springfield Union*, June 23, 1877, cols. 5-6, p. 4.

"The Modern Increase in the Average Life," *Springfield Union*, September 4, 1873, cols. 4-5, p. 4.

"The Modern Revival of Muscle," *Springfield Union*, July 17, 1873, cols. 6-7, p. 2.

"Moral and Religious Revivals," *Springfield Union*, February 21, 1874, col. 5, p. 4.

"Moral Murder as a Fine Art," *Springfield Union*, August 20, 1874, col. 4, p. 4.

"Morality and Politics," *Springfield Union*, November 17, 1876, col. 6, p. 2.

"Moralities in Politics," *Springfield Union*, November 17, 1876, col. 5, p. 2.

"Morbid Criticism," *Springfield Union*, February 2, 1875, cols. 2-3, p. 4.

"More English Lectures," *Springfield Union*, April 22, 1873, col. 1, p. 2.

"More Elbow Room," *Springfield Union*, March 5, 1874, cols. 4-5, p. 4.

"More School Superintendents Called For," *Springfield Union*, July 7, 1877, cols. 6-7, p. 4.

"More Talks about 'Individualism' and Common Sense," *New Nation*, III, 13 (April 1, 1893), col. 1, p. 167.

"A Much Needed Educative Reform," *Springfield Union*, August 8, 1874, cols. 4-5, p. 4.

"Must Man Be Master or Servant," *New Nation*, II, 35 (August 27, 1892), cols. 1-2, p. 543.

"Mr. Edward Atkinson's Little Stove," *New Nation*, I, 13 (April 25, 1891), col. 2, p. 206.

"Mr. Foulke on Individualism," *New Nation*, III, 10 (March 11, 1893), col. 2, p. 131.

"Mr. Gladden Attacks the Principle of Economic Equality," *New Nation*, III, 17 (April 29, 1893), col. 1, p. 216.

"Mr. Howells' Great Nationalistic Story," *New Nation*, III, 41 (October 14, 1893), p. 458.

"National Forests," *New Nation*, I, 46 (December 12, 1891), col. 2, p. 731.

"The National Sin of Calumny," *Springfield Union*, May 18, 1875, quoted in A. E. Morgan, *Edward Bellamy*, pp. 123-24.

"Nationalism and Anarchy," *New Nation*, I, 46 (December 12, 1891), col. 1, p. 727.

"Nationalism and Civil Service Reform," *New Nation*, I, 49 (December 19, 1891), col. 2, p. 743—col. 1, p. 744.

"Nationalism and the European System of Pensioning Workmen," *New Nation*, I, 30 (August 22, 1891), col. 2, p. 472.

"Nationalism and the Liquor Question," *New Nation*, I, 21 (June 20, 1891), cols. 1-2, p. 326.

"Nationalism and the Persecution of the Jews," *New Nation*, I, 18 (May 30, 1891), col. 2, p. 277.

"Nationalism in a Nutshell," *New Nation*, I, 37 (October 10, 1891), col. 2, p. 590.

"Nationalism Logically Implied in Individualism," *New Nation*, I, 2 (February 13, 1892), col. 1, p. 98.

"A Nationalist Text From Calvin's City," *New Nation*, II, 46 (November 12, 1892), col. 2, p. 674—col. 1, p. 675.

"The Nationalist the True Conservative Party," *New Nation*, III, 4 (January 28, 1893), col. 2, p. 49.

"Nationalists Are Color Blind," *New Nation*, I, 36 (October 3, 1891), col. 1, p. 567.

"The Nation's Idol," *Springfield Union*, June 14, 1877, col. 7, p. 2.

"New Books," *Springfield Union*, July 12, 1873, col. 4, p. 2.

"New Books," *Springfield Union*, June 17, 1873, col. 3, p. 2.

"New Books and Magazines," *Springfield Union*, August 20, 1872, col. 4, p. 2.

"New Books and Magazines," *Springfield Union*, September 20, 1872, col. 3, p. 2.

"A New England Country Parson," *Springfield Union*, November 14, 1877, cols. 5-6, p. 4.

"The New Magazines," *Springfield Union*, November 17, 1877, cols. 2-3, p. 4.

"The New Nation," *New Nation*, I, 1 (January 31, 1891), col. 2, p. 10.

"New Publication," *Springfield Union*, August 30, 1872, col. 2, p. 3.

"News from Nowhere," *New Nation*, I, 3 (February 14, 1891), col. 1, p. 47.

"Newspapers Under Nationalism," *New Nation*, I, 41 (November 7, 1891), cols. 1-2, p. 468.

"The New York Standard Suspends," *New Nation*, II, 37 (September 20, 1892), col. 2, p. 567.

"A Non Sequitur," *Springfield Union*, February 15, 1873, col. 1, p. 2.

"Not Too Soon," *New Nation,* III, 49 (December 9, 1893), col. 2, p. 523.

"The Novelists and the Critics," *Springfield Union,* March 21, 1877, col. 7, p. 4.

"Now Is the Accepted Time," *Springfield Union,* October 1, 1873, col. 6, p. 2.

"Objections to National Ownership of the Railroads," *New Nation,* III, 17 (April 29, 1893), pp. 213-214.

"The Old Faith and the New," *Springfield Union,* December 23, 1873, cols. 5-6, p. 2.

"The Old Patriotism and the New," *New Nation,* III, 27 (July 8, 1893), pp. 333-4.

"The Old and the New," *Springfield Union,* October 23, 1873, col. 4, p. 5.

"One of the A. B. C's," *New Nation,* I, 34 (September 19, 1891), col. 2, p. 536.

"The Only Prevention of Prostitution," *New Nation,* I, 44 (November 28, 1891), col. 1, p. 694.

"The Only Respect in Which a Republic Is Better than a Monarchy," *New Nation,* III, 4 (January 28, 1893), cols. 1-2, p. 52.

"An Opportune Time for the State Life Insurance Company," *New Nation,* II, 23 (June 4, 1892), col. 2, p. 354—col. 1, p. 355.

"The Opportunity of the Workman and of the Church," *Springfield Union,* December 4, 1873, cols. 3-4, p. 4.

"The Order of Enoch: A New Phase of Mormonism," *Springfield Union,* April 19, 1874, col. 4, p. 4.

"Outdoor Life in the Summer," *Springfield Union,* May 23, 1877, col. 7, p. 4.

"Our Children Must Be Educated," *Springfield Union,* November 24, 1874, col. 4, p. 6.

"Our Present Social System 'An Agreement with Death and a Covenant with Hell,'" *New Nation,* II, 16 (April 16, 1892), col. 2, p. 241—col. 1, p. 242.

"Our Unemployed Young Men," *Springfield Union,* September 19, 1874, col. 4, p. 6.

"Out of the Fashion—Out of the World," *Springfield Union,* May 10, 1873, col. 1, p. 7.

"Overgrown Fortunes a Social Injury," *Springfield Union,* June 17, 1893, cols. 1-2, p. 2.

"Over Production and Over Trading," *Springfield Union,* July 20, 1875, cols. 5-6, p. 4.

"Overworked Children in Our Mills," *Springfield Union,* June 5, 1873, col. 1, p. 2.

"The Patrons of Husbandry," *Springfield Union,* February 10, 1874, col. 4, p. 3.

"A People's Party Hymn Criticized," *New Nation,* I, 38 (October 17, 1891), cols. 1-2, p. 600.

"The Pestilence at Memphis," *Springfield Union,* October 17, 1873, col. 7, p. 2.

"The Philosophy of Competition," *New Nation,* I, 17 (April 23, 1892), col. 1, p. 259.

"Physical Health as a Moral Factor," *Springfield Union,* July 19, 1873, col. 5, p. 4.

"The Piece-Meal Process," *New Nation,* I, 44 (January 28, 1891), cols. 1-2, p. 695.

"A Picture of Labor," *New Nation,* I, 39 (October 24, 1891), col. 1, p. 616.

"A Pleasant but Sad Seduction," *Springfield Union,* September 9, 1876, col. 5, p. 4.

"The Plea of Insanity," *Christian Union,* May 8, 1872.

"Plenty of Room at the Top," *New Nation,* II, 32 (August 6, 1892), col. 2, p. 500.

"Points to Be Remembered," *New Nation,* III, 44 (November 4, 1893), col. 1, p. 483.

"The Poor Man's Banker," *Springfield Union,* February 23, 1875, cols. 4-5, p. 4.

"The Powerlessness of Congressional Majorities," *New Nation,* II, 11 (March 18, 1893), cols. 1-2, p. 143.

"Practical Dress Reform," *Springfield Union,* December 19, 1874, col. 1, p. 5.

"Practical Questions about Railroad Nationalization," *New Nation,* III, 35 (September 2, 1893), cols. 1-2, p. 410.

"The Present Status of the 'Woman Movement'," *Springfield Union,* October 15, 1873, col. 2, p. 7.

"Preserving Our Forests," *New Nation,* I, 37 (October 10, 1891), cols. 1-2, p. 587.

"Prison Reform and the Proposed Means," *Springfield Union,* February 17, 1874, col. 4, p. 4.

"Professor David Swing and the Chicago Presbytery," *Springfield Union*, May 5, 1874, cols. 2-3, p. 4.

"Professor Huxley Furnishes Us with an Argument," *New Nation*, III, 23 (June 10, 1893), col. 1, p. 288—col. 2, p. 287.

"Property Is Power," *New Nation*, I, 12 (April 14, 1891), col. 1, p. 190.

"Proportional Representation," *New Nation*, II, 30 (July 23, 1892), col. 2, p. 466, cols. 1-2, p. 467.

"Protection at the South," *Springfield Union*, September 6, 1876, col. 3, p. 4.

"The Psychology of Spencer," *Springfield Union*, October 18, 1873, cols. 6-7, p. 4.

"Pulpit and Plow," *Springfield Union*, May 31, 1873, col. 1, p. 2.

"Punishment and Insanity," *Springfield Union*, January 22, 1876, cols. 3-4, p. 4.

"Put Yourself in His Place," *Springfield Union*, August 18, 1874, cols. 5-6, p. 4.

"Putting on the Screws," *Springfield Union*, June 23, 1877, col. 6, p. 4.

"Puzzles in Morals," *Springfield Union*, June 1, 1875, cols. 4-5, p. 4.

"The Question of Incentives Once More," *New Nation*, I, 12 (April 18, 1891), col. 2, p. 189.

"The Question of Residence Under Nationalism," *New Nation*, III, 3 (January 14, 1893), col. 2, p. 15—col. 1, p. 16.

"The Rage for Office and Title," *Springfield Union*, October 2, 1873, col. 5, p. 4.

"The Rain-fall Declining from Year to Year," *Springfield Union*, November 16, 1876, col. 2, p. 6.

"Reading the Newspapers," *Springfield Union*, July 14, 1874, col. 2, p. 6.

"Real Independence," *Springfield Union*, January 20, 1877, col. 4, p. 5.

"Reason to Thank God," *New Nation*, III, 42 (October 21, 1893), p. 466.

"Recent Miracles," *Springfield Union*, August 11, 1874, col. 4, p. 4.

"Referendum in Nebraska," *New Nation*, I, 2 (February 7, 1891), col. 2, p. 21.

"A Reform Worth Having," *Springfield Union*, July 13, 1876, cols. 5-6, p. 2.

"The Reign of the Hucksters," *New Nation*, II, 1 (January 2, 1892), col. 2, p. 5.

"A Reign of Terror Ended," *Springfield Union*, March 17, 1877, col. 7, p. 5—col. 1, p. 6.

"Religion and Science," *Springfield Union*, March 30, 1875, col. 5, p. 4.

"Religious Nonsense and Religious Common Sense," *Springfield Union*, November 22, 1873, col. 6, p. 4.

"Religious Sensuousness," *Springfield Union*, August 22, 1877, cols. 6-7, p. 4.

"Religious Service for the Masses," *Springfield Union*, November 7, 1872, col. 1, p. 2.

"Rents and Ownership," *Springfield Union*, September 25, 1875, cols. 5-6, p. 4.

"A Republic Without Virtue," *Springfield Union*, June 5, 1874, col. 2, p. 4.

"Responsibility in Mental Disease," *Springfield Union*, May 12, 1874, col. 3, p. 4.

"The Revision of the Bible," *Springfield Union*, July 13, 1872, col. 2, p. 2.

"Riches and Rottenness," *Springfield Union*, November 14, 1877, col. 4, p. 5.

"The Right to Labor—Work for the Unemployed—What Can and Ought to Be Done About It," *New Nation*, II, 2 (January 2, 1892), col. 2, p. 18.

"The Rising Generation," *Springfield Union*, February 7, 1877, cols. 5-6, p. 4.

"Ritualism and Rutism," *Springfield Union*, February 20, 1875, col. 4, p. 5.

"The Root and Cause of all Panics, Crises, and Hard Times and the Remedy," *New Nation*, III, 32 (August 12, 1893), col. 1, p. 387.

"The Root of the Present Social Discontent," *New Nation*, I, 25 (July 8, 1891), col. 2, p. 389—cols. 1-2, p. 390.

"A Sensible City Fashion and Why Don't the Country Adopt It?" *Springfield Union*, February 19, 1874, col. 7, p. 4.

"Sense and Nonsense, About Servants," *Springfield Union*, August 16, 1873, col. 5, p. 4.

"Serbonian Bogs," *Springfield Union*, April 7, 1874, cols. 4-6, p. 4.

"Several Questions Answered," *New Nation*, I, 24 (July 11, 1891), col. 1, p. 374.

"Several Stock Objections to Nationalism Objected To," *New Nation*, I, 44 (November 28, 1891), pp. 697-699.

"Sex in Education," *Springfield Union*, December 27, 1873, cols. 6-7, p. 4.

"Sex in Industry," *Springfield Union*, May 13, 1875, cols. 6-7, p. 4.

"Schools of Instruction in Theology," *Springfield Union*, May 28, 1873, cols. 1-2, p. 2.

"Science and Sentiment," *Springfield Union*, December 29, 1875, col. 5, p. 2.

"The Scientific Basis of Economic Equality," *New Nation*, II, 25 (June 18, 1892), cols. 1-2, p. 388—col. 1, p. 389.

"Scientific Farming," *Springfield Union*, November 3, 1875, cols. 2-3, p. 4.

"The Shadow of the Man on Horseback," *New Nation*, II, 46 (November 12, 1892), cols. 1-2, p. 675.

"Shall Public Business Be Conducted by Public Employees," *New Nation*, I, 41 (November 7, 1891), cols. 1-2, p. 647.

"Shall We Call Them Servants," *Springfield Union*, September 26, 1877, col. 5, p. 4.

"The Shame and Salvation of Popular Government," *Springfield Union*, March 4, 1873, col. 1, p. 2,

"Should Every Boy Learn a Trade? And How Shall He Find Out What He Is Best Fitted For?" *New Nation*, II, 36 (September 3, 1893), cols. 1-2, p. 557.

"Small Help in a Good Education," *New Nation*, III, 13 (April 1, 1893), col. 2, p. 167—col. 1, p. 168.

"The Social Conscience in Advance of the Individual Conscience," *New Nation*, III, 50 (December 16, 1893), col. 2, p. 531.

"Socialism Abroad," *New Nation*, I, 42 (November 14, 1891), cols. 1-2, p. 663.

"Socialism and Nationalism," *New Nation*, IV, 4 (January 27, 1894), col. 1, p. 38.

"The Society for the Prevention of Cruelty to Children," *Springfield Union*, December 28, 1874, col. 4, p. 7.

"The Solution and the Only One of the Unemployed Problem," *New Nation*, III, 36 (September 9, 1893), col. 2, p. 417—cols. 1-2, p. 418.

"Some Account of Eugen Richter's Anti-Socialist Romance," *New Nation*, III, 22 (June 6, 1892), col. 2, p. 275.

"Some Common Adulteries," *Springfield Union*, May 9, 1877, col. 7, p. 4.

"Some Facts About Trusts," *New Nation*, II, 13 (March 26, 1892), col. 1, p. 195.

"Some Good Words Spoiled," *Springfield Union*, June 22, 1876, col. 4, p. 4.

"Some Hints About Ventilation," *Springfield Union*, November 20, 1873, cols. 3-4, p. 4.

"Some Points of Nationalism Argued Out," *New Nation,* I, 31 (August 29, 1891), col. 2, p. 486.

"Spots on the Sun," *New Nation,* I, 9 (March 28, 1891), col. 2, p. 142.

"Springfield Shylocks," *Springfield Union,* January 5, 1873, col. 1, p. 2.

"The Springtime," *Springfield Union,* May 19, 1877, cols. 6-7, p. 4.

"The Spirit and Logic of Nationalism," *New Nation,* II, 9 (February 27, 1892), col. 2, p. 129.

"Spiritualism and Science," *Springfield Union,* July 14, 1874, cols. 5-6, p. 4.

"The State of the Labor Market," *Springfield Union,* February 7, 1874, col. 1, p. 4.

"Statistics of Children," *Springfield Union,* November 29, 1876, col. 4, p. 4.

"Stirpiculture," *Springfield Union,* October 2, 1875, col. 3, p. 4.

"Striking Hard Pan," *Springfield Union,* March 15, 1873, col. 1, p. 2.

"Suicide in New York," *Springfield Union,* January 8, 1873, col. 2, p. 2.

"Suicides," *Springfield Union,* November 18, 1873, col. 4, p. 4.

"Sunday School Songs," *Springfield Union,* November 11, 1873, cols. 6-7, p. 4.

"The Swedish Civil Service," *Springfield Union,* November 21, 1877, col. 4, p. 4.

"A System Without Government of Any Sort," *New Nation,* III, 4 (October 21, 1893), col. 2, p. 467.

"Taking the Election," *Springfield Union,* November 15, 1876, col. 2, p. 4.

"Talks on Nationalism," *The New Nation,* 1891: Mr. Smith and Successful Business Man *re* Motivation of Labor, I, 3 (February 14, 1891); Mr. Smith and Minister *re* Nationalism as Christianity, I, 4 (February 21, 1891); Mr. Smith and Public Speaker *re* Individuality, I, 5 (February 28, 1891); Mr. Smith and Sceptic *re* Brotherhood of Man, I, 6 (March 7, 1891); Mr. Smith and Evolutionist, I, 7 (March 14, 1891); Mr. Smith *re* Governmental Paternalism, I, 8 (March 21, 1891); Mr. Smith and Believer in the Bible, I, 9 (March 28, 1891); Mr. Smith *re* Variety in Life, I, 10 (April 4, 1891); Mr. Smith and Stickler for Private Ownership, I, 11 (April 11, 1891); Mr. Smith and Woman's Rights Advocate, I, 12 (April 18, 1891); Mr. Smith and Workingman, I, 13 (April 25, 1891); Mr. Smith and Father of Family, I, 14 (May 2, 1891); Mr. Smith *re* Changing Human Nature, I, 15 (May 9, 1891); Mr. Smith *re* Charity, I, 16 (May 16, 1891); Mr. Smith *re* Spencer and Fear of Despotism in New

State, I, 17 (May 23, 1891); Mr. Smith *re* Prevention of Cruelty to Animals, I, 18 (May 30, 1891); Mr. Smith and Malthus, I, 19 (June 6, 1891); Mr. Smith *re* Inventions, I, 20 (June 13, 1891); Mr. Smith *re* Money, I, 21 (June 20, 1891); Mr. Smith Talks with College Man about Opportunity, I, 22 (June 27, 1891); Mr. Smith and Tariff Reformer, I, 23 (July 4, 1891); Mr. Smith and Prohibitionist, I, 24 (July 11, 1891); Mr. Smith *re* Immigration Restrictions, I, 25 (July 18, 1891); Mr. Smith *re* Economic Equality, I, 26 (July 25, 1891); Mr. Smith Defines Difference Between Communism, Socialism and Nationalism, I, 27 (August 1, 1891); Mr. Smith and Investment Banker, I, 28 (August 8, 1891); Mr. Smith *re* Servant Question, I, 29 (August 13, 1891); Mr. Smith *re* Pensions for All, I, 30 (August 22, 1891); Mr. Smith and Farmer, I, 31 (August 29, 1891); Mr. Smith and Dress Reformer, I, 37 (October 10, 1891).

Talks on Nationalism. Foreword by William P. Harvey. Reprints from *The New Nation.* Chicago: Peerage Press, 1938.

"Tea Table Talk," Springfield *Daily News,* September 24, 1880, cols. 2-3, p. 1.

"Tea Table Talk," Springfield *Daily News,* October 26, 1880, col. 3, p. 3.

"Tea Table Talk," Springfield *Daily News,* November 11, 1880, col. 2, p. 3.

"Tea Table Talk," Springfield *Daily News,* November 13, 1880, col. 2, p. 3.

"Tea Table Talk," Springfield *Daily News,* January 14, 1881, col. 2, p. 3.

"These Dreadful Days," *Springfield Union,* October 26, 1872, col. 1, p. 2.

"Three Epitaphs," Springfield *Penny News,* March 6, 1880, col. 2, p. 4.

"Time Lost by Slow Travel," *Springfield Union,* January 4, 1873, col. 2, p. 2.

"Tinkering the Constitution," *Springfield Union,* December 5, 1876, col. 5, p. 2.

"Traveller from Altruria," *New Nation,* II, 48 (November 26, 1892), pp. 701-702.

"Treasures for the Taking," *Springfield Union,* July 10, 1875, cols. 2-3, p. 6.

"Trial by Jury," *Springfield Union,* February 8, 1873, cols. 1-2, p. 2.

"The Tribute of a Philosopher to Religion," *Springfield Union,* December 3, 1874, cols. 4-5, p. 4.

"The True Mission of the Teacher," *Springfield Union,* September 3, 1874, col. 4, p. 4.

"The Truth Shall Make You Free," *New Nation,* II, 12 (March 19, 1892), col. 1, p. 180—col. 2, p. 179.

"The Topic of the Hour," *Springfield Union,* November 10, 1874, cols. 5-6, p. 4.

"Too Many College Men Already," *New Nation,* I, 37 (October 10, 1891), col. 1, p. 583—col. 2, p. 582.

"The Torpedo as a Peace Maker," *Springfield Union,* June 20, 1877, col. 3, p. 4.

"Touching Things Spiritual," *Springfield Union,* November 27, 1875, cols. 3-4, p. 4.

"Towards a Solution," *Springfield Union,* August 4, 1877, cols. 6-7, p. 4.

"The Tweedle-dee Party and the Tweedle-dum Party," *New Nation,* I, 36 (October 3, 1891), col. 1, p. 568.

"Two Good Christians," *Springfield Union,* April 25, 1877, col. 3, p. 6.

"Two Types of Reformers," *Springfield Union,* September 25, 1873, col. 4, p. 4.

"Two Ways of Looking at It and the Right Way," *New Nation,* III, 13 (April 1, 1893), col. 1, p. 166.

"The Unfitness of Things," *Springfield Union,* May 11, 1875, cols. 3-4, p. 4.

"The Useful Should Be Ornamental," *Springfield Union,* January 27, 1874, cols. 5-6, p. 4.

"Useful Wishes and Useful Work," *Springfield Union,* July 23, 1874, cols. 3-4, p. 4.

"The Uses of Leisure," *Springfield Union,* July 7, 1874, cols. 5-6, p. 4.

"Vacation Philosophy," *Springfield Union,* August 2, 1876, col. 5, p. 4.

"Vacations for Tired People," *Springfield Union,* July 14, 1877, col. 6, p. 4.

"The Value of a Public Brand," *New Nation,* III, 37 (September 16, 1893), col. 1, p. 427.

"Vanderbilt's Way," *Springfield Union,* August 1, 1877, col. 7, p. 4.

"Variety in Unity," *Springfield Union,* October 7, 1873, cols. 4-5, p. 4.

"A Victim to American Eating Habits," *Springfield Union,* November 23, 1875, cols. 5-6, p. 4.

"Von Moltke's Criticism of Our Army," *Springfield Union,* August 3, 1875, col. 7, p. 4.

"Walking," *Springfield Union,* September 5, 1877, cols. 4-5, p. 4.

"The War for Woman's Independence Must Become Socialistic," *New Nation,* III, 43 (October 28, 1893), col. 2, p. 774.

"Water, Water Everywhere and Not a Drop to Drink," *Springfield Union,* August 16, 1873, cols. 4-5, p. 4.

"Was It Worth It?" *Springfield Union,* October 24, 1874, col. 5, p. 4.

"Wastes and Burdens of Society," *Springfield Union,* November 15, 1877, col. 3, p. 4.

"We Accept the Title," *New Nation,* I, 23 (July 4, 1891), col. 2, p. 359.

"Wealth and Sensual Pleasures," *Springfield Union,* February 24, 1873, col. 1, p. 2.

"Well Done, Mr. Andrews, but Look at Home," *New Nation,* II, 23 (June 4, 1892), col. 2, p. 353—col. 1, p. 354.

"What Mr. Joel Benton Thinks Nationalism Is Like," *New Nation,* III, 3 (January 21, 1893), cols. 1-2, p. 34.

"What Ought to be Done for the Unemployed," *New Nation,* III, 50 (December 16, 1893), cols. 1-2, p. 530.

"What Our Young Men Should Resolve to Become," *Springfield Union,* March 17, 1874, cols. 4-5, p. 4.

"What Reading for the Young," *Springfield Union,* August 15, 1877, cols. 5-6, p. 4.

"What the Grangers Say of Themselves," *Springfield Union,* February 7, 1874, col. 5, p. 4.

"When Will the Other Churches Wake Up," *New Nation,* I, 16 (May 16, 1891), cols. 1-2, p. 247.

"Where Are They," *Springfield Union,* November 18, 1872, col. 1, p. 2.

"Whitefield One of the Founders of the American Nationality," *Springfield Union,* October 8, 1873, cols. 6-7, p. 2.

"Who Has Got to Pay?" *Springfield Union,* July 25, 1877, col. 4, p. 4.

"Wholesome Heat and Enough of It," *Springfield Union,* October 20, 1874, col. 3, p. 4.

"Who Shall Be the City Physician," *Springfiield Union,* January 17, 1873, col. 1, p. 2.

"Who Should Not Marry," *Springfield Union,* September 30, 1873, cols. 4-5, p. 4.

"Why All Women Should Be Nationalists," *New Nation,* II, 23 (June 14, 1892), cols. 1-2, p. 355.

"Why Co-operation Does Not Always Succeed," *Springfield Union,* December 13, 1877, col. 7, p. 2—col. 1, p. 3.

"Why Don't God Kill the Devil," *Springfield Union,* July 13, 1876, cols. 6-7, p. 2.

"Why Every Workingman Should Be a Nationalist," *New Nation,* III, 15 (April 15, 1893), col. 1, p. 193.

"Why Not Have Candor in Party Platforms," *Springfield Union,* September 8, 1877.

"Why Should Not the Function of the Government 'Include Support of the People'?" *New Nation,* III, 15 (April 15, 1893), cols. 1-2, p. 192.

"Why We Cannot Agree with the Tribune," *New Nation,* I, 16 (May 16, 1891), col. 3, p. 247—col. 1, p. 248.

"Why Workingmen Should Favor All Propositions for Public Operation of Business," *New Nation,* II, 10 (March 11, 1893), col. 2, p. 129—cols. 1-2, p. 130.

"Will Erotic Crimes Ever Become Unknown," *New Nation,* I, 29 (August 15, 1891), cols. 1-2, p. 456.

"Will the Lesson Be Heeded," *Springfield Union,* November 21, 1872, col. 1, p. 2.

"Will the World Be Over-Peopled Under Nationalism," *New Nation,* III, 5 (February 4, 1893), cols. 1-2, p. 51.

"Winter Occupations," *Springfield Union,* December 26, 1875, col. 4, p. 4.

"Woman as an Inventor," Springfield *Daily News,* December 1, 1880, col. 6, p. 1.

"Woman's Extravagance," *Springfield Union,* October 25, 1873, col. 6, p. 4.

"The Woman's Congress," *Springfield Union,* October 17, 1873, col. 7, p. 2.

"Woman Suffrage," *Springfield Union,* November 25, 1872, col. 1, p. 2.

"Women Before the Law," *Springfield Union,* February 26, 1874, col. 4, p. 4.

"Woodman, Spare That Tree," *Springfield Union,* July 7, 1873, col. 6, p. 6.

"A Word About Co-operative Colonies," *New Nation,* I, 14 (March 2, 1891), p. 222.

"The Word 'Obey' in the Marriage Ceremony," *New Nation,* II, 25 (June 18, 1892), col. 1, p. 387.

"A Word of Explanation," *New Nation,* III, 30 (July 29, 1893), col. 2, p. 370.

"Work for Women," *Springfield Union,* March 15, 1873, col. 1, p. 2.

"The World's Fair of 1893 and the World's Fair of 2000AD," *New Nation,* III, 18 (May 6, 1893), col. 1, p. 227.

"Worth a Thanksgiving," *New Nation,* III, 47 (November 25, 1893), col. 1, p. 507.

"Wrestling with a Holiday," *Springfield Union,* April 3, 1874, cols.
4-5, p. 4.

"Writing One's Own Obituary," *Springfield Union,* July 15, 1876, col. 5,
p. 4.

"The Zone System with a Local Application," *New Nation,* I, 35 (September 26, 1891), cols. 1-2, p. 551.

Unpublished Manuscripts, Letters, and Journals of
Edward Bellamy

Bellamy manuscripts, letters, journals deposited at Houghton Library,
Harvard University, Cambridge, Massachusetts.

Letters and journal of Edward Bellamy, Bellamy Family, 75 Avon Place,
Springfield, Massachusetts.

Letters of Edward Bellamy to William Dean Howells, William Dean
Howells manuscript collection, Houghton Library, Harvard University,
Cambridge, Massachusetts.

Letters of Edward Bellamy to Thomas Wentworth Higginson, Thomas
Wentworth Higginson manuscript collection, Houghton Library,
Harvard University, Cambridge, Massachusetts.

Letter of Edward Bellamy to Edgar Yates, Massachusetts Historical Society, Boston, Massachusetts.

BIBLIOGRAPHY

Books about Bellamy, Utopias, and the Period

Adams, Frederick B., Jr., *Radical Literature in America*. Stamford, Conn.: Overbrook Press, 1939.

Arnavon, Cyrille. *Les Lettres américaines devant la Critique Francaise*. Société d'Edition Les Belle Lettres, 1951.

Bellamy, Charles J. *The Breton Mills*. New York: G. P. Putnam's Sons, 1879.

———— *An Experiment in Marriage*. Albany, New York: Albany Book Co., 1889.

———— *The Way Out*. New York: G. P. Putnam's Sons, 1884.

———— *Were They Sinners?* Springfield, Mass.: Authors' Publishing Co., 1890.

Berneri, Marie Louise. *Journey Through Utopia*. London: Routledge and Kegan Paul, Ltd., 1950.

Bloomfield, Paul. *Imaginary Worlds, or the Evolution of Utopia*. London: Hamish Hamilton, 1932.

Boyle, James. *What Is Socialism?* New York: The Shakespeare Press, 1912.

Brooks, John Graham. *The Social Unrest*. 2d ed. New York: The Macmillan Co., 1909.

Buber, Martin. *Paths in Utopia*. Translated by R. F. C. Hull. London: Routledge and Kegan Paul, 1949.

Calverton, V. F. *Where Angels Dared to Tread*. Indianapolis: Bobbs-Merrill Co., 1941.

Cargill, Oscar. *Intellectual America*. New York: The Macmillan Co., 1941.

Commager, Henry S. *The American Mind*. New Haven: Yale University Press, 1950.

Cook, Joseph. *Boston Monday Lectures*. Boston: Houghton, Mifflin and Co., 1880.

Coombs, Edith I. (ed.) *America Visited*. New York: The Book League of America, n.d.

Cullen, Alexander. *Adventures in Socialism*. London: A. & C. Black, 1910.

Dombrowski, James. *The Early Days of Christian Socialism in America.* New York: Columbia University Press, 1936.

Donner, H. W. *Introduction to Utopia.* London: Sidgwick and Jackson, Ltd., 1945.

Dorfman, Joseph. *The Economic Mind in American Civilization, 1865-1918.* Vol. I. New York: The Viking Press, 1949.

———— *Thorstein Veblen and His America.* New York: The Viking Press, 1947.

Ely, Richard T. *French and German Socialism in Modern Times.* New York: Harper and Brothers, 1883.

———— *The Labor Movement in America.* New York: Thomas Y. Crowell & Co., 1886.

———— *Recent American Socialism.* Johns Hopkins University Studies in Historical and Political Science, Third Series, No. IV. Baltimore: Johns Hopkins University, 1885.

———— *Socialism.* New York: Thomas Y. Crowell & Co., 1894.

Filler, Louis. *Crusaders for American Liberalism.* New York: Harcourt, Brace & Co., 1939.

Gide, Charles. *Communist and Co-operative Colonies.* Translated by Ernest F. Row. London: George Harrap & Co., 1930.

Grahamme, Stewart. *Where Socialism Failed.* New York: McBride, Nast & Co., 1912.

Gray, Alexander. *The Socialist Tradition.* New York: Longmans, Green & Co., 1946.

Griffin, C. S. *Nationalism.* Boston: C. S. Griffin, 1889.

Gronlund, Lawrence. *The Co-operative Commonwealth in Its Outlines. An Exposition of Modern Socialism.* Boston: Lee & Shepard, 1884.

———— *Our Destiny. The Nationalist,* Vol. II, 4 (March, 1890) to Vol. III, 2 (September, 1890).

Harris, George. *Inequality and Progress.* Boston: Houghton, Mifflin & Co., 1897.

Hicks, Granville. *The Great Tradition.* New York: Macmillan Co., 1933.

Hillquit, Morris. *History of Socialism in the United States.* New York: Funk & Wagnalls, 1903.

———— *Socialism in Theory and Practice.* New York: Macmillan Co., 1919.

Hooker, Richard. *The Story of an Independent Newspaper. One Hundred Years of the Springfield Republican. 1824-1924.* New York: Macmillan Co., 1924.

James, Henry Ammon. *Communism in America.* New York: Henry Holt & Co., 1879.

James, Henry. *Substance and Shadow.* Boston: Ticknor & Fields, 1866.

———— *Christianity, the Logic of Creation.* New York: D. Appleton & Co., 1857.

Jevons, H. Stanley. *Economic Equality in the Co-operative Commonwealth.* London: Methuen & Co., Ltd., 1933.

Johnson, L. L. *Chicopee Illustrated.* Holyoke, Mass.: Transcript Publishing Company, 1896.

Josephson, Matthew. *The Robber Barons: The Great American Capitalists, 1861-1901.* New York: Harcourt, Brace and Co., 1934.

Kahn, Hans. *Prophets and Peoples: Studies in Nineteenth Century Nationalism.* New York: Macmillan Co., 1946.

Kaufmann, Rev. M. *Utopias: or, Schemes of Social Improvements from Sir Thomas More to Karl Marx.* London: Kegan Paul & Co., 1879.

Kelly, Edmond. *Twentieth Century Socialism.* New York: Longmans, Green & Co., 1913.

Kirkup, Thomas. *History of Socialism.* 5th ed. London: Adam and Charles Black, 1913.

Laidler, Harry W. *A History of Socialist Thought.* Crowell's Social Science Series. New York: Thomas Y. Crowell Co., 1927.

Madison, Charles A. *Critics and Crusaders.* New York: Henry Holt & Co., 1947.

Mann, Arthur. *Yankee Reformers in the Urban Age.* Cambridge: Harvard University Press, 1954.

Macy, John. *Socialism in America.* New York: Doubleday, Page & Co., 1916.

Mannheim, Karl. *Ideology and Utopia.* New York: Harcourt Brace, 1949.

Mannin, Ethel. *Bread and Roses.* London: Macdonald and Co., 1944?

Markham, S. F. *A History of Socialism.* New York: Macmillan & Co., 1931.

Martin, Fred R. *Fool's Gold.* New York: Madison and Marshall, Inc., 1936.

Mason, Alpheus Thomas. *Security Through Freedom.* Ithaca: Cornell University Press, 1955.

Masso, Gildo. *Education in Utopia.* New York: Bureau of Publications, Teachers College, Columbia University, 1927.

Morgan, Arthur E. *Edward Bellamy.* New York: Columbia University Press, 1944.

———— *The Philosophy of Edward Bellamy.* New York: King's Crown Press, 1945.

———— *Nowhere Was Somewhere.* Chapel Hill: The University of North Carolina Press, 1946.

———— *Plagiarism in Utopia.* Yellow Springs, Ohio: 1944.

Moore, David A. *The Age of Progress.* New York: Sheldon, Blakeman & Co., 1856.

Morton, A. L. *The English Utopia.* London: Lawrence and Wishart, 1952.

Mott, Frank Luther. *A History of American Magazines.* Cambridge: Harvard University Press, 1938.

Mumford, Lewis. *The Story of Utopias.* New York: Peter Smith, 1941.

Nevins, Allan. *The Evening Post: A Century of Journalism.* New York: Boni and Liveright, 1922.

Nordhoff, Charles. *The Communistic Societies of the United States.* New York: Harper and Brothers, 1875.

Oneal, James, and Werner, Gustave A. *American Communism.* New York: Dutton & Co., 1947.

Overstreet, H. A. *We Move in New Directions.* New York: W. Norton & Co., 1933.

Palmer, Mrs. Clara Skeele. *Annals of Chicopee Street.* Springfield, Mass.: Henry R. Johnson, 1899.

Parrington, Vernon L. *American Dreams: A Study of American Utopias.* Providence, Rhode Island: Brown University, 1947.

Quint, Howard. *The Forging of American Socialism.* Columbia: University of South Carolina, 1953.

Rae, John. *Contemporary Socialism.* New York: Charles Scribner's Sons, 1910.

Russell, Charles Edward. *Bare Hands and Stone Walls.* New York: Charles Scribner's Sons, 1933.

Ruyer, Raymond. *L'Utopie et les Utopies.* Paris: Presses Universitaires de France, 1950.

Sanders, George A. *Reality.* Cleveland: The Burrows Brothers Company, 1898.

Savelle, Max. *Seeds of Liberty: The Genesis of the American Mind.* New York: Alfred A. Knopf, 1948.

Seagar, Allan. *They Worked for a Better World.* New York: Macmillan Co., 1939.

Seldes, G. V. *The Stammering Century.* New York: John Day Co., 1928.

Schiffman, Joseph, ed. "Introduction," *Edward Bellamy, Selected Writings on Religion and Society*. New York: Liberal Arts Press, 1955.

Schlesinger, Arthur M. *Political and Social History of the United States, 1829-1925*. New York: Macmillan Co., 1930.

Schneider, Herbert W. *A History of American Philosophy*. New York: Columbia University Press, 1946.

Shaw, G. B. *et al. Socialism: The Fabian Essays*. Boston: Charles E. Brown & Co., 1894.

Shlakman, Vera. *Economic History of a Factory Town: A Study of Chicopee, Massachusetts*. Smith College Studies in History, Vol. XX, Nos. 1-4. Northampton, Mass.: Department of History, October, 1934—July, 1935.

Skelton, O. D. *Socialism: A Critical Analysis*. Boston: Houghton and Mifflin Co., 1911.

Sotheran, Charles. *Horace Greeley and Other Pioneers of American Socialism*. 2nd. ed. New York: Mitchell Kennerly, 1915.

Spargo, John. *Americanism and Social Democracy*. New York: Harper and Brothers, 1918.

Symes, Lillian, and Travers, Clement. *Rebel America: The Story of Social Revolt in the United States*. New York: Harper and Brothers, 1934.

Tawney, R. H. *Religion and the Rise of Capitalism*. Pelican Books. New York: Penguin Books, Inc., 1947.

Taylor, Walter Fuller. *The Economic Novel in America*. Chapel Hill: The University of North Carolina Press, 1942.

Thomas, Norman. *America's Way Out*. New York: Macmillan Co., 1931.

Wagner, Donald O. (ed.) *Social Reformers: Adam Smith to John Dewey*. New York: Macmillan Co., 1934.

Walsh, Correa Maylan. *Socialism*. New York: Sturgis and Walton Co., 1917.

Webb, Sidney. *Socialism in England*. 2nd. ed. London: Swan Sonnenschein & Co., 1893.

Wells, H. G. *The Outlook for Homo Sapiens and The New World Order*. London: Secker and Warburg, 1946.

Wheeler, David Hilton. *Our Industrial Utopia and Its Unhappy Citizens*. Chicago: A. C. McClurg & Co., 1895.

Whitman, John Pratt. *Utopia Dawns*. Boston: Utopia Publishing Co., 1934.

Anonymous Articles in Periodicals

"Announcement of an Excellent Publication," *New Nation,* I, 12 (April 18, 1891), p. 182.

"The Annual Town Reports," *Springfield Union,* March 28, 1877, col. 2, p. 8.

"Another Co-operative Colony," *New Nation,* I, 11 (April 11, 1891), p. 177.

"Arnold J. Toynbee," *Time,* Atlantic Edition, LVIII, 18 (October 29, 1951), col. 3, p. 23.

"An Attempt to Fool the Public," *New Nation,* III, 47 (November 25, 1893), p. 507.

"Attitude of the Press," *Nationalist,* II, 3 (February, 1890), p. 121; II, 4 (March, 1890), p. 143; II, 1 (August, 1890), pp. 37-38, 39-40; I, 6 (October, 1889), p. 220; II, 2 (January, 1890), p. 80.

"Beecher on Fisk," *Springfield Union,* January 22, 1872, col. 4, p. 2.

"Buying the Boston and Albany Railroad," *New Nation,* I, 17 (May 23, 1891), col. 2, p. 261.

"Chicopee Items," *Springfield Union,* August 5, 1879, col. 3, p. 4.

"City Items," *Springfield Union,* April 4, 1878, col. 1, p. 4; April 18, 1878, col. 1, p. 4; March 2, 1878, col. 2, p. 8; January 14, 1878, col. 1, p. 4.

"The Commonwealth of Jesus," *New Nation,* I, 7 (March 14, 1891), p. 113.

"Communistic Settlements," *Encyclopedia of Social Sciences* (1929), IV, p. 100.

"Co-operative Cooking," *New Nation,* II, 7 (February 13, 1893), p. 106.

"The Cradle of Liberty Rocked," *New Nation,* I, 38 (October 17, 1891), pp. 606-8.

"The Daily News for 1881," Springfield *Daily News,* January 27, 1881, col. 2, p. 4.

"Death of George W. Houghton," *New Nation,* I, 12 (April 18, 1891).

"Does Farming Pay?" *New Nation,* III, 10 (March 11, 1893), p. 133.

"Domestic Co-operation Experiments," *New Nation,* I, 13 (April 25, 1891), p. 198.

"Do Not Trade Our Heritage of Liberty for Autocracy, White Urges Kansas University Seniors," *Arkansas City Traveler,* June 12, 1934.

[Editorial Comment] *Springfield Union,* January 25, 1871, col. 1, p. 2.

"Editorial Notes," *Nationalist,* II, 3 (February, 1890), p. 116; I, 12 (April, 1891), p. 188; II, 5 (April, 1890), p. 187; I, 1 (May, 1889), p. 22; II, 4 (March, 1890), p. 140.

"Editor's Portfolio," "A Plain Talk with Mr. Bellamy," *Good House-keeping,* X, 9 (March 1, 1890), pp. 213-215.

"The Week," "Edward Bellamy," *The Outlook,* LIX, 4 (May 28, 1898), pp. 204-5.

"Edward Bellamy," *The American Fabian,* June, 1898, reprinted in *Edward Bellamy Speaks Again,* pp. 19-22.

"Edward Bellamy," *Springfield Union,* 1888, Bellamy Family Clippings.

"Equality," *Saturday Review* (London), LXXXIV, 2176 (July 10, 1897), pp. 45-46.

"Faneuil Hall Ablaze," *New Nation,* II, 15 (April 15, 1892), pp. 230-234.

"A Fine Infant," *New Nation,* I, 11 (April 11, 1891), p. 172.

"Francis E. Willard A Nationalist," *New Nation,* I, 7 (March 14, 1891), col. 1, p. 102.

"The Icarians," "Current Topics," *Nationalist,* III, 3 (October, 1890), p. 1199.

"The Ideal Always," Hartford, Connecticut, *Examiner,* July 5, 1889, Bellamy Family Files.

"The Inaugural Address," *Springfield Union,* March 5, 1873, col. 1, p. 2.

"James Russell Lowell's Looking Forward," *New Nation,* I, 33 (October, 1891), col. 2, p. 520.

"The Late Mr. Bellamy," *The Critic,* XXXII, 849 (May 28, 1898), pp. 362-363.

"Literary Notices," *Nationalist,* III, 1 (August, 1890), pp. 53-54; III, 5 (January, 1890), p. 359.

"A Look Ahead," *The Literary World,* XIX, 6 (March 7, 1888), pp. 85-86.

"Looking Beyond," *New Nation,* I, 43 (November 21, 1891), p. 683.

"Massachusetts at It Again," *New Nation,* II, 38 (September 17, 1892), p. 582.

"Miss Ludington's Sister," *The Literary World,* XV, 16 (August 9, 1884), p. 255.

"Moonblight," *New Nation,* III, 23 (June 10, 1893), p. 288.

Morning Herald, re Judge Wells, Bellamy Clippings, Houghton Library, Harvard University.

"Mr. Bellamy's Critics," *Lend-a-Hand,* VI, 1 (January, 1891).

"Mrs. Edward Bellamy," *Literary Digest,* CXVII (June 23, 1934), p. 11.

"Mrs. Woodhull on Free Love," *Springfield Union,* February 5, 1872, col. 2, p. 2.

"Nationalism at the Boston Anniversaries," *Nationalist,* I, 3 (July, 1889), p. 86.

"Nationalism in Politics," *New Nation,* II, 43 (October 22, 1892), pp. 643-645.

"Nationalist Publications," *New Nation,* I, 36 (October 3, 1891), p. 565.

"Nationalist Drift," *New Nation,* I, 5 (February 28, 1891), col. 2, p. 73.

"Nationalists in Council," *New Nation,* II, 20 (July 23, 1892), p. 469.

"News from the Clubs," *New Nation,* I, 18 (May 30, 1891), p. 289.

"News of the Movement," *Nationalist,* I, 1 (May, 1889), pp. 23-27; I, 4 (August, 1889), p. 127.

"Our Anniversary," "Editorial Notes," *Nationalist,* II, 1 (December, 1889), p. 35.

"Philip Meyer's Scheme," *New Nation,* III, 14 (April 8, 1893), p. 182.

"Publisher's Notice," Springfield *Daily News,* October 18, 1880, col. 1, p. 2.

"Recent Novels," *The Nation,* XXVII, 686 (August 22, 1878), p. 118.

"Reviews," *Nationalist,* I, 2 (June, 1889), p. 63.

"A Rousing Meeting at Lynn," *New Nation,* I, 40 (October 31, 1891), p. 636.

"The Second Anniversary of Nationalism," *New Nation,* I, 19 (June 6, 1891), p. 303.

"Scientific Intelligence, Paper Window Shutters," *Springfield Union,* January 11, 1873.

"The Significance of the New Party," *New Nation,* I, 34 (September 19, 1891), p. 539.

"Some Early Fruits," "Current Topics," *Nationalist,* III, 3 (October, 1890), pp. 197-8

"Third Party in Many States," "A Glance the Country Over," *New Nation,* I, 10 (April 4, 1891), p. 149.

"Trend of the Periodicals," *New Nation,* I, 13 (April 25, 1891), col. 1, p. 210; I, 5 (February 28, 1891), cols. 1-3, p. 74.

"Unequal Burdens and Benefits Under Competition," *New Nation,* I, 47 (December 19, 1891), p. 749.

"We Trust This Is Not Sound Theosophy," *New Nation,* II, 50 (December 10, 1892), p. 723.

"Well Done, Rhode Island," *New Nation*, I, 7 (March 14, 1891), p. 108.
" 'Which Wins?'—A Timely Book," *New Nation*, I, 23 (July 4, 1891), p. 360.

Signed Articles in Magazines and Journals

Arden, Edward. "Some Propositions of Nationalism," *The Chautauquan*, XIV, 4 (January, 1892), pp. 437-441.

Austin, Henry. "Edward Bellamy," *National Magazine*, IX, 1 (October, 1898), pp. 69-71

Baxter, Sylvester. "What Is Nationalism?" *The Nationalist*, I, 1 (May, 1889), pp. 2-12.

———— "Shall We Adopt the Swiss Referendum," *New Nation*, I, 1 (January 31, 1891), cols. 1-3, p. 15—cols. 1-2, p. 16.

———— "The Author of 'Looking Backward,' " *New England Magazine*, ns. I (September, 1889), pp. 92-98.

Becker, George J. "Edward Bellamy: Utopia, American Plan," *Antioch Review* (Summer, 1954), pp. 181-194.

Bisbee, Rev. R. E. "Some Characteristics of Edward Bellamy," *Coming Age*, I, 2 (February, 1899), p. 181.

Bliss, Rev. W. D. P. "A Study of the Present Situation," *The Dawn*, III, 21 (April, 1892), pp. 5-6.

Bradlaugh, C. "Socialism: Its Fallacies and Dangers," *North American Review*, CXLIV, 362 (January, 1887), pp. 12-21.

Bridges, John Ransom. "Nationalistic Socialism," *The Arena*, I, 2 (January, 1890), pp. 184-195.

———— "The Changes of Fifty Years," *The Nationalist*, I, 6 (October, 1889), pp. 227-230.

Broderick, George C. "Democracy and Socialism," *The Nineteenth Century*, XV, 86 (April, 1884), pp. 626-664.

Bryan, Clark W. "Edward Bellamy," "Editor's Portfolio," *Good Housekeeping*, X, 4 (December 21, 1889), pp. 95-6.

Burnham, Collins G. "The City of Chicopee," *The New England Magazine*, ns. XVIII, 3 (May, 1898), pp. 361-379.

Chadburn, Charles N. "Will It Destroy Individuality?" *The Nationalist*, II, 6 (May, 1890), pp. 187-193.

Chamberlain, Arthur. "A Communication: Christian Nationalism," *Andover Review* (Boston), SV, 90 (June, 1891), pp. 659-662.

Cheney, Walter L. "The Effect of Our Patent Laws," *The Nationalist*, I, 2 (June, 1889), pp. 52-54.

Coleman, McAlister, "Bellamy's Utopia," *The Nation,* CLIX, 27 (December 30, 1944), p. 803.

Cooper, John A. "Edward Bellamy," *Canadian Magazine,* IX, 4 (August, 1897), pp. 344-46.

Coursen, Alfred C. "Is Bellamy's Idea Feasible?" *The Arena,* XXI, 5 (May, 1899), pp. 344-46.

Cox, Jesse. "Stinted Production," *The Nationalist,* I, 3 (July, 1889), pp. 76-81.

Cressy, Rev. C. A. "A New Industrial System," *The Nationalist,* III, 3 (October, 1890), pp. 158-165.

E. L. H. W. "Home Correspondence," "Woman's Press Association and Mr. Bellamy's Domestic Service Problem," *Good Housekeeping,* X, 11 (March 29, 1890), p. 262.

Dawes, Anna L. "Mr. Bellamy and Christianity," *Andover Review,* CL, 88 (April, 1891), pp. 413-418.

Day, Clive. "Capitalistic and Socialistic Tendencies in the Puritan Colonies," *Annual Report of the American Historical Association for the Year 1920,* Vol. I, pp. 223-235.

deLaveleye, Emile. "Two New Utopias," *Littell's Living Age,* CLXXXIV, 2381 (February 15, 1890), pp. 381-399.

Dewey, John. "A Great American Prophet," *Common Sense,* April, 1934, reprint, Bellamy Files, Springfield Massachusetts, pp. 1-4.

Diaz, Abby Morton. "The Why and Wherefore," *The Nationalist,* II, 1 (December, 1889), pp. 5-10.

Feet, Sherman W. "The Credit System of Sonaloa," *Nationalist,* III, 7 (February, 1891), pp. 433-438.

Fellner, Dr. Ernst. "The Psychology of Socialism," *The Hibbert Journal,* XLVI, 2 (January, 1948), pp. 138-145.

Filler, Louis. "Edward Bellamy and the Spiritual Unrest," *American Journal of Economics and Sociology,* VIII (April, 1949), pp. 239-249.

Forbes, Alyn. "The Literary Quest for Utopias," *Social Forces,* VI, 2 (December, 1927), pp. 179-189.

Ford, Mary H. "A Feminine Iconoclast," *The Nationalist,* 1, 7 (November, 1889), pp. 252-257.

Foss, S. W. "Can We Popularize Absolute Justice?" *The Nationalist,* I, 3 (July, 1889), pp. 74-75.

Foster, Rev. E. P. "Nationalism: Behind the Mask," *Arena,* II, 11 (October, 1890), pp. 588-591.

Garrison, William L. "The Mask of Tyranny," *Arena,* I, 5 (April, 1890), pp. 553-559.

Georgii, Max. "Co-operative Society of Ghent," *The Nationalist*, II, 2 (January, 1890), pp. 53-57.

Green, Mason A. "Unconscious Nationalism in Our American System of Government," *New Englander and Yale Review*, ns. XVI, 229 (February, 1890), pp. 97-106.

Gronlund, Laurence. "Nationalism," *Arena*, I, 2 (January, 1890), pp. 165-153.

————— "The Nationalization of Industry," *Nationalist*, I, 2 (June, 1889), pp. 33-36.

————— "A Reply to Dr. Heber Newton," *Nationalist*, I, 4 (September, 1889), pp. 158-161.

Hale, E. E. "The Best Government," *Nationalist*, I, 2 (June, 1889), pp. 37-40.

————— "The Pilgrim's Life in Common," *New England Magazine*, ns. I, 1 (September, 1889), pp. 27-30.

Hamilton, Edward, and Hale, E. E., *et al.* "Destitution in Boston with Striking Illustrations and Practical Suggestions," *Arena*, II, 12 (November, 1890), pp. 733-751.

Harris, W. T. "Edward Bellamy's Vision," *Forum*, VIII (October, 1889), pp. 199-200.

Harvey, W. P. "Current Economic Issues Raised by Edward Bellamy Back in 1887," *The Railroad Trainman*, LV, 1 (January, 1938), pp. 21-22.

Henderson, C. R. "Fact and Fiction in Social Study," *The Dial*, XXIII, 266 (July 16, 1897), pp. 48-50.

Higginson, T. W. "Step by Step," *Nationalist*, I, 4 (September, 1889), pp. 145-148.

Higgs, William. "Bellamy: Objections to His Utopia," *New Englander and Yale Review*, LII, 240 (March, 1890), pp. 231-239.

Holyoake, George J. "State Socialism," *The Nineteenth Century*, V, 27 (June, 1879), pp. 1114-1120.

Howe, Julia Ward. "Women in the Professions," *Chautauquan*, VII, 8 (May, 1887), pp. 460-462.

Howells, William Dean. "Edward Bellamy," *Atlantic Monthly*, LXXXII (July, 1898), pp. 253-256, reprinted from "Edward Bellamy," *The Blindman's World*, pp. V—XIII.

Hudson, James F. "The Anthracite Coal Pool," *North American Review*, CXLIV, 362 (January, 1887), pp. 43-54.

Kouwenhoven, John A. (ed.) "America on the Move," *Harper's Magazine*, CCI, 1205 (October, 1950), pp. 97-144.

Levi, A. W. "Edward Bellamy, Utopian," *Ethics*, LV (January, 1945), pp. 131-144.

Livermore, Mary A. "Co-operative Housekeeping," *The Chautauquan*, VI, 7 (April, 1886), pp. 396-399.

Lynes, Russell. "The Age of Taste," *Harper's Magazine*, CCI, 1205 (October, 1950), pp. 60-73.

Madison, Charles A. "Edward Bellamy, Social Dreamer," *New England Quarterly*, XV (September, 1942), pp. 444-446.

Maher, Michael. "Socialist's Dream," *The Month*, LXXII, 319 (January, 1891), pp. 1-9; 320 (February, 1891), pp. 173-188.

Martin, J. J. "The Co-operative Commonwealth, The Kaweah Colony," *Nationalist*, I, 6 (October, 1889), pp. 204-208.

Morgan, A. E. "An Early American Social Revolt," *Survey Graphic*, XXIX, 12 (December, 1940), pp. 618-619.

Morris, William. "Looking Backward," *Commonweal*, V, 180 (June 22, 1889), pp. 194-195.

Orme, John. "Labor and Nationalism in Great Britain," *New Nation*, I, 4 (February 21, 1891), p. 641.

Orvis, John. "Social Transition," *Nationalist*, III, 1 (August, 1890), pp. 1-16.

Ridpath, J. C. "Is the Prophet Dead?" *Arena*, XX, 2 (August, 1898), pp. 284-288; reprinted in *Edward Bellamy Speaks Again*, pp. 217-228.

Ross, J. Elliot. "On Rereading Bellamy," *Commonweal*, XXIII, 16 (February 14, 1936), pp. 432-434.

Russell, Frances E. "Mrs. Russell Defends Bellamyism," *National Single Taxer*, September 1, 1897, p. 10

Sadler, Elizabeth. "One Book's Influence: Edward Bellamy's 'Looking Backward,' " *New England Quarterly*, XVII, 4 (December, 1944), pp. 530-555.

Schiffman, Joseph, "Edward Bellamy's Altruistic Man," *American Quarterly*, VI (Fall, 1954), pp. 195-209.

———— "Edward Bellamy's Religious Thoughts," *PMLA*, LXVIII (September, 1953), pp. 716-732.

Schindler, Solomon. "First Steps in Nationalism," *Arena*, XIII, 1 (June, 1895), pp. 26-30.

———— "Dr. Leete's Letter to Julian West," *Nationalist*, III, 2 (September, 1890), pp. 81-86.

Schoenlank, Bruno. "Socialism in Germany," *New Nation*, I, 8 (March 21, 1891), p. 130.

Sedgwick, A. G. "Bellamy's Utopia," *The Nation, LXV,* 1678 (August 26, 1897), pp. 170-171.

Shurter, Robert L. "The Literary Work of Edward Bellamy," *American Literature,* V, 3 (November, 1933), pp. 229-234.

———— "Utopian Novel in America," *South Atlantic Quarterly,* XXXIV (April, 1935), pp. 137-144.

———— "Writing of 'Looking Backward,'" *South Atlantic Quarterly,* XXXVIII (July, 1939), pp. 255-261.

Smith, Goldwin. "Prophet of Unrest," *The Forum,* IX, 6 (August, 1890), pp. 599-614.

Spencer, Edward Glenfoun. "Birth of Industrial Co-operation," *The Nationalist,* II, 7 (June, 1890), pp. 215-221.

Spahr, C. B. "Socialism, Nationalist and Christian," *The Nation,* XLVIII, 1250 (June 13, 1889), pp. 478-479.

Sinclair, Upton. "The World as I Want It," *Forum,* XCII, 3 (September, 1934), p. 157.

Tarbell, Ida M. "New Dealers of the 'Seventies: Henry George and Edward Bellamy," *Forum,* XCII, 3 (September, 1934), pp. 133-140.

Taylor, Bruce R. "Communistic Settlements in America," *Encyclopedia of Religion and Ethics* (1910), III, p. 783.

Timsol, Robert. "Back from Altruria," *Lippincott's Magazine,* LXI, (February, 1898), pp. 274-279.

Vassault, F. I. "Nationalism in California," *Overland Monthly,* ns. XV, 90 (June, 1890), pp. 659-661.

Wakeman, Thaddeus B. "Politics and the People," *Nationalist,* II, 1 (December, 1889), pp. 11-17.

———— "Decline of the Farmer," *Nationalist,* I, 17 (November, 1889), pp. 233-237.

Walker, F. A. "Bellamy and the New Nationalist Party," *Atlantic Monthly,* LXV, 388 (February, 1890), pp. 248-262.

Williams, Henry M. "Palaces and Hovels," *Nationalist,* I, 7 (November, 1889), pp. 250-251.

Willis, Frederick M. "The Sphere of the State," *Nationalist,* II, 5 (April, 1890), pp. 155-162.

Willard, C. F. "A Retrospect," *Nationalist,* II, 1 (December, 1889), pp. 37-40.

Willard, Cyrus. "The Nationalist Club of Boston," *Nationalist,* I, 1 (May, 1889), pp. 16-20.

Willard, Frances E. "An Interview with Edward Bellamy," *Our Day,* IV, 24 (December, 1889), pp. 539-542.

Works, Austin M. "Builders of a Brave New World," *Scholastic,* XXIII, 16 (January 27, 1934), p. 16.

Woods, Katharine P. "Edward Bellamy: Author and Economist," *The Bookman,* VII, 5 (July, 1898), pp. 398-401.

Pamphlets

Austin, Henry. *Address of Henry Austin Before the Second Nationalist Club of Boston at Twilight Hall. August 25, 1890.* Published by the Second Nationalist Club of Boston, n.d. John Crerar Library, Chicago, Illinois.

Barnes, Charles E. *Would Nationalism Destroy Individuality. Read Before the A to Z Club, Lansing, Michigan, December 5, 1889.* Lansing: Robert Smith and Co., n.d. John Crerar Library, Chicago, Illinois.

Boynton, Thomas J. *Guesses in Social Science. Remarks Delivered before the Unitarian Society at Florence, Massachusetts, August 15, 1869.* Chicago: Rand, McNally & Company, 1869.

Clark, F. C. *A Neglected Socialist: Wilhelm Weitling.* Publication of the American Academy of Political and Social Science, No. 144, April 9, 1895, pp. 66-87. Philadelphia, American Academy of Political and Social Science.

Colville, W. J. *Nationalism or the Next Step in Civilization. An Inspirational Address Delivered in Twilight Hall, Boston, Massachusetts, September 30, 1890.* Published by the Second Nationalist Club, Boston, n.d.

Constitution of the First Nationalist Club of Jersey City, New York: Arthur & Vonnell, 1890. John Crerar Library, Chicago, Illinois.

Constitution of the Nationalist Club of Philadelphia. Philadelphia: George F. Lasher, 1890. John Crerar Library, Chicago, Illinois.

Corbin, Caroline Fairfield. *"The Position of Women in Utopia."* Chicago: 1901.

Declaration of Constitution of the Nationalist Club, No. 1, of Washington, D. C., Adopted January 31, 1889. Washington: Gibsen Bros., 1889. John Crerar Library, Chicago, Illinois.

Declaration of Principles and Constitution of the Nationalist Club, No. 1, of Washington, D. C. Revised April 16, 1890. Washington: Press of the Craftsman, 1890. John Crerar Library, Chicago, Illinois.

Draper, Frank W., M. D. *The Homes of the Poor in Our Cities.* Report of the Massachusetts State Board of Health, 1873, pp. 396-441.

Edson, Jacob. *Nationalism. An Address to the Second Nationalist Club of Boston, Massachusetts.* Published by the Second Nationalist Club of Boston, n.d. John Crerar Library, Chicago, Illinois.

The Edward Bellamy Association of New York. Publication of the Edward Bellamy Association of New York, 193—

Ehmann, John. *Does Socialism Intend to Abolish Private Property?* Lecture Delivered Before Cincinnati and Newport Section of Socialistic Labor Party, n.p., n.d. Boston Public Library, Boston, Massachusetts.

Faris, Clyde Richey. *Bellamy or Chaos—Which?* Kansas City, Missouri: The Peerage Press, 1941.

Fawcett, Henry. *State Socialism and the Nationalization of Land.* London: Macmillan & Co., 1883.

Gilruth, T. W. *Nationalist Pamphlet.* Kansas City, Missouri: January, 1890. John Crerar Library, Chicago, Illinois.

Green, Mason A. *Nearer Than a Dream.* John Crerar Library, Chicago, Illinois.

Haller, William. *German Socialism in America: a Reply to an Article in the North American Review for April and May, 1879.* Cincinnati: Press of Harpel & Skillman, 1879.

Hartford Nationalist Club Declaration of Principles, Constitution, and By-Laws. Hartford, Connecticut: 1889. John Crerar Library, Chicago, Illinois.

Haskell, Burnette G. *Poverty Can Be Abolished. Praecipe of the San Francisco Nationalist Club.* 2d. edition of 20,000. San Francisco, The Printery of Truth, 1889.

The Industrial Evolution: Nationalism and Some of Its Features. Publication of the Nationalist Club, No. I, of Cincinnati, Ohio: n.d. John Crerar Library, Chicago, Illinois.

Judah, N. J. *The 'ABC' of Nationalism.* John Crerar Library, Chicago, Illinois.

Nationalism: Address of the Nationalist Club of Baltimore. Its Aims and Purposes. n.d. John Crerar Library, Chicago, Illinois.

Platform of the Nationalist Party of California. Los Angeles, California: Weekly Nationalist, n.d. John Crerar Library, Chicago, Illinois.

Principles of Nationalism and Constitution of the Nationalist Club of Baltimore. Baltimore: Press of Heal and Son, 1892. John Crerar Library, Chicago, Illinois.

Rooms of the New York Nationalist Club, No. 7. New York, 1896. John Crerar Library, Chicago, Illinois.

San Francisco Nationalist Club. 1889-1890. John Crerar Library, Chicago, Illinois.

What Is Nationalism? A Paper Read Before the San Francisco Nationalist Club, November 4, 1889. San Francisco: The Pacific Union, 1889. John Crerar Library, Chicago, Illinois.

What Nationalism Is: The American Cure for Monopoly and Anarchy. Opinions on the Movement from the Leading American Literary and Social Authorities: E. E. Hale, Mary Livermore, Col. T. W. Higginson, et al. Pacific Nationalist Tracts, No. I. Publication of the Nationalist Club of Oakland, Calfornia: 1889. John Crerar Library, Chicago, Illinois.

What Nationalists Have to Say. Tract No. I. Supplement to the Weekly Nationalist. Los Angeles: Nationalist Co-operative Publishing Co., n.d. John Crerar Library, Chicago, Illinois.

Jungst, W. *Are the Aims of Socialism Justifiable or Not? An Essay Delivered Before the Popular Science Society.* Cincinnati: Cincinnati Volksfreund, 1875.

Kent, Alexander. *Is the Competitive System of Industry Christian? A Sermon by Rev. Alexander Kent, of Washington, D. C., Pastor of the Universalist Church and President of Nationalist Club No. I. Delivered February 24, 1889.* Washington, D. C.: Rufus H. Darby, Printer, n.d. John Crerar Library, Chicago, Illinois.

———— "The Good Time Coming," Reprinted from *The Weekly Examiner,* April 28, 1889, Hartford, Connecticut. Nationalist Tracts, No. 3. John Crerar Library, Chicago, Illinois.

King, James Clement. *Some Elements of National Solidarity.* Chicago, Illinois: The University of Chicago, 1935.

Lindblom, Robert. *Nationalism. Before the 'Sunset Club,' February 27, 1890.* Chicago, n.p., n.d.

Willard, Frances E. *The Coming Brotherhood.* National Leaflet No. 36. Chicago: National W. C. T. U. by the Woman's Temperance Publication Association, n.d.

Wilshire, H. G. *The Poor Farmer and Why He Is Poor.* Fullerton, California: Nationalist Publication Company, 1890. John Crerar Library, Chicago, Illinois.

Unpublished Manuscripts

Bellamy, Mrs. Edward. "Edward Bellamy's Background and Character," Speech of Mrs. Edward Bellamy, Bellamy Family Files, Springfield, Massachusetts, pp. 1-5.

Bellamy, Mrs. Edward, and Earnshaw, Mrs. Marion. "Notebook of Reminiscences Relating to Edward Bellamy," Bellamy Family Files, Springfield, Massachusetts.

Blufarb, Douglas. "The Mind of Edward Bellamy," Honors Essay, Department of History and Literature, Harvard College, March 1, 1939, pp. I-LI, 1-158.

"Charvat Broadcast," Morgan Collection, Houghton Library, Springfield, Massachusetts.

Earnshaw, Mrs. Marion Bellamy. "Edward Bellamy, My Father, the Man," Speech of Mrs. Marion Earnshaw, Bellamy Family Files, pp. 1-3.

George, James T. "Edward Bellamy and the Nationalist Movement," Divisional Honors Essay, Amherst College, May, 1938, pp. 1-149.

Green, Mason. "Edward Bellamy: A Biography of the Author of *Looking Backward,*" Houghton Library, Harvard University, I-IX, pp. 9-207.

Letters of others to Edward Bellamy, Bellamy Manuscript Collection, Houghton Library, Harvard University.

Letters of others relating to Edward Bellamy or to his influence, Bellamy Family Files, Springfield, Massachusetts.

Letters of others relating to Edward Bellamy written to Arthur Morgan, Morgan Collection, Houghton Library, Harvard University.

Luntz, Lester. "Daniel De Leon and the Movement for Social Reform, 1886-1889." Columbia University, New York, 1939, pp. 1-47.

Schiffman, Joseph. "Edward Bellamy: Literary Aspects of an Original Mind," New York University, Thesis for Doctor of Philosophy, 1951.

Scott, Alexander. Broadcast *re* Edward Bellamy by the President of the Bellamy Society, Wellington, New Zealand, September, 1936, Bellamy Family Files, Springfield, Massachusetts.

Smith, Walter A. "The Religion of Edward Bellamy," Columbia University, Master of Arts Thesis, June, 1937, I-VI, pp. 1-107.

Willard, Cyrus Field. "Autobiography of Cyrus F. Willard," Morgan Collection, Houghton Library, Harvard University, pp. 1-207.

Collections of Newspaper Clippings

Clippings relating to Edward Bellamy, Bellamy Family Files, Springfield, Massachusetts.

Clippings relating to reviews and criticisms of Edward Bellamy, Bellamy Collection, Houghton Library, Harvard University, Cambridge, Massachusetts.

Clippings relating to Edward Bellamy, Chicopee Public Library, Chicopee, Massachusetts.

Scrapbook of B. F. Thompson, Volume III, 1898-1909, Connecticut Valley Historical Association Library, Springfield, Massachusetts.

Scrapbook of Mrs. Luther Goodspeed, Connecticut Valley Historical Association Library, Springfield, Massachusetts.

INDEX